A MAP OF
TWENTIETH-CENTURY
THEOLOGY

A MAP OF TWENTIETH-CENTURY THEOLOGY

READINGS FROM KARL BARTH TO RADICAL PLURALISM

Edited and Introduced by

CARL E. BRAATEN

and

ROBERT W. JENSON

FORTRESS PRESS   Minneapolis

To LaVonne
and
Blanche

A MAP OF TWENTIETH-CENTURY THEOLOGY
Readings from Karl Barth to Radical Pluralism

Copyright © 1995 Augsburg Fortress. All rights reserved. Except for brief quotations in critical articles or reviews, no part of this book may be reproduced in any manner without prior written permission from the publisher. Write: Permissions, Augsburg Fortress, 426 S. Fifth St., Box 1209, Minneapolis, MN 55440.

The editors gratefully acknowledge permissions to reprint received from publishers listed in the Acknowledgments, which constitute an addition to this page.

Cover photos: Albert Schweitzer (Bettmann Archives); Karl Barth; Rudolf Bultmann (Edward C. Hobbs); Karl Rahner (Andes Press Agency)

Cover design: Judy Swanson

Library of Congress Cataloging-in-Publication Data

A map of twentieth-century theology : readings from Karl Barth to
   radical pluralism / edited and introduced by Carl E. Braaten and
   Robert W. Jenson.
    p.   cm.
  Includes bibliographical references and index.
  ISBN 0-8006-2686-9 (alk. paper)
  1. Theology, Doctrinal.   2. Theology, Doctrinal—History—20th
century—Sources.   I. Braaten, Carl E., 1929–   .   II. Jenson,
Robert W.
BR53.M38   1995
230' .09' 04—dc20   95-19864
                                         CIP

The paper used in this publication meets the minimum requirements of American National Standard for Information Sciences—Permanence of Paper for Printed Library Materials, ANSI Z329.4—1984.

Manufactured in the U.S.A.   AF 1–2686
99   98   97   96   95   1   2   3   4   5   6   7   8   9   10

Contents

Preface   ix

Introduction   1
    The Background of Twentieth-Century Theology

PART ONE   DIALECTICAL THEOLOGY
**   AND ITS DESCENDANTS**   13

1. **The Crisis in Theology**   15
    Editors' Introduction

    1. Albert Schweitzer, The Quest of the Historical Jesus   18
    2. Karl Barth, The Strange New World within the Bible   21
    3. Ernst Troeltsch, The Absoluteness of Christianity   31

2. **Dialectical Theology**   39
    Editors' Introduction

    4. Karl Barth, The Epistle to the Romans   42
    5. Rudolf Bultmann, The Question of "Dialectical"
       Theology   50
    6. Emil Brunner, Nature and Grace   54

3. **New Systematics**   62
    Editors' Introduction

    7. Karl Barth, Church Dogmatics   65
    8. Paul Tillich, Systematic Theology   80

4. **Theologies of Secularization**   94
    Editors' Introduction

    9. Dietrich Bonhoeffer, Letters to Eberhard Bethge   98
   10. Friedrich Gogarten, Secularization and
       Christian Faith   107

CONTENTS

5. The New Hermeneutics   115
    Editors' Introduction

    11. Rudolf Bultmann, The Problem of Hermeneutics   119
    12. Gerhard Ebeling, The Word of God and Hermeneutics   130
    13. Ernst Fuchs, The Essence of the "Language Event" and
        Christology   138

6. Eschatological Theology   147
    Editors' Introduction

    14. Wolfhart Pannenberg, Revelation as History   151
    15. Jürgen Moltmann, Theology of Hope   160
    16. Johannes Metz, The Church and the World in Light of
        "Political Theology"   168

7. Trinitarian Theology   179
    Editors' Introduction

    17. Karl Barth, The Doctrine of the Trinity   182
    18. Karl Rahner, The Trinity   190
    19. Eberhard Jüngel, The Doctrine of the Trinity   196

PART TWO   ALTERNATIVE PARADIGMS
              IN THEOLOGY   207

8. Theology of Religions   209
    Editors' Introduction

    20. Paul Tillich, The Significance of the History of
        Religions for the Systematic Theologian   213
    21. Hendrik Kraemer, Christian Attitudes toward
        Non-Christian Religions   222
    22. Karl Rahner, Christianity and the
        Non-Christian Religions   231

9. Confessional Theologies   247
    Editors' Introduction

    23. Werner Elert, The Revelation of God   252
    24. Anders Nygren, Agape and Christianity   262
    25. William Temple, The Person of Christ   268

10. Transcendental Thomism   276
    Editors' Introduction

    26. Bernard J. F. Lonergan, Method in Theology   281
    27. Karl Rahner, Knowledge of God   289

CONTENTS

11. **Theology and Language**   300
    Editors' Introduction

    28. Antony Flew, R. M. Hare, and Basil Mitchell,
        The University Discussion   305
    29. Ian T. Ramsey, Religious Language   313
    30. Paul Ricoeur, Myth and Symbol   319

12. **Process Theology**   328
    Editors' Introduction

    31. Pierre Teilhard de Chardin, Evolution and the
        Christian Future   332
    32. Alfred North Whitehead, God and the World   340
    33. Charles Hartshorne, The Divine Self-Creation   349

13. **Neo-Protestantism in America**   352
    Editors' Introduction

    34. Walter Rauschenbusch, Theology and the Social Gospel   356
    35. H. Richard Niebuhr, Revelation and Radical Monotheism   361
    36. Reinhold Niebuhr, Human Nature and Politics   367
    37. Carl F. H. Henry, God, Revelation and Authority   377

Acknowledgments   383

Index   387

Preface

A *Map of Twentieth-Century Theology* charts the roads that have led to the present situation of theology. It offers readings that cover the most significant developments in twentieth-century theology up to the emergence of the current radical pluralism. The readings are selected from the formative writings of the principal theologians of the period. At each branch in a road, the next group of selections is introduced by an essay that interprets the basic themes and trends represented in it.

Every teacher of theology knows how difficult it is to introduce students to the fundamental theological events and ideas that have shaped our present situation. This volume places in the hands of students readings that contain the generative ideas of the leading schools of thought, from the crisis in theology in the first decades of the century to the rise of the radical pluralism that is the distinguishing feature of present-day theology. Without some road map, contemporary students often find it difficult to make meaningful contact with the theological giants of the era just passed. They tend to become dependent on sweeping generalizations and second-hand slogans. The difficulty is compounded by the fact that many truly historic documents are out of print.

Where there is selection there must be criteria. The editors disclaim any intentional ideological control over the choices made. The criteria have instead been pedagogical: to show how we have arrived where we are. The question was always: What must be included to enable necessary knowledge of our immediate theological history? To display the chain of links between the present and the past? Our aim has been to counteract the amnesia that enervates so much contemporary theology.

The introductory essays explain the reasons for the individual selections. That there is a predominance of German theologians cannot be helped; it simply is the ways things unfolded until the center of gravity of creative theology shifted to the United States. This shift brought with it the explosion of pluralism that characterizes the present situation. The readings break off at the threshold of popular contemporary currents: liberationism, feminism, multiculturalism, environmentalism, deconstructionism, neo-liberalism, etc. Important individual German and American theologians of the just-ending generation are also omitted. We break off where we do because these movements and thinkers are readily accessible through current publications and are commonly taught in theological seminaries and departments of religion.

PREFACE

The texts are taken from standard editions of authors' works, as cited in the Acknowledgments. Because the selections even in translation cover such a broad historical period, there were in the originals considerable differences of style (including punctuation, spelling, capitalization, and footnoting). We have modified some of the texts in order to achieve a modicum of stylistic consistency but without seeking complete uniformity and without affecting the content. In particular, we have not attempted to render the selections gender-free since to do so would have required substantial rewriting with the possibility of altering the original meaning. Biblical citations have been allowed to stand in the form given by the selected texts, without striving for consistency of style or translation. Where necessary, however, we have corrected chapter and verse references to correspond to modern English editions. Capitalization has been held to a minimum throughout, and footnotes have been eliminated. Omitted passages are marked by ellipses. During the earlier periods of the preparation, some of our students helped with work on the texts; the contribution of one, Stephen Verkouw, then a student at Gettysburg Seminary, deserves explicit mention.

Carl E. Braaten
Robert W. Jenson

Introduction

The Background of
Twentieth-Century Theology

I

Every period in the church's history provides Christian theology with challenges of its own particular sort. Perhaps we may say that Western modernity's
challenges have been to the faith's *plausibility* within Western culture. The
eighteenth-century European and North American Enlightenment undid the
culturally established ways in which Western Christianity had assured itself that
its talk of God could responsibly be taken for truth and that the authority of the
Bible was appropriate. So corrosive indeed were the Enlightenment's effects on
the established life of Christianity, that by the opening of the nineteenth century
European and North American elites generally took it for granted that Christianity's day was over.

We predict and God disposes. The nineteenth century proved in fact to be
one of the great periods of Christian intellectual and missionary expansion.
And the intellectual side of this feat was achieved by creative confrontation
with the Enlightenment.

For our purposes, we may characterize the Enlightenment quite simply.
The seventeenth century had witnessed the first great explosion of modern science. The eighteenth-century Enlightenment consisted in being mightily impressed by science's achievements and in adopting a general intellectual
policy shaped by this awe. For our particular purposes, we may describe this
policy under two headings: (a) suspicion of tradition, and (b) reshaping of the
West's established enterprise of comprehensive understanding, usually called
metaphysics.

II

The new science was based on only a few methodological commitments. One
was culturally determinative: rigorous determination not to take things at face

1

value. The archetypical and inspiring case of such "critique of appearances" was Copernican astronomy. It certainly appears that the sun goes round the earth; astronomy was rescued from sterility by persistence in the question, "Yes, but does it really? Let us look again."

It was inevitable that once Europe and America had seen how the critique of appearances produced abundant new understanding of the world in which we live—and vastly improved technology based on this understanding— the dream should arise of extending the policy to the knowledge and improvement of human personal life and society. Pursuit of this dream was the great intellectual enterprise of the Enlightenment.

But what is *humanity's* face value? What are *our* initial "appearances"? In the essential temporality of our life, it is the tradition of the past that is our face value. When we ask, "What are humans?" we have no other place to look for an initial presentation than to parents and then generally to humans who came before us. Thus, the critique of appearances, applied to human life, became the critique of tradition. Humankind generally supposes that an opinion's establishment in tradition is the very thing that makes it plausible. "Enlightened" Westerners came to suppose the opposite.

The critique of tradition poses theological problems in several ways. Very directly, trust in the traditional teaching of the church will be replaced by suspicion, and the dissolution of dogma has been a continuing phenomenon of the modern period. A "modern" theology is one that proposes some way of dealing with the resulting void.

Most specifically, the critique of tradition attacks the identification of God, which in any religion is accomplished by tradition. Indeed, every actual religion simply *is* a historical tradition that identifies God in some way, as "Marduk, the primal Hydrologist," or "the God of Israel, who raised Jesus from the dead."

This point was not always apparent to the Enlighteners themselves; some of them thought there was or could be a functioning religion natural to humankind and therefore independent of tradition, a religion that worshipped a God identified only generically. The attempt to practice such religion, however, demonstrated its emptiness: to worship as Benjamin Franklin did and not to worship at all quickly work out to much the same thing. Actually to *pray* to and be *blessed* by God, we must identify which God we intend as the true one, among the multitude of candidates. A prayer is an address to someone, and one god's blessing is another god's curse.

The "natural" religion of Enlightened religionists first emptied the churches by depriving its adherents of trust in the specifically identified God there worshipped, and then displayed its own insipidity. The spiritual void these events left in Western culture has been the chief theological and philosophical preoccupation of the nineteenth and twentieth centuries.

III

Christianity's talk of God had been plausible not only because it was anchored in tradition, but also because it belonged to a comprehensive interpretation of reality. The classic metaphysical thinking of the West claimed insight by which the world immediately knowable as the deep structure of that world, and the reality of God, could all be interpreted within one discourse and with one standard of truth. It was supposed that such various truths as that water runs downhill and beauty is good and Jesus is Son of God, must all somehow make one truth together. The Enlightenment attacked also this context of theology.

Some Enlighteners, noting the great differences between the cognitive procedures of metaphysics and those of science, became metaphysical skeptics. It certainly seems to the human mind that, for example, every event must have a cause and that this connection itself must then have a Cause. But such things can hardly be established by scientific procedure, and if science is to be our one paradigm of truth, such things cannot be established at all. Thereupon, critical reason suspects: perhaps the only reason we think such things is that human minds need to think them. David Hume (1711–1776) and Immanuel Kant (1724–1804) were the great leaders down this path; on it, talk of God lost much of its old context.

Other Enlighteners made a metaphysics of their own that was to be "scientific." The metaphysically impressive aspect of the world as science made it known was its *order*. So much of the world had heretofore resisted humanity's longing for order that the new science seemed actively revelatory, unveiling a blessed vision of harmony. Every vision of universal harmony is at its heart poetic; it explicates some "root metaphor." The new science did not itself provide such a metaphor, but the technology based on it seemed to.

Seventeenth-century physics is called mechanics because its laws explain the behavior of machines. And a machine *can* be a metaphor of harmony: it is put together of numerous and disparate parts and encompasses great contending dynamisms, yet is itself stable and constrains all forces to one end.

If God's creation is a universal machine, God must be a universal Engineer; some Enlighteners tried to worship just such a God. A good engineer's creation does not need frequent repair or adjustment; an omnipotent Engineer's creation would never need it. Therefore, the God of the machine-cosmos cannot be active in creation once it is there; every "intervention" would only show that God had been incompetent in the first place.

Thus, this metaphysics does have place for a God but not for the Christian God. The God of the Bible cannot be cast as a perfect Engineer: his very deity is invested in interruptions and new beginnings, in forgiveness and resurrection. If the universe is envisioned as a machine, the God of the Bible must appear incompetently godly.

3

Two great efforts to meet these challenges were launched in the late eighteenth and early nineteenth centuries, and set the pattern for all that followed. One was the work of the theologian Friedrich Schleiermacher (1768–1834), the other of the philosopher Georg Friedrich Wilhelm Hegel (1770–1831). The Enlightenment began with writers in the English language and only later was exported to French and German territories. It was in Germany that integration of Christian faith and Enlightenment was persistently attempted, and this effort made Germany the center of the theological world for a century and a half.

Friedrich Schleiermacher was a leading participant in the burgeoning intellectual and artistic life of turn-of-the-century Germany. The book that made him the "church father of the nineteenth century" appeared in 1799: *On Religion: Speeches to Its Cultured Despisers.*

Schleiermacher did not defend traditional interpretations of God; he assumed that the Enlightenment had undone them for the class to which he belonged and for which he wrote. He accepted that religion could be defended neither as a metaphysical sort of knowledge nor, as the proponents of "natural" religion often thought, as a necessary correlate of morality. But knowledge and moral action are not, he said, the whole or center of life, and it is the great error of the Enlightenment to suppose that they are.

Through the last quarter of the eighteenth century, a new ideal of humanity had been taking shape in artistic and intellectual Germany. Its chief articulator was perhaps Johann Gottfried Herder (1744–1803); its paradigmatic embodiment was the great Johann Wolfgang von Goethe (1749–1832). These artist-philosophers envisaged the human person as a being of infinitely diverse potentialities, whose calling is the maximal unfolding of these potentialities and their simultaneous integration into harmony. That is, the human person is to be his or her own work of art, of the kind that occupies time, as do music or poetry or drama. We may say that the new ideal was of a human life as a self-composed Mozart symphony.

In effect, the *Speeches* said to their readers: Do you indeed want your life to be an achievement of musical-dramatic coherence? Is Goethe your model? Then you must—surprising though it may be to you—cultivate your religious life. You think religion irrelevant only because you are, despite your enthusiasm for such as Goethe, still bound to the Enlightenment's superficial vision of humanity, in which religion has no proper place. But in religion and only in religion can the events and aspects of a life, through time, cohere to make a beautiful whole.

Religion's utterances, interpreted as would-be factual statements, as metaphysics, said Schleiermacher, are indeed unverifiable. And morality needs no support of divine rewards; it is rather spoiled by such. But religion is in fact neither of these. Religion is rather a mode of "feeling," of "taste" or "sense." Along with knowledge and practice, feeling is a third mode of human existence in its own right.

Schleiermacher's "feeling" has little directly to do with "emotion." We are closer to his use when we speak of someone having "a feel" for color, or cultivating "a taste" for oysters. "Feeling" is a contact with reality that is more primitive than knowledge or choice yet somehow already encompasses both. Just as such, it is the conscious person's unity with himself or herself, the mode of experience that is present in every experience and in which particular experiences can therefore be possessed together as belonging to the person. Moreover, as the experience in which cognitive and active experiences of the world originate and are not yet divided, feeling is also the point of the conscious person's unity with the world, in which knowing and acting first become possible.

As the unity of my experience in itself and as the unity of my experience with its object, feeling is thus conscious being's grasp of *wholeness*. And so there is *religion*. Religion, says Schleiermacher, is feeling for "the universal," for the "unbounded." Religion is the sense of the coherence of things, by which alone we in fact venture from moment to moment. It is therefore a fundamental function of human being, a mode of experience necessarily co-present in every experience, a grasp of reality without which conscious life would fall apart into temporal fragments of knowing and doing. Therefore, we cannot not be religious; we can only be richly or poorly religious. And God is the word by which we aim ourselves toward that infinite with which—in every religion—we feel ourselves at one, but which we can never know or act upon.

Religion, however, is never actual except as some particular religion, for to become actual it must embrace knowing and doing, and these are always of particulars, never of the whole as such. Actual religion always belongs to some community united by a common particular focus of religious feeling. Our actual choice, therefore, is among historically actual religions; and our challenge is to embrace a religion that fulfills the religious function copiously and precisely. Theology is a description of the knowings and doings that characterize some such particular religion. What specifies Christianity among the religions is, Schleiermacher thinks, plain: the concentration of all religious feeling on the figure of Christ.

Through the nineteenth century, there were few who simply adopted Schleiermacher's whole proposal. But the main features of his *procedure* were instantly and almost universally adopted and enabled the theological enterprise's new beginning; these define what historians of theology call "Neo-Protestantism." There could be and were many succeeding and competing sorts of Neo-Protestant theology, united and defined as such only by sharing in Schleiermacher's procedure.

Neo-Protestant method begins with an analysis of human being, which locates in us a necessary and paramount experiential function—whether feeling or some other—and finds in it a place for "religion." This analysis does not need to be done transcendentally as by Schleiermacher himself; it can be done psychologically, sociologically, or metaphysically, or even read from the Bible or church tradition. Next, history is identified as the realm within which actual religions appear. One can then make a particular religion plausible by showing how it fulfills the religious function. Finally, theology is critical self-reflection of the particular religion itself.

Hegel has a different place in the history of theology. There were more avowed "Hegelians" among the theologians of the nineteenth century than there were material imitators of Schleiermacher, but within the theology of the church it was Schleiermacher and not Hegel who provided the common basis. In the broader intellectual life of Germany and North America, on the other hand, Hegel's influence was extraordinary.

Hegelianism itself ceased to dominate around the middle of the century, but many movements of nineteenth- and twentieth-century continental philosophy—existentialism, Marxism, personalism, or the stream through Nietzsche and Heidegger—may each be described as a fragment of the Hegelian system gone off on its own. And whenever theologians have turned against Neo-Protestantism—as decisively at the beginning of our century—these movements and Hegel himself have regularly offered resource.

Hegel met the Enlightenment head-on. Christianity, in his judgment, could not be restored by negotiating with "natural" religion, or by seeking a realm of religion's own not subject to the Enlightenment's critique, such as "feeling." Instead, Hegel built yet one more—the last, it is often thought—in the great sequence of the West's metaphysical systems, to be the context and explication of Christianity's knowledge of God. And he built it by taking the crisis of metaphysical thinking into the system itself.

Hume and Kant had apparently shown that what human subjects take for metaphysical truths are merely the necessary demands of subjectivity itself: we think, for example, that all events have causes because otherwise we could not *think* events at all. Very well, said Hegel—and other German "idealists" with him—that only means that reality taken whole *is* the self-expression of Subjectivity. So all events do indeed have causes, because were it not for the structure of Mind that demands causes there would be no events to lack them.

The "religious" word for the Mind that thus expresses itself in all things is God. Philosophy and religion have the same matter, but in different forms. Philosophy grasps eternal truth in thought; religion, in symbols and stories. This distinction was to cast a long shadow over the twentieth century, in, for instance, the debates over "demythologizing."

Enlighteners who created a mechanistic worldview pitted metaphysical truth and historical freedom against each other, thereby excluding the biblical God from metaphysical truth. Hegel attacked directly, constructing a metaphysics in which historical eventfulness is itself the model of encompassing truth. Hegel analyzed the movement of history, precisely in its unpredictability and contradictoriness—in its seeming irrationality—for its *own* sort of sense.

Thus, for example, the way in which, during Hegel's lifetime, the French monarchy had provoked its opposite, popular revolutionary government, which then produced in Napoleon a synthesis of both, has, said Hegel, its own logic — the famous logic of "thesis," "antithesis," and "synthesis." This is not the logic of abstract reasoning but the logic of *creative* reasoning, of "spirit." *Spirit* is the lively order that emerges in all reality, of which mechanical orderliness is but a passing aspect. And again, the religious word for the Spirit that by and through all reality brings forth its own opposite and then reconciles that opposite to itself within itself, is *God*.

IV

The Enlightenment's direct challenge to the authority of tradition, and its challenge to the faith's metaphysical plausibility, came together in the center of Christian theology, the doctrine of Christ. The critical spirit of the Enlightenment created, as Gotthold Lessing (1729–1781) wrote, an "ugly ditch" between the new historical mode of thinking and the dogmatic Christology of the church. Lessing formulated the problem that became critical for all subsequent theology as a sharp distinction between "accidental truths of history and necessary truths of reason."

Applied to Christology, this distinction created a dualism between the "historical Jesus" and the "Christ of faith." Traditional Christology had read the Gospels' narratives about Jesus within a system of concepts that identified Jesus Christ as one person who is both fully human and fully divine. As long as this Christology remained in force, it could scarcely occur to anyone to search for a human Jesus of history as he might have been before he became the object of faith and the content of doctrine.

But critique of tradition could not spare the sources that told the story of Jesus of Nazareth. Immanuel Kant, in the important essay, "What Is Enlightenment?" defined Enlightenment as coming of age, as emancipation from adolescent dependence on authorities. "*Sapere aude!* 'Have courage to use your own reason' — that is the motto of the Enlightenment." The Bible became the test case. All the latest critical methods and concepts were applied to the sacred texts, without reservation. "Criticism does not recognize infallible texts."

Thus Lessing's ditch widened, and became a huge gap between christological doctrine and the historical Jesus. If the gap could not be bridged, Christianity itself would be the victim for having failed to meet the challenge of critical historical consciousness.

The New Testament provided two forms of the basic christological proposition essential to faith: John 1:14, "The Word became flesh," and 2 Corinthians 5:19, "God was in Christ." From the beginning of theology, these propositions were understood to assert a special unity of Jesus with God. In speaking of Christ, both the unity (more stated by the Johannine passage) and the duality (more apparent in the passage from Corinthians) had to be maintained. If the unity of God with Jesus is wrongly stressed, the temptation is to overshadow his real humanity, his flesh and blood; those in the ancient church who fell to this temptation were called "monophysites," and accused of "docetism." If the duality is wrongly stressed, the view results that Jesus is a human being at best very intimately related to God; no real incarnation occurs. This position was called "Nestorianism" in the ancient church; the extreme form that treats Jesus simply as an exceptional human has been called "ebionitism."

Friedrich Schleiermacher, in *The Christian Faith*, identified docetism and ebionitism as perennial heresies, also in his own time. The nineteenth century's struggle to reach a modern understanding of Christ oscillated between these docetic and ebionitic poles; underlying both was an understanding of God that made his union with humanity an ontological impossibility. Theologians of the eighteenth and nineteenth centuries inherited an idea of God as utterly immutable and impassible, and thus incapable of entering the realm of finite and contingent human persons. The Word could not really *become* flesh and Jesus not really *be* God. The old adage that "the finite is not capable of the infinite" ruled. Thus, while many of these theologians rejected the Christology of the ancient church on account of its use of Hellenistic metaphysical concepts like "being" and "hypostasis," their difficulty with the Incarnation was in large part due to assumptions about God inherited from the same Hellenistic philosophy.

Immanuel Kant believed he could spell out the meaning of Christianity as a "religion within the limits of reason alone." This religion enshrines the idea of the moral person as well pleasing to God. Every human is drawn by this ideal, but Kant considered Jesus its most perfect example. In principle, however, the moral ideal is universal, and needs no historical example to be present in human reason. We may think of "Christ" as an eternal ideal only incidentally connected to the individual Jesus. Since Jesus was no other than human for Kant, Kant's Christology could be called ebionitic. But since he has the concept of an ideal Christ, as the real object of faith, who is represented by but not embodied in the person of Jesus, his Christology is also docetic.

Kant's merely ethical Christology was quickly transcended by the more powerful views of Schleiermacher and Hegel. Schleiermacher's account of Christianity was radically christocentric: what is unique to Christianity is that everything in it is related to the redemption achieved by Jesus of Nazareth. Thus, he started his system of Christian doctrine with the present experience of redemption shared by the Christian community, and moved inferentially backward to ask: Who and what must Jesus have been to explain the Christian experience of salvation? The answer was that Jesus is the original and creative model of the redeemed life that he inspires in his followers. His uniqueness lies in his perfect consciousness of God, and in this sense he may be called divine.

Schleiermacher's critics were quick to point out that Jesus' awareness of God, no matter how constant, does not make him categorically more than human. To call Jesus God on this account is pious hyperbole. Schleiermacher could not accept the dogmatic formula of "one person in two natures" because he felt it contradictory and illogical, but even more because he found it unnecessary to account for contemporary christocentric religious experience.

Hegel took a different path. From his transcendental point of departure, Hegel constructed a speculative theory of the Christian doctrines of Trinity and of Christology. The Absolute, "God the Father," objectifies itself and so posits another, the eternal "Son of God," the world of finitude in distinction from the Infinite. Next, the difference between the Father and the Son is overcome in the "Spirit," the principle of return and reconciliation.

Some theologians rejoiced to see such a beautiful overcoming of the gap between Christianity and modern philosophy: what Christians mean by the incarnation of God, and the history of being, are reconciled in a universal synthesis. But what does all this speculation from above have to do with the lowly man from Nazareth? Hegel seemed to bypass the concrete person of Jesus. Lessing's point was apparently vindicated again: there can be no essential connection between facts of history and truths of reason. But the Christian gospel is not based in a philosophical synthesis of deity and humanity but in the Word become a historical individual.

Hegel's metaphysical Christology provoked strong reaction from three sides: (a) Positivist historicism turned away from *a priori* philosophy to establish what "really happened" in the history of Jesus; (b) a lone protester in Denmark, Søren Kierkegaard (1813–1855), rebelled against universal historical systems in the name of the concrete particularity of Jesus Christ in whom the eternal God appeared in human time; and (c) a third front was opened by confessional theologians who tried to integrate the new emphasis on the historical Jesus into the framework of traditional Christology. Thus, for example, Gottfried Thomasius (1802–1873) advanced a "kenotic" Christology according to which the eternal Logos emptied himself of his cosmological attributes, limiting himself to a human finite life that could occur in history. All three of these lines continue in various twentieth-century schools of theology.

"Historical-critical" positivism aimed to build Christology directly on the life of Jesus. The beginning of "the quest for the historical Jesus" coincided with the breakup of Protestant orthodoxy; the new scholarship attempted to view Christ from a historical, not a dogmatic, perspective. The goal was to approximate as closely as possible a kind of cinematographic reproduction of the life of Jesus, free of dogmatic prejudices. The interest of these biographers was far from purely antiquarian. Most of the "life of Jesus" scholars were religiously motivated: they hoped to draw a true-to-life picture of Jesus relevant to modern times. They searched for natural explanations of myths and miracles. They wanted to base piety directly on the religion and morality of Jesus rather than on later "mythological" or dogmatic constructions. They widened the ditch between the Jesus of the Gospels and the Christ of the Creeds.

Not only dogmatic Christology had to be smashed to enable the quest for the historical Jesus but also the orthodox doctrine of Scripture's inspiration and plenary inerrancy. Freedom to study Scripture critically, without dogmatic restriction, was achieved in a series of fierce battles against orthodox theologians. In order to write a biography of Jesus, scholars had to decide which sources were reliable. Thus, the root of modern biblical criticism is the religious drive to discover the personality, religious experience, and teaching of Jesus. If these could be recovered, historical critics assumed, Christianity could again be at home in a world shaped by enlightened and emancipated reason.

The more scholars examined the sources for a life of Jesus, the more they realized that the sources have many gaps. Periods of Jesus' life receive no mention at all; at best, there are a few clues here and there. For the rest, scholars had to supplement the evidence with inferences from modern psychology, on the principle of analogy. In consequence, as Albert Schweitzer (1875–1965) was to show, their portrayals of Jesus' experience and teaching regularly bore striking resemblance to their own.

Kierkegaard was a solitary thinker whose struggle with the Hegelian system was to receive belated worldwide recognition in twentieth-century existentialism. His thought turned on Lessing's challenge to cross the "ugly ditch" between historical facts and eternal truths. The answer for Kierkegaard was the "leap of faith." The ditch could be bridged neither by metaphysical speculation nor by historical demonstration. History can at most prove that Jesus Christ was a great man. But it cannot prove he was God incarnate. Christ is "the absolute paradox" who cannot be reached by reason, metaphysical or historical.

Kierkegaard minted the coins that became current in dialectical and existentialist theology: "infinite qualitative difference," "the moment," "incognito," "paradox," "encounter" and the like. They were calculated to break the christological hold of both absolute idealism and positivistic historicism. Faith needs no external props or authorities to gain access to the living Christ of the Bible. External assurances can at most provide "approximate" certainty, too weak a foundation for the hope of eternal life. Faith has to overcome the objective uncertainty of the historical brute fact that the God-man appeared as a particular person of the past, that the eternal God has entered historical time. That eternity has entered time without canceling it is a paradox that can be believed only in its offensiveness.

The nineteenth century did not harbor only rationalists, idealists, and historicists. There were conservative and pietist theologians who clung to the Bible's authority and interpreted it by the Creeds. Theologians of the "Erlangen School" made the most influential attempts to combine the classical traditions with Schleiermacher's experiential theological method and the historical study of Scripture, creating the "history of salvation" scheme of theology that was to be popular also in the twentieth century.

V

Thus, after Schleiermacher and Hegel, various theological movements, of which we have described only a few, proposed bridges over the "ugly ditch." Kierkegaard's call for a leap of faith seemed to leave matters hanging in the air. Attempts to discover a more secure location for faith and theology, even an "invulnerable sphere," can be classified as subjectivist and objectivist.

Subjectivist or "expressivist" projects interpret theology as the expression of the theologian's experience of faith. The Bible and church tradition enter only subsequently; they are expressions of previous Christian experience, and so can confirm or possibly correct what any individual theologian derives from his or her experience. This approach was initiated by Schleiermacher and continued by the Erlangen School and by "liberals" such as Wilhelm Herrmann (1846–1922). (We will come to other liberals in the first chapter.) Finally, such interpretation leaves faith to rely on itself as the creator of its own basis and contents.

An opposite approach was the quest for objective supports on which to rest the relation between faith and God. Martin Luther had said that faith and God belong together: your God is where you put your faith. But what mediates the two? What holds God and faith together? We have already mentioned the nineteenth century's most modern attempt to locate a basis for faith in objective fact: the "life of Jesus" movement. Leopold von Ranke (1794–1866) defined history as the science that discovers what "really" happened in the past. This positivistic historicism presented a tempting option for theology: an alternative to the seeming arbitrariness of mysticism, rationalism, or dogmatism. In the historical facts underlying the layers of later interpretation, contemporary faith could find a sure basis backed by scientific scholarship. But this ally proved fickle. If historical scholarship could provide an objective basis for faith, it could as easily withdraw it; thus, faith was suspended in endless uncertainty. Those who sought refuge from dogmatism in historicism merely exchanged one system of authority for another.

Through the century, circles of Protestant orthodoxy remained, as another objectivism. These looked to the Bible as an absolute guarantee of faith and doctrine. The doctrine of verbal inspiration was intended to underwrite that guarantee, providing faith with a high threshold of objectivity. But faith's confidence in divine revelation itself must then be shaken as soon as the accuracy of any statement in the Bible is doubted. Thus, orthodox theologians engaged in a continuous battle against biblical scholarship and, in the end, could offer no deterrent to subjectivism.

Roman Catholicism offered a more massive system of objective supports. Protestantism's struggles in the encounter with modernity were addressed by Roman Catholic authorities in a series of decrees and encyclicals, once even requiring of priests and teachers an "oath against modernism." This defense was maintained virtually to the time of the Second Vatican Council, when the flood-gates opened.

VI

We can tarry no longer with the nineteenth century. Its detailed history is rich and fascinating, but is not the one we have to tell. In the introductory essay to the first set of readings, we will describe the beginning of specifically twentieth-century theology as the crisis of the nineteenth century's Neo-Protestantism. The crisis was partly internal: the problems that worked themselves to the fore had been inherent in the ways Schleiermacher and Hegel made the Christian God newly plausible. And the crisis was partly a matter of historical events whose challenge Neo-Protestantism could not meet.

PART ONE

DIALECTICAL THEOLOGY AND ITS DESCENDANTS

1

The Crisis in Theology

The last great school of Neo-Protestantism was the "liberal" theology, prominent in the decades around the turn of the century, so called because of its moral coherence with liberalism generally, that is, with the politics and economics of the bourgeoisie. Among the Neo-Protestant schools, the liberal theology was distinguished by the particular analysis of human existence with which it began and by the particular way in which it asserted the historicality of religion.

Hegelianism and other idealist projects had fallen out of favor, perhaps largely because of sheer conceptual ponderousness. And, with Darwinism, mechanistic interpretations of the world again came to seem unavoidable. Those we call the "liberal" theologians were unwilling to retreat to feeling or a similar refuge. Instead, such theologians as Albrecht Ritschl (1822–1889), Ernst Troeltsch (1865–1923), and Adolf von Harnack (1851–1930) turned to Immanuel Kant's moralism for their initiating analysis of human life.

Kant had worked to invalidate mechanistic metaphysics by invalidating metaphysics in general. It indeed appears to us that, for example, all events must have a cause, and that this circumstance must itself have a Cause, whether God or impersonal law. But, said Kant, this is an appearance imposed by the necessities not of reality somehow "out there" but of our reality as subjects; except through such framing concepts as "cause," we would not experience such things as "events" at all. We must resist the temptation to think that the guiding concepts of our own subjectivity enable knowledge of reality "out there," given by the nature and relations of those concepts themselves. To continue the central example: the circumstance that we must indeed think all events have causes does not enable knowledge that there is in fact a universal Cause.

Kant did not undertake the critique of metaphysics in order to abolish all talk of God but to enable a new, a-metaphysical location for it. Although the idea of a universal personal Cause cannot be known to correspond in metaphysical fashion to anything other than itself, it is a necessary postulate within *moral* subjectivity; and there, moreover, it is *true* in the way appropriate to moral conviction. Nor do we thereby make God a postulate of

15

merely individual aspiration, for a conviction is moral precisely insofar as it is asserted as a rule for all.

The most influential systematician of liberalism, Albrecht Ritschl, found his foundational analysis of human existence in these Kantian principles. Humanity's specific reality is its calling to establish the "kingdom of God," that is, according to Ritschl, the realm of rationally dictated political and social love. This is the kingdom of *God* in that it is possible for us to act freely in the world, despite the natural determinism that rules all events in it, if we trust a Will who at once commands the "values" that are the goals of our free action and ordains the natural law that governs the world. This *trust* is our entire relation to God and does not constitute knowledge of any "object."

For this, we must in fact be *able* to trust God; it is at this point that liberalism's particular christocentrism and particular use of history enter. All Protestantism has insisted that the ability to trust God is the great gift bestowed by Jesus Christ. But how do we come in contact with Jesus, in order to receive it? Jesus, said the liberals, is a historical figure if he is anything at all; therefore, at least our initial contact with him must be of the same sort as is our contact with any historical figure. And in the world after the Enlightenment, such contact can with honesty be claimed only by critical investigation of the historical sources. "Historical-critical" study of the New Testament to find the "real," that is, the "historical" Jesus, was for liberalism a sort of fundamental sacrament, the action by which we meet the Lord. And when we do then find the historical Jesus, we find one who proclaimed the kingdom of a loving God and died in testimony to that love.

Liberalism was undone by a remarkable coincidence of events: discoveries made by historical-critical biblical scholarship itself, world political catastrophe, certain liberal intellectuals' own theological analysis of the nature of history, and the political and religious radicalization of a small group of younger liberals. Therewith the theology specific to the twentieth century began. Where the impact of these events was not so strongly felt, as in much of the English-speaking church, liberalism has continued as the ordinary theology; and we will in Part Two consider this and closely related alternative paradigms. But the theology precipitated by revolt against nineteenth-century principles has been the century's new and defining current.

Already in 1892, the great liberal New Testament scholar, Johannes Weiss (1868–1916), demonstrated in *Die Predigt Jesu vom Reich Gottes (Jesus' Proclamation of the Kingdom of God)* that the historical Jesus was no liberal and that the kingdom of God he proclaimed was not to be set up in this world by human moral action but was to replace this world by the action of God. A decisive similar blow was struck by Albert Schweitzer (1875–1965) whose *Von Reimarus zu Wrede* (translated as *The Quest of the Historical Jesus*), published in 1906, showed that liberal portraits of the

"historical Jesus" had been works of ideological imagination, and that the historical Jesus, insofar as he can be known at all, presents a mystery of apocalypticism utterly useless to our projects of self-improvement.

Not just the specific liberal theology, but the whole Neo-Protestant project depended on seeing Christianity as one phenomenon in the history of religion and on arguing in one way or another for its superiority within the offerings of that history. Ernst Troeltsch (1865–1923), one of the towering figures of modern intellect, devoted his life to the problems of such argument. He concluded that when reality is grasped in its full historicity, no case can be made for the superiority of one religion over another. *Die Absolutheit des Christentums und die Religionsgeschichte* (translated as *The Absoluteness of Christianity,* 1902), brought the nineteenth century's historicism to its climax and final problem.

Then, in 1914, the liberally cultivated nations of Europe fell to slaughtering one another, for no ascertainable reason and with unprecedented ferocity. Where this event was experienced directly, it became hard to hope for a kingdom of mutual love and justice to be established by human liberality.

Meanwhile, a young Swiss had been studying theology with Adolf von Harnack at Berlin and Wilhelm Herrmann (1846–1922) at Marburg. Then, to be seasoned for an expected academic career, he had taken a parish in his native Switzerland. Von Harnack and Troeltsch expected great things of him.

Karl Barth (1886–1968) became Protestant pastor of Safenwil, a small industrial city in Switzerland, in 1911. He came to his parish trained to cultivate the Christian religion and the ethical enthusiasm this religion was supposed to enable. Pastoral experience at Safenwil broke this understanding of his calling and of the Christian faith, radicalizing him theologically, politically, and personally.

In the parish, he had to preach regularly and was expected to expound set texts. Fulfilling this responsibility, he came to read the Bible differently than as a source of historical knowledge about Jesus' religion and ethics. The Bible, he discovered, is indeed about something called the kingdom of God, but what that might be came to puzzle him deeply; it was plainly *not* what liberalism proclaimed as the goal of our religious and moral quest or activism. Barth found the Bible in general surprising, a "strange new *world*" that one would have to inhabit to understand, a world in which everything seemed to go differently than in the world of self-fulfillment construed by the European bourgeoisie, a world given meaning not by our religious quest for God but by God's sovereign grasp on us.

Moreover, it quickly became clear to Barth that his working-class parishioners, in their unmistakable economic and political exploitation, had more urgent concerns than the cultivation of religious experience. Nor was a kingdom of God constructed as the religious fruition of the liberal

political-economic project something for which they were likely to be enthusiastic, it being the agents of that project who oppressed them. Hope
for a kingdom only God could bring seemed more to the point, even the
political and economic point.

Then World War I broke out, and Barth had to watch German liberal
culture enthusiastically enlist in the service of blind nationalism. To his horror, most of his old teachers signed a famous "Declaration of German Intellectuals" on behalf of "emperor and fatherland."

Thus, Barth's radicalization came from all sides. Yet, for him, it made but
one experience, which left him in the midst of parish duties with no concept of what he was there to accomplish, except that it was not what he had
thought it was and it had to do with entering the Bible's strange new reality.
Politically, he became a social democrat, that is, a non-Communist Marxist.
As a proper young academic, he did his theological struggling in print, producing, among other essays, those translated in the collection *The Word of
God and the Word of Man.*

These early essays were read and understood as something new and
began to establish Barth as a rallying center for others discomfited like
himself. In 1921, he was called, without a doctorate, to the first of several
teaching posts in Germany. There, events were again to overtake him, and
he would become a theological leader of the churchly resistance to Adolf
Hitler and the drafter of the *Barmen Declaration.* In 1922, he published
the book that would make him the leader of a generation of theological
revolutionaries, the second attempt at a commentary on Paul's letter to
the Romans.

1. Albert Schweitzer, *The Quest of the Historical Jesus*

We modern theologians are too proud of our historical method, too proud of our
historical Jesus, too confident in our belief in the spiritual gains which our historical theology can bring to the world. The thought that we could build up by
the increase of historical knowledge a new and vigorous Christianity and set free
new spiritual forces, rules us like a fixed idea, and prevents us from seeing that
the task which we have grappled with and in some measure discharged is only
one of the intellectual preliminaries of the great religious task. We thought that it
was for us to lead our time by a roundabout way through the historical Jesus, as
we understood him, in order to bring it to the Jesus who is a spiritual power in
the present. This roundabout way has now been closed by genuine history.

There was a danger of our thrusting ourselves between men and the Gospels,
and refusing to leave the individual man alone with the sayings of Jesus.

There was a danger that we should offer them a Jesus who was too small, because we had forced him into conformity with our human standards and human

psychology. To see that, one need only read the Lives of Jesus written since the sixties, and notice what they have made of the great imperious sayings of the Lord, how they have weakened down his imperative world-contemning demands upon individuals, that he might not come into conflict with our ethical ideals, and might tune his denial of the world to our acceptance of it. Many of the greatest sayings are found lying in a corner like explosive shells from which the charges have been removed. No small portion of elemental religious power needed to be drawn off from his sayings to prevent them from conflicting with our system of religious world-acceptance. We have made Jesus hold another language with our time from that which he really held. . . .

In the course of the critical study of the Life of Jesus, after a resistance lasting for two generations, during which first one expedient was tried and then another, theology was forced by genuine history to begin to doubt the artificial history with which it had thought to give new life to our Christianity, and to yield to the facts, which, as Wrede strikingly said, are sometimes the most radical critics of all. History will force it to find a way to transcend history, and to fight for the lordship and rule of Jesus over this world with weapons tempered in a different forge.

We are experiencing what Paul experienced. In the very moment when we were coming nearer to the historical Jesus than men had ever come before, and were already stretching out our hands to draw him into our own time, we have been obliged to give up the attempt and acknowledge our failure in that paradoxical saying: "If we have known Christ after the flesh yet henceforth know we him no more." And further we must be prepared to find that the historical knowledge of the personality and life of Jesus will not be a help, but perhaps even an offence to religion.

But the truth is, it is not Jesus as historically known, but Jesus as spiritually arisen within men, who is significant for our time and can help it. Not the historical Jesus, but the spirit which goes forth from him and in the spirits of men strives for new influence and rule, is that which overcomes the world. . . .

Jesus as a concrete historical personality remains a stranger to our time, but his spirit, which lies hidden in his words, is known in simplicity, and its influence is direct. Every saying contains in its own way the whole Jesus. The very strangeness and unconditionedness in which he stands before us makes it easier for individuals to find their own personal standpoint in regard to him.

Men feared that to admit the claims of eschatology would abolish the significance of his words for our time; and hence there was a feverish eagerness to discover in them any elements that might be considered not eschatologically conditioned. When any sayings were found of which the wording did not absolutely imply an eschatological connexion, there was a great jubilation — these at least had been saved uninjured from the coming *debacle*.

But in reality that which is eternal in the words of Jesus is due to the very fact that they are based on an eschatological worldview, and contain the expression of a mind for which the contemporary world with its historical and social circumstances no longer had any existence. They are appropriate, therefore, to any world, for in every world they raise the man who dares to meet their challenge, and does not turn and twist them into meaninglessness, above his world and his time, making him inwardly free, so that he is fitted to be, in his own world and in his own time, a simple channel of the power of Jesus.

Modern Lives of Jesus are too general in their scope. They aim at influencing, by giving a complete impression of the life of Jesus, a whole community. But the historical Jesus, as he is depicted in the Gospels, influenced individuals by the individual word. They understood him so far as it was necessary for them to understand, without forming any conception of his life as a whole, since this in its ultimate aims remained a mystery even for the disciples.

Because it is thus preoccupied with the general, the universal, modern theology is determined to find its world-accepting ethic in the teaching of Jesus. Therein lies its weakness. The world affirms itself automatically; the modern spirit cannot but affirm it. But why on that account abolish the conflict between modern life, with the world-affirming spirit which inspires it as a whole, and the world-negating spirit of Jesus? Why spare the spirit of the individual man its appointed task of fighting its way through the world-negation of Jesus, of contending with him at every step over the value of material and intellectual goods—a conflict in which it may never rest? For the general, for the institutions of society, the rule is: affirmation of the world, in conscious opposition to the view of Jesus, on the ground that the world has affirmed itself! This general affirmation of the world, however, if it is to be Christian, must in the individual spirit be Christianized and transfigured by the personal rejection of the world which is preached in the sayings of Jesus. It is only by means of the tension thus set up that religious energy can be communicated to our time. There was a danger that modern theology, for the sake of peace, would deny the world-negation in the sayings of Jesus, with which Protestantism was out of sympathy, and thus unstring the bow and make Protestantism a mere sociological instead of a religious force. There was perhaps also a danger of inward insincerity, in the fact that it refused to admit to itself and others that it maintained its affirmation of the world in opposition to the sayings of Jesus, simply because it could not do otherwise.

For that reason, it is a good thing that the true historical Jesus should overthrow the modern Jesus, should rise up against the modern spirit and send upon earth, not peace, but a sword. He was not teacher, not a casuist; he was an imperious ruler. It was because he was so in his inmost being that he could think of himself as the Son of Man. That was only the temporally conditioned expression of the fact that he was an authoritative ruler. The names in which men expressed their recognition of him as such, Messiah, Son of Man, Son of God, have become for us historical parables. We can find no designation which expresses what he is for us.

He comes to us as One unknown, without a name, as of old, by the lake-side, he came to those men who knew him not. He speaks to us the same words: "Follow thou me!" and sets us to the tasks which he has to fulfill for our time. He commands. And to those who obey him, whether they be wise or simple, he will reveal himself in the toils, the conflicts, the sufferings which they shall pass through in his fellowship, and, as an ineffable mystery, they shall learn in their own experience Who he is.

2. Karl Barth, *The Strange New World within the Bible*

We are to attempt to find an answer to the question, What is there within the Bible? What sort of house is it to which the Bible is the door? What sort of country is spread before our eyes when we throw the Bible open?

We are with Abraham in Haran. We hear a call which commands him: Get thee out of thy country, and from thy kindred, unto a land that I will show thee! We hear a promise: I will make of thee a great nation. And Abraham believed in the Lord; and he counted it to him for righteousness. What is the meaning of all this? We can but feel there is something behind these words and experiences. But what?

We are with Moses in the wilderness. For forty years, he has been living among the sheep, doing penance for an over-hasty act. What change has come over him? We are not told; it is apparently not our concern. But suddenly there comes to him also a call: Moses, Moses!—a great command: Come now therefore, and I will send thee unto Pharaoh, that thou mayest bring forth my people, the children of Israel, out of Egypt!—and a simple assurance: Certainly I will be with thee. Here again are words and experiences which seem at first to be nothing but riddles. We do not read the like either in the daily papers or in other books. What lies behind?

It is a time of severe oppression in the land of Canaan. Under the oak at Ophrah stands the farmer's son, Gideon. The "angel of the Lord" appears to him, and says, The Lord is with thee, thou mighty man of valor. He sees nothing amiss in protesting, If the Lord be with us, why then is all this befallen us? But "The Lord" knows how to bring him to silence: Go in this thy might, and *thou* shalt save Israel from the hand of the Midianites: have not *I* sent thee?

In the tabernacle at Shiloh lies the young Samuel. Again a call: Samuel, Samuel! And the pious priest Eli, to whom he runs, wisely advises him to lie down again. He obeys and sleeps until, the call returning and returning, he can no longer sleep; and the thought comes to the pious Eli: It might be! And Samuel must hear and obey.

We read all this, but what do we read behind it? We are aware of something like the tremors of an earthquake or like the ceaseless thundering of ocean waves against thin dikes; but what really is it that beats at the barrier and seeks entrance here? . . .

Then come the incomprehensible, incomparable days, when all previous time, history, and experience seem to stand still—like the sun at Gibeon—in the presence of a man who was no prophet, no poet, no hero, no thinker, and yet all of these and more! His words cause alarm, for he speaks with authority and not as we ministers. With compelling power, he calls to each one: Follow me! Even to the distrustful and antagonistic he gives an irresistible impression of "eternal life." "The blind receive their sight, and the lame walk, the lepers are cleansed, and the deaf hear, the dead are raised up, and the poor have the gospel preached to them." "Blessed is the womb that bore thee," cry the people. And the quieter and lonelier he becomes, and the less real "faith" he finds in the world about him, the stronger through his whole being peals one triumphant note: "I am the resurrection and the life! Because I live—ye shall live also!"

And then comes the echo, weak enough, if we compare it with that note of Easter morning—and yet strong, much too strong for our ears, accustomed as they are to the weak, pitiably weak tones of today—the echo which this man's life finds in a little crowd of folk who listen, watch, and wait. Here is the echo of the first courageous missionaries who felt the necessity upon them to go into all the world and preach the gospel to every creature. Here is the echo of Paul: "The righteousness of God is revealed! If any man be in Christ, he is a new creature. And he which hath begun a good work in you will finish it!" Here is the deep still echo of John: "Life was manifested. . . . We beheld his glory. . . . Now are we the sons of God. . . . And this is the victory that overcometh the world, even our faith."

The echo ceases. The Bible is finished.

Who is the man who spoke such words and lived such a life, who set these echoes ringing? And again we ask: What is there within the Bible? What is the significance of the remarkable line from Abraham to Christ? What of the chorus of prophets and apostles? And what is the burden of their song? What is the one truth that these voices evidently all desire to announce, each in its own tone, each in its own way? What lies between the strange statement, In the beginning God created the heavens and the earth, and the equally strange cry of longing, Even so, come, Lord Jesus! What is there behind all this, that labors for expression?

It is a dangerous question. We might do better not to come too near this burning bush. For we are sure to betray what is—behind *us!* The Bible gives to every man and to every era such answers to their questions as they deserve. We shall always find in it as much as we seek and no more: high and divine content if it is high and divine content that we seek; transitory and "historical" content, if it is transitory and "historical" content that we seek—nothing whatever, if it is nothing whatever that we seek. The hungry are satisfied it is surfeiting before they have opened it. The question, What is within the Bible? has a mortifying way of converting itself into the opposing question, Well, what are you looking for, and who are you, pray, who make bold to look?

But in spite of all this danger of making embarrassing discoveries in ourselves, we must yet trust ourselves to ask our question. Moreover, we must trust ourselves to reach eagerly for an answer which is really much too large for us, for which we really are not ready, and of which we do not seem worthy, since it is a fruit which our own longing, striving, and inner labor have not planted. What this fruit, this answer, is, is suggested by the title of my address: within the Bible there is a strange new world, the world of God. This answer is the same as that which came to the first martyr, Stephen: Behold, I see the heavens opened and the Son of man standing on the right hand of God. Neither by the earnestness of our belief nor by the depth and richness of our experience have we deserved the right to this answer. What I shall have to say about it will be only a small and unsatisfying part of it. We must openly confess that we are reaching far beyond ourselves. But that is just the point: if we wish to come to grips with the contents of the Bible, we must dare to reach far beyond ourselves. The Book admits of nothing less. For, besides giving to every one of us what he rightly deserves—to one, much, to another, something, to a third, nothing—it leaves us no rest whatever, if we are in earnest, once with our shortsighted eyes and awkward fingers we have found the answer in it that *we* deserve. Such an answer is something but, as we soon realize, not everything. It may satisfy us for a few years, but we simply cannot be content with it forever. Ere long the Bible says to us, in a manner candid and friendly enough, with regard to the "versions" we make of it: "These may be you, but they are not I! They may perhaps suit you, meeting the demands of your thought and temperament, of your era and your 'circle,' of your religious or philosophical theories. You wanted to be mirrored in me, and now you have really found in me your own reflection. But now I bid you come seek *me*, as well. Seek what is here." It is the Bible itself, it is the straight inexorable logic of its onmarch which drives us out beyond ourselves and invites us, without regard to our worthiness or unworthiness, to reach for the last highest answer, in which all is said that can be said, although we can hardly understand and only stammeringly express it. And that answer is: A new world, the world of God. There is a spirit in the Bible that allows us to stop a while and play among secondary things as is our wont—but presently it begins to press us on; and however we may object that we are only weak, imperfect, and most average folk, it presses us on to the primary fact, whether we will or no. There is a river in the Bible that carries us away, once we have entrusted our destiny to it—away from ourselves to the sea. The Holy Scriptures will interpret themselves in spite of all our human limitations. We need only dare to follow this drive, this spirit, this river, to grow out beyond ourselves toward the highest answer. This daring is *faith*; and we read the Bible rightly, not when we do so with false modesty, restraint, and attempted sobriety, for these are passive qualities, but when we read it in faith. And the invitation to dare and to reach toward the highest, even though we do not deserve it, is the expression of *grace* in the Bible; the Bible unfolds to us as we are met, guided, drawn on, and made to grow by the grace of God.

What is there within the Bible? *History!* The history of a remarkable, even unique, people; the history of powerful, mentally vigorous personalities; the history of Christianity in its beginnings—a history of men and ideas in which anyone who considers himself educated must be interested, if for no other reason than because of its effects upon the times following and the present time.

Now one can content himself for a time with this answer and find in it many true and beautiful possibilities. The Bible is full of history: religious history, literary history, cultural history, world history, and human history of every sort. A picture full of animation and color is unrolled before all who approach the Bible with open eyes.

But the pleasure is short-lived: the picture, on closer inspection, proves quite incomprehensible and flat, if it is meant only for history. The man who is looking for history or for stories will be glad after a little to turn from the Bible to the morning paper or to other books. For when we study history and amuse ourselves with stories, we are always wanting to know: How did it all happen? How is it that one event follows another? What are the natural causes of things? *Why* did the people speak such words and live such lives? It is just at the most decisive points of its history that the Bible gives no answer to our Why. Such is the case, indeed, not only with the Bible, but with all the truly decisive men and events of history. The greater a crisis, the less of an answer we get to our inquisitive Why. And vice versa: the smaller a man or an era, the more the "historians" find to explain and establish. But the Bible meets the lover of history with silences quite unparalleled.

Why was it that the Israelitish people did not perish in the Egyptian bondage, but remained a people, or rather, in the very deepest of their need, became one? Why? There was a reason! Why is it that Moses was able to create a law which for purity and humanity puts us moderns only to shame? There was a reason! Why is it that Jeremiah stands there during the siege of Jerusalem with his message of doom, an enemy of the people, a man without a country? Why Jesus' healing of the sick, why his messianic consciousness, why the resurrection? Why does a Saul become a Paul? Why that other-worldly picture of Christ in the fourth gospel? Why does John on the Isle of Patmos—ignoring the Roman Empire in its very heyday—see the holy city, new Jerusalem, coming down from God out of heaven, prepared as a bride adorned for her husband? There was a reason!

How much trouble the Bible makes the poor research workers! There was a reason (with an exclamation point)! is hardly an adequate answer for a history; and if one can say of the incidents of the Bible only There was a reason! its history is in truth stark nonsense. Some men have felt compelled to seek grounds and explanations where there were none, and what has resulted from that procedure is a history in itself—an unhappy history into which I will not enter at this time. The bible itself, in any case, answers our eager Why neither like a sphinx,

24

with There was a reason! nor, like a lawyer, with a thousand arguments, deductions, and parallels, but says to us, The decisive cause is *God.* Because *God* lives, speaks, and acts, there was a reason . . . !

To be sure, when we hear the word "God," it may at first seem the same as There was a reason! In the leading articles of our dailies, and in the primary history readers of our Aargau schools one does not expect to have events explained by the fact that "God created," or "God spoke!" When God enters, history for the while ceases to be, and there is nothing more to ask; for something wholly different begins—a history with its own distinct grounds, possibilities, and hypotheses.

The paramount question is whether we have understanding for this different, new world, or good will enough to meditate and enter upon it inwardly. Do we desire the presence of "God"? Do we dare to go whither evidently we are being led? That were "faith"! A new world projects itself into our old ordinary world. We may reject it. We may say, It is nothing; this is imagination, madness, this "God." But we may not deny nor prevent our being led by Bible "history" far out beyond what is elsewhere called history—into a new world, into the world of God.

We might also say, There is *morality* within the Bible. It is a collection of teachings and illustrations of virtue and human greatness. No one has ever yet seriously questioned the fact that in their way the men of the Bible were good representative men, from whom we have an endless amount to learn. Whether we seek practical wisdom or lofty examples of a certain type of heroism, we find them here forthwith.

And again in the long run we do not. Large parts of the Bible are almost useless to the school in its moral curriculum because they are lacking in just this wisdom and just these "good examples." The heroes of the Bible are to a certain degree quite respectable, but to serve as examples to the good, efficient, industrious, publicly educated, average citizen of Switzerland, men like Samson, David, Amos, and Peter are very ill fated indeed. . . . How shall we find in the life and teaching of Jesus something to "do" in "practical life"? Is it not as if he wished to say to us at every step "What interest have I in your 'practical life'? I have little to do with that. Follow after *me* or let me go my way!"

At certain crucial points, the Bible amazes us by its remarkable indifference to our conception of good and evil. Abraham, for instance, as the highest proof of his faith desires to sacrifice his son to God; Jacob wins the birthright by a refined deception of his blind father; Elijah slays the four hundred and fifty priests of Baal by the brook Kishon. Are these exactly praiseworthy examples?

And in how many phases of morality the Bible is grievously wanting! How little fundamental information it offers in regard to the difficult questions of business life, marriage, civilization, and statecraft, with which we have to struggle! To mention only a single problem, but to us today a mortal one: how unceremoniously and constantly war is waged in the Bible! Time and again, when this question comes up, the teacher or minister must resort to various kinds of extra-biblical material, because the New as well as the Old Testament almost completely breaks down at this point. Time and again, serious Christian people who seek "comfort" and "inspiration" in the midst of personal difficulties will quietly close their Bibles. . . . Time and again, the Bible gives us the impression that it contains no instructions, counsels, or examples whatsoever, either for individuals or for nations and governments; and the impression is correct. It offers us not at all what we first seek in it.

Once more we stand before this "other" new world which begins in the Bible. In it the chief consideration is not the doings of man but the doings of God—not the various ways which we may take if we are men of good will, but the power out of which good will must first be created—not the unfolding and fruition of love as we may understand it, but the existence and outpouring of eternal love, of love as God understands it—not industry, honesty, and helpfulness as we may practice them in our old ordinary world, but the establishment and growth of a new world, the world in which God and *his* morality reign. In the light of this coming world a David is a great man in spite of his adultery and bloody sword: blessed is the man unto whom the Lord imputeth not iniquity! Into this world, the publicans and the harlots will go before your impeccably elegant and righteous folk of good society! In this world, the true hero is the lost son, who is absolutely lost and feeding swine—and not his moral elder brother! The reality which lies behind Abraham and Moses, behind Christ and his apostles, is the world of the Father, in which morality is dispensed with because it is taken for granted. And the blood of the New Testament which seeks inflow into our veins is the will of the Father which would be done on earth as it is in heaven.

We may have grasped this as the meaning of the Bible, as its answer to our great and small questions, and still say: I do not need this; I do not desire it; it tells me nothing; I cannot get anywhere with it! It may be that we really cannot get anywhere with it on our present highways and byways—on our byways of church and school, for example, and, in many instances, on the byway of the personal life which we have been traveling with such perseverance. There are blind alleys of a thousand types, out of which the way into the kingdom of heaven can at first lead only backwards. And it is certain that the Bible, if we read it carefully, makes straight for the point where one must decide to accept or to reject the sovereignty of God. This is the new world within the Bible. We are offered the magnificent, productive, hopeful life of a grain of seed, a new beginning, out of which all things shall be made new. One cannot learn or imitate this life of the divine seed in the new world. One can only let it live, grow, and ripen within him. One can only believe—can only hold the ground whither he has been led. Or not believe. There is no third way.

Let us seek our way out on still another side: let us start with the proposition that in the Bible we have a revelation of true *religion*, of religion defined as what we are to think concerning God, how we are to find him, and how we are to conduct ourselves in his presence. . . . The Bible as a "source-book for godly living"—how much has been said and written upon this theme in the last years! And such the Bible is. It is a treasury of truth concerning the right relation of men to the eternal and divine—but here too the same law holds: we have only to seek honestly and we shall make the plain discovery that there is something greater in the Bible than religion and "worship." Here again we have only a kind of crust which must be broken through.

We have all been troubled with the thought that there are so many kinds of Christianity in the world—Catholic Christianity and Protestant, the Christianities of the various communions and of the "groups" (*Richtungen*) within them, the Christianity of the old-fashioned and the Christianity of the modern—and all, all of them appealing with the same earnestness and zeal to the Bible. Each insists, *Ours* is the religion revealed in the Bible, or at least its most legitimate successor. And how is one to answer? Does it not require a generous bit of effrontery to say, We Protestants, or we members of such and such a communion or society are right, for such and such reasons; and all the others are wrong? When once one knows how easy it is to find "reasons," the pleasure of participating in this eternal game begins to pall.

Then shall we take the position that fundamentally we are all right? Shall we dip our hands into that from which the spirit of the Bible silently turns away, the dish of tolerance which is more and more being proclaimed, especially in our nation church, as the highest good?

Or may we all, jointly and severally, with our various views and various forms of worship, be—wrong? The fact is that we must seek our answer in this direction—"Yea, let God be true, but every man a liar." All religions may be found in the Bible, if one will have it so; but when he looks closely, there are none at all. There is only—the "other," new, greater world! When we come to the Bible with our questions—How shall I think of God and the universe? How arrive at the divine? How present myself?—it answers us, as it were, "My dear sir, these are *your* problems: you must not ask *me!* Whether it is better to hear mass or hear a sermon, whether the proper form of Christianity is to be discovered in the Salvation Army or in 'Christian Science,' whether the better belief is that of old Reverend Doctor Smith or young Reverend Mr. Jones, whether your religion should be more a religion of the understanding, of the will, or of the feelings, you can and must decide for yourself. If you do not care to enter upon *my* questions, you may, to be sure, find in me all sorts of arguments and quasi-arguments for one or another standpoint, but you will not then find what is really here." We shall find ourselves only in the midst of a vast human controversy and far, far away from reality, or what might become reality in our lives.

It is not the right human thoughts about God which form the content of the Bible, but the right divine thoughts about men. The Bible tells us not how we should talk with God but what he says to us; not how we find the way to him, but how he has sought and found the way to us; not the right relation in which we must place ourselves to him, but the covenant which he has made with all who are Abraham's spiritual children and which he has sealed once and for all in Jesus Christ. It is this which is within the Bible. The word of God is within the Bible.

Our grandfathers, after all, were right when they struggled so desperately in behalf of the truth that there is revelation in the Bible and not religion only, and when they would not allow facts to be turned upside down for them even by so pious and intelligent a man as Schleiermacher. And our fathers were right when they guarded warily against being drawn out upon the shaky scaffolding of religious self-expression.

The more honestly we search the Scriptures, the surer, sooner or later, comes the answer: The right forms of worship and service? — "they are they which testify of *Me!*" We seek ourselves — we find God; and having done so stand before him with our religions, Christianities, and other notions, like blundering scholars with their A B C's. Yet we cannot be sad about it but rejoice that we have found, among all lesser considerations, the chief one, without which every form of religion, even the most perfect, is only a delusion and a snare. This chief consideration contains, again, the living grain of seed out of which a right relation to God, a service of God "in spirit and in truth," necessarily must issue, whether we lay stress more upon this detail or that. The word of God! The standpoint of God!

Once more we have every liberty of choice. We may explain: "I cannot get anywhere with this: the conception of the 'word of God' is not part of my philosophy. I still prefer the old ordinary Christianity of my kind of 'worship' and my own particular standpoint." Or we may be willing to hear what "passeth all understanding"; may desire in the power of God and the Savior to let it grow and ripen within us according to the laws of the great life process set forth in the Bible; may obey the spirit of the Book and acknowledge God to be right instead of trying to prove ourselves right; may dare — to believe. Here we find ourselves faced once more by the question of faith. But without anticipating our answer to it, we may rest assured that in the Bible, in both the Old and the New Testaments, the theme is, so to speak, the religion of God and never once the religion of the Jews, or Christians, or heathen; that in this respect, as in others, the Bible lifts us out of the old atmosphere of man to the open portals of a new world, the world of God.

But we are not yet quite at an end. We have found in the Bible a new world, God, God's sovereignty, God's glory, God's incomprehensible love. Not the history of man but the history of God! Not the virtues of men but the virtues of him who hath called us out of darkness into his marvelous light! Not human standpoints but the standpoint of God!

Now, however, might not a last series of questions arise: Who then is God? What is his will? What are his thoughts? What is the mysterious "other," new, greater world which emerges in the Bible beyond all the ways of men, summoning us to a decision to believe or not to believe? In whom did Abraham believe? For whom did the heroes fight and conquer? Whom did the prophets prophesy?

In whose power did Christ die and rise again? Whose name did the Apostles proclaim? The contents of the Bible are "God." But what is the content of the contents? Something "new" breaks forth! But what is the new?

To these questions there is a series of ready answers, serious and well-founded answers taken from the Bible itself, answers to which we must listen: God is the Lord and Redeemer, the Savior and Comforter of all the souls that turn to him; and the new world is the kingdom of blessedness which is prepared for the little flock who escape destruction. Is not this in the Bible? . . . Again: God is the fountain of life which begins its quiet murmuring when once we turn away from the externalities of the world and bow before him in silence; and the new world is the incomparable peace of such a life hid with Christ in God. Is not this also in the Bible? . . . Again: God is the Lord of the heaven which awaits us, and in which, when our journey through the sorrows and imperfections of this life is done, we are to possess and enjoy our citizenship; and the new world is just this blessed other life, the "still eternity" into which the faithful shall one day enter. This answer also comes directly from the Bible.

These are true enough answers. But are they *truth*? Are they the whole truth? Can one read or hear read even as much as two chapters from the Bible and still with good conscience say, God's word went forth to humanity, his mandate guided history from Abraham to Christ, the Holy Spirit descended in tongues of fire upon the apostles at Pentecost, a Saul became a Paul and traveled over land and sea—all in order that here and there specimens of men like you and me might be "converted," find inner "peace," and by a redeeming death go some day to "heaven." Is *that* all? Is *that* all of God and his new world, of the meaning of the Bible, of the content of the contents? The powerful forces which come to expression in the Bible, the movements of peoples, the battles, and the convulsions which take place before us there, the miracles and revelations which constantly occur there, the immeasurable promises for the future which are unceasingly repeated to us there—do not all these things stand in a rather strange relation to so small a result—if that is really the only result they have? Is not God greater than that? Even in these answers, earnest and pious as they may be, have we not measured God with our own measure, conceived God with our own conceptions, wished ourselves a God according to our own wishes? When we begin to read the Bible carefully, must we not grow beyond these answers, too?

Must we not also grow beyond the strange question, Who is God? As if we could dream of asking such a question, having willingly and sincerely allowed ourselves to be led to the gates of the new world, to the threshold of the kingdom of God! There one asks no longer. There one sees. There one hears. There one has. There one knows. There one no longer gives his petty, narrow little answers. The question, Who is God? and our inadequate answers to it come only from our having halted somewhere on the way to the open gates of the new world; from our having refused somewhere to let the Bible speak to us candidly; from our having failed somewhere truly to desire to—believe. At the point of halt the truth

29

again becomes unclear, confused, problematical—narrow, stupid, high-church, nonconformist, monotonous, or meaningless. "He that hath *seen* me hath *seen* the Father." That is it: when we allow ourselves to press on to the highest answer, when we find God in the Bible, when we dare with Paul not to be disobedient to the heavenly vision, then God stands before us as he really is. "Believing, ye *shall* receive!" God is *God*.

But who may say, I believe?—"Lord, I believe; help thou mine unbelief." It is because of our unbelief that we are so perplexed by the question, Who is God?— that we feel so small and ashamed before the fullness of the Godhead which the men and women of the Bible saw and proclaimed. It is because of our unbelief that even now I can only stammer, hint at, and make promises about that which would be opened to us if the Bible could speak to us unhindered, in the full fluency of its revelations.

Who is God? The heavenly Father! But the heavenly Father even upon *earth*, and upon earth really the *heavenly* Father. He will not allow life to be split into a "here" and "beyond." He will not leave to death the task of freeing us from sin and sorrow. He will bless us, not with the power of the church but with the power of life and resurrection. In Christ he caused his word to be made flesh. He has caused eternity to dawn in place of time, or rather upon time—for what sort of eternity were it which should begin "afterwards!" He purposes naught but the establishment of a new *world*.

Who is God? The Son who has become "the mediator for my soul." But more than that: He has become the mediator for the whole world, the redeeming Word, who was in the beginning of all things and is earnestly expected by all things. He is the redeemer of my brothers and sisters. He is the redeemer of a humanity gone astray and ruled by evil spirits and powers. He is the redeemer of the groaning creation about us. The whole Bible authoritatively announces that God must be all in all; and the events of the Bible are the beginning, the glorious beginning of a new *world*.

Who is God? The spirit in his believers, the spirit

> by which we own
> The Son who lived and died and rose;
> Which crystal clear from God's pure throne
> Through quiet hearts forever flows.

But God is also that spirit (that is to say, that love and good will) which will and must break forth from quiet hearts into the world outside, that it may be manifest, visible, comprehensible: behind the tabernacle of God is with men! The Holy Spirit makes a new heaven and a new earth and, therefore, new men, new families, new relationships, new politics. It has no respect for old traditions simply because they are traditions, for old solemnities simply because they are solemn, for old powers simply because they are powerful. The *Holy* Spirit has respect only for truth, for itself. The Holy Spirit establishes the righteousness of heaven in the midst of the unrighteousness of earth and will not stop nor stay until all that is dead has been brought to life and a new *world* has come into being.

This is within the Bible. It is within the Bible for us. For it we were baptized. Oh, that we dared in faith to take what grace can offer us!

I need not suggest that we all have need of this. We live in a sick old world which cries from its soul, out of deepest need: Heal me, O Lord, and I shall be healed! In all men, whoever and wherever and whatever and however they may be, there is a longing for exactly this which is here within the Bible. We all know that.

And now hear: "A certain man made a great supper, and bade many; and sent his servant at suppertime to say to them that were hidden, Come, for all things are now ready! . . ."

3. Ernst Troeltsch, *The Absoluteness of Christianity*

The modern idea of history, which depends on critical source-analysis and on conclusions derived from psychological analogy, is the history of the development of peoples, spheres of culture, and cultural components. It dissolves all dogmas in the flow of events and tries sympathetically to do justice to all phenomena, first measuring them by their own criteria and then combining them into an overall picture of the continuous and mutually conditioning factors in all individual phenomena that shape the unfolding development of mankind. This overall picture, steadily pursued despite the incompleteness and uncertainty of our knowledge, is today, with all its different stages of development, the presupposition of every judgment concerning the norms and ideals of mankind. For this reason the modern idea of history is no longer merely one aspect of a way of looking at things or a partial satisfaction of the impetus to knowledge. It is, rather, the foundation of all thinking concerning values and norms. It is the medium for the self-reflection of the species upon its nature, origins, and hopes.

It is easy to see how Christianity is affected by this mode of thought which is entirely free as regards the outcome of specific investigations and yet bound to definite methodological presupposition. Christianity, like all great religious movements, has from the outset possessed a naive certainty as to its normative truth. Apologetic reflections have fortified this confidence since the earliest times by contrasting Christianity with everything non-Christian as a whole. In this way the latter became more and more a homogeneous mass of human error while the former became more and more a divinely ordained institution, recognizable as such on the basis of external and internal miracle. Ecclesiastical philosophy and theology then perfected the concept of the church. Founded as an absolute miracle and authenticating itself in the miracles of conversion and the sacraments, the church was conceived as a supernatural institution that stands within history but does not derive from history. Ordinary history with its merely human and humanly conditioned truths is, according to this view, the sphere of sin and error. Only history as written by the church gives truth that is absolutely certain, though not absolutely exhaustive, because it works with powers that derive not from history but directly from God.

The modern idea of history, however, has had a radically dissolving effect on this apologetic structure of thought. Opposition to the rationalistic watering down of Christianity, often thought of as a kind of restoration of church-oriented theology, led to a revival of the notion of the historical uniqueness of Christianity. But this in turn simply led to the incorporation of Christianity as one individual phenomenon that history has brought forth, even though the Christian phenomenon was not to be declared false on the basis of extraneous normative concepts. In particular, it led to the incorporating of Christianity into the context of the history of religions. The apologetic wall of division, the wall of external and internal miracle, has slowly been broken down by this idea of history, for no matter what one may otherwise think about miracles, it is impossible for historical thought to believe the Christian miracles but deny the non-Christian. Again, however frequently one may discern something supernatural in the ethical power of the inner life, no means exist by which to construe the Christian's elevation above sensuality as supernatural while interpreting that of Plato or Epictetus as natural. . . .

Once the modern idea of history made it impossible to prove the normative value of Christian thought by the means the church had traditionally used, attempts were made to reach the goal by yet another path. Its starting point was the concept of a total history of mankind with history taken as a dynamic principle in its own right. The history of mankind was viewed casually and teleologically as a single whole. Within this whole, the ideal of religious truth was thought of as moving forward in gradual stages, and at one definite point, namely, in the historical phenomenon of Christianity, it was deemed to have reached absolute form, that is, the complete and exhaustive realization of its principle.

This approach remained true to the Enlightenment and its incorporating of Christianity into the religions of the world. It also remained true to the historico-critical way of viewing Christianity. Because the totality of history in general and the history of religion in particular were comprehended by an all-embracing intuition and were brilliantly interpreted, it was expected that this approach would overcome the tension between the multiplicity of history and its relative, individual forms. It was to do so by means of the concept of a universal principle that bore within itself the law of its movement from lower, obscure, and embryonic beginnings to complete, clear, and conscious maturity—a universal principle represented as a normative power actualizing itself by degrees in the course of history. In this way Christianity was held up as the actualization of the principle of religion, the absolute religion in antithesis to mediated and veiled expressions of this principle. There exists, in reality, only one religion, namely, the principle or essence of religion, and this principle of religion, this essence of religion, is latent in all historical religions as their ground and goal. In Christianity, this universally latent essence, everywhere else limited by its media, has appeared in untrammeled and exhaustive perfection. If Christianity is thus identical with this principle of religion that is elsewhere implicit and that comes to complete explication only in Christianity, then the Christian religion is of course normative religious truth. Thus the older apologetic speculation, which opposed history, has been replaced by a new one that is on the side of history. Thus too, in fact, the concept of a principle of Christianity that is at the same time the realization of the principle of religion as such has become the foundation of the modern apologetic. . . .

The basic ideas of this interpretation are clear. First, it subordinates history to the concept of a universal principle which represents a uniform, homogeneous, law-structured, and self-actuating power that brings forth individual instances of itself. Second, it elevates this concept of a universal principle to that of a norm and ideal representing what is of permanent value in all events. Third, it binds these two concepts together by means of a theory of evolutionary development. This implies, as the fourth basic idea, both a perfect congruity between the results of the law-regulated causal process as brought forth in accordance with the concept of the universal principle and the successive creation of value as produced in accordance with the concept of absolute realization.

The irrefutable objections to this interpretation are, however, equally clear. The modern idea of history knows no universal principle on the basis of which the content and sequence of events might be deduced. It knows only concrete, individual phenomena, always conditioned by their context and yet, at bottom, undeniable and simply existent phenomena. For this reason, the modern understanding of history knows no values or norms that coincide with actual universals. It knows them, rather, strictly as universally valid ideas, or ideas purporting to be universally valid, which invariably appear in individual form and make their universal validity known by their resistance to the merely existent. For all these reasons the modern understanding of history knows no evolutionary development in which an actual, law-regulated universal principle produces values that are universally authentic. It knows, finally, no absolute realization of such a universal principle within the context of history where, as a matter of fact, only phenomena that are uniquely defined and limited and thus possess individual character are brought forth at any given point. . . .

It becomes evident that the concepts men sought to weld together in a theory of this kind have now come apart. The concept of that which is really and authentically universal in the basic and characteristic phenomena of religion and the concept of a norm governing authoritative religious truth were appended to each distinctive, historical religion seen as a concrete, individual phenomenon. These concepts, precisely because their definitions are so obscure and uncertain, show clearly how impossible it is to take a universal principle or essence and suddenly give it normative status or, conversely, to defend the concept of a normative principle by reference to its concurrent property of being a universal one.

Even more serious, in the second place, is what happens with regard to the absolute realization of this universal principle in the process of historical development. Here two possibilities exist. On the one hand, greater emphasis may be laid on the causal aspect of the universal principle. In this case, however, its absolute realization is embodied only in the sequence of historical configurations taken as a whole. Among these configurations, then, there can obviously be no absolute religion in which this principle or essence is exclusively and exhaustively realized. "The idea prefers not to pour out all its abundance into one individual specimen." However plausible such a view may appear to the historian, since it enables him to form conceptions freely and impartially, it can hardly suffice for him who sees in religion not merely an object of historical inquiry but a question of life itself and who for this reason is even less inclined to forget the teleological aspect of the universal principle. Yet at the same time it is the historian himself who cannot evade the teleological problem, inasmuch as he pursues his labors not merely for the sake of gaining knowledge of things past but rather for the sake of comprehending the values that gradually make themselves known in history.

If the aspect of gradual manifestation is given the stronger emphasis, however, then the second possibility comes into view. One senses that he is indeed oriented toward a goal, but he feels that until the end of history is reached, he ought not to speak of an absolute religion but should await it in close conjunction with the end of all history. There must be complete twilight before the owl of Minerva can begin its flight in the land of the realized absolute principle. But if that is how matters stand, how can the universal principle be characterized with sufficient certainty as long as its definitive realization still lies far off in the incalculable distance? And if the character of the universal principle cannot be determined with certainty how then can its stages be described with certainty—those stages by which it has moved toward realization up to the present time and among which we are supposed to make a choice? Precisely for this reason, the attempt to demonstrate a religion as absolute never continues long with one historical religion but tends to become a projection of the religion of the future. The impracticability of this concept of absolute realization is made unmistakably evident, however, by the fact that these depictions of the coming religion, each of which is set forth as the goal of the evolutionary process, are mutually inconsistent. As a result, there is great disparity in the determination and evaluation of the stages that lead to this goal, the highest being the one on which we are supposed to take our stand.

More specifically, the modern study of history gives no indication whatever of any graded progression such as this theory might lead us to expect. History manifests no gradual ascent to higher orientations as far as the vast majority of mankind is concerned. Only at special points do higher orientations burst forth, and then in a great, soaring development of their uniquely individual content.

34

By no means, however, are the great religions that burst forth in this way related to each other in a stage-by-stage causal process. They stand, rather, in a parallel relationship. The only path to an understanding of their relationship in terms of value is toil and inner moral struggle, not schemes of progressive development like those that are always being constructed. Since it is no longer merely the history of religion in the Near East and in the cultures around the Mediterranean but also the world of the East Asian religions that stands before our eyes, we can no longer deceive ourselves about this matter. Thus even with regard to this aspect, our conclusion is that while the modern study of history cannot avoid forming concepts of normative principles, it cannot arrive at such concepts by proofs for the absolute realization of a universal principle.

Most problematic of all, in the third place, is the interpreting of Christianity as the absolute religion. This holds true not only because, as suggested above, no such demonstration is possible in historical terms, but above all because the impossibility of uniting a theoretically conceived universal principle with a concrete, individual, historical configuration becomes directly discernible at this point. Of course all religious men naturally understand that Christianity is a dynamic religious orientation of great significance, that it is under all circumstances an eminent religious truth. Yet it is also evident that Christianity in every age, and particularly in its period of origin, is a genuinely historical phenomenon—new, and large, in its consequences, but profoundly and radically conditioned by the historical situation and environment in which it found itself as well as by the relations it entered into in its further development. It presupposes the breakdown of the ethnic religions of antiquity and also of the naive values that had sprung up with them. It likewise presupposes the new religious movements that emerged from this rubble and gravitated toward Christianity as the most powerful force. Indeed, these movements may possibly have participated in some way in Christianity's earliest, formative history.

In its central concepts, moreover, Christianity is clearly determined in a radical sense by the eschatological ideas that were a source of strength to Israel in this situation. It was in connection with these ideas that Christianity first articulated its purely inward and ethical faith. At this particular juncture, however, the early Christian ethic was so strongly stamped by the expectation of the end of the world and of standing in the presence of God, as well as by indifference to all earthly values, that it took on the religious harshness and one-sidedness that is possible only in such situations and under such presuppositions. Yet no sooner had Christianity freed itself from these first popular and mythical forms and disclosed its concern for humane and inward values than it drew to itself the closely related ethics of Platonism and Stoicism together with the metaphysics of idealism and the teleology of Aristotelianism. Thus it showed again, by virtue of these relations, that it was a thoroughly concrete, limited, and conditioned movement.

And so it continues to the present day. Nowhere is Christianity the absolute religion, an utterly unique species free of the historical conditions that comprise its environment at any given time. Nowhere is it the changeless, exhaustive, and unconditioned realization of that which is conceived as the universal principle of religion.

To be sure, it is necessary to seek out the controlling idea of Christianity and to understand, as far as possible, the development and continuation of Christianity in view of the content of this idea. But this controlling idea must be derived strictly from Christianity, which means that it is at every moment intimately interwoven with quite definite historical conditions. Like all other ideas, it lives by virtue of its involvement in a historical context and thus always in completely individual, historical forms. Conversely, this controlling idea is falsified and placed in an utterly artificial relationship to its own reality if it is contrived from without as the absolute idea of religion and then injected into Christianity. . . .

Thus our conclusion may be expressed as follows: Whatever the permanent significance of the concept of evolutionary development may be, it is not to be worked out in the form of a sequence that assumes a congruity between causality and finality and thus seems to make possible a theoretical computation of the value of the various stages. It is not to be used to prove the absoluteness of any one religion as the definitive realization of the principle of religion itself.

It is evident, therefore, that the attempt to present Christianity as the absolute religion is untenable. The fathers of the theology of evolutionary development found it possible to put a construction like this on Christianity only because the history of religion of their day was still quite undeveloped and provincial. Equally important, their historical research into Christian religion still fluctuated between rationalistic-pragmatic explanations of individual phenomena, on the one hand, and poetic-intuitive improvisations, on the other. Only through the mist of historical knowledge that was still quite hazy could the rainbow of such speculation shine.

Moreover, these theologians still stood under the influence of an older habit of thought that saw Christianity as the divine realization of natural religion, of the Logos, and of the natural moral law. Their "essence of religion," seen from that angle, was simply the poetic idea of natural religion made perfect and introduced into history by God. Thus old habits of thought still have power even over those who have broken away from them at critical points. Furthermore, in their use of this construction, these men were obliged to attach significant qualifications to it. . . .

The personalistic redemption-religion of Christianity is the highest and most significantly developed world of religious life that we know, being grounded in the prophets and in Jesus, possessing its primary and classical attestation in the Bible, and having disclosed a wealth of potentialities in its fusion with the culture of antiquity and with that of the Germanic tribes of western Europe. The authentic life it contains will endure in every conceivable future development. Its authentic life may be assimilated by such development, but it will never be annulled. And if it is incumbent upon us to consider the possibility of a disruption and decline of culture and of religious development, we still have every reason to believe that this authentic life will reappear and make a fresh start in a form analogous to the Christianity we know.

That is our situation, and only in this sense is it possible to affirm the "absoluteness of Christianity." This judgment issues from a joining together of absolute decision in the present with an interpretation of the developmental process that affirms historical relativity. It cannot emerge from repeated demonstrations of how Christianity, taken as an isolated object, produces an impression of absolute miracle, nor can it be deduced from the developmental process as a certain and verifiable law. In both positions something authentic has been recognized, but neither is exhaustive; instead, each must be worked out in and with the other. The "absoluteness" to which this inquiry has led us is simply the highest value discernible in history and the certainty of having found the way that leads to perfect truth. . . .

The religious man wants to possess truth, genuinely desires to find God, yearns to cling to an authentic revelation and manifestation of God. For this, however, does he require an absolute religion, a knowledge of God that exhausts its essence and idea, that is withdrawn from all change and enrichment, that overleaps the bounds of history? Or if, with an admittedly quite unjustified attenuating of the word, one defines absolute religion as meaning only that pinnacle of religious knowledge which has definitely been reached and can never be surpassed, is the principal thing one needs for his own religious life the certainty that subsequent generations will never attain a higher knowledge of God? Is there not contained in such demands all too much of the natural, human presumptuousness that would vault over the boundaries and conditionality of life and transpose itself at once to the perfect goal where there is a cessation of toil, conflict, and difficulty over this matter of truth? Is not this presumptuousness unbecoming, especially in the faithful, who, because of their own spiritual struggles and their own lack of conviction and strength, ought to understand how deceptive the riddle of earthly life is better than the superficial crowd that strives self-confidently for perfect solutions? Does it not reflect more timidity and inner uncertainty for one to become completely certain about a religious orientation whose power he has actually experienced only when he knows that it must be experienced in this way, in this historical context, and in this form of thought? that it must be experienced as we ourselves experience it today?

Is not the principal need of the religious man, rather, the real and innermost certainty of having encountered God and heard his voice? of following, from among the mandates of God of which he becomes aware, those that strike him as particularly plain, simple, and impelling? of committing to God the question of how he will proceed from this point on? If so, can he not be certain that what he has felt inwardly and tested in experience as the truth of life can never in all eternity become untruth? Can it be a threat to him if it is sheer faith which asserts that beyond the revelation of God in Jesus there is nothing higher to be hoped for in our entire range of vision? That assertion is, to be sure, only a statement of probability. But is this probability something we may snobbishly scorn or disdain when our knowledge is still so obscure and confused that all confidence in the existence and victory of the Spirit is itself a probability judgment only partially supported by observation and experience? when even the boldest theories of religion have attained no further than the instinctive probability judgment that God would not undertake such a display of miraculous powers and extraordinary manifestations twice or even more frequently?

With statements of this kind, we have admittedly made a transition from scientific discourse to religious: from scientific substantiation by means of universal principles, laws, and necessary relations, to religious reflection upon the immediate value of a religious orientation for our life and feeling. It is the tone of the sermon or meditation that we have sounded. However, in view of the question under consideration, it can hardly be otherwise. The only kind of person who might wish to have it differently is the "scientistic" fanatic, who refuses to trust his own beliefs and values unless he has first translated them into seemingly scientific propositions, but as long as that eludes him, renounces any direct affirmation of life. . . .

All that the Christian needs, therefore, is the certainty that within the Christian orientation of life there is an authentic revelation of God and that nowhere is a greater revelation to be found. This certainty he can discover even in a purely historical consideration of Christianity. In such a consideration the faith in God that animated Jesus and his followers encounters him with a power that is irresistibly transforming, profoundly moving, and binding in the highest degree. With complete composure, he can consign to the world to come the absolute religion that represents not struggling faith but changeless and certain knowledge of the truth.

2

Dialectical Theology

It is a repeated phenomenon of theological history: one book marks an epoch. Anselm's *Why God Became Man* and Schleiermacher's *Speeches on Religion* may serve as examples. *Der Römerbrief* (1922), by Karl Barth, translated as *Commentary on Romans* (hereinafter, *Romans*), is another. The book made the decisive break between the characteristic theologies of the nineteenth and twentieth centuries.

The theology of *Romans* was promptly labeled "dialectical," and readers will see why. The work is a dizzying spin of positions and counterpositions, of dicta and paradoxes. "Dialectic" has been practiced through Western intellectual history; since Socrates, a *conversation* of position and counterposition, of question and answer and new question, has been seen as the proper philosophical method. Dialectic can be closed or open; the meeting of position and counterposition can eventuate in synthesis or sheerly in a new question. Through the time of his radicalization, Barth studied Plato and "the Danish Socrates," Søren Kierkegaard, to learn a dialectic very different from Hegel's, one not only open but actively hostile to all synthesis.

Romans is intended as an assault on the reader. Its dialectic is a conscious renewal of Socrates' attack on Athenian certainties. It does not seek to provide the reader with information or theory but rather to derange his or her religious assumptions. As Socrates elicited self-contradictions to deconstruct the claim that what justice meant in Athens is what justice means in itself, so Barth's whirl of paradoxes intends to undo any direct identity between what faith can mean within the Christian *religion* and what it truly means, in the Christian *gospel*. Liberal theology is never indicted by name, but it is the clear model of the Christian religiosity Barth assails.

Romans adopts Schleiermacher's understanding of religion as the essential and crowning human possibility, and then reverses the value signs. Religion is, just as Neo-Protestantism supposed, our unquenchable and ennobling longing for the eternal totality beyond our temporal being, in which alone our lives can come together. Just so, said Barth, religion is the attempt to use eternity for our temporal purposes, and so denies what it seeks. We cannot but dream of God, and indeed not to dream of God

39

would be to sink below humanity; but precisely because our gods are indeed our dreams, they are idols.

Romans teaches no system; it wills to destroy all systems. But Barth did write, in the Foreword to one edition, "If I have a system, it consists in what Kierkegaard named 'the infinite qualitative difference' between time and eternity. . . ." We are on the one side of this difference and God is on the other. Religion is our attempt to bridge the separation, to seek and find God that we may be saved from the emptiness of mere temporality. But religion does indeed *bridge* the difference, that is, it creates a synthesis of time and eternity. This mixture is the being of the idols, who, just because they are *almost*-gods, cannot but be tyrants.

Eternity does touch time, else we would not be distressed in our temporality and would seek nothing beyond ourselves. But because eternity is infinitely other than time, it touches time without verging on it. *Romans* is full of images and other evocations of this relation between eternity and time, but perhaps one is plainest. Eternity touches time, Barth says, as a tangent line touches a circle. There is indeed a geometrical *point* that is both on the circle and on the line, yet this meeting has no *extension* on either. The religious attempt to live at once on the circle and on the line falsely projects the line's eternity onto some part of the temporal circle— or, what is the same, falsely projects the circle's finitude onto some part of the line. Either way, a confusion of eternity and time results, populated by the half-gods of religion. "The eternal and fundamental Presupposition of the Creator turns into a thing in itself, over and among the things . . . , even if it is the highest. . . . The Unapproachable and therefore infinitely Near turns into a—forever uncertain—object of our experience."

Perhaps Barth might better have spoken of a cylinder and a tangent plane. Beings inhabiting the surface of a cylinder-world would find their movements stopped when they came to the line of tangency. Yet they would have no purchase on the impediment, and every attempt to deal with it as if it were an object of the cylinder-world would but generate illusion. The line of tangency of eternity to time, says Barth in *Romans,* is "the line of death." Religion is the hopeless and disastrous quest to get some purchase on death.

"Ungod," the almost-God of the middle realm religion creates and inhabits, is not nothing. God could have let Ungod be nothing—and with him us, since now it is Ungod from whom we in fact draw our existence. But it is at once our God-inflicted disaster, "the final consequence of the divine wrath," *and* the continuing possibility of our salvation, that "in fact it is still always God we run into," that also "Ungod" is God, "God in his wrath . . . , God who can now only say No."

That we in practice think of God as if he occupied some stretch of time, as if he were a creature, that we do do not, indeed cannot, think otherwise of God than of ourselves, works out on two lines. The one is that of the vulgar Enlightenment, of what is mostly taught in our schools and presupposed by the shapers of culture. "In place of the holy God enters fate, matter, the universe, accident." "Thrown . . . on itself, humanity faces the meaninglessly reigning powers of the universe." The other way is that of those who still want to be religious. "The deified powers of nature and the soul are gods now and rule the atmosphere of our lives—as Jupiter and Mars, Isis and Osiris, Cybele and Attis."

Christ, according to *Romans*, is the Savior because he fully occupies and so manifests the line of death, closing off our evocation of religion's middle realm. He perfects religion by bringing it definitively to its inevitable failure; he "bridges over the distance between God and man in that he tears it open." At the line of death, we apprehend final negation—which just because it is *final* is *God's* negation, so that we do after all meet God. "The No which meets us is God's No. What we lack is just what helps us. . . . Exactly because God's No is complete, it is also his Yes." God "acknowledges us as his own in that he takes and keeps his distance from us."

Barth compared the publication of *Romans* to groping in a dark church, accidentally yanking the bell rope, and bringing the whole town running. The book became the banner of a generation of the young pastors and academics of German-speaking Protestantism. These "dialectical theologians"—some of whom did not themselves write in particularly dialectical fashion—came together to publish a journal and so identified themselves as a movement. *Zwischen den Zeiten* published for ten years, and ceased publication when those whom *Romans* had gathered moved again apart.

Of the "dialectical theologians," Rudolf Bultmann (1884–1976) was already an established scholar of the New Testament when *Zwischen den Zeiten* was founded. The essay reprinted here is among several in which Bultmann defended *Romans* and its author against the attack of the theological establishment. Friedrich Gogarten (1887–1967), from whose later work we will bring a selection in a later chapter, was perhaps the greatest enthusiast of "dialectic" and "crisis"—which perhaps led to his disastrous initial support for Hitler's crisis-politics and to consequent lifelong hatred by Barth. Paul Tillich (1886–1965), from whose writings later chapters will bring samples, was always a bit on the edge of the dialectical movement. Emil Brunner (1889–1966), who would later be greatly influential in "Neo-Orthodox" circles, wrote "Nature and Grace" in the classic spirit of the period.

The dialectical theology was above all a polemical movement, determined to end what Barth and his allies took to be an epochal theological mistake, the interpretation of the gospel as an aid to religion. Once the polemic was accomplished and the dialecticians had to say with what *affirmations* they proposed to replace Neo-Protestantism, they quickly discovered they had few in common. None renounced the dialectical theology's negations, except perhaps Tillich. But in the years following 1930, each had to seek his own way to theological construction, in the rubble-field their polemics had left. The ways they variously found have provided the chief characteristic options of mid-twentieth-century theology. Each has begun with an answer to the question: How shall we construct theology, without retreating to what *Romans* demolished?

By hindsight, we can easily see that the dialectical theology could not be more than the theology of a moment. Like its predecessor Neo-Protestantism, it was a methodologically christocentric theology. Yet it was crippled precisely in its ability to speak of Christ. Christ was said to be Savior as the perfect occupant of the line of death. Thus, dialectical theology could not speak of the risen Christ as other than the perpetual actuality of his own death; it could not speak of him *as living*. Yet it did not have the alternative available to its liberal antagonists; it could not, like the liberals, make the historical Jesus the Savior, for the historical Jesus did not yet occupy the line of death.

The great achievement of dialectical theology was that it took the Enlightenment's critique of religion all the way—Barth and the others had been reading also Ludwig Feuerbach (1804–1872) and the historian Franz Overbeck (1837–1905), Friedrich Nietzsche's friend. *All* religion, most especially including the Christian religion, is unveiled as human projection of metaphorical entities half-eternal and half-temporal. Christianity is indeed unique—not, however, because it is the absolute version of religion, but because as a religion it harbors and sometimes releases religion's one great adversary, the gospel. The gospel proclaims as Lord one crucified by the earnest and accomplished representatives of that religion evoked precisely by God's authentic self-revelation. But when one has made all that plain, what does one say next?

4. Karl Barth, *The Epistle to the Romans*

Paul is authorized to deliver—the Gospel of God. He is commissioned to hand over to men something quite new and unprecedented, joyful and good,—the truth of God. Yes, precisely—of God! The Gospel is not a religious message to inform mankind of their divinity or to tell them how they may become divine. The Gospel proclaims a God utterly distinct from men. Salvation comes to them from him, because they are, as men, incapable of knowing him, and because they have no right to claim anything from him. The Gospel is not one thing in the midst of other things, to be directly apprehended and comprehended. The Gospel is the Word of the Primal Origin of all things, the Word which, since it is ever new, must ever be received with renewed fear and trembling. The Gospel is therefore not an event, nor an experience, nor an emotion—however delicate! Rather, it is the clear and objective perception of what eye hath not seen nor ear heard. Moreover, what it demands of men is more than notice, or understanding, or sympathy. It demands participation, comprehension, cooperation; for it is a communication which presumes faith in the living God, and which creates that which it presumes. . . .

In this name two worlds meet and go apart, two planes intersect, the one known and the other unknown. The known plane is God's creation, fallen out of its union with him, and therefore the world of the "flesh" needing redemption, the world of men, and of time, and of things—our world. This known plane is intersected by another plane that is unknown—the world of the Father, of the Primal Creation, and of the final Redemption. The relation between us and God, between this world and his world, presses for recognition, but the line of intersection is not self-evident. The point on the line of intersection at which the relation becomes observable and observed is Jesus. . . . The point on the line of intersection is no more extended onto the known plane than is the unknown place of which it proclaims the existence. . . .

The plane which is known to us, he intersects vertically, from above. Within history, Jesus as the Christ can be understood only as Problem or Myth. As the Christ he brings the world of the Father. But we who stand in this concrete world know nothing, and are incapable of knowing anything, of that point above, and the corresponding discerning of it from below. The Resurrection is the revelation: the disclosing of Jesus as the Christ, the appearing of God, and the apprehending of God in Jesus. . . .

God is the unknown God, and, precisely because he is unknown, he bestows life and breath and all things. Therefore the power of God can be detected neither in the world of nature nor in the souls of men. It must not be confounded with any high, exalted force, known or knowable. The power of God is not the most exalted of observable forces, nor is it either their sum or their fount. Being completely different, it is the *crisis* of all power, that by which all power is measured, and by which it is pronounced to be both something and—nothing, nothing, and—something. It is that which sets all these powers in motion and fashions their eternal rest. It is the Primal Origin by which they all are dissolved, the consummation by which they all are above—supernatural!—these limited and limiting powers. It is pure and pre-eminent and—beyond them all. It can neither be substituted for them nor ranged with them, and, save with the greatest caution, it cannot even be compared with them. The assumption that Jesus is the Christ (1:4) is, in the strictest sense of the word, an assumption, void of any content that can be comprehended by us. . . .

The Resurrection, that is our escape, is also the barrier—and the barrier is also the escape. The No which confronts us is *God's* No. What we are not given, is also what helps us. What limits us, is new territory. What abrogates all worldly truth, is also the foundation. Precisely because God's No is total, it is also his Yes! . . .

Our arrogance demands, besides everything else, knowledge of and access to a super-world. Our deeds cry for deeper foundation, for transcendent praise and reward. Our lust for life wants pious moments too, wants prolongation into eternity. When we "believe" in him, we justify, enjoy and honor ourselves. . . . We mistake time for eternity. That is our disobedience—and that is relationship with God, this side of Resurrection. . . .

They changed the glory of the incorruptible—for an image of the corruptible. That is to say, the understanding of what is characteristic of God was lost. They had lost their knowledge of the crevasse, the polar zone, the desert barrier, which must be crossed if men are really to advance from corruption to incorruption. The distance between God and man had no longer its essential, sharp, acid, and disintegrating ultimate significance. The difference between the incorruption, the pre-eminence and originality of God, and the corruption, the boundedness and relativity of men had been confused. Once the eye, which can perceive this distinction, has been blinded, there arises in the midst, between here and there, between us and the "Wholly Other," a mist or concoction of religion in which, by a whole series of skillful assimilations and mixings more or less strongly flavored with sexuality, sometimes the behavior of men or of animals is exalted to be an experience of God, sometimes the Being, and Existence of God is "enjoyed" as a human or animal experience. In all this mist the prime factor is provided by the illusion that it is possible for men to hold communication with God or, at least, to enter into a covenant relationship with him without miracle—vertical from above, without the dissolution of all concrete things, and apart from *the* truth which lies beyond birth and death. But, on whatever level it occurs, if the experience of religion is more than a void, or claims to contain or possess or to "enjoy" God, it is a shameless and abortive anticipation of that which can proceed from the unknown God alone. In all this busy concern with concrete things there is always a revolt against God. For in it we assist at the birth of the "No-God," at the making of idols. Enveloped in mist, we forgot not merely that all passes to corruption is a parable, but also that it is only a parable. . . .

God does not live by the idea of justice with which we provide him. He is his own justice. he is not one cause among many; he is not the final solution which we propound to the problem of life. Therefore his appearance is incomprehensible and without known occasion, and his judgment is according to his own justice. And yet, there is a claim to salvation from the wrath of God: the claim is where every claim is surrendered and broken down by God himself; where his negation is final and his wrath unavoidable; when God is recognized as God. The claim is where the history of the relation between God and man begins; where there is no history to record, because it only occurs, and occurs eternally. The claim is when men dare—but even this is no recipe for blessedness but only the eternal ground of its perception—to go forth into the fresh air and to love the undiscoverable God. And this occurrence is—in Jesus Christ. . . .

In Jesus we have discovered and recognized the truth that God is found everywhere and that, both before and after Jesus, men have been discovered by him. In him we have found the standard by which all discovery of God and all being discovered by him is made known as such; in him we recognize that this finding and all being found is the truth of the order of eternity. Many live their lives in the light of redemption and forgiveness and resurrection; but that we have eyes to see their manner of life we owe to the One. In his light we see light.

That it is the Christ whom we have encountered in Jesus is guaranteed by our finding in him the sharply defined, final interpretation of the Word of the faithfulness of God to which the Law and the Prophets bore witness. His entering within the deepest darkness of human ambiguity and abiding within it is the faithfulness. The life of Jesus is perfected obedience to the will of the faithful God. Jesus stands among sinners as a sinner; he sets himself wholly under the judgment under which the world is set; he takes his place where God can be present only in questioning about him; he takes the form of a slave; he moves to the cross and to death; his greatest achievement is a negative achievement. He is not a genius, endowed with manifest or even with occult powers; he is not a hero or leader of men; he is neither poet nor thinker:—My God, my God, why hast thou forsaken me? Nevertheless, precisely in this negation, he is the fulfillment of every possibility of human progress, as the Prophets and the Law conceive of progress and evolution, because he sacrifices to the incomparably Greater and to the invisibly or psychic possibility, because there is no conceivable human possibility of which he did not rid himself.

Our experience is what is not our experience. Our religion consists in the abolition of our religion. Our law is the radical invalidation of all human experiencing, knowing, having and doing. Nothing human remains that wants to be more than emptiness, lack, possibility and reference. . . . Faith remains only as faith, without value in itself (including the power of humility!), without wanting to be anything at all, whether before God or humanity.

All religion "reckons" *either* with . . . somehow perceptible human behavior that can claim to inspire divine approval . . . , *or* with a change of human behavior emanating from God, that becomes perceptible and recognizable as such in the world. For all religion, there is, apart from the "moment" when a human standing naked before God is clothed by him . . . , a *before* and an *after* the moment . . . , that is not altogether unlike it. . . .

Do we make the law of none effect through faith? If we thrust the Resurrection into history, if we set the presupposition which is in Jesus within the sequence of events, if we weave the paradox of faith into human spiritual experience, we introduce, as it were, a specter which devours every living thing. The world would then disappear before God, creation before redemption, experience before apprehension, content before form, and the law would be made of none effect before the sole reality, before the faithfulness of the Lawgiver, which is, however, visible to faith alone. How could we protect such a notion and the criticism which proceeds from it from the dualism of Gnosticism? We could in no way protect it, if the radicalism which here appears be not the extreme radicalism. A negation which remains side by side with the position it negates must itself be negated, and is therefore no truly radical negation. Resurrection ceases to be resurrection, if it be some abnormal event side by side with other events. What, in that case, did rise again . . .

By faith we attain the status of those who have been declared righteous before God. By faith we are what we are not. Faith is the predicate of which the new man is the subject. Projected into the midst of human life, the new man seems no more than a void, his "passionate motions of eternity" (Kierkegaard) are invisible. Seen from the human side, he is incomprehensible, a mere negation; and yet, it is this which marks him out for what he is. He is the zero-point between two branches of a hyperbola stretching to infinity; and being this, he is, in unimaginable fashion, both end and beginning. The new subject, being that which is radically and absolutely "other," must therefore be contrasted with what I am; it is, in fact, what I am not. Nevertheless, I am this new subject; because, since faith is the predicate, an identity is established between me and it. . . .

The truth is, however, comprehensible to us only at its starting-point. And this starting-point means for us the end of the old man. This is the only aspect of the truth visible to us; only in the Cross of Christ can we comprehend the truth and meaning of his Resurrection. We can only believe in what is new, and, moreover, our capacity reaches no further than to believing that we do believe. The point where faith and unbelief part company can be defined neither psychologically nor historically. . . .

Whatever is in the world is given over to the way of the world. It precisely does not procure for us the promise, the kinship of Abraham, but does indeed, if it is to be understood not in its worth as witness but in its worth as reality, procure God's wrath. . . . All religion stands under this rule, insofar as it is historical, temporal, perceptible reality—also true, upright and deep religion, also the religion of Abraham and the prophets, also the religion of the Letter to the Romans, and obviously of all books about the Letter to the Romans. . . .

It takes the . . . catastrophe even of the human religious possibility, for the turn of God's No into his Yes to accomplish itself, for grace to be grace. . . . Grace is grace only there, where the religious possibility, taken with complete seriousness, standing in its full power and development—is given up! . . .

The new world is the Kingdom of God and the sphere of his sovereignty and power. As new men, we stand at its threshold. God himself, and God alone, wills and elects, creates and redeems. We were concerned with the genuineness of the movement from Adam to Christ, when, associating like to like, we finally brought the whole possibility of religion under the general heading of "The reign of sin unto death." This was essential, in order that we might confront everything with its opposite—with grace which reigns through righteousness unto eternal life—through Jesus Christ our Lord. Grace is not grace, if he that receives it is not under judgment. Righteousness is not righteousness, if it be not reckoned to the sinner. Life is not life, if it be not life from death. And God is not God, if he be not the End of men. We have seen the old world as a completely closed circle from which we have no means of escape. But, because we have perceived this, we are able to recognize—in the light of the Resurrection of Jesus from the dead—the power and meaning of the Coming Day: the Day of the New World and of the New Man. . . .

Grace is the crisis from death to life. Death is therefore at once the absolute demand and the absolute power of obedience over against sin. No tension or polarity is possible between grace and sin; there can be no adjustment or equilibrium or even temporary compromise between them. As men under grace, we cannot admit or allow grace and sin to be two alternative possibilities or necessities, each with its own rights and properties. For this reason, the Gospel of Christ is a shattering disturbance, an assault which brings everything into question. For this reason, nothing is so meaningless as the attempt to construct a religion out of the Gospel, and to set it as one human possibility in the midst of others. Since Schleiermacher, this attempt has been undertaken more consciously than ever before in Protestant theology—and it is the betrayal of Christ. The man under grace is engaged unconditionally in a conflict. This conflict is a war of life and death, a war in which there can be armistice, no agreement—and no peace. . . .

All human possibilities, including the possibility of religion, have been offered and surrendered to God on Golgotha. Christ, who was born under the law (Gal. 4:4); Christ, who submitted, as did all the pious of Israel, to John's baptism of repentance; Christ, the prophet, the wise man, the teacher, the friend of men, the Messiah-King, dies, that the Son of God may live. Golgotha is the end of law and the frontier of religion. In the slain Christ-according-to-the-law, the last and noblest human possibility, the possibility of human piety and belief and enthusiasm and prayer, is fulfilled by being evacuated. And it is evacuated because the man Jesus, in spite of all that he is and has and does, gives honor to God, and to God alone. With this human body of Christ we also are dead to the law, for we have been removed from that life under the dominion of law, which is death. Looking outward from the Cross, we observe religion, as a concrete thing of soul and sense, as a particular aspect of human behavior, to have been—taken out of the way (Col. 2:14). Men do not stand upright before God in virtue of their religion, any more than they stand upright before him in virtue of any other human property. They stand upright before him in virtue of that divine nature by which also Christ stood when his "religious consciousness" was the recognition that he was abandoned by God. In the slain body of Christ, we perceive the nonexistence of men and supremely of religious (!) men; and we also perceive atonement, forgiveness, justification, and redemption. From death comes life; and what death is, is made known to us in the death of Christ. . . .

47

DIALECTICAL THEOLOGY

We have now reached the point where we are bound to discuss the effective meaning and significance of that last and noblest human possibility which encounters us at the threshold and meeting-place of two worlds, but which, nevertheless, remains itself on this side the abyss dividing sinners from those who are under grace. Here, at the turning point, grace and law—religion—the first invisibility and the last visible thing, confront each other. Grace is the freedom of God by which men are seized. Within the sphere of psycho-physical experience this seizure is, however, nothing but vacuum and void and blankness. The seizure, therefore, lies on the other side of the abyss. Though religion and law appear to concern that relationship between men and God with which grace is also concerned, yet in fact they do not do so. Law and religion embrace a definite and observable disposition of men in this world. They hold a concrete position in the world, and are, consequently, things among other things. They stand, therefore, on this side the abyss, for they are not the presupposition of all things. . . .

The veritable crisis under which religion stands consists first in the impossibility of escape from it as long as a man liveth; and then in the stupidity of any attempt to be rid of it, since it is precisely in religion that men perceive themselves to be bounded as men of the world by that which is divine. Religion compels us to the perception that God is not to be found in religion. Religion makes us to know that we are competent to advance no single step. Religion, as the final human possibility, commands us to halt. Religion brings us to the place where we must wait, in order that God may confront us—on the other side of the frontier of religion. The transformation of the "No" of religion into the divine "Yes" occurs in the dissolution of this last observable human thing. It follows, therefore, that there can be no question of our escaping from this final thing, ridding ourselves of it, or putting something else in its place. . . .

What we here and now, in the psychic-historical reality of this humanity in the world, as the act of turning to that foreign land that is after all our homeland, can least omit to do—precisely that is as act, as the positing of reality, the supreme betrayal of its own presupposition.

Religion is anything but harmony with myself or perhaps with the Infinite. In religion there is no room for noble feelings and superior humanity. Let naive Middle-Europeans and Westerners think that, so long as they still can. In religion is the abyss; in religion is horror. In religion, demons are seen—Ivan Karamazov and Luther! . . .

What was it that the law could not do? As we shall hear later, it could not make men free. That is to say, the law could not set human feet upon the rock of Eternity and rid them of the sentence of death which had been pronounced over them. No religion is capable of altering the fact that the behavior of men is a behavior apart from God. All that religion can do is to expose the complete godlessness of human behavior. As a concrete human being and having and doing, religion is—flesh; it shares, that is to say, in the profligacy and essential worldliness of everything human, and is in fact the crown and perfection of human achievement. Religion neither overcomes human worldliness nor transfigures it; not even the religion of Primitive Christianity or of Isaiah or of the Reformers can rid itself of this limitation. Nor is it merely fortuitous that an odor of death seems, as it were, to hang about the very summits of religion. There proceeds, for example, from Zwingli an insipid bourgeoisdom, from Kierkegaard the poison of a too intense pietism, from Dostoevsky an hysterical world-fatigue, from the Blumhardts, father and son, a far too easy complacency. Woe be to us, if from the summits of religion there pours forth nothing but—religion! . . .

Jesus Christ is shown forth and accredited as the Son of God, because in his Sonship sin-controlled flesh becomes a parable or likeness. What is human and worldly and historical and "natural" is shown to be what it veritably is in its relation to God the Creator—only a transparent thing, only an image, only a sign, only something relative. . . .

God, the true limit and true beginning of all that we are, have and do, confronting humanity and all that is human in infinite qualitative difference, never ever identical with what we call God or experience and adore as God, the unconditional "Stop!" to all human agitation and the unconditional "Forward!" to all human peace, the Yes in our No and the No in our Yes, the First and the Last and therefore the Unknown, never ever an entity in the middle-realm we know, God the Lord, the Creator and Redeemer—that is the living God! . . .

The church confronts the Gospel as the last human possibility confronts the impossible possibility of God. The abyss which is here disclosed is like to none other. Here breaks out the veritable God-sickness: for the church, situated on this side of the abyss which separates men from God, is the place where the eternity of revelation is transformed into a temporal, concrete, directly visible thing in this world. In the church, the lightning from heaven becomes a slow-burning, earth-made oven, loss and discovery harden into a solid enjoyment of possession; divine rest is changed into human discomfort, and divine disquiet into human repose. In the church, the "Beyond" is transfigured into a metaphysical "something," which, because it is contrasted with this world, is no more than an extension of it. In the church, all manner of divine things are possessed and known, and are therefore not possessed and not known. In the church, the unknown beginning and end are fashioned into some known middle position, so that men do not require to remember always that, if they are to become wise, they must die. In the church, faith, hope, and love are directly possessed, and the kingdom of God directed awaited, with the result that men band themselves together to inaugurate it, as though it were a thing which men could have and await and work for. To a greater or lesser extent, the church is a vigorous and extensive attempt to humanize the divine, to bring it within the sphere of the world of time and things, and to make it a practical "something," for the benefit of those who cannot live with the Living God, and yet cannot live without God (the Grand Inquisitor!). To sum up; the church is the endeavor to make the incomprehensible and unavoidable Way intelligible to men. In all this busy activity, the

Catholic church has been granted very considerable success, whereas Protestantism has had to suffer much more severely from the fact that what is so dear to the heart of a churchman is unattainable. From this it is obvious that the opposition between the church and the Gospel is final and all-embracing; the Gospel dissolves the church, and the church dissolves the Gospel. . . .

The theme of the church is the very Word of God—the Word of Beginning and End, of the Creator and Redeemer, of Judgment and Righteousness; but the theme is proclaimed by human lips and received by human ears. The church is the fellowship of men who proclaim the Word of God and hear it. It follows from this situation that, when confronted by the adequacy of the Word of God, human lips and ears must display their inadequacy; that, though men are bound to receive and proclaim the Truth as it is with God, as soon as they do receive it and do proclaim it it ceases to be the Truth; that, however true the theme of the church may be, as the theme of the church it is untrue. This is at once the miracle and the tribulation of the church, for the church is condemned by that which establishes it, and is broken in pieces upon its foundations. . . .

A church daring enough . . . to renounce all effort to achieve or demonstrate perceptible goals and results, to cultivate the experience of God by energetic critique of all mere experience, to cultivate religion by unabashed relativizing of all religion, to cultivate the pious human (that stiff-necked variety of the species human!) by tirelessly confronting him with the heathen, tax-collectors, Spartacists, imperialists, capitalists and other unsympathetic types whom God justifies . . .—that would be the church of faith. . . .

The catastrophe of the church means that there is no point from which God can be excluded—For of him and through him and unto him are all things (11:36). Through him the task of the church becomes inevitable. But he is the impossibility which deprives the church of the possibility of fulfilling its task. He renders men guilty in their attempt to fulfill it, and holds them bound and helpless, as with fetters of iron. By thus binding them, he makes himself known as the One God, beyond human misery and guilt, and as the goal of human hope. The same God who selects Saul also rejects him in order that he may select David. Why should this be? Simply because he is God—My soul truly waiteth still upon God, for of him cometh my salvation. This intolerable behavior is divine. God's action requires that men should be still; and in this stillness hope is possible and necessary. Were the action of God less intolerable, it would not be divine, and men would have to do otherwise than be still and hope.

5. Rudolf Bultmann, *The Question of "Dialectical" Theology*

When Socrates set out to find truth in the Discourses, his underlying notion was that the individual man, in his empirical state, does not have truth at his disposal, but that it can come to light in dialogue, in conversation. The individual has no criterion for truth and falsehood; if in dialogue, however, one convinces or per-suades the other, this constitutes a criterion. In continuous dialogue, in ques-tioning and answering, in testing and convicting, the truth must become progressively evident. The underlying conviction in this situation is that the truth was present from the beginning, but concealed, and that such dialogue par-takes of this truth. But there is something else here; in subsequent speaking, truth is still present only in concealment, since the questioning and answering goes on and on. Knowledge achieves the presuppositions necessary for the valid-ity of its assertions only step by step; furthermore, we must strive to find the pre-suppositions which lie deeper within the subject, in order finally to approach the presupposition which needs no other presupposition. This process is unending, and yet meaningful, for ἀλήθεια (truth) is the infinite goal, not as something which can always become a datum (even if in the infinite), but as something im-manent in the entire process of dialogue (thinking). It is the "undefined middle" at any given time between two assertions. Only, one should never forget that the entire process of knowledge is dialectic, a dialogue in which no assertion taken in itself may claim absolute truth, but is truth only in relation to the middle. This relation is guaranteed by the fact that every statement must be confronted by its opposite—that it is our task to find the opposite of every statement. Truth which is known at a specific time is therefore certainly never reality, but always and only possibility. Moreover, one can demonstrate that two (or more) actual persons are not necessary to the concept of discourse, but that thinking as such is discourse which may just as well happen in monologue. The duality of dialogue has mean-ing only in guaranteeing the dialectic character of speaking or thinking as such.

It is also valid to say that question is answer, and answer is question in this di-alogue. For if the immanent movement of logos occurs in the interchange of question and answer, then every question insofar as it, as individual logos, shares in the logos of the whole releases as an answer the corresponding movement of the developing process of thought. A question contains, then, not an accidental answer, but the necessary one. The answer is determined by the question, just as the question was determined by the answer in the previous stage, and just as the new answer must open up a new question. Thus, the relation here to a presup-position (ultimately, to *the* presupposition) is basically a posing of the presuppo-sition itself through speech, insofar as every logos shares in the total logos. We are not speaking of the accidental posing of a "working hypothesis" by some thinking individual, but of the immanent presupposition posed by all speech which claims to be true. . . .

In "dialectic" theology also one is concerned with a dialogue based on the presupposition that no individual assertion is itself true or has general validity, but that it achieves its meaning only in connection with a counterassertion on the basis of the relation of both assertions to an undefined middle. In "dialectic" theology also one speaks of the question being the answer and vice versa. But at this point it becomes clear that despite all this outward similarity something fundamentally different is involved, so that we must ask whether it is really justifiable to speak of "dialectic" theology at all. So long as the meaning of what is said is not misunderstood, however, the question is ultimately immaterial.

It is clear that we "dialecticians" use this language which says the question is the answer and vice versa only in relation to one particular question—the decisive question of man in his existence. And there is likewise one particular answer—the justification of the sinner by God. Indeed, the answer immediately becomes a question again if man comprehends it; that is, if he understands it as a statement which is disconnected from the actual event it signifies. But it does not become a new question; it is the old one, and similarly, the answer it contains is not a new one, but the old. Thus, it is not a matter of a developing process of thought, but of a continuing point or, if you prefer, of a circling about one midpoint. Every attempt "to advance" would be futile, since the person supposedly advancing sees himself immediately pushed back to the old question.

The question, in fact, is not asked from man's point of view at all, nor is the answer determined by man's questioning. As long as *man* questions, the answer is not the question; the answer can be the question only if God has done the asking; that is, what is in question is the real man in his specific situation, not abstract man. Since man's existence is not at his disposal (he does not stand *alongside* it, but *in* it; he *lives* it, he *is* it as it takes place), he recognizes the question under which he stands (namely, that he is a sinner) only when God shows it to him. If God shows it to him, then the question is the answer; not, to be sure, because the question is eliminated or transcended, that is, understood as a step toward the answer in the continuous process of knowing, but the answer must, in fact, *be* the question; in other words, it is the sinner who is justified.

So the essence of the answer, which is also the question, is not constituted by the movement of the logos or consolidated by the logos; it is rather the existential concreteness of man's being, which is seen not in the logos but in his historical reality unfolding between birth and death. Truth, which is the issue here, is not an abstract possibility, but a concrete reality. Just as the question in which we are immersed is our existential situation (whether we are aware of it or not), and is neither our subjective questioning nor a stage in the sweep of the conceptual process, so the answer is only really spoken by God—it is an event in which our existence is grounded anew. . . .

It is an *eternal* event, insofar as it never creates an actual state (neither in the empirical history of humanity nor in the history of the individual) which would be an intellectual or mental datum; it is an event continually renewed by the miracle of the Holy Spirit. But it is an eternal *event*, not something made perceptible as the eternal movement of the *logos*, but something real insofar as it comes from God and becomes an event in our temporality through the miracle of the Holy Spirit. But it is just this concept of eternal event which allows the dialectic process (let us not say method) to appear as the appropriate parlance of theology. To speak of such an eternal event as though it held still even for one moment for us to examine it and solidify it into an assertion is to falsify it; only the constant reservation that it is not meant in this way can justify my speaking about it. This reservation comes into operation in setting up the counterassertion to the initial assertion. How this process appears is shown by Barth, to the extent that one can "show" such a thing—basically, one cannot, since absolutely nothing can be demonstrated in the abstract. Dialogue is no fiction here; it involves the constant situation of assertion and counterassertion about what is said by and to a specific person. On the contrary, it is the monologue form of theological development that is fiction.

This "dialectic" is no less than a dialogue which, as such, sets up its own presuppositions. But the theological dialectician is not permitted to do this; that is, he cannot give meaning and truth (meaning and truth—reality!) to his speaking, because the presupposition is not at his disposal. His speaking is never anything but a witness to God's truth, which lies "in the middle." This truth is truly the event from God; it is God's act, which is neither presupposed for the speaker as the immanent law of thought which gives every statement its meaning, nor imagined as perfect knowledge at the end of the infinite path of all discourse; rather, it is something which happens (in time), something to which the speaker relates himself and to which he refers. And it is not because he must always say something new and true of God that his speaking becomes a process ad infinitum, but because he must continually guard the reference to what happens against being misunderstood as a reference to an objectively demonstrable fact of the history of humanity or the soul; it is after all an eternal event! . . .

When the discourse of theology refers to an occurrence (arising from God) as its presupposition, then the object of theology, insofar as God is spoken of in theology, allows fundamentally no discourse at all (we can go this far as dialecticians), and the only appropriate form for speaking of him is that of message, of proclamation. But "dialectic" theology is aware of its direct association with proclamation (as its presupposition, not its consequence). . . .

Our "dialectic" process does not have the least intention of establishing faith by the via dialectica or of replacing faith by it; it seeks rather to elevate itself on the basis of faith and attempts to speak in a compatible manner.

The decisive question, however, is still the following: In what way is revelation "presupposed" in theology? In what way are concrete authority and concrete obedience expressed in it? . . .

A false concept of revelation issues from the concept of man's being as an essence which assumes its definite place in the cosmos in the graduated structure of modes of being, and has the possibility of comprehending the entire cosmic order of being by speculative thinking, and even of elevating its own mode of being to one that is higher and nearer the divine mode. . . .

Revelation, then, is a cosmic transaction (just as man is a cosmic creature), which took place once and continues working in the form of a causal process (how else?). . . .

In truth, we are not speaking here of concrete authority and concrete obedience, since we are not speaking of concrete man. For concrete man cannot be understood as an essence which has its place and thus its security in a cosmic order of being. Concrete man exists only in the specificity of his temporal being, in his historical nature—and that means in full uncertainty. Because his existence is always in time and therefore in constant flux, it is impossible for him to be incorporated into an order of being. And not only could he know nothing about a revelation that was a cosmic event, but it would not concern him in the least. Our opinion is that one speaks of the real man only if one sees that man is subject to time in a specific way. And if revelation is God's eternal event, an event which enters into our time, our history, then revelation is available to theological talk as a "presupposition" only when it pleases God to set up this presupposition, when he allows it to happen in the working of his Holy Spirit. Obedience is indeed not something that can be calculated as a datum at our disposal; whether or not it is present in our theology is decided by God. The authority to be expressed in theology is not our authority, but God's; that is, it is not a direct authority controlled by theology, but the authority of the Spirit over which we have no control. In other words, participation in the Logos is not direct, but is man's participation in the Spirit of God. . . .

But if God is the object of our human speaking, then in order to avoid philosophical dialectic and speculation, we must not forget that we are speaking of ourselves. And it is enough to say that that does not mean to speak of our experiences. It should be equally clear that we are then speaking of our reality, in which alone we have our being before God. For "the one who is god in isolation is not God. He could also be something different. The God who reveals himself is God." The phrase "who reveals himself" means, to be sure, the one who addresses our reality. As Herrmann expressed it: "What an almighty being is in himself remains hidden to us. He appears in that which he brings about for us. We can say of God only what he does in relation to us." Or, as we find it in Luther: "And here we also see that to believe in Christ does not mean to believe that Christ is a person who is both God and man—that helps no one; it is to believe that the same person, who proceeds from God for our sakes and has come into the world and then leaves the world and goes to the Father, is Christ." Or, finally, as Melanchthon said, "*Christum cognoscere id est beneficia eius cognoscere*" (to know Christ is to know his benefits).

6. Emil Brunner, *Nature and Grace*

The Issue between Karl Barth and Myself

The credit of having given back to Protestant theology its proper theme and subject-matter is due, without qualification and, if I may use the expression, without competition, to Karl Barth. It is not as though there were not before him, and to some extent beside him, men who also knew the proper theme and subject. . . .

But they were unable to break through the front of theological modernism. A task such as this demanded greater mental impetus and this Karl Barth possessed. Within the space of a few years he completely changed the Protestant theological situation. Even where he was not acknowledged, his influence was very considerable. To-day we struggle no longer, as we did fifteen years ago, concerning "religion," but concerning the "Word of God"; no longer concerning the *deus in nobis*, but concerning the revelation in Jesus Christ. To put it briefly: no longer concerning the themes of the enlightenment, but concerning the theme of the Bible itself. We others who have assisted Barth in this struggle have all of us first had our eyes opened by him, even though some have never publicly acknowledged Barth.

But the fact that we are to-day again concerned with the message of the Bible and the Reformation is not all. . . .

We are not concerned with Luther nor with Lutheranism, but with that hard truth and message of Luther's concerning *sola gratia*, which is so greatly opposed to the thought of our time—with Christ crucified as the only salvation of the world and with justification by faith alone. We are concerned with the doctrine that in all questions of the church's proclamation Holy Scripture alone is the ultimate standard. We are concerned with the message of the sovereign, freely electing grace of God. Of his free mercy God gives to man, who of himself can do nothing towards his own salvation, to man, whose will is not free but in bondage, his salvation in the Cross of Christ and by the Holy Spirit who enables him to assimilate this word of the Cross. We are therefore also concerned with the freedom of the church, which has its basis and its justification, its law and its possibility purely and solely in this divine revelation. Therefore it is not tied at all to nations and states. It is above all nations and states without any possibility of accepting from them any law or commission. We are concerned with the fact that the proclamation of the church has not two sources and norms, such as, e.g., revelation *and* reason or the Word of God *and* history, and that ecclesiastical or Christian action has not two norms, such as, e.g., commandments *and* "Ordinances." The struggle against this "and" is the struggle of Elijah on Mount Carmel against the halting between two opinions and therefore it is the struggle for the glory of the true God. In all this there is between me and Barth no difference of opinion, except the one on the side of Barth that there is a difference of opinion. All I can say is: No, there is none. . . .

Barth's False Conclusions

I have repeatedly pointed out that most theology is made necessary by heretics using the terms of the true faith, while meaning by them something other than the plain words can signify. Not open heresy but hidden heresy is the real danger in the church; it is the internal enemy, ever more dangerous than the external. Hence it is understandable that suspicion belongs as it were to the professional virtues of the good theologian. It is a fact that he is called to be a guardian, and as the bodyguard of any great man of this world look upon every one who is near him with suspicion until they have convinced themselves of his harmlessness, so also the theologian must act—not as a man but as a bearer of his office. Therefore I cannot agree with those who reproach Barth with this "heresy-hunting." It is the result of his great devotion to his subject, and this not even his most embittered adversaries have been able to deny him. If I reproach Barth with anything at all it is with this, that he would like it best to carry out this guardian's duty alone, and that if anyone wishes to call his attention to a mistake he is not ready to believe that he, Barth, could be in error; and that in this matter he puts into practice the not very biblical maxim of William Tell that "the strong man is strongest alone." Apart from that the difference between us is purely objective and theological and can only be removed if we test it anew by that standard which we both acknowledge.

From the doctrine of *sola gratia* and the position of the Bible as the sole ultimate standard of truth Barth draws the following conclusions:

1. Since man is a sinner who can be saved only by grace, the image of God in which he was created is obliterated entirely, i.e., without remnant. Man's rational nature, his capacity for culture and his humanity, none of which can be denied, contain no traces or remnants whatever of that lost image of God.

2. Since we acknowledge scriptural revelation as the sole norm of our knowledge of God and the sole source of our salvation, every attempt to assert a "general revelation" of God in nature, in the conscience and in history, is to be rejected outright. There is no sense in acknowledging two kinds of revelation, one general and one special. There is only one kind, namely the one complete revelation in Christ.

3. Accordingly we have to draw the following conclusion from the acknowledgment of Christ as the sole saving grace of God: there is no grace of creation and preservation active from the creation of the world and apparent to us in God's preservation of the world. For otherwise we would have to acknowledge two or even three kinds of grace, and this would contradict the oneness of the grace of Christ.

4. Accordingly there is no such thing as God's ordinances of preservation, which we could know to be such and in which we could recognize the will of God which is normative of our own action. A *lex naturae* of this kind which is derived from creation can be introduced into Christian theology only *per nefas*, as a pagan thought.

5. For the same reason it is not permissible to speak of the "point of contact" for the saving action of God. For this would contradict the sole activity of the saving grace of Christ, which is the centre of the theology of the Bible and the Reformation. . . .

My Counter-Theses and Their Proof

1. The question concerning the *imago Dei* seems to be ultimately nothing but a dispute about words. I agree with Barth in teaching that the original image of God in man has been destroyed, that the *justitia originalis* has been lost and with it the possibility of doing or even of willing to do that which is good in the sight of God, and that therefore the free will has been lost. Barth himself does not deny that even sinful and unredeemed man is capable of doing and thinking what is reasonable, and that in spite of their questionable nature humanity and culture are not simply to be dismissed as of no value from the point of view of revelation. It might therefore appear as of no account whether we would connect these abilities, which even natural man has, with the original image of God or not. Why should we be concerned to introduce here the dangerous and vague concept of the remnant of the *imago?* We shall discuss the purpose of this in the last chapter. Here I shall justify myself by saying the following:

We have to consider the image of God in man in two ways: one formal and one material. The formal sense of the concept is the human, i.e. that which distinguishes man from all the rest of creation, whether he be a sinner or not. Even the Old Testament speaks of man's likeness to God in this sense. It signifies above all the superiority of man within creation. Thus in the two important passages (Genesis 1:26 and Ps. 8) man has not, even as a sinner, ceased to be the central and culminating point of creation. This superior position in the whole of creation, which man still has, is based on his special relation to God, i.e. on the fact that God has created him for a special purpose—to bear his image. This *function* or calling as a bearer of the image is not only not abolished by sin; rather is it the presupposition of the ability to sin and continues within the state of sin. We can define this by two concepts: the fact that man is a subject and his responsibility. Man has an immeasurable advantage over all other creatures, even as a sinner, and this he has in common with God: he is a subject, a rational creature. The difference is only that God is the original, man a derived subject. Not even as a sinner does he cease to be one with whom one can speak, with whom therefore also God can speak. And this is the very nature of man: to be responsible. Even as a sinner man is responsible. Upon these two characteristics, that of his capacity for words and that of responsibility, which in their turn are closely interrelated, depends not only man's special position but also the connection between this special position and the form of the redeeming revelation, namely that God becomes man.

If the formal side of the *imago Dei* is thus conceived, it does not in any way result in an encroachment upon the material concept of *justitia originalis*, nor in the lessening of the weight of the statement that this *justitia originalis* is completely lost. Therefore we do not use the questionable concept of the "remnant" which would suggest a quantitative and therefore relative concept of sin. We distinguish categorically: formally the *imago* is not in the least touched—whether

57

sinful or not, man is the subject and is responsible. Materially the *imago* is completely lost, man is a sinner through and through and there is nothing in him which is not defiled by sin. To formulate it differently: as before, man is a person, i.e. he is in a derived sense that which God is originally. Yet he is not a personal person but an anti-personal person; for the truly personal is existence in love, the submission of the self to the will of God and therefore an entering into communion with one's fellow-creature because one enjoys communion with God. This *quid* of personality is negatived through sin, whereas the *quod* of personality constitutes the *humanum* of every man, also that of the sinner.

2. The world is the creation of God. In every creation the spirit of the creator is in some way recognizable. The artist is known by all his works. So much do the Scriptures of the Old and New Testament testify to the fact that this applies also in our world, which is the stage on which we sinful creatures act, that it is unnecessary to quote any special passages in support. The praise of God through his creation is also an integral part of the Christian liturgy from the earliest times and throughout all centuries. Scripture itself says so and upbraids man for not acknowledging it, and it expects from him as a believer that he should take part in this praise of God through his creation. Therefore it seems to me a queer kind of loyalty to Scripture to demand that such a revelation should not be acknowledged, in order that the significance of biblical revelation should not be minimized.

Wherever God does anything, he leaves the imprint of his nature upon what he does. Therefore the creation of the world is at the same time a revelation, a self-communication of God. This statement is not pagan but fundamentally Christian. But nowhere does the Bible give any justification for the view that through the sin of man this perceptibility of God in his works is destroyed, although it is adversely affected. Rather does it say this, that surprisingly enough sin makes man blind for what is visibly set before our eyes. The reason why men are without excuse is that they will not know the God who so clearly manifests himself to them. . . .

The difficult question is therefore not whether there are two kinds of revelation. The reply to this question must on the basis of Scripture once and for all be a positive one. The question is rather how the two revelations, that in creation and that in Jesus Christ, are related. The first answer—again one which is universally Christian and also obviously biblical—is that for us sinful men, the first, the revelation in creation, is not sufficient in order to know God in such a way that this knowledge brings salvation. Furthermore, we have to make the significant distinction between the subjective and the objective factor in this interrelation of knowledge. According to St. Paul the revelation of God in his creation would be sufficient for every one to know therein the Creator according to his majesty and wisdom. But sin dulls man's sight so much that instead of God he "knows" or "fancies" gods. We may correctly characterize the objective and subjective factors thus: man misrepresents the revelation of God in creation and turns it into idols. In any case he is unable to know God, who in Jesus Christ reveals himself to him anew according to his true nature, which even in creation is partially hidden.

But in faith, taking our stand upon the revelation in Jesus Christ, we shall not be able to avoid speaking of a double revelation: of one in creation which only he can recognize in all its magnitude, whose eyes have been opened by Christ; and of a second in Jesus Christ in whose bright light he can clearly perceive the former. This latter revelation far surpasses that which the former was able to show him, and moreover it points to a third revelation, the beatific vision, which again will be entirely different from the second and yet will not deny it, but only confer upon it its ineffable perfection. . . .

3. Wherever both the omnipotent creator and sin are taken equally seriously, there must needs arise a third concept, that of God's gracious preservation. God is present even to his sinful creature which is far removed from him. This incongruence of divine presence and human distance is highly important. . . . Preserving grace does not abolish sin but abolishes the worst consequences of sin. The grace of preservation for the most part consists in that God does not entirely withdraw his grace of creation from the creature in spite of the latter's sin. In part, however, in that, agreeably to the state of sin, he provides new means for checking the worst consequences of sin, e.g. the State. . . .

4. Within the sphere of this preserving grace belong above all those "ordinances" which are the constant factors of historical and social life, and which therefore form a basic part of all ethical problems. There are certain ordinances, such as e.g. Matrimony and the State, without which no communal life is conceivable, that could in any way be termed human. These ordinances vary in dignity.

Monogamous marriage, for example, is of higher dignity than the State because, as an institution, as an ordinance, it is—apart from special concrete cases—unrelated to sin. (This is independent of the way in which its humane necessity may be proved, i.e. is made known to us.) Therefore it has from of old been called an "ordinance of creation." This means simply that the Christian, who recognizes the creator only in Jesus Christ, also recognizes the ordinance of matrimony to have been instituted by the creator. The distinction between this "ordinance of creation" from a mere "ordinance of preservation" relative to sin, such as the State, is made for sound theological reasons. It is necessary for a Christian *theologia naturalis*, i.e. for Christian theological thinking which tries to account for the phenomena of natural life. Matrimony is a "natural" ordinance of the creator because the possibility of and the desire for its realization lies within human nature and because it is realized to some extent by men who are ignorant of the God revealed in Christ.

For this reason there lies over these ordinances a twilight which cannot be dispelled. They are given by God. They are realized naturally. For their realization not only the natural impulse is necessary but also the *humanum*. They can be recognized as necessities and as goods by natural man. But—and this is the critical point: only by means of faith can their significance be perfectly understood and therefore it is only by means of faith that they can be realized according to the will of him who has instituted them. Nevertheless, i.e. although they are understood correctly only in faith, they are and remain for the believer divine ordinances of *nature*. This means that they do not belong to the realm of redemption, of the church, but belong to the realm of divine preservation, in which natural impulse and reason are constituent factors. All human arts by which man, thanks to the divine grace of preservation, maintains himself, are performed by instinct or by reason. Similarly all these ordinance, whether they be "ordinances of creation" or "ordinances of preservation" in the narrower sense, are created and maintained by instinct and reason. Even the believer, who by reason of his faith understands their ultimate sense better than the unbeliever, cannot but allow his instinct and his reason to function with regard to these ordinances, just as in the arts. And finally it is true that only by means of faith, i.e. through Christ, their relation to the loving will of God can be rightly understood. Nevertheless through the preserving grace of God they are known also to "natural man" as ordinances that are necessary and somehow holy and are by him respected as such. For it is peculiar to the preserving grace of God that he does his preserving work both by nature acting unconsciously and by the reason of man.

5. No one who agrees that only human subjects but not stocks and stones can receive the Word of God and the Holy Spirit can deny that there is such a thing as a point of contact for the divine grace of redemption. This point of contact is the formal *imago Dei*, which not even the sinner has lost, the fact that man is man, the *humanitas* in the two meanings defined above: capacity for words and responsibility. Not even sin has done away with the fact that man is receptive of words, that he and he alone is receptive of the Word of God. But this "receptivity" must not be understood in the material sense. This receptivity says nothing as to his acceptance or rejection of the Word of God. It is the purely formal possibility of his being addressed. This possibility of his being addressed is also the presupposition of man's responsibility. Only a being that can be addressed is responsible, for it alone can make decisions. Only a being that can be addressed is capable of sin. But in sinning, while being responsible, it somehow or other knows of its sin. This knowledge of sin is a necessary presupposition of the understanding of the divine message of grace. It will not do to kill the dialectic of this knowledge of sin by saying that knowledge of sin comes only by the grace of God. This statement is as true as the other, that the grace of God is comprehensible only to him who already knows about sin. The case is similar to that of the divine ordinances or of the law: Natural man knows them and yet does not know them. If he did not know them, he would not be human: if he really knew them, he would not be a sinner. This dichotomy is itself the essence of the state of sin. *Without* knowledge of God there can be no sin: sin is always "in the sight of

God." *In* sin there can be no knowledge of God, for the true knowledge of God is the abolition of sin. This dialectic must not be one-sidedly abolished. On the contrary it must be strongly insisted upon. For only in this dialectic does the responsibility of faith become clear. He who does not believe is himself guilty. He who believes knows that it is pure grace.

It is impossible to deny this point of contact of divine grace, i.e. it is possible to do so only by a misunderstanding. The misunderstanding always arises out of the lack of a distinction between the formal and the material definitions. We said above that materially there is no more *imago Dei*, whereas formally it is intact. Similarly we must say that materially there is no point of contact, whereas formally it is a necessary presupposition. The Word of God does not have to create man's capacity for words. He has never lost it, it is the presupposition of his ability to hear the Word of God. But the Word of God itself creates man's ability to believe the Word of God, i.e. the ability to hear it in *such a way* as is only possible in faith. It is evident that the doctrine of *sola gratia* is not in the least endangered by such a doctrine of the point of contact. . . .

3

New Systematics

Of those who joined in the "dialectical" revolt, two afterwards produced major systems of theology in the classic mode: Karl Barth, the center of the movement, and Paul Tillich, the most loosely affiliated. In purpose, intellectual style and procedure, material teaching, and even sheer bulk, the two works are appropriately different. Yet both result from the same need: to create theology that could be taught and serve the church, while not transgressing the limits and insights set in the dialectical experience.

The positions of the dialectical theology itself were systematically maintained in more original form by the "Bultmann school," in which the distinction between exegetical and constructive theology continued to be overridden as in *Romans* itself. "The systematician of the Bultmann school," Gerhard Ebeling (1912–), has recently published a full system. This type of theology, including Ebeling's own very important thought is, however, perhaps more characteristically represented in other literary and disciplinary forms, and will be so represented here.

I

Barth himself found his way to theological construction by yet another reversal of Schleiermacher. Neo-Protestantism had established the cognitive status of Christian claims by finding a place for them within the presupposed general truth of human religiosity. Neo-Protestantism told first the supposedly true story of humanity and its quest for God, and then tried to establish the truth of Christ by showing his place in that story. It was precisely this procedure that "dialectical" critique had destroyed. Now Barth asked, Why not do it just the other way around?

Why not first tell the story of Christ, and claim truth for our knowledge of God by showing *our* place and the place of our knowledge in *his* story? Why should we rely on supposed truth prior to the gospel? If the gospel is true, must not the world in fact have such truth as it possesses from precisely that reality which the gospel narrates? Thus the *Church Dogmatics* became one vast telling and retelling of the story of Christ as the encompassing truth about all things.

As Barth came to understand the assertions of faith, they have their *own* internal coherence, and we show faith's rationality by tracing the spider-web of this coherence. Moreover, the inner coherence of the faith is not merely that of a conceptual system that may nevertheless lack reference, for the whole is what it is exactly as it is witness to an event external to it, an event that demands this witness and no other.

The event in question is, of course, the death and resurrection of Christ. Thus we come to the way Barth found to maintain the dialectical theology's insights. In his writings from 1931 on, and particularly in the *Church Dogmatics,* Barth in effect translated the dialectics of time and eternity into Christology. Time and eternity join without joining, along the tangent of death, not as a general divide between God and creatures but as the structure of the God-man's existence, as the death and resurrection of this one person. Thus the time-eternity dialectic no longer functions to exclude us from God, but precisely to include us in him, while the absolute distinction is still maintained.

An ambiguity of Barth's earlier thinking, one that has occasioned much misunderstanding in English-speaking theology, is thus dispelled. Does Barth oppose religion's quest for God because he thinks God and we are so far apart that the effort is *hopeless?* Or is it instead because he thinks that God is not absent in the first place, so that a quest is *unnecessary?* English and American comment mostly supposed that Barth meant the former, but Barth's later work makes it inescapably plain that he meant rather the latter. The "infinite qualitative *difference*" between God and creature is not at all a *distance.* Indeed, in that the difference constitutes the being of Christ, precisely the difference brings God near. The religious quest has its evil results because it denies that God is with us and supposes we must go looking for him.

The *Church Dogmatics,* to which Barth devoted his life from 1932 on, is the longest such work ever written. It is structured as a series of "volumes," each of which grew in the writing into a multivolumed part of the work. Volume I, in two actual volumes, is the introduction to the whole, but a very different sort of introduction: it contains the doctrine of Trinity and the doctrine of revelation. That is, it introduces the whole by identifying the God about whom the work is to speak, and by describing how it happens that we do and can speak of him. Volume II, also in two volumes, contains that part of the doctrine of God not anticipated in Volume I: the doctrine of his being, attributes, and will. Volume III, in *four* volumes, is on creation; Barth's wind is strengthening. Volume IV, in three completed volumes (one again subdivided) and the fragment of a fourth, contains the doctrine of reconciliation. A Volume V was to have treated eschatology.

The *Church Dogmatics* is desperately systematic: every proposition leads to every other, in a dense network of mutual implication. But it does not proceed from premises at the beginning to conclusions along the way; rather, each of the "volumes" is effectively an entire systematic theology, built around its particular topic and beginning theological reflection anew. One can therefore begin reading the work at the beginning of any volume; none requires knowledge of previous parts, except insofar as all require the fundamental identification of God accomplished in Volume I, Book 1.

In making a selection for this volume, we have perhaps chosen more conventionally than would have been necessary. It would have been possible, and probably more faithful to the spirit of the work, to plunge readers directly into, for example, Barth's astonishing doctrine of creation, or his revolutionary treatment of predestination. But we have instead chosen sections more calculated to lead easily into the whole: Barth's description of the discipline of churchly theology, and his interpretation of the beginning of theology, the fact that we do know God.

II

Paul Tillich did not attempt full-scale systematic construction until after his emigration to America. In Germany and during the earlier part of his American second career, he had been above all a theologian of culture, interpreting politics and the arts by insight given with the gospel. (Because his theological interpretation of politics called for "Christian socialism," he had to flee the Nazi state.)

Tillich's *Systematic Theology* has in fact directly continued his theological interpretation of Western culture, simply turning to the intellectual heart of the culture, its philosophical tradition. Thus, in the first volume, he deals with "reason," "being," and "God," in each case drawing his meanings and orderings more from the main line of Western philosophical reflection than from Scripture or creed, yet always seeking positions coherent with the biblical and churchly "kerygma."

What Tillich calls the "central" parts of the work have a "trinitarian structure:" "Being and God," "Existence and Christ," and "Life and the Spirit." These are preceded by an epistemological part, "Reason and Revelation," consisting of discussions that systematically belong in the three trinitarian sections but are gathered here for pedagogical and apologetic purposes. A fifth part is on "History and the Kingdom of God."

To understand the system, we must be clear that its trinitarianism has little to do with the church's doctrine of Trinity—which indeed is hardly discussed. This "trinitarian" structure is determined rather by the moments of being, existence, and life in the dialectic of the Absolute, as perennially envisaged in the Western metaphysical tradition. This accounts also for the somewhat isolated position of the system's fifth part, which deals with "the historical aspect of life," with the "symbol 'Kingdom of God.'" In the church's doctrine, it is precisely God's history that necessitates the doctrine of Trinity; for Tillich, the "historical aspect" must be treated outside the "trinitarian structure which determines the central parts."

Tillich's own way of maintaining the achievements of the dialectical theology appears most plainly in two further systematic structures of his work. In each part of the *Systematic Theology,* the philosophical tradition delivers precisely a *question,* to which Christian answers are sought; that is, the whole system is a dialectic. These questions, moreover, are those of *existential,* and therefore intrinsically open, philosophical reflection. So, to "the question implied in . . . finitude," God is the answer; to the question of "existential self-estrangement," Christ is the answer; to the question of life's "ambiguity," Spirit is the answer.

Tillich's great influence is perhaps not so much exercised by particular theological propositions espoused in the *Systematic Theology* as by certain of the work's systematic moves and conceptual themes. We will simply list the chief of these: the notion of the "theological circle" and of the asking of "ultimately concerned" questions as the way in which one occupies this circle; the "method of correlation" as the proposed appropriate method of "apologetic" theology, according to which one pairs existential questions posed by existence itself with answers proposed by the gospel; the claim that it is the "biblical *picture*" of Jesus "as the Christ" that is the revelatory and saving event, rather than whatever happened historically in first-century Palestine, and the correlated way in which resurrection, kingdom of God, and the like are presented as "symbols;" and, finally, the central soteriological category of "new being," the overcoming within existence of existential estrangement from being.

7. Karl Barth, *Church Dogmatics*

The Church, Theology, Science

Dogmatics is a theological discipline. But theology is a function of the church.

The church confesses God, by the fact that she speaks of God. She does so first of all through her existence in the action of each individual believer. And she does so in the second place through her special action as a community; in proclamation by preaching and administration of the Sacrament, in worship, in instruction, in her mission work within and without the church, including loving activity among the sick, the weak, and those in jeopardy. Fortunately the church's reality does not coincide exactly with her action. But her action does coincide with the fact that alike in her existence in believers and in her communal existence as such, she speaks about God. . . .

But by her very confession of God, the church also confesses to the humanity and likewise to the responsibility of her action. She is aware of her exposure to fierce temptation in speaking of God, aware also that she has to reckon with God for her speaking. The first, last, and decisive answer to this double compulsion consists in the fact that she finds his grace sufficient, whose strength is mighty in the weak. Yet in virtue of her very contentment with that, she recognizes and undertakes, as an active church, a further human task, the task of criticizing and revising her language about God. This confronts us with the concept of theology in the strictest and proper meaning of the word. . . .

The church produces theology in this special and peculiar sense, by subjecting herself to a self-test. She faces herself with the question of truth, i.e. she measures her action, her language about God, against her existence as a church.

The question of truth, with which theology is throughout concerned, is the question as to the agreement between the language about God peculiar to the church and the essence of the church. The criterion of Christian language, in past and future as well as at the present time, is thus the essence of the church, which is Jesus Christ, God in his gracious approach to man in revelation and reconciliation. Has Christian language its source in him? Does it lead to him? Does it conform to him? None of these questions can be put without the others, but each in all its force must be put independently. . . .

Since the church in putting the question of truth in this triple sense is acting not arbitrarily but relevantly, this self-test of hers acquires the character of a scientific undertaking, which as such ranks independently along with other human undertakings of a like or similar kind, as this special, or theological "science." As to both claims, the claim of theology to be a "science" and her claim to a separate place alongside the other "sciences," these can of course only be upheld practically and with reservations. . . .

It might be that philosophy, or historical science or sociology or psychology or pedagogics, or all of them together, working in the sphere of the church, would undertake the task of measuring the church's language about God against her essence as a church, and thus render a special theology superfluous. In reality theology does not find itself in possession of special keys for special doors! Neither has it at its disposal a basis of knowledge, which might not straightway be realized in every other science, nor is it aware of an objective area, which is necessarily hidden away from any other science whatsoever. It would have to ignore the factual nature of revelation as an event, the possibility of grace and thereby its own nature, were it to dream of such an assertion. . . .

As a matter of practice the other sciences have not recognized and assumed the task of theology as their own. True, the language of the church about God has long been criticized from many quarters, and attempts have been made to correct it. But what must be done here is to criticize and revise it from the standpoint of the essence of the church, of Jesus Christ as her foundation, her end and her content. Practically it is the case (although it does not admit of proof as a necessary matter of principle), that the historian, educationist, and so one, and not least the philosopher himself, for all their goodwill in taking this matter into account, always, within the framework of their own science, speak past the problem here confronting them. In other words, they judge the church's language about God on principles foreign to it, instead of on its own principles, and thus increase instead of diminishing the harm on account of which the church needs a critical science. . . .

The case is also somewhat similar with the question whether theology is a "science" at all. This question is never a vital question for theology. There is no fundamental necessity, there are no inner grounds to cause it to claim membership of this genus. . . .

If theology allows itself to be called or calls itself a science, it cannot at the same time take over the obligation to submit to measurement by the canons valid for other sciences.

Likewise it cannot justify itself before the other sciences on the score of setting up for discussion on its own side a concept of science which does not exclude but includes a good theology. To put itself in a systematic relationship with the other sciences, theology would have to regard its own special existence as fundamentally necessary. That is exactly what it cannot do. It absolutely cannot regard itself as a member of an ordered cosmos, but only as a stop-gap in an unordered one.

Dogmatics as an Inquiry

Dogmatics is the self-test to which the Christian church puts herself in respect of the content of her peculiar language about God. Our object, the proper content of this language, we call "dogma."

Dogmatics as an inquiry presupposes the ascertainability by man of the proper content of Christian language about God. It makes this presupposition because it believes, in the church and with the church, in Jesus Christ, as the revealing and reconciling approach of God to man. Language about God has the proper content, when it conforms to the essence of the church, i.e. to Jesus Christ. . . .

Dogmatics presupposes that as God in Jesus Christ is the essence of the church, that is, as he has promised himself to the church, he is the truth; and not merely in himself, but (we do know him, and we know him only, in faith in Jesus Christ) also and precisely the truth for us. . . .

In, with, and beneath the human question dogmatics speaks of the divine answer. In investigating it, it is also aware of it. In learning it, it is already teaching it. In human uncertainty, like any other science, it establishes the most certain truth, which long ago came to light. . . .

As an inquiry dogmatics presupposes that the proper content of Christian language about God must be known humanly. Christian language must be investigated as to its conformity to Christ. In this conformity it is by no means presented to us obviously or free from difficulties. The finally and adequately given divine answer is the counterpart of the human question which retains its faithfulness throughout unwearied, honest advance, of the cry that is sincere even amid the loftiest attainments, "not as though I had already attained!" True, dogmatics receives the measure with which it measures in an act of human appropriation. Therefore it must be an inquiry. It knows the light that is perfect in itself, that discovers all in a flash. But it knows it only in the prism of this act, which, however radically or existentially it may be regarded, is a human act, offering in itself no sort of surety for the correctness of the appropriation in question, being rather fallible and therefore itself in need of criticism and revision, of repeated and ever closer retesting. The creaturely form which God's revealing action comes to take in dogmatics is therefore not that of knowledge attained in a flash, which it would have to be to correspond to the divine gift, but a laborious advance from one partial human insight to another, intending but by no means guaranteeing an "advance!"

The essence of the church is Jesus Christ, and is therefore irremovably a divine-human Person, the action of God on man, an action in distinction from which human appropriation, as actually attested in the very "dogmas" believed in by the church, may be termed worthy, respectable but by no means "infallible," and so not withdrawn from further interrogation as to "whether that is the relation." The concept "truths of revelation," in the sense of Latin propositions given and sealed once for all by divine authority in wording and meaning, is theologically impossible, if it be the case that revelation has its truth in the free decision of God, made once for all in Jesus Christ, and for that very reason and in that way strictly future for us, and must become true in the church from time to time in the intractable reality of faith. Truth of revelation is the freely acting God, himself and quite alone. Results of dogmatic work, like the dogmas underlying the creeds, which are venerable results, because gained in the common knowledge of the church at a definite time, may and should guide our own dogmatic work, but never replace it at any point in virtue of their authority. . . .

Dogmatics as an Act of Faith

Dogmatics is a part of the work of human knowledge. But this part of the work of human knowledge comes under a special decisive limitation. It demands of course, like all work of human knowledge, the intellectual faculties of attention and concentration, of understanding and judgment. Like all serious work of human knowledge it demands the best will to utilize these faculties and, finally, surrender of the entire personality to such utilization. But over and above this it presupposes Christian faith, which even in the deepest and purest surrender to this task in itself does not by any means just happen. In fact dogmatics is a function of the Christian church. The church tests herself by essaying dogmatics. To the church is given the promise of the criterion for Christian faith, namely, the revelation of God. The church can ply dogmatics. Even in the church dogmatics need not be the work of a special theological science. Yet dogmatics is impossible outside the church. To be in the church means to be called upon with others through Jesus Christ. To act in the church means to act in obedience to this call. This obedience to the call of Christ is faith. In faith the judgment of God is acknowledged and his grace praised. In faith self-testing is necessary in view of responsibility before God. . . . Faith is the determination of human action by the essence of the church, that is by Jesus Christ, by the gracious approach of God to man. In faith and only in faith is human action related to the essence of the church, to the revealing and reconciling action of God. Thus dogmatics is only possible as an act of faith, in the determination of human action by listening, and as obedience towards Jesus Christ. . . .

Now faith is not the sort of determination of human action that man can apply to his action at will, or that, once received, he can maintain at will. It is rather itself the gracious approach of God to man, the free personal presence of Jesus Christ in man's action. Thus we assert that dogmatics presupposes faith, presupposes the determination of human action through listening, and as obedience to the essence of the church; whence we assert that at every step and proposition it presupposes the free grace of God, which may from time to time be given or else refused, as the object and meaning of this human action. It depends from time to time upon God and not upon us, whether our hearing is real hearing, our obedience real obedience, whether our dogmatics is blessed and hallowed as knowledge of the proper content of Christian language, or is idle speculation. . . .

The church can and ought to undertake and carry through her self-test on her own responsibility, by human application of human means. But whether in so doing she is acting as the church and so is discerning God in faith, whether the result of her action is therefore just and weighty criticism or revision, and not a worse devastation of Christian language, does not lie within her province. Obviously the givenness of the special and decisive conditions of dogmatics, the decision from time to time of what is or is not the truth in dogmatics, are matters of divine predestination. Fear of the Lord must ever and anon repeatedly be the beginning of wisdom here.

The Election of Jesus Christ

The election of grace is the eternal beginning of all the ways and works of God in Jesus Christ. In Jesus Christ God in his free grace determines himself for sinful man and sinful man for himself. He therefore takes upon himself the rejection of man with all its consequences, and elects man to participation in his own glory.

Jesus Christ, Electing and Elected

Between God and man there stands the person of Jesus Christ, himself God and himself man, and so mediating between the two. In him God reveals himself to man. In him man sees and knows God. In him God stands before man and man stands before God, as is the eternal will of God, and the eternal ordination of man in accordance with this will. In him God's plan for man is disclosed, God's judgment on man fulfilled, God's deliverance of man accomplished, God's gift to man present in fullness, God's claim and promise to man declared. In him God has joined himself to man. And so man exists for his sake. It is by him, Jesus Christ, and for him and to him, that the universe is created as a theatre for God's dealings with man and man's dealings with God. The being of God is his being, and similarly the being of man is originally his being. And there is nothing that is not from him and by him and to him. He is the Word of God in whose truth everything is disclosed and whose truth cannot be over-reached or conditioned by any other word. He is the decree of God behind and above which there can be no earlier or higher decree and beside which there can be no other, since all others serve only the fulfillment of this decree. He is the beginning of God before which there is no other beginning apart from that of God within himself. Except, then, for God himself, nothing can derive from any other source or look back to any other starting point. He is the election of God before which and without which and beside which God cannot make any other choices. Before him and without him and beside him God does not, then, elect or will anything. And he is the election (and on that account the beginning and the decree and the Word) of the free grace of God. For it is God's free grace that in him he elects to be man and to have dealings with man and to join himself to man. He, Jesus Christ, is the free grace of God as not content simply to remain identical with the inward and eternal being of God, but operating *ad extra* in the ways and works of God. And for this reason, before him and above him and beside him and apart from him there is no election, no beginning, no decree, no Word of God. . . .

God elects. It is this that precedes absolutely all other being and happening. And at this point both subject and predicate clearly lead us beyond time and beyond the nexus of the created world and its history. They lead us to the sphere where God is with himself, the sphere of his free will and pleasure. And this sphere is his eternity, which gives to the world and time and all that is in them their origin, their direction and their destiny. . . . But there is a temptation here, . . . temptation to think of this sphere as at once empty and undetermined. It is the temptation to think of God the Father, Son and Holy Spirit merely as a Subject which can and does elect, a Subject which is furnished, of course, with supereminent divine attributes, but which differs from other such subjects only by the fact that in its election it is absolutely free. . . . This construction has been very influential in the history of the doctrine. And it can still actually be a temptation, and a temptation which we must recognize and resist. . . .

The choice or election of God is basically and properly God's decision that as described in John 1:1–2 the Word which is "the same," and is called Jesus, should really be in the beginning, with himself, like himself, one with himself in his deity. And for this reason it is *per se* an election of grace. . . .

In the beginning, before time and space as we know them, before creation, before there was any reality distinct from God which could be the object of the love of God or the setting for his acts of freedom, God anticipated and determined within himself (in the power of his love and freedom, of his knowing and willing) that the goal and meaning of all his dealings with the as yet nonexistent universe should be the fact that in his Son he would be gracious towards man, uniting himself with him. In the beginning it was the choice of the Father himself to establish this covenant with man by giving up his Son for him, that he himself might become man in the fulfillment of his grace. In the beginning it was the choice of the Son to be obedient to grace, and therefore to offer up himself and to become man in order that this covenant might be made a reality. In the beginning it was the resolve of the Holy Spirit that the unity of God, of Father and Son should not be disturbed or rent by this covenant with man, but that it should be made the more glorious, the deity of God, the divinity of his love and freedom, being confirmed and demonstrated by this offering of the Father and this self-offering of the Son. This choice was in the beginning. As the subject and object of this choice, Jesus Christ was at the beginning. He was not at the beginning of God, for God has indeed no beginning. But he was at the beginning of all things, at the beginning of God's dealings with the reality which is distinct from himself. Jesus Christ was the choice or election of God in respect of this reality. He was the election of God's grace as directed towards man. He was the election of God's covenant with man. . . .

In its simplest and most comprehensive form the dogma of predestination consists, then, in the assertion that the divine predestination is the election of Jesus Christ. But the concept of election has a double reference—to the elector and to the elected. And so, too, the name of Jesus Christ has within itself the double reference: the One called by this name is both very God and very man. Thus the simplest form of the dogma may be divided at once into the two assertions that Jesus Christ is the electing God, and that he is also elected man. . . .

Jesus Christ is the electing God. We must begin with this assertion because by its content it has the character and dignity of a basic principle, and because the other assertion, that Jesus Christ is elected man, can be understood only in the light of it.

We may notice at once the critical significance of this first assertion in its relation to the traditional understanding of the doctrine. In particular, it crowds out and replaces the idea of a *decretum absolutum*. That idea does, of course, give us an answer to the question about the electing God. It speaks of a good-pleasure of God which in basis and direction is unknown to man and to all beings outside God himself. This good-pleasure is omnipotent and incontrovertible in its decisions. If we are asked concerning its nature, then ultimately no more can be said than that it is divine, and therefore absolutely supreme and authoritative. But now in the place of this blank, this unknown quantity, we are to put the name of Jesus Christ. . . .

Jesus Christ was in the beginning with God. He was so not merely in the sense that in view of God's eternal knowing and willing all things may be said to have been in the beginning with God, in his plan and decree. . . . He was also in the beginning with God as "the first-born of every creature" (Col. 1:15), himself the plan and decree of God, himself the divine decision with respect to all creation and its history whose content is already determined. All that is embraced and signified in God's election of grace as his movement towards man, all that results from that election and all that is presupposed in such results—all these are determined and conditioned by the fact that that election is the divine decision whose content is already determined, that Jesus Christ is the divine election of grace.

Thus Jesus Christ is not merely one object of the divine good-pleasure side by side with others. On the contrary, he is the sole object of this good-pleasure, for in the first instance he himself is this good-pleasure, the will of God in action. He is not merely the standard or instrument of the divine freedom. He is himself primarily and properly the divine freedom itself in its operation *ad extra*. He is not merely the revelation of the mystery of God. He is the thing concealed within this mystery, and the revelation of it is the revelation of himself and not of something else. He is not merely the Reconciler between God and man. First, he is himself the reconciliation between them. And so he is not only the Elected. He is also himself the Elector, and in the first instance his election must be understood as active. It is true that as the Son of God given by the Father to be one with man, and to take to himself the form of man, he is elected. It is also true that he does not elect alone, but in company with the electing of the Father and the Holy spirit. But he does elect. The obedience which he renders as the Son of God is, as genuine obedience, his own decision and electing, a decision and electing no less divinely free than the electing and decision of the Father and the Holy Spirit. Even the fact that he is elected corresponds as closely as possible to his own electing. In the harmony of the triune God he is no less the original Subject of this electing than he is its original object. And only in this harmony can he really be its object, i.e. completely fulfill not his own will but the will of the Father, and thus confirm and to some extent repeat as elected man the election of God. This all rests on the fact that from the very first he participates in the divine election; that election is also his election; that it is he himself who posits this beginning of all things; that it is he himself who executes the decision which issues in the establishment of the covenant between God and man; that he too, with the Father and the Holy Spirit, is the electing God. . . .

The election of Jesus Christ is the eternal choice and decision of God. And our first assertion tells us that Jesus Christ is the electing God. We must not ask concerning any other but him. In no depth of the godhead shall we encounter any other but him. There is no such thing as Godhead in itself. Godhead is always the godhead of the Father, the Son, and the Holy Spirit. But the Father is the Father of Jesus Christ and the Holy Spirit is the Spirit of the Father and the

Spirit of Jesus Christ. There is no such thing as a *decretum absolutum*. There is no such thing as a will of God apart from the will of Jesus Christ. . . .

Christ reveals to us our election as an election which is made by him, by his will which is also the will of God. He tells us that he himself is the One who elects us. In the very foreground of our existence in history we can and should cleave wholly and with full assurance to him because in the eternal background of history, in the beginning with God, the only decree which was passed, the only Word which was spoken and which prevails, was the decision which was executed by him. As we believe in him and hear his Word and hold fast by his decision, we can know with a certainty which nothing can ever shake that we are the elect of God.

Jesus Christ is elected man. In making this second assertion we are again at one with the traditional teaching. . . .

Now without our first assertion we cannot maintain such a position. For where can Jesus Christ derive the authority and power to be Lord and Head of all others, and how can these others be elected "in him," and how can they see their election in him the first of the elect, and how can they find in his election the assurance of their own, if he is only the object of election and not himself its Subject, if he is only an elect creature and not primarily and supremely the electing Creator? . . . In one and the same person he must be both elected man and the electing God. Thus the second assertion rests on the first, and for the sake of the second the first ought never to be denied or passed over.

Because of this interconnexion we must now formulate the second statement with rather more precision. It tells us that before all created reality, before all being and becoming in time, before time itself, in the pretemporal eternity of God, the eternal divine decision as such has as its object and content the existence of this one created being, the man Jesus of Nazareth, and the work of this man in his life and death, his humiliation and exaltation, his obedience and merit. It tells us further that in and with the existence of this man the eternal divine decision has as its object and content the execution of the divine covenant with man, the salvation of all men. In this function this man is the object of the eternal divine decision and foreordination. Jesus Christ, then, is not merely one of the elect but *the* elect of God. From the very beginning (from eternity itself), as elected man he does not stand alongside the rest of the elect, but before and above them as the One who is originally and properly the Elect. From the very beginning (from eternity itself), there are no other elect together with or apart from him, but, as Eph.1:4 tells us, only "in" him. "In him" does not simply mean with him, together with him, in his company. Nor does it mean only through him, by means of that which he as elected man can be and do for them. "In him" means in his person, in his will, in his own divine choice, in the basic decision of God which he fulfills over against every man. What singles him out from the rest of the elect, and yet also, and for the first time, unites him with them, is the fact that as elected man he is also the electing God, electing them in his own humanity. In that he (as God) wills himself (as man), he also wills them. And so they are elect "in him," in and with his own election. . . .

But the elected man Jesus was foreordained to suffer and to die. That is how his selection, and sending, and, as we have seen, his election, are understood in the new Testament. The free grace of God directed in him towards the creature took on this form from the very first (from all eternity). According to Phil. 2:6f. it is obedience unto death, even unto the death of the cross, to which the Son of God predestines himself when he empties himself of his divine form of being. And this predestining is the content of the divine decree at the beginning of all things. "The Word became flesh" (John 1:14). This formulation of the message of Christmas already includes within itself the message of Good Friday. For "all flesh is as grass." The election of the man Jesus means, then, that a wrath is kindled, a sentence pronounced and finally executed, a rejection actualized. It has been determined thus from all eternity. From all eternity judgment has been foreseen—even in the overflowing of God's inner glory, even in the ineffable condescension of God's embracing of the creature, even in the fullness of self-giving by which God himself wills to become a creature. For theologically the election of the man Jesus carries within itself the election of a creation which is good according to the positive will of God and of man as fashioned after the divine image and foreordained to the divine likeness (reflection). But this involves necessarily the rejection of Satan, the rebel angel who is the very sum and substance of the possibility which is not chosen by God (and which exists only in virtue of this negation); the very essence of the creature in its misunderstanding and misuse of its creation and destiny and in its desire to be as God, to be itself a god. Satan (and the whole kingdom of evil, i.e., the demonic, which has its basis in him) is the shadow which accompanies the light of the election of Jesus Christ (and in him of the good creation in which man is in the divine image). And in the divine counsel the shadow itself is necessary as the object of rejection. To the reality of its existence and might and activity (only, of course, in the power of the divine negation, but to that extent grounded in the divine will and counsel) testimony is given by the fall of man, in which man appropriates to himself the satanic desire. When confronted by Satan and his kingdom, man in himself and as such has in his creaturely freedom no power to reject that which in his divine freedom God rejects. Face to face with temptation he cannot maintain the goodness of his creation in the divine image and foreordination to the divine likeness. This is done by the elected man Jesus (Matt. 4:1-11). In himself and as such man will always do as Adam did in Gen. 3. And for this reason, according to the will and counsel of God, man in himself and as such incurs the rejection which rests upon his temptation and corruption. He stands under the wrath which is God's only answer to the creature which abuses and dishonours its creatureliness. Exposed to the power of the divine negation, he is guilty of death. But it is this very man in himself and as such who in and with the election of the man Jesus is loved of God from all eternity and elected to fellowship with him: he who was powerless against the insinuations of the tempter and seducer; he who in his actual temptation and seduction became the enemy of God; he who incurred rejection and became guilty of death. In this one man Jesus, God puts at the head and in the place of all other men the One who has the same power as himself to reject Satan and to maintain and not surrender the goodness of man's divine creation and destiny; the One who according to Matt. 4 actually does this, and does it for all who are elected in him, for man in himself and as such who does not and cannot do it of himself. The rejection which all men incurred, the wrath of God under which all men lie, the death which all men must die, God in his love for men transfers from all eternity to him in whom he loves and elects them, and whom he elects at their head and in their place. God from all eternity ordains this obedient One in order that he might bear the suffering which the disobedient have deserved and which for the sake of God's righteousness must necessarily be borne. Indeed, the very obedience which was exacted of him and attained by him was his willingness to take upon himself the divine rejection of all others and to suffer that which they ought to have suffered. He is elected, and he maintains the goodness of man's divine creation and destiny, not for his own sake but . . . for the sake of man in himself and as such. He, the Elect, is appointed to check and defeat Satan on behalf of all those that are elected "in him," on behalf of the descendants and confederates of Adam now beloved of God. . . .

Against the aggression of the shadow-world of Satan which is negated by him and which exists only in virtue of this negation, God must and will maintain the honour of his creation, the honour of man as created and ordained for him, and his own honour. God cannot and will not acquiesce in the encroachment made with the fall of man. On the contrary, it must be his pleasure to see that Satan and all that has its source and origin in him are rejected. But this means that God must and will reject man as he is in himself. And he does so. But he does it in the person of the elected man Jesus. And in him he loves man as he is in himself.

The Eternal Will of God in the Election of Jesus Christ

We may begin with an epistemological observation. Our thesis is that God's eternal will is the election of Jesus Christ. At this point we part company with all previous interpretations of the doctrine of predestination. In these the Subject and object of predestination (the electing God and elected man) are determined ultimately by the fact that both quantities are treated as unknown. We may say that the electing God is a supreme being who disposes freely according to his own omnipotence, righteousness and mercy. We may say that to him may be ascribed the lordship over all things, and above all the absolute right and absolute power to determine the destiny of man. But when we say that, then ultimately and fundamentally the electing God is an unknown quantity. On the other hand, we may say that elected man is the man who has come under the eternal good-pleasure of God, the man whom from all eternity God has foreordained to fellowship with himself. But when we say that, then ultimately and fundamentally elected man is also an unknown quantity. . . . In the sharpest contrast to this view our thesis that the eternal will of God is the election of Jesus Christ means that we deny the existence of any such twofold mystery.

In this antithesis it is not a matter of the mystery of God's freedom in his eternal will concerning man. We have to do with this mystery too—the mystery of God, and the mystery of man which arises as man is caught up by the eternal will of God into God's own mystery. But what matters here is really the nature of this one and twofold mystery, whether it is incomprehensible light or incomprehensible darkness. What matters is whether at this point we have to recognize and respect the majesty of a God who is known to us or whether we have to recognize and respect the majesty of a God who is not known to us. Again, what matters is whether the man confronted by the majesty of that God is known or not known to us. . . .

Where the parting of the ways comes is in the question of the relationship between predestination and Christology. Is there any continuity between the two? Is there a continuity between the christological centre and *telos* of the temporal work of God which was so clearly recognized by the older theologians, and the eternal presupposing of that work in the divine election which was no less clearly recognized by them? Is there the continuity which would mean necessarily the expounding of predestination in the light of Christology and the understanding of Jesus Christ as the substance of predestination? . . .

Is Jesus Christ really the One who was, and is, and is to come, or is he not? And if he is, what constraint or authority is there that we should not think through to the ultimate meaning of the "he was," not go back to the real beginning of all things in God, i.e., not think of the divine foreordination, the divine election of grace, as something which takes place in him and through him? . . .

With the traditional teaching, and the testimony of Scripture, we think of predestination as eternal, preceding time and all the contents of time. We also think of it as divine, a disposing of time and its contents which is based on the omnipotence of God and characterized by his constancy (or "immutability"). With the strict exponents of tradition, and especially with the Supralapsarians of the seventeenth century, we think of it as the beginning of all things, i.e., the beginning which has no beginning except in God's eternal being in himself; the beginning which in respect of God's relationship with the reality which is distinct from himself is preceded by no other beginning; the beginning which is itself the beginning of this relationship as such; the beginning which everything else included or occurring within this relationship can only follow, proceeding from it and pointing back to it. . . .

But we depart from tradition when we say that for us there is no obscurity about this good-pleasure of the eternal will of God. It is not a good-pleasure which we have to admire and reverence as divine in virtue of such obscurity. . . . God is the self-revealing God, and as such he is the electing God. The eternal will of God which is before time is the same as the eternal will of God which is above time, and which reveals itself as such and operates as such in time. In fact, we perceive the one in the other. For God's eternity is one. God himself is one. He may only be known either altogether or not at all. When he is known he is known all at once and altogether. But these are secondary and derivative considerations which would have no force at all unless they were supported by the fact of the revelation of God. This fact has as such the character of completeness. Revealing to us the fullness of the one God, it discloses to us not only what the will of God is, but also what it was and what it will be. . . .

If we hold fast the revelation of God as the revelation of his eternal will and good-pleasure, if we acknowledge God's freedom in the revelation in which he has proclaimed and enacted it, then as the beginning of all things with God we find the decree that he himself in person, in the person of his eternal Son, should give himself to the son of man, the lost son of man, indeed that he himself in the person of the eternal Son should *be* the lost Son of Man. In the beginning with God, i.e., in the resolve of God which precedes the existence, the possibility and the reality of all his creatures, the very first thing is the decree whose realization means and is Jesus Christ. This decree is perfect both in subject and object. It is the electing God and also the elected man Jesus Christ, and both together in the unity of the one with the other. It is the Son of God in his whole giving of himself to the Son of Man, and the Son of Man in his utter oneness with the Son of God. This is the covenant of grace which is perfected and sealed in the power of God's free love, established openly and unconditionally by God himself and confirmed with a faithfulness which has no reserve. And this decree is really the first of all things. It is the decision between God and the reality distinct from himself. It is a decision which is the basis of all that follows. . . . The will of God is Jesus Christ, and this will is known to us in the revelation of Jesus Christ. If we acknowledge this, if we seriously accept Jesus Christ as the content of this will, then we cannot seek any other will of God, either in heaven or earth, either in time or eternity. . . .

The eternal will of God in the election of Jesus Christ is his will to give himself for the sake of man as created by him and fallen from him. According to the Bible this was what took place in the incarnation of the Son of God, in his death and passion, in his resurrection from the dead. We must think of this as the content of the eternal divine predestination. The election of grace in the beginning of all things is God's self-giving in his eternal purpose. His self-giving: God gave—not only as an actual event but as something eternally foreordained—God gave his only begotten Son. God sent forth his own Word. And in so doing he gave himself. He gave himself up. He hazarded himself. He did not do this for nothing, but for man as created by him and fallen away from him. This is God's eternal will. . . .

What was it that God elected in the eternal election of Jesus Christ? When we asked concerning the content of predestination in our previous expositions we could never give a single answer but only a double. Primarily God elected or predestinated himself. God determined to give and to send his Son. God determined to speak his Word. The beginning in which the Son became obedient to the Father was with himself. The form and concretion of his will, the determination of his whole being, was reached in himself. All God's freedom and love were identical with this decree, with the election of Jesus Christ. That is the one side of the matter. And the other is that God elected man, this man. God's decision and ordination concerned this man. He predestinated his own Son to existence as the son of David. . . . There is already, in origin and from all eternity, this twofold reference, a double predestination. It is obvious that when we confess that God has elected fellowship with man for himself we are stating one thing, and when we confess that God has elected fellowship with himself for man we are stating quite another. Both things together are the divine election. But obviously if its object is twofold so too is its content. It is one thing for God to elect and predestinate himself to fellowship with man, and quite another for God to predestinate man to fellowship with himself. Both are God's self-giving to man. But if the latter means unequivocally that a gift is made to man, the former certainly does not mean that God gives or procures himself anything—for what could God give or procure himself in giving to man a share in his own being? What we have to consider under this aspect is simply God's hazarding of his Godhead and power and status. For man it means an infinite gain, an unheard-of advancement, that God should give himself to him as his own possession, that God should be his God. But for God it means inevitably a certain compromising of himself that he should determine to enter into this covenant. Where man stands only to gain, God stands only to lose. And because the eternal divine predestination is identical with the election of Jesus Christ, its twofold content is that God wills to lose in order that man may gain. There is a sure and certain salvation for man, and a sure and certain risk for God. . . .

What was involved, then, when God elected to become the Son of Man in Jesus Christ? In giving himself to this act he ordained the surrender of something, i.e., of his own impassibility in face of the whole world which because it is not willed by him can only be the world of evil. In himself God cannot be affected either by the possibility or by the reality of that will which opposes him. He cannot be affected by any potentiality of evil. In him is light and no darkness at all. But when God of his own will raised up man to be a covenant-member with himself, when from all eternity he elected to be one with man in Jesus Christ, he did it with a being which was not merely affected by evil but actually mastered by it. . . . God does not merely give himself up to the risk and menace, but he exposes himself to the actual onslaught and grasp of evil. For if God himself became man, this man, what else can this mean but that he declared himself guilty of the contradiction against himself in which man was involved; that he submitted himself to the law of creation by which such a contradiction could be accompanied only by loss and destruction; that he made himself the object of the wrath and judgment to which man had brought himself; that he took upon himself the rejection which man had deserved. . . .

When we say that God elected as his own portion the negative side of the divine predestination, the reckoning with man's weakness and sin and inevitable punishment, we say implicitly that this portion is not man's portion. In so far, then, as predestination does contain a No, it is not a No spoken against man. In so far as it does involve exclusion and rejection, it is not the exclusion and rejection of man. In so far as it is directed to perdition and death, it is not directed to the perdition and death of man. . . . Rejection cannot again become the portion or affair of man. The exchange which took place on Golgotha, when God chose as his throne the malefactor's cross, when the Son of God bore what the son of man ought to have borne, took place once and for all in fulfillment of God's eternal will, and it can never be reversed. There is no condemnation—literally none—for those that are in Christ Jesus. For this reason faith in the divine predestination as such and *per se* means faith in the nonrejection of man, or disbelief in his rejection. Man is not rejected. In God's eternal purpose it is God himself who is rejected in his Son. . . .

We now turn to the other aspect of this same reality. What did God elect in the election of Jesus Christ? We have said already that not only did he elect fellowship with man for himself, but he also elected fellowship with himself for man. . . . All god's willing is primarily a determination of the love of the Father and the Son in the fellowship of the Holy Ghost. How, then, can its content be otherwise than good? How can it be anything else but glory—a glory which is new and distinctive and divine? But in this primal decision God does not choose only himself. In this choice of self he also chooses another, that other which is man. Man is the outward cause and object of this overflowing of the divine glory. God's goodness and favour are directed towards him. In this movement God has not chosen and willed a second god side by side with himself, but a being distinct from himself. And in all its otherness, as his creature and antithesis, this being has been ordained to participation in his own glory, the glory to which it owes its origin. It has been ordained to exist in the brightness of this glory and as the bearer of its image. In all its otherness it is predestined to receive the divine good which has been revealed and communicated. This is what is ordained for man in the primal decision of the divine decree. . . .

We state at once that we have to do here with the positive content, the Yes of predestination. We have to do with what is primary and proper to it, its meaning and end. For the fact that God willed and chose man with this ordination, the fact that he predestinated him to be a witness of his glory, and therefore to blessedness and eternal life, meant inevitably that he was foreordained to danger and trouble. Man was willed and chosen by God with his limitations, as a creature which could and would do harm to God by the application, or rather the misuse, of its freedom. The danger-point of man's susceptibility to temptation, and the zero-point of his fall, were thus included in the divine decree. In their own way they were even the object of the divine will and choice. This is also true. This second aspect accompanies the first like a shadow preceding and following.

In ordaining the overflowing of his glory God also and necessarily ordains that this glory, which in himself, in his inner life as Father, Son, and Holy Spirit, cannot be subjected to attack or disturbance, which in himself cannot be opposed, should enter the sphere of contradiction where light and darkness are marked off from each other; where what God wills, the good, stands out distinctively from what he does not will, the evil; where by the very existence of good there is conceded to evil and created for it a kind of possibility and reality of existence; where it can and does enter in as a kind of autonomous power, as Satan. The possibility of existence which evil can have is only that of the impossible, the reality of existence only that of the unreal, the autonomous power only that of impotence. But these as such it can and must have. How can God ordain the overflowing of his glory, how can he choose the creature man as witness to this glory, without also willing and choosing its shadow, without conceding to and creating for that shadow—not in himself, but in the sphere of the outward overflowing of his glory—an existence as something yielding and defeated, without including the existence of that shadow in his decree? Without evil as "permitted" in this sense there can be no universe or man, and without the inclusion of this "permission" God's decree would be something other than it actually is. It should be perfectly clear, however, that the overflowing and the shadow are the will of God at a completely different level and in a completely different sense. The positive will and choice of God is only the overflowing of his glory and the blessedness and eternal life of man. Even in his permitting of man's liability to temptation and fall, even in his permitting of evil, this is always what God wills. The divine willing of evil has, then, no proper or autonomous basis in God. It is not, as it were, an independent light in God which shines or is suddenly kindled at this point. God wills evil only because he wills not to keep to himself the light of his glory but to let it shine outside himself, because he wills to ordain man the witness of this glory. There is nothing in God and nothing in his willing and choosing *ad extra* to which either evil or the doer of evil can appeal, as though evil too were divinely created, as though evil too had in God a divine origin and counterpart. God wills it only as a shadow which yields and flees. And he wills it only because he wills the shining of only the one true light, his own light, and because he wills to reveal and impart this light. . . .

8. Paul Tillich, *Systematic Theology*

Message and Situation

Theology, as a function of the Christian church, must serve the needs of the church. A theological system is supposed to satisfy two basic needs: the statement of the truth of the Christian message and the interpretation of this truth for every new generation. Theology moves back and forth between two poles, the eternal truth of its foundation and the temporal situation in which the eternal truth must be received. Not many theological systems have been able to balance these two demands perfectly. Most of them either sacrifice elements of the truth or are not able to speak to the situation. Some of them combine both shortcomings. Afraid of missing the eternal truth, they identify it with some previous theological work, with traditional concepts and solutions, and try to impose these on a new, different situation. They confuse eternal truth with a temporal expression of this truth. This is evident in European theological orthodoxy, which in America is known as fundamentalism. . . .

"Situation," as one pole of all theological work, does not refer to the psychological or sociological state in which individuals or groups live. It refers to the scientific and artistic, the economic, political, and ethical forms in which they express their interpretation of existence. The "situation" to which theology must speak relevantly is not the situation of the individual as individual and not the situation of the group as group. Theology is neither preaching nor counseling; therefore, the success of a theology when it is applied to preaching or to the care of souls is not necessarily a criterion of its truth. The fact that fundamentalist ideas are eagerly grasped in a period of personal or communal disintegration does not prove their theological validity, just as the success of a liberal theology in periods of personal or communal integration is no certification of its truth. The "situation" theology must consider is the creative interpretation of existence, an interpretation which is carried on in every period of history under all kinds of psychological and sociological conditions. The "situation" certainly is not independent of these factors. However, theology deals with the cultural expression they have found in practice as well as in theory and not with these conditioning factors as such. Thus theology is not concerned with the political split between East and West, but it is concerned with the political interpretation of this split. Theology is not concerned with the spread of mental diseases or with our increasing awareness of them, but it is concerned with the psychiatric interpretation of these trends. The "situation" to which theology must respond is the totality of man's creative self-interpretation in a special period. Fundamentalism and orthodoxy reject this task, and, in doing so, they miss the meaning of theology. . . .

The Theological Circle

Attempts to elaborate a theology as an empirical-inductive or a metaphysical-deductive "science," or as a combination of both, have given ample evidence that no such an attempt can succeed. In every assumedly scientific theology there is a point where individual experience, traditional valuation, and personal commitment must decide the issue. . . .

In both the empirical and the metaphysical approaches, as well as in the much more numerous cases of their mixture, it can be observed that the a priori which directs the induction and the deduction is a type of mystical experience.

Whether it is "being-itself" (Scholastics) or the "universal substance" (Spinoza), whether it is "beyond subjectivity and objectivity" (James) or the "identity of spirit and nature" (Schelling), whether it is "universe" (Schleiermacher) or "cosmic whole" (Hocking), whether it is "value creating process" (Whitehead) or "progressive integration" (Wieman), whether it is "absolute spirit" (Hegel) or "cosmic person" (Brightman)—each of these concepts is based on an immediate experience of something ultimate in value and being of which one can become intuitively aware. . . . The theological concepts of both idealists and naturalists are rooted in a "mystical a priori," an awareness of something that transcends the cleavage between subject and object. And if in the course of a "scientific" procedure this a priori is discovered, its discovery is possible only because it was present from the very beginning. This is the circle which no religious philosopher can escape. And it is by no means a vicious one. . . .

But the circle within which the theologian works is narrower than that of the philosopher of religion. He adds to the "mystical a priori" the criterion of the Christian message. While the philosopher of religion tries to remain general and abstract in his concepts, as the concept "religion" itself indicates, the theologian is consciously and by intention specific and concrete. . . .

The doctrine of the theological circle has a methodological consequence: neither the introduction nor any other part of the theological system is the logical basis for the other parts. Every part is dependent on every other part. The introduction presupposes the Christology and the doctrine of the church and vice versa. The arrangement is only a matter of expediency.

Two Formal Criteria of Every Theology

This, then, is the first formal criterion of theology: *The object of theology is what concerns us ultimately. Only those propositions are theological which deal with their object in so far as it can become a matter of ultimate concern for us.* . . .

The question now arises: What is the content of our ultimate concern? What *does* concern us conditionally? The answer, obviously, cannot be a special object, not even God, for the first criterion of theology must remain formal and general. If more is to be said about the nature of our ultimate concern, it must be derived from an analysis of the concept "ultimate concern." *Our ultimate concern is that which determines our being or not-being. Only those statements are theological which deal with their object in so far as it can become a matter of being or not-being for us.* This is the second formal criterion of theology.

Theology and Christianity

If taken in the broadest sense of the word, theology, the *logos* or the reasoning about *theos* (God and divine things), is as old as religion. Thinking pervades all the spiritual activities of man. Man would not be spiritual without words, thoughts, concepts. This is especially true in religion, the all-embracing function of man's spiritual life. . . .

Every myth contains a theological thought which can be, and often has been, made explicit. Priestly harmonizations of different myths sometimes disclose profound theological insights. Mystical speculations, as in Vedanta Hinduism, unite meditative elevation with theological penetration. Metaphysical speculations, as in classical Greek philosophy, unite rational analysis with theological vision. Ethical, legal, and ritual interpretations of the divine law create another form of theology on the soil of prophetic monotheism. All this is "theo-logy," *logos* of *theos*, a rational interpretation of the religious substance of rites, symbols, and myths.

Christian theology is no exception. It does the same thing, but it does it in a way which implies the claim that it is *the* theology. The basis of this claim is the Christian doctrine that the Logos became flesh, that the principle of the divine self-revelation has become manifest in the event "Jesus as the Christ." If this message is true, Christian theology has received a foundation which transcends the foundation of any other theology and which itself cannot be transcended. Christian theology has received something which is absolutely concrete and absolutely universal at the same time. No myth, no mystical vision, no metaphysical principle, no sacred law, has the concreteness of a personal life. In comparison with a personal life everything else is relatively abstract. And none of these relatively abstract foundations of theology has the universality of the Logos, which itself is the principle of universality. In comparison with the Logos everything else is relatively particular. Christian theology is *the* theology in so far as it is based on the tension between the absolutely concrete and the absolutely universal. . . .

It seems paradoxical if one says that only that which is absolutely concrete can also be absolutely universal and vice versa, but it describes the situation adequately. Something that is merely abstract has a limited universality because it is restricted to the realities from which it is abstracted. Something that is merely particular has a limited concreteness because it must exclude other particular realities in order to maintain itself as concrete. Only that which has the power of representing everything particular is absolutely concrete. And only that which has the power of representing everything abstract is absolutely universal. This leads to a point where the absolutely concrete and the absolutely universal are identical. And this is the point at which Christian theology emerges, the point which is described as the "Logos who has become flesh." The Logos doctrine as the doctrine of the identity of the absolutely concrete with the absolutely universal is not one theological doctrine among others; it is the only possible foundation of a Christian theology which claims to be *the theology*.

Theology and Philosophy

Theology claims that it constitutes a special realm of knowledge, that it deals with a special object and employs a special method. This claim places the theologian under the obligation of giving an account of the way in which he relates theology to other forms of knowledge. He must answer two questions: What is the relationship of theology to the special sciences (*Wissenschaften*) and what is its relationship to philosophy? The first question has been answered implicitly by the preceding statement of the formal criteria of theology. If nothing is an object of theology which does not concern us ultimately, theology is unconcerned about scientific procedures and results and vice versa. Theology has no right and no obligation to prejudice a physical or historical, sociological or psychological, inquiry. And no result of such an inquiry can be directly productive or disastrous for theology. The point of contact between scientific research and theology lies in the philosophical element of both the sciences and theology. . . .

Philosophy asks the question of reality as a whole; it asks the question of the structure of being. And it answers in terms of categories, structural laws, and universal concepts. It must answer in ontological terms. Ontology is not a speculative-fantastic attempt to establish a world behind the world, it is an analysis of those structures of being which we encounter in every meeting with reality. . . .

Theology necessarily asks the same question, for that which concerns us ultimately must belong to reality as a whole; it must belong to being. Otherwise we could not encounter it, and it could not concern us. Of course, it cannot be one being among others; then it would not concern us infinitely. It must be the ground of our being, that which determines our being or not-being, the ultimate and unconditional power of being. But the power of being, its infinite ground or "being-itself," expresses itself in and through the structure of being. Therefore, we can encounter it, be grasped by it, know it, and act toward it. Theology, when dealing with our ultimate concern, presupposes in every sentence and structure of being, its categories, laws, and concepts. Theology, therefore, cannot escape the question of being any more easily than can philosophy. . . .

Philosophy and theology ask the question of being. But they ask it from different perspectives. Philosophy deals with the structure of being in itself; theology deals with the meaning of being for us. From this difference convergent and divergent trends emerge in the relation of theology and philosophy.

The first point of divergence is a difference in the cognitive attitude of the philosopher and the theologian. Although driven by the philosophical *eros*, the philosopher tries to maintain a detached objectivity toward being and its structures. He tries to exclude the personal, social, and historical conditions which might distort an objective vision of reality. His passion is the passion for a truth which is open to general approach, subject to general criticism, changeable in accordance with every new insight, open and communicable. . . .

The theologian, quite differently, is not detached from his object but is involved in it. He looks at his object (which transcends the character of being an object) with passion, fear, and love. This is not the *eros* of the philosopher or his passion of objective truth; it is the love which accepts saving, and therefore personal, truth. The basic attitude of the theologian is commitment to the content he expounds. Detachment would be a denial of the very nature of this content. The attitude of the theologian is "existential." He is involved—with the whole of his existence, with his infinitude and his anxiety, with his self-contradictions and his despair, with the healing forces in him and in his social situation. Every theological statement derives its seriousness from these elements of existence. The theologian, in short, is determined by his faith. Every theology presupposes that the theologian is in the theological circle. This contradicts the open, infinite, and changeable character of philosophical truth.

The second point of divergence between the theologian and the philosopher is the difference in their sources. The philosopher looks at the whole of reality to discover within it the structure of reality as a whole. He tries to penetrate into the structures of being by means of the power of his cognitive function and its structures. He assumes—and science continuously confirms this assumption—that there is an identity, or at least an analogy, between objective and subjective reason, between the *logos* of reality as a whole and the *logos* working in him. Therefore, this *logos* is common; every reasonable being participates in it, uses it in asking questions and criticizing the answers received. There is no particular place to discover the structure of being; there is no particular place to stand to discover the categories of experience. The place to look is all places; the place to stand is no place at all; it is pure reason.

The theologian, on the other hand, must look where that which concerns him ultimately is manifest, and he must stand where its manifestation reaches and grasps him. The source of his knowledge is not the universal *logos* but the Logos "who became flesh," that is, the *logos* manifesting itself in a particular historical event. And the medium through which he receives the manifestation of the *logos* is not common rationality but the church, its traditions and its present reality. He speaks in the church about the foundation of the church. And he speaks because he grasped, by the power of this foundation and by the community built upon it, the concrete *logos* at which the philosopher looks, through rational detachment.

The third point of divergence between philosophy and theology is the difference in their content. Even when they speak about the same object, they speak about something different. The philosopher deals with the categories of being in relation to the material which is structured by them. He deals with causality as it appears in physics or psychology; he analyzes biological or historical time; he discusses astronomical as well as microcosmic space. He describes the epistemological subject and the relation of person and community. He presents the characteristics of life and spirit in their dependence on, and independence of, each other. He defines nature and history in their mutual limits and tries to penetrate into ontology and logic of being and nonbeing. . . . The theologian, on the other hand, relates the same categories and concepts to the quest for a "new being." His assertions have a soteriological character. He discusses causality in relation to a *prima causa*, the ground of the whole series of causes and effects; he deals with time in relation to eternity, with space in relation to man's existential homelessness. He speaks of the self-estrangement of the subject, about the spiritual center of personal life, and about community as a possible embodiment of the "New Being." He relates the structures of life to the creative ground of life and the structures of spirit to the divine Spirit. He speaks of the participation of nature in the "history of salvation," about the victory of being over nonbeing. Here also the examples could be increased indefinitely; they show the sharp divergence of theology from philosophy with respect to their content.

The Method of Correlation

Systematic theology uses the method of correlation. It has always done so, sometimes more, sometimes less, consciously, and must do so consciously and outspokenly, especially if the apologetic point of view is to prevail. The method of correlation explains the contents of the Christian faith through existential questions and theological answers in mutual interdependence. . . .

The answers implied in the event of revelation are meaningful only in so far as they are in correlation with questions concerning the whole of our existence, with existential questions. Only those who have experienced the shock of transitoriness, the anxiety in which they are aware of their finitude, the threat of nonbeing, can understand what the notion of God means. Only those who have experienced the tragic ambiguities of our historical existence and have totally questioned the meaning of existence can understand what the symbol of the Kingdom of God means. Revelation answers questions which have been asked and always will be asked because they are "we ourselves." Man is the question he asks about himself, before any question has been formulated. It is, therefore, not surprising that the basic questions were formulated very early in the history of mankind. Every analysis of the mythological material shows this. Nor is it surprising that the same questions appear in early childhood, as every observation of children shows. Being human means asking the questions of one's own being and living under the impact of the answers given to this question. And, conversely, being human means receiving answers to the question of one's own being and asking questions under the impact of the answers.

In using the method of correlation, systematic theology proceeds in the following way: it makes an analysis of the human situation out of which the existential questions arise, and it demonstrates that the symbols used in the Christian message are the answers to these questions. The analysis of the human situation is done in terms which today are called "existential." Such analyses are much older than existentialism; they are, indeed, as old as man's thinking about himself, and they have been expressed in various kinds of conceptualization since the beginning of philosophy. Whenever man has looked at his world, he has found himself in it as a part of it. But he also has realized that he is a stranger in the world of objects, unable to penetrate it beyond a certain level of scientific analysis. And then he has become aware of the fact that he himself is the door to the deeper levels of reality, that in his own existence he has the only possible approach to existence itself. This does not mean that man is more approachable than other objects as material for scientific research. The opposite is the case! It does mean that the immediate experience of one's own existing reveals something of the nature of existence generally. Whoever has penetrated into the nature of his own finitude can find the traces of finitude in everything that exists. And he can ask the question implied in his finitude as the question implied in finitude universally. In doing so, he does not formulate a doctrine of man; he expresses a doctrine of existence as experienced in him as man. . . .

The analysis of the human situation employs materials made available by man's creative self-interpretation in all realms of culture. Philosophy contributes, but so do poetry, drama, the novel, therapeutic psychology, and sociology. The theologian organizes these materials in relation to the answer given by the Christian message. In the light of this message he may make an analysis of existence which is more penetrating than that of most philosophers. Nevertheless, it remains a philosophical analysis. The analysis of existence, including the development of the questions implicit in existence, is a philosophical task, even if it is performed by a theologian. . . . As a theologian he does not tell himself what is philosophically true. As a philosopher he does not tell himself what is theologically true. But he cannot help seeing human existence and existence generally in such a way that the Christian symbols appear meaningful and understandable to him. . . .

The Christian message provides the answers to the questions implied in human existence. These answers are contained in the revelatory events on which Christianity is based. . . . Their content cannot be derived from the questions, that is, from an analysis of human existence. They are "spoken" to human existence from beyond it. Otherwise, they would not be answers, for the question is human existence itself. But the relation is more involved than this, since it is correlation. There is a mutual dependence between question and answer. In respect to content the Christian answers are dependent on the revelatory events in which they appear; in respect to form they are dependent on the structure of the questions which they answer. God is the answer to the question implied in human finitude. This answer cannot be derived from the analysis of existence. However, if the notion of God appears in systematic theology in correlation with the threat of nonbeing which is implied in existence, God must be called the infinite power of being which resists the threat of nonbeing. In classical theology this is being-itself. If anxiety is defined as the awareness of being finite, God must be called the infinite ground of courage. In classical theology this is universal providence. If the notion of the kingdom of God appears in correlation with the riddle of our historical existence, it must be called the meaning, fulfillment, and unity of history. In this way an interpretation of the traditional symbols of Christianity is achieved which preserves the power of these symbols and which opens them to the questions elaborated by our present analysis of human existence.

The New Being in Jesus as the Christ

According to eschatological symbolism, the Christ is the one who brings the new eon. When Peter called Jesus "the Christ," he expected the coming of a new state of things through him. This expectation is implicit in the title "Christ." But it was not fulfilled in accordance with the expectations of the disciples. The state of things, of nature as well as of history, remained unchanged, and he who was supposed to bring the new eon was destroyed by the powers of the old eon. This meant that the disciples either had to accept the breakdown of their hope or radically transform its content. They were able to choose the second way by identifying the New Being with the being of Jesus, the sacrificed. In the Synoptic records Jesus himself reconciled the messianic claim with the acceptance of a violent death. The same records show that the disciples resisted this combination. Only the experiences which are described as Easter and Pentecost created their faith in the paradoxical character of the messianic claim. It was Paul who gave the theological frame in which the paradox could be understood and justified. One approach to the solution of the problem was to state the distinction between the first and the second coming of the Christ. The new state of things will be created with the second coming, the return of the Christ in glory. In the period between the first and the second coming the New Being is present in him. He is the Kingdom of God. In him the eschatological expectation is fulfilled in principle. Those who participate in him participate in the new Being, though under the condition of man's existential predicament and, therefore, only fragmentarily and by anticipation.

New Being is essential being under the conditions of existence, conquering the gap between essence and existence. For the same idea Paul uses the term "new creature," calling those who are "in" Christ "new creatures." "In" is the preposition of participation; he who participates in the newness of being which is in Christ has become a new creature. It is a creative act by which this happens. Inasmuch as Jesus as the Christ is a creation of the divine Spirit, according to Synoptic theology, so is he who participates in the Christ made into a new creature by the Spirit. The estrangement of his existential from his essential being is conquered in principle, i.e., in power and as in beginning. The term "New Being," as used here, points directly to the cleavage between essential and existential being—and is the restorative principle of the whole of this theological system. The New Being is new in so far as it is the undistorted manifestation of essential being within and under the conditions of existence. It is new in two respects: it is new in contrast to the merely potential character of essential being;

and it is new over against the estranged character of existential being. It is actual, conquering the estrangement of actual existence. . . .

The Expressions of the New Being in Jesus as the Christ

Jesus as the Christ is the bearer of the New Being in the totality of his being, not in any special expressions of it. It is his being that makes him the Christ because his being has the quality of the New Being beyond the split of essential and existential being. From this it follows that neither his words, deeds, or sufferings nor what is called his "inner life" make him the Christ. They are all expressions of the New Being, which is the quality of his being, and this, his being, precedes and transcends all its expressions. This assertion can serve as a critical tool against several inadequate ways of describing his character as the Christ.

The first expression of the being of Jesus as the Christ is his words. The word is the bearer of spiritual life. The importance of the spoken word for the religion of the New Testament cannot be overestimated. The words of Jesus, to cite but two examples of many, are called "words of eternal life," and discipleship is made dependent upon "holding to his words." And he himself is called "the Word." It is just this last instance that shows it is not his words which make him the Christ but his being. This is metaphorically called "the Word" because it is the final self-manifestation of God to humanity. His being, which is called "the Word," expresses itself also in his words. But, as the Word, he is more than all the words he has spoken. This assertion is the basic criticism of a theology which separates the words of Jesus from his being and makes him into a teacher, preacher, or prophet. This theological tendency, as old as the church, is represented by ancient and modern rationalism. It came to the foreground in the so-called "liberal theology" of the nineteenth century. But its theological significance is surpassed by its influence on the popular mind. It plays a tremendous role in the piety of daily life, particularly in those groups for whom Christianity has become a system of conventional rules commanded by a divine teacher. . . . This view is obviously a relapse to the legalistic type of self-salvation. . . . It is the replacement of Jesus as the Christ by the religious and moral teacher called Jesus of Nazareth. Against such theology and its popularized application, one must hold to the principle that "being precedes speaking". . . .

The second expression of the New Being in Jesus as the Christ is his deeds. They also have been separated from his being and made into examples to be imitated. He is not considered to be a lawgiver but as himself being the new law. . . . *Imitatio Christi* is often understood as the attempt to transform one's life into a copy of the life of Jesus, including the concrete traits of the biblical picture. But this contradicts the meaning of these traits as parts of his being within the picture of Jesus the Christ. These traits are supposed to make translucent the New Being, which is his being. As such, they point beyond their contingent character and are not instances to imitate. . . .

The third expression of the New Being in Jesus as the Christ is his suffering. It includes his violent death and is a consequence of the inescapable conflict between the forces of existential estrangement and the bearer of that by which existence is conquered. Only by taking suffering and death upon himself could Jesus be the Christ, because only in this way could he participate completely in existence and conquer every force of estrangement which tried to dissolve his unity with God. The significance of the Cross in the New Testament picture of Jesus as the Christ induced orthodox theologians to separate both suffering and death from his being and to make these his decisive function as the Christ within the frame of a sacrificial theory. This is partially justifiable; for, without the continuous sacrifice of himself as a particular individual under the conditions of existence to himself as the bearer of the New Being, he could not have been the Christ. He proves and confirms his character as the Christ in the sacrifice of himself as Jesus to himself as the Christ. But it is not justifiable to separate this sacrificial function from his being, of which it is actually an expression. . . . The suffering on the Cross is not something additional which can be separated from the appearance of the eternal God-Manhood under the conditions of existence; it is an inescapable implication of this appearance. Like his words and his deeds, the suffering of Jesus as the Christ is an expression of the New Being in him. . . .

The term "New Being," when applied to Jesus as the Christ, points to the power in him which conquers existential estrangement or, negatively expressed, to the power of resisting the forces of estrangement. To experience the New Being in Jesus as the Christ means to experience the power in him which has conquered existential estrangement in himself and in everyone who participates in him. "Being," if used for God or divine manifestations, is the power of being or, negatively expressed, the power of conquering nonbeing. The word "being" points to the fact that this power is not a matter of someone's good will but that it is a gift which precedes or determines the character of every act of the will. In this sense, one can say that the concept of the New Being re-establishes the meaning of grace.

The New Being in Jesus as the Christ as the Conquest of Estrangement

The New Being in the Christ and the Marks of Estrangement. — In all its concrete details the biblical picture of Jesus as the Christ confirms his character as the bearer of the New Being or as the one in whom the conflict between the essential unity of God and man and man's existential estrangement is overcome. Point by point, not only in the Gospel records but also in the Epistles, this picture of Jesus as the Christ contradicts the marks of estrangement. . . .

According to the biblical picture of Jesus as the Christ, there are, in spite of all tensions, no traces of estrangement between him and God and consequently between him and himself and between him and his world (in its essential nature).

The paradoxical character of his being consists in the fact that, although he has only finite freedom under the conditions of time and space, he is not estranged from the ground of his being. There are no traces of unbelief, namely, the removal of his personal center from the divine center which is the subject of his infinite concern. Even in the extreme situation of despair about his messianic work, he cries to his God who has forsaken him. In the same way the biblical picture shows no trace of *hubris* or self-elevation in spite of his awareness of his messianic vocation. In the critical moment in which Peter first calls him the Christ, he combines the acceptance of this title with the acceptance of his violent death, including the warning to his disciples not to make his messianic function public. . . . Nor is there any trace of concupiscence in the picture. This point is stressed in the story of the temptation in the desert. Here the desires for food, acknowledgment, and unlimited power are used by Satan as the possible weak spots in the Christ. As the messiah, he could fulfill these desires. But then he would have been demonic and would have ceased to be the Christ. . . .

The reality of the temptations of Christ.—Since Jesus as the Christ is finite freedom, he also confronts real temptation. Possibility is itself temptation. And Jesus would not represent the essential unity between God and man (Eternal God-Manhood) without the possibility of real temptation. A Monophysitic tendency, which runs through all church history, including theologians and popular Christianity, has tacitly led many to deny that the temptations of the Christ were serious. They could not tolerate the full humanity of Jesus as the Christ, his finite freedom, and, with it, the possibility of defeat in temptation. Unintentionally, they deprived Jesus of his real finitude and attributed a divine transcendence to him above freedom and destiny. The church was right, though never fully successful, in resisting the Monophysitic distortion of the picture of Jesus as the Christ. . . .

The marks of his finitude.—The seriousness of the temptation of the Christ is based on the fact that he is finite freedom. The degree to which the biblical picture of Jesus as the Christ stresses his finitude is remarkable. As a finite being, he is subject to the contingency of everything that is not by itself but is "thrown" into existence. He has to die, and he experiences the anxiety of having to die. This anxiety is described by the evangelists in the most vivid way. It is not relieved by the expectation of resurrection "after three days," or by the ecstasy of a substitutional self-sacrifice, or even by the ideal of the heroism of wise men such as Socrates. Like every man, he experiences the threat of the victory of nonbeing over being, as, for instance, in the limits of the span of life given to him. As in the case of all finite beings, he experiences the lack of a definite place. From his birth on, he appears strange and homeless in his world. He has bodily, social, and mental insecurity, is subject to want, and is expelled by his nation. In relation to other persons, his finitude is manifest in his loneliness, both in respect to the masses and in respect to his relatives and disciples. He struggles to make them understand, but during his life he never succeeds. . . .

In relation to reality as such, including things and persons, he is subject to uncertainty in judgment, risks of error, the limits of power, and the vicissitudes of life. The Fourth Gospel says of him that he *is* truth, but this does not mean that he *has* omniscience or absolute certainty. He *is* the truth in so far as his being— the New Being in him—conquers the untruth of existential estrangement. But being the truth is not the same as knowing the truth about all finite objects and situations. Finitude implies openness to error, and error belongs to the participation of the Christ in man's existential predicament. . . .

His participation in the tragic element of existence. —Every encounter with reality, whether with situations, groups, or individuals, is burdened with practical and theoretical uncertainty. This uncertainty is caused not only by the finitude of the individual but also by the ambiguity of that which a person encounters. Life is marked by ambiguity, and one of the ambiguities is that of greatness and tragedy. . . .

The first and historically most important example in this area is the conflict of Jesus with the leaders of his nation. The ordinary Christian view is that their hostility toward him is unambiguously their religious or moral guilt. They decided against him, although they could have decided for him. But this "could" is just the problem. It removes the tragic element which universally belongs to existence. It places the leaders out of the context of humanity and makes them into representatives of unambiguous evil. But there is no unambiguous evil. This is acknowledged by Jesus when he refers to the traditions and when he expresses that he belongs to the "house of Israel." Although continuously persecuted by the Jews, Paul witnesses to their zeal to fulfill the law of God. The Pharisees were the pious ones of their time, and they represented the law of God, the preparatory revelation, without which the final revelation could not have happened. If Christians deny the tragic element in the encounter between Jesus and the Jews (and analogously between Paul and the Jews), they are guilty of a profound injustice. . . .

His permanent unity with God. —The conquest of existential estrangement in the New Being, which is the being of the Christ, does not remove finitude and anxiety, ambiguity and tragedy; but it does have the character of taking the negativities of existence into unbroken unity with God. The anxiety about having to die is not removed; it is taken into participation in the "will of God," i.e., in his directing creativity. His homelessness and insecurity with respect to a physical, social, and mental place are not diminished but rather increased to the last moment. Yet they are accepted in the power of a participation in a "transcendent place," which in actuality is no place but the eternal ground of every place and of every moment of time. His loneliness and his frustrated attempts in trying to be received by those to whom he came do not suddenly end in a final success; they are taken into the divine acceptance of that which rejects God, into the vertical line of the uniting love which is effective where the horizontal line from being to being is barred. Out of his unity with God he has unity with those who are separated from him and from one another by finite self-relatedness and existential self-seclusion. Both error and doubt equally are not removed but are taken into the participation in the divine life and thus indirectly into the divine omniscience. Both error and truth are taken into the transcendent truth. Therefore, we do not find symptoms of repression of doubt in the picture of Jesus as the Christ. Those who are not able to elevate their doubts into the truth which transcends every finite truth must repress them. They perforce become fanatical. Yet no traces of fanaticism are present in the biblical picture. Jesus does not claim absolute certitude for a finite conviction. He rejects the fanatical attitude of the disciples toward those who do not follow him. In the power of a certitude which transcends certitude and incertitude in matters of religion as well as secular life, he accepts incertitude as an element of finiteness. This also refers to the doubt about his own work—a doubt which breaks through most intensively on the Cross but still does not destroy his unity with God.

4

Theologies of Secularization

The strong emphasis of dialectical theology on the radical transcendence and otherness of God after World War I gave way to an equally radical stress on the immanence of God in various theologies of secularization after World War II. Dietrich Bonhoeffer (1906–1945) coined the formula that captured the imagination of all the theologians of secular Christianity: "the Beyond in the midst of our life." God's transcendence is not to be found above and beyond human existence, life, and history, but in their very midst. Under the influence of Friedrich Gogarten (1887–1976), Rudolf Bultmann (1884–1976) and, above all, Dietrich Bonhoeffer, there arose, not only in Germany but also in England and the United States, various types of theology in which secularization became a positive concept, indicating a legitimate Christian development within world history and not merely a falling away from the faith.

Karl Barth's theology was a formative influence in the background of this new affirmation of secularity. His criticism of religion, his rejection of natural theology, and his christocentric approach were key starting points for all the theologians of secularization, although Barth ultimately could not speak favorably of the novel directions in which his erstwhile friends and followers were to develop these common themes. The secular theologians, all in various ways ex-Barthians, believed that Barth had removed faith from the realm of everyday life and thus had exaggerated God's transcendence at the expense of divine presence in the world. Thus, the new theology of secularization can be seen as a rebellion against the theology of Karl Barth, even while being profoundly indebted to his break with liberal Protestantism and his christocentric dogmatics.

I

Although "secularization" became one of the slogans of contemporary theological discussion, its usage continues to be notoriously ambiguous. This is due in part to its lexical origin and history of translation, and in part to the variety of meanings and connotations, negative and positive, the word has acquired in the history of the church and its encounter with modernity.

94

The word "secularization" stems from the Latin *saeculum* and *saecularis* and originally referred to a period of time, such as a generation, age, or epoch. In medieval Latin, however, under the influence of Augustine's usage, the word was narrowed to mean simply "world" or "worldly," in distinction from "church" or "religious." In standard English usage the word "secular" can have a purely neutral descriptive meaning as in "secular clergy," priests whose ministries are in the world and not bound by monastic rules. The word also and more commonly has acquired a negative meaning, as antithetical to sacred things, opposed to church teachings and religious principles, as in "secular humanism."

The task of clarifying the meaning of "secularization" is, however, more than linguistic. The matter is complicated by long centuries of conflict between religious and civil authorities, papacy and empire, church and state, in securing and maintaining influence in all areas of life, in politics, economics, education, and culture. With the Enlightenment and the French Revolution, the process of secularization came increasingly to mean the privatization of religion, the removal of ecclesiastical control over public life, and belief in complete autonomy for human life. When taken to its logical extreme, "secularism" results—an outlook that aims to direct all human activities and social institutions in complete subjection to the canons of reason and science, without reference to God or religion.

II

There is widespread agreement that the outlook of our age is predominantly secular. But how to characterize this phenomenon more precisely has been much disputed. Careful analysis must attempt to distinguish among words like secular, secularity, secularism, and secularization, and this proves necessary if theology is to welcome the secularization of our age as compatible with biblical faith and Christian doctrine. This is what the theologians of secularization attempted to do.

Dietrich Bonhoeffer, the young German theologian murdered by the Nazis just a few days before the Allies liberated the camp where he was imprisoned, has provided the greatest stimulus to rethinking the relation of Christian faith to the modern historical process of secularization. In his last letters and papers from prison, which we have excerpted for this chapter, Bonhoeffer coined new phrases that became the pegs on which a whole school of followers hung their ideas. Expressions like "religionless Christianity" and "the world come of age" were Bonhoeffer's attempt to describe a new understanding of God's relation to the world that would dispense with concepts of God as a "working hypothesis," "stop-gap," or "tutor."

Bonhoeffer believed that people of today are becoming "radically religionless," but this does not necessarily mean that they must turn away from Christianity. In his view, not only secularists without faith but Christians are becoming "religionless." The concept of a "religionless Christianity" would strike traditional theology as an oxymoron, in that Christianity itself would seem to be that particular religion in which God's revelation has entered human experience. Bonhoeffer, of course, had read and was convinced by Barth's radical critique of religion made in the name of Christian faith. For Barth, religion was the means that people used to make their own way to God, thus bypassing the very revelation by which God has already come upon the human world. In his *Church Dogmatics,* Barth treated religion under the heading, "The Revelation of God as the Abolition of Religion." Thus, for Bonhoeffer also, religion was something primarily negative that needs to be overcome and canceled by faith.

For nearly two thousand years, Christianity has presented itself in the garments of religion, but now the age of religion is supposedly disappearing or has already disappeared. Accordingly, religion is but a time-conditioned and transitory element in the history of humanity that Christianity dare no longer presuppose as universally timeless. So Bonhoeffer asked the question in his prison papers, "What will it mean to be Christian in a world without religion?" What will it mean to pray or to preach without any religious props or propositions? For Bonhoeffer, the elements of religion that are fading away are metaphysics, individualism, and inwardness; by these means liberal theology had tried to keep a special space for religion in the world. Bonhoeffer praised Barth for being the first theologian to begin the criticism of religion, but he felt that Barth did not go far enough; in rejecting religion and natural theology, he left the world to its own devices and did not show concretely how Christ is Lord of this "world come of age."

The interrelated concepts of "religionless Christianity" and "the world come of age" led Bonhoeffer to propose a "nonreligious interpretation of the Bible," even more radical in his view than Bultmann's program of demythologization by means of existentialist categories. Bonhoeffer accused Bultmann too of not having gone far enough, still clinging in some way to the older liberal religious misunderstanding of Christianity. Had Bonhoeffer survived to work out a fully systematic theology along the new lines laid down in his prison letters, the result would not in any case have been discontinuous with the dominant theme of his entire life and theological authorship—"the Lordship of Christ in the world come of age."

III

Friedrich Gogarten was the pioneer of the new and positive affirmation of secularization that characterizes so much of twentieth century theology. In the 1920s, Gogarten first became known as one of the dialectical theologians, a collaborator of Karl Barth. His break with Barth occurred in a dispute over the place of anthropology in theology. Gogarten, along with Brunner and Bultmann, held that theology presupposes some prior understanding of human existence, since the truth in which the Christian believes is a historical one which can only be grasped historically. Barth saw in this a repetition of the error of the liberal tradition, starting with Schleiermacher, that based theology on a philosophical anthropology, moving from a prior general concept of a *homo religiosus* to the *homo christianus.* Gogarten agreed that theology must not derive its anthropology from sources outside of theology, but because theological concepts do not fall down from heaven, they are bound up with the world of human language and need to be investigated for the understanding of human existence implied in them.

After his break with Barth, Gogarten experienced many phases in his development, including a notorious endorsement of the infamous German Christians and their opposition to the Confessing Church and its theological leader, Karl Barth. To his credit, he broke with the German Christians when it became clear that they wanted to get rid of the Old Testament and exclude persons of Jewish extraction from the church. After World War II, Gogarten in his old age got his second theological wind, allying himself with Bultmann's existentialist interpretation of history and Christian faith. In this final period of his career, he turned his thoughts to a positive advocacy of secularization. It may be said that his insistence on the "worldliness of the world," as seen from the perspective of Christian faith, became his most distinctive contribution to twentieth-century theology.

Secularization, not to be confused with secularism, can be affirmed in a peculiar theological sense as the legitimate historical outcome of biblical faith and the Christian doctrine of creation. The beating heart of Gogarten's entire theology was the Lutheran doctrine of salvation by grace through faith apart from works of the law. By denying that works possess any saving efficacy, faith secures their worldly significance. That is, faith secularizes them, keeping them down to earth, strictly something for this *saeculum,* divested of all "religious" meaning as duties that must be performed to be saved. Such secularization or historization—the words are virtually synonymous for Gogarten—of faith's relation to the world belongs to the essence of Christian faith, but when cut loose from Christian faith secularization degenerates into secularism, by which humans proclaim themselves autonomous lords over the world and wrapped up in themselves. In not being "free for God" as his creatures, taking responsibility for the world as God's creation, they end in bondage to themselves.

IV

In the 1960s, the theology of secularization reached Britain and America in full force in various new and radical permutations. All of them were inspired by Bonhoeffer's call for a religionless Christianity attuned to a secular age. The first expression of the radical wing of the Barth, Bultmann, Gogarten, and Bonhoeffer legacy announced itself as the theology of the death-of-God or Christian atheism, in books and articles by William Hamilton and Thomas J. J. Altizer. Paul van Buren, John A. T. Robinson, and Harvey Cox added impetus to a thoroughgoing secular interpretation of the Christian message, catapulting the death-of-God movement and radical theology into the popular media, epitomized by *Time* magazine's cover story, in October 1965, "Is God Dead?" Robinson's *Honest to God* and Harvey Cox's *The Secular City* were extremely popular versions of secular Christianity, but once exposed to the sustained scrutiny of theological criticism their influence proved to be short-lived. Rather than building on the strengths of their dialectical and neo-orthodox predecessors, they represented more a return to the accommodationism of liberal Protestantism, with its confidence in historical progress and cultural optimism. That the American secular theologians failed to provide an adequate solution to the problem of Christian faith in a secular age is signaled by the fact that they soon moved beyond the secular to new experiments in theology.

9. Dietrich Bonhoeffer, *Letters to Eberhard Bethge*

You would be surprised, and perhaps even worried, by my theological thoughts and the conclusions that they lead to; and this is where I miss you most of all, because I don't know anyone else with whom I could so well discuss them to have my thinking clarified. What is bothering me incessantly is the question what Christianity really is, or indeed who Christ really is, for us today. The time when people could be told everything by means of words, whether theological or pious, is over, and so is the time of inwardness and conscience — and that means the time of religion in general. We are moving towards a completely religionless time; people as they are now simply cannot be religious any more. Even those who honestly describe themselves as "religious" do not in the least act up to it, and so they presumably mean something quite different by "religious."

Our whole nineteen-hundred-year-old Christian preaching and theology rest on the "religious *a priori*" of mankind. "Christianity" has always been a form — perhaps the true form — of "religion." But if one day it becomes clear that this *a priori* does not exist at all, but was a historically conditioned and transient form of human self-expression, and if therefore man becomes radically religionless — and I think that that is already more or less the case (else how is it, for example, that this war, in contrast to all previous ones, is not calling forth any "religious" reaction?)—what does that mean for "Christianity"? It means that the foundation is taken away from the whole of what has up to now been our "Christianity," and that there remain only a few "last survivors of the age of chivalry," or a few intellectually dishonest people, on whom we can descend as "religious." Are they to be the chosen few? Is it on this dubious group of people that we are to pounce in fervour, pique, or indignation, in order to sell them our goods? Are we to fall upon a few unfortunate people in their hour of need and exercise a sort of religious compulsion on them? If we don't want to do all that, if our final judgment must be that the western form of Christianity, too, was only a preliminary stage to a complete absence of religion, what kind of situation emerges for us, for the church? How can Christ become the Lord of the religionless as well? Are there religionless Christians? If religion is only a garment of Christianity—and even this garment has looked very different at different times—then what is a religionless Christianity?

Barth, who is the only one to have started along this line of thought, did not carry it to completion, but arrived at a positivism of revelation, which in the last analysis is essentially a restoration. For the religionless working man (or any other man) nothing decisive is gained here. The questions to be answered would surely be: What do a church, a community, a sermon, a liturgy, a Christian life mean in a religionless world? How do we speak of God—without religion, i.e. without the temporally conditioned presuppositions of metaphysics, inwardness, and so on? How do we speak (or perhaps we cannot now even "speak" as we used to) in a "secular" way about "God"? In what way are we "religionless-secular" Christians, in what way are we the ἐκ-κλησία, those who are called forth, not regarding ourselves from a religious point of view as specially favoured, but rather as belonging wholly to the world? In that case Christ is no longer an object of religion, but something quite different, really the Lord of the world. But what does that mean? What is the place of worship and prayer in a religionless situation? Does the secret discipline, or alternatively the difference (which I have suggested to you before) between penultimate and ultimate, take on a new importance here? . . .

The Pauline question whether περιτομή [circumcision] is a condition of justification seems to me in present-day terms to be whether religion is a condition of salvation. Freedom from περιτομή is also freedom from religion. I often ask myself why a "Christian instinct" often draws me more to the religionless people than to the religious, by which I don't in the least mean with any evangelizing intention, but, I might almost say, "in brotherhood." While I'm often reluctant to mention God by name to religious people—because that name somehow seems to me here not to ring true, and I feel myself to be slightly dishonest (it's particularly bad when others start to talk in religious jargon; I then dry up almost completely and feel awkward and uncomfortable)—to people with no religion I can on occasion mention him by name quite calmly and as a matter of course. Religious people speak of God when human knowledge (perhaps simply because they are too lazy to think) has come to an end, or when human resources fail—in fact it is always the *deus ex machina* that they bring onto the scene, either for the apparent solution of insoluble problems, or as strength in human failure—always, that is to say, exploiting human weakness or human boundaries. Of necessity, that can go on only till people can by their own strength push these boundaries somewhat further out, so that God becomes superfluous as a *deus ex machina*. I've come to be doubtful of talking about any human boundaries (is even death, which people now hardly fear, and is sin, which they now hardly understand, still a genuine boundary today?). It always seems to me that we are trying anxiously in this way to reserve some space for God; I should like to speak of God not on the boundaries but at the centre, not in weaknesses but in strength; and therefore not in death and guilt but in man's life and goodness. As to the boundaries, it seems to me better to be silent and leave the insoluble unsolved. Belief in the resurrection is *not* the "solution" of the problem of death. God's "beyond" is not the beyond of our cognitive faculties. The transcendence of epistemological theory has nothing to do with the transcendence of God. God is beyond in the midst of our life. The church stands not at the boundaries where human powers give out, but in the middle of the village. That is how it is in the Old Testament, and in this sense we still read the New Testament far too little in the light of the Old. How this religionless Christianity looks, what form it takes, is something that I'm thinking about a great deal, and I shall be writing to you again about it soon. It may be that on us in particular, midway between East and West, there will fall a heavy responsibility. . . .

A few more words about "religionlessness." I expect you remember Bultmann's essay on the "demythologizing" of the New Testament? My view of it today would be, not that he went "too far," as most people thought, but that he didn't go far enough. It's not only the "mythological" concepts, such as miracle, ascension, and so on (which are not in principle separable from the concepts of God, faith, etc.), but "religious" concepts generally, which are problematic. You can't, as Bultmann supposes, separate God and miracle, but you must be able to interpret and proclaim *both* in a "nonreligious" sense. Bultmann's approach is fundamentally still a liberal one (i.e. abridging the gospel), whereas I'm trying to think theologically.

What does it mean to "interpret in a religious sense"? I think it means to speak on the one hand metaphysically, and on the other hand individualistically. Neither of these is relevant to the biblical message or to the man of today. Hasn't the individualistic question about personal salvation almost completely left us all? Aren't we really under the impression that there are more important things than that question (perhaps not more important than the *matter* itself, but more important than the *question!*)? I know it sounds pretty monstrous to say that. But, fundamentally, isn't this in fact biblical? Does the question about saving one's soul appear in the Old Testament at all? Aren't righteousness and the Kingdom

100

of God on earth the focus of everything, and isn't it true that Rom. 3:24 ff. is not an individualistic doctrine of salvation, but the culmination of the view that God alone is righteous? It is not with the beyond that we are concerned, but with this world as created and preserved, subjected to laws, reconciled, and restored. What is above this world is, in the gospel, intended to exist for this world; I mean that, not in the anthropocentric sense of liberal, mystic pietistic, ethical theology, but in the biblical sense of the creation and of the incarnation, crucifixion, and resurrection of Jesus Christ.

Barth was the first theologian to begin the criticism of religion, and that remains his really great merit; but he puts in its place a positivist doctrine of revelation which says, in effect, "Like it or lump it": virgin birth, Trinity, or anything else; each is an equally significant and necessary part of the whole, which must simply be swallowed as a whole or not at all. That isn't biblical. There are degrees of knowledge and degrees of significance; that means that a secret discipline must be restored whereby the *mysteries* of the Christian faith are protected against profanation. The positivism of revelation makes it too easy for itself, by setting up, as it does in the last analysis, a law of faith, and so mutilates what is— by Christ's incarnation!—a gift for us. In the place of religion there now stands the church—that is in itself biblical—but the world is in some degree made to depend on itself and left to its own devices, and that's the mistake.

I'm thinking about how we can reinterpret in a "worldly" sense—in the sense of the Old Testament and of John 1.14—the concepts of repentance, faith, justification, rebirth, and sanctification. I shall be writing to you about it again. . . .

Now for some further thoughts about the Old Testament. Unlike the other oriental religions, the faith of the Old Testament isn't a religion of redemption. It's true that Christianity has always been regarded as a religion of redemption. But isn't this a cardinal error, which separates Christ from the Old Testament and interprets him on the lines of the myths about redemption? To the objection that a crucial importance is given in the Old Testament to redemption (from Egypt, and later from Babylon—cf. Deutero-Isaiah) it may be answered that the redemptions referred to here are *historical*, i.e. on *this* side of death, whereas everywhere else the myths about redemption are concerned to overcome the barrier of death. Israel is delivered out of Egypt so that it may live before God as God's people on earth. The redemption myths try unhistorically to find an eternity after death. Sheol and Hades are no metaphysical constructions, but images which imply that the "past," while it still exists, has only a shadowy existence in the present.

The decisive factor is said to be that in Christianity the hope of resurrection is proclaimed, and that that means the emergence of a genuine religion of redemption, the main emphasis now being on the far side of the boundary drawn by death. But it seems to me that this is just where the mistake and the danger lie. Redemption now means redemption from cares, distress, fears, and longings, from sin and death, in a better world beyond the grave. But is this really the essential character of the proclamation of Christ in the gospels and by Paul? I should say it is not. The difference between the Christian hope of resurrection and the mythological hope is that the former sends a man back to his life on earth in a wholly new way which is even more sharply defined than it is in the Old Testament. The Christian, unlike the devotees of the redemption myths, has no last line of escape available from earthly tasks and difficulties into the eternal, but, like Christ himself ("My God, why has thou forsaken me?"), he must drink the earthly cup to the dregs, and only in his doing so is the crucified and risen Lord with him, and he crucified and risen with Christ. This world must not be prematurely written off; in this the Old and New Testaments are at one. Redemption myths arise from human boundary-experiences, but Christ takes hold of a man at the centre of his life. . . .

Now I will try to go on with the theological reflections that I broke off not long since. I had been saying that God is being increasingly pushed out of a world that has come of age, out of the spheres of our knowledge and life, and that since Kant he has been relegated to a realm beyond the world of experience. Theology has on the one hand resisted this development with apologetics, and has taken up arms—in vain—against Darwinism, etc. On the other hand, it has accommodated itself to the development by restricting God to the so-called ultimate questions as a *deus ex machina*; that means that he becomes the answer to life's problems, and the solution of its needs and conflicts. So if anyone has no such difficulties, or if he refuses to go into these things, to allow others to pity him, then either he cannot be open to God; or else he must be shown that he is, in fact, deeply involved in such problems, needs, and conflicts, without admitting or knowing it. If that can be done—and existentialist philosophy and psychotherapy have worked out some quite ingenious methods in that direction—then this man can now be claimed for God, and methodism can celebrate its triumph. But if he cannot be brought to see and admit that his happiness is really an evil, his health sickness, and his vigour despair, the theologian is at his wits' end. It's a case of having to do either with a hardened sinner of a particularly ugly type, or with a man of "bourgeois complacency," and the one is as far from salvation as the other.

You see, that is the attitude that I am contending against. When Jesus blessed sinners, they were real sinners, but Jesus did not make everyone a sinner first. He called them away from their sin, not into their sin. It is true that encounter with Jesus meant the reversal of all human values. So it was in the conversion of Paul, though in his case the encounter with Jesus preceded the realization of sin. It is true that Jesus cared about people on the fringe of human society, such as harlots and tax-collectors, but never about them alone, for he sought to care about man as such. Never did he question a man's health, vigour, or happiness, regarded in themselves, or regard them as evil fruits; else why should he heal the sick and restore strength to the weak? Jesus claims for himself and the Kingdom of God the whole of human life in all its manifestations. . . .

102

The displacement of God from the world, and from the public part of human life, led to attempts to keep his place secure at least in the sphere of the "personal," the "inner," and the "private." And as every man still has a private sphere somewhere, that is where he was thought to be the most vulnerable. The secrets known to a man's valet—that is, to put it crudely, the range of his intimate life, from prayer to his sexual life—have become the hunting-ground of modern pastoral workers. In that way they resemble (though with quite different intentions) the dirtiest gutter journalists—do you remember the *Wahrheit* and the *Glocke*, which made public the most intimate details about prominent people? In the one case it's social, financial, or political blackmail and in the other, religious blackmail. Forgive me, but I can't put it more mildly.

From the sociological point of view this is a revolution from below, a revolt of inferiority. Just as the vulgar mind isn't satisfied till it has seen some highly placed personage "in his bath," or in other embarrassing situations, so it is here. There is a kind of evil satisfaction in knowing that everyone has his failings and weak spots. In my contracts with the "outcasts" of society, its "pariahs," I've noticed repeatedly that mistrust is the dominant motive in their judgment of other people. Every action, even the most unselfish, of a person of high repute is suspected from the outset. These "outcasts" are to be found in all grades of society. In a flower-garden they grub around only for the dung on which the flowers grow. The more isolated a man's life, the more easily he falls a victim to this attitude.

There is also a parallel isolation among the clergy, in what one might call the "clerical" sniffing-around-after-people's-sins in order to catch them out. It's as if you couldn't know a fine house till you had found a cobweb in the furthest cellar, or as if you couldn't adequately appreciate a good play till you had seen how the actors behave off-stage. It's the same kind of thing that you find in the novels of the last fifty years, which do not think they have depicted their characters properly till they have described them in their marriage-bed, or in films where undressing scenes are thought necessary. Anything clothed, veiled, pure, and chaste is presumed to be deceitful, disguised, and impure; people here simply show their own impurity. A basic antisocial attitude of mistrust and suspicion is the revolt of inferiority.

Regarded theologically, the error is twofold. First, it is thought that a man can be addressed as a sinner only after his weaknesses and meannesses have been spied out. Second, it is thought that a man's essential nature consists of his inmost and most intimate background; that is defined as his "inner life," and it is precisely in those secret human places that God is to have his domain!

On the first point it is to be said that man is certainly a sinner, but is far from being mean or common on that account. To put it rather tritely, were Goethe and Napoleon sinners because they weren't always faithful husbands? It's not the sins of weakness, but the sins of strength, which matter here. It's not in the least necessary to spy out things; the Bible never does so. (Sins of strength: in the genius, *hubris*; in the peasant, the breaking of the order of life — is the decalogue a peasant ethic? —; in the bourgeois, fear of free responsibility. Is this correct?)

On the second point: the Bible does not recognize our distinction between the outward and the inward. Why should it? It is always concerned with *anthropos teleios*, the *whole* man, even where, as in the Sermon on the Mount, the decalogue is pressed home to refer to "inward disposition." That a good "disposition" can take the place of total goodness is quite unbiblical. The discovery of the so-called inner life dates from the Renaissance, probably from Petrarch. The "heart" in the biblical sense is not the inner life, but the whole man in relation to God. But as a man lives just as much from "outwards" to "inwards" as from "inwards" to "outwards," the view that his essential nature can be understood only from his intimate spiritual background is wholly erroneous.

I therefore want to start from the premise that God shouldn't be smuggled into some last secret place, but that we should frankly recognize that the world, and people, have come of age, that we shouldn't run man down in his worldliness, but confront him with God at his strongest point, that we should give up all our clerical tricks, and not regard psychotherapy and existentialist philosophy as God's pioneers. The importunity of all these people is far too unaristocratic for the Word of God to ally itself with them. The Word of God is far removed from this revolt of mistrust, this revolt from below. On the contrary, it reigns. . . .

Now for a few more thoughts on our theme. I'm only gradually working my way to the nonreligious interpretation of biblical concepts; the job is too big for me to finish just yet.

On the historical side: There is one great development that leads to the world's autonomy. In theology one sees it first in Lord Herbert of Cherbury, who maintains that reason is sufficient for religious knowledge. In ethics it appears in Montaigne and Bodin with their substitution of rules of life for the commandments. In politics Machiavelli detaches politics from morality in general and founds the doctrine of "reasons of state." Later, and very differently from Machiavelli, but tending like him towards the autonomy of human society, comes Grotius, setting up his natural law as international law, which is valid *etsi deus non daretur*, "even if there were no God." The philosophers provide the finishing touches: on the one hand we have the deism of Descartes, who holds that the world is a mechanism, running by itself with no interference from God; and on the other hand the pantheism of Spinoza, who says that God is nature. In the last resort, Kant is a deist, and Fichte and Hegel are pantheists. Everywhere the thinking is directed towards the autonomy of man and the world.

(It seems that in the natural sciences the process begins with Nicolas of Cusa and Giordano Bruno and the "heretical" doctrine of the infinity of the universe. The classical *cosmos* was finite, like the created world of the Middle Ages. An infinite universe, however it may be conceived, is self-subsisting, *etsi deus non daretur*. It is true that modern physics is not as sure as it was about the infinity of the universe, but it has not gone back to the earlier conceptions of its finitude.)

God as a working hypothesis in morals, politics, or science, has been surmounted and abolished; and the same thing has happened in philosophy and religion (Feuerbach!). For the sake of intellectual honesty, that working hypothesis should be dropped, or as far as possible eliminated. A scientist or physician who sets out to edify is a hybrid.

Anxious souls will ask what room there is left for God now; and as they know of no answer to the question, they condemn the whole development that has brought them to such straits. I wrote to you before about the various emergency exits that have been contrived; and we ought to add to them the *salto mortale* [death-leap] back into the Middle Ages. But the principle of the Middle Ages is heteronomy in the form of clericalism; a return to that can be a counsel of despair, and it would be at the cost of intellectual honesty. It's a dream that reminds one of the song O *wusst' ich doch den Weg zuruck, den weiten Weg ins Kinderland.* There is no such way—at any rate not if it means deliberately abandoning our mental integrity; the only way is that of Matt. 18:3, i.e. through repentance, through *ultimate* honesty.

And we cannot be honest unless we recognize that we have to live in the world *etsi deus non daretur.* And this is just what we do recognize—before God! God himself compels us to recognize it. So our coming of age leads us to a true recognition of our situation before God. God would have us know that we must live as men who manage our lives without him. The God who is with us is the God who forsakes us (Mark 15:34). The God who lets us live in the world without the working hypothesis of God is the God before whom we stand continually. Before God and with God we live without God. God lets himself be pushed out of the world onto the cross. He is weak and powerless in the world, and that is precisely the way, the only way, in which he is with us and helps us. Matthew 8:17 makes it quite clear that Christ helps us, not by virtue of his omnipotence, but by virtue of his weakness and suffering.

Here is the decisive difference between Christianity and all religions. Man's religiosity makes him look in his distress to the power of God in the world: God is the *deus ex machina.* The Bible directs man to God's powerlessness and suffering; only the suffering God can help. To that extent we may say that the development towards the world's coming of age outlined above, which has done away with a false conception of God, opens up a way of seeing the God of the Bible, who wins power and space in the world by his weakness. This will probably be the starting-point for our "secular interpretation." . . .

[The Christian] must therefore really live in the godless world, without attempting to gloss over or explain its ungodliness in some religious way or other. He must live a "secular" life, and thereby share in God's sufferings. He *may* live a "secular" life (as one who has been freed from false religious obligations and inhibitions). To be a Christian does not mean to be religious in a particular way, to make something of oneself (a sinner, a penitent, or a saint) on the basis of some method or other, but to be a man—not a type of man, but the man that

Christ creates in us. It is not the religious act that makes the Christian, but participation in the sufferings of God in the secular life. That is *metanoia*: not in the first place thinking about one's own needs, problems, sins, and fears, but allowing oneself to be caught up into the way of Jesus Christ, into the messianic event, thus fulfilling Isa. 53. Therefore "believe in the gospel," or, in the words of John the Baptist, "Behold, the Lamb of God, who takes away the sin of the world" (John 1:29). (By the way, Jeremias has recently asserted that the Aramaic word for "lamb" may also be translated "servant"; very appropriate in view of Isa. 53!)

This being caught up into the messianic sufferings of God in Jesus Christ takes a variety of forms in the New Testament. It appears in the call to discipleship, in Jesus' table-fellowship with sinners, in "conversions" in the narrower sense of the word (e.g. Zacchaeus), in the act of the woman who was a sinner (Luke 7)—an act that she performed without any confession of sin, in the healing of the sick (Matt. 8:17; see above), in Jesus' acceptance of children. The shepherds, like the wise men from the East, stand at the crib, not as "converted sinners," but simply because they are drawn to the crib by the star just as they are. The centurion of Capernaum (who makes no confession of sin) is held up as a model of faith (cf. Jairus). Jesus "loved" the rich young man. The eunuch (Acts 8) and Cornelius (Acts 10) are not standing at the edge of an abyss. Nathaniel is "an Israelite indeed, in whom there is no guile" (John 1:47). Finally, Joseph of Arimathea and the women at the tomb. The only thing that is common to all these is their sharing in the suffering of God in Christ. That is their "faith." There is nothing of religious method here. The "religious act" is always something partial; "faith" is something whole, involving the whole of one's life. Jesus calls men, not to a new religion, but to life.

But what does this life look like, this participation in the powerlessness of God in the world? I will write about that next time, I hope. Just one more point for today. When we speak of God in a "nonreligious" way, we must speak of him in such a way that the godlessness of the world is not in some way concealed, but rather revealed, and thus exposed to an unexpected light. The world that has come of age is more godless, and perhaps for that very reason nearer to God, than the world before its coming of age. Forgive me for still putting it all so terribly clumsily and badly, as I really feel I am. But perhaps you will help me again to make things clearer and simpler, even if only by my being able to talk about them with you and to hear you, so to speak, keep asking and answering. . . .

During the last year or so I've come to know and understand more and more the profound this-worldliness of Christianity. The Christian is not a *homo religious*, but simply a man, as Jesus was a man—in contrast, shall we say, to John the Baptist. I don't mean the shallow and banal this-worldliness of the enlightened, the busy, the comfortable, or the lascivious, but the profound this-worldliness, characterized by discipline and the constant knowledge of death and resurrection. I think Luther lived a this-worldly life in this sense.

I remember a conversation that I had in America thirteen years ago with a young French pastor. We were asking ourselves quite simply what we wanted to do with our lives. He said he would like to become a saint (and I think it's quite likely that he did become one). At the time I was very impressed, but I disagreed with him, and said, in effect, that I should like to learn to have faith. For a long time I didn't realize the depth of the contrast. I thought I could acquire faith by trying to live a holy life, or something like it. I suppose I wrote *The Cost of Discipleship* as the end of that path. Today I can see the dangers of that book, though I still stand by what I wrote.

I discovered later, and I'm still discovering right up to this moment, that it is only by living completely in this world that one learns to have faith. One must completely abandon any attempt to make something of oneself, whether it be a saint, or a converted sinner, or a churchman (a so-called priestly type!), a righteous man. . . .

10. Friedrich Gogarten, *Secularization and Christian Faith*

Contemporary history is more and more marked by the peculiar phenomenon called secularization. Originally, secularization meant the process by which something that served several purposes of worship was taken over for secular purposes. Such secularization took place, for instance, during the time of the Reformation when monasteries were closed and their buildings, the produce of their lands, and their other properties were used for secular purposes. More recently, however, secularization has come to be understood as a cultural process: the transposition of originally Christian ideas, insights, and experiences into those of human reason in general. Spiritual phenomena, ideas, and insights which until now were held to be revelations and immediate emanations from God and thus only available through faith, become, through secularization, insights which are available to reason independently of faith by virtue of reason's secular power. Independent and self-sufficient reason takes the place of revelation and of divinely wrought faith. This causes a change not only in the source and the means of these insights but also in their content. What is recognized and experienced by reason changes from a divine to a human reality; the reality which thus far was caused solely by God and hence accessible only through faith now becomes a reality caused by man by virtue of his reason. Man now assumes the responsibility to fashion this reality on the basis of his rational insights and experiences.

The manifold elements of this phenomena are recognized with increasing clarity in modern thought and can generally be understood as part of a single movement through which a profound transformation of man and the world takes place. The relationship of man to himself and to the world is fundamentally being changed. This change is very peculiar because ideas and insight of Christian origin determine this relationship of man to himself and the world which has assumed a new meaning through secularization. On the other hand, this relationship is totally different from that conceived by the Christian faith where it is God who places man into this relationship to himself and the world so that man may experience in this relationship his dependence upon God. On the contrary it is his independence which man now realizes in this secularized relationship to himself and the world. The change which takes place in secularization is perhaps most remarkable in that the radical meaning of man's independence as it developed in the modern world could only have been brought about by the insights and experiences made available by the Christian faith.

These peculiarities and apparent contradictions raise the crucial question whether secularization is alien and opposed to the nature of the Christian faith, imposed on it and hence destructive toward it, or whether secularization as a process naturally derives from the nature of Christian faith. In the latter case, there would be the further question whether this process shows that the Christian faith does not have the power to shape the world and hence was deformed and finally destroyed when with the beginning of the modern era the world and its reality imposed itself upon man with the irrefutable claim for objective knowledge and action, generated by its own resources; or, on the contrary, whether secularization represents the first massive effort to shape the world by the forces of the Christian faith albeit with all the dangers and errors which inevitably accompany such an undertaking. The question of the meaning of secularization in terms of its relation to the Christian faith is all the more urgent since today the dangers which are connected with secularization are becoming increasingly visible. Can man, who through secularization has become the independent lord over the world and himself, fulfill the task confronting him; or, having undertaken this task in the name of freedom, is he about to destroy this freedom in a most gruesome way? This question becomes more crucial every day.

Today we can no longer ignore the insight that freedom is only possible for man in the context of relationship. Moreover, this cannot be a relationship which man imposes on himself, but one which irrevocably is imposed on him. In a secularized world, however, such a relationship cannot and should not exist. This insight might lead to the conclusion that the only possibility to avoid disaster would be to reverse the process of secularization. Such a solution of the problem is too simple, for the obvious reason that historical events of this sort cannot be reversed. Secularization, however, is a historical event of worldwide dimensions; since it is the transformation of Christian insights and experiences on the basis of revelation and faith into those of general human reason, this also means the transformation from insights and experiences concerning the reality of God into those of man's reality.

Furthermore, a plea for the reversal of the process of secularization overlooks the possibility, suggested by the results of the inquiries into the history of thought, that this process is an outgrowth of Christian faith. For if it were assumed that secularization is a phenomenon of disintegration, it would have its origin in Christian faith, which then would have failed to shape the world and its reality according to its own insights and experiences once it took resolutely into account the ideas and forces which it had aroused. Consequently, we would be faced with either of two alternatives. Either we would have to reject the Christian faith as an appropriate means for shaping the world. This would imply the judgment that the Christian ideas which, although transformed, became effective in secularization have falsified and distorted the shaping of the world, undertaken in modern times by the world's own secular forces. Or we would have to renounce the attempt to shape the world out of the perspective of the Christian faith. Its effect upon modern life, visible in the phenomena of secularization, would then have to be explained as misunderstandings of the Christian faith. Faith would be understood exclusively in otherworldly terms and any thought concerned with the care for this world would be rejected as deviation from the one thing necessary.

This understanding of the Christian faith would be common to both alternatives and so would be the judgment that secularization as an attempt of the Christian faith to influence the shaping of the world is misdirected. In the first case this faith would have undertaken something foreign to its nature. Therefore, secularization should be completed in the direction of a further and finally total de-Christianization of the Christian ideas which had already been transformed. In the second instance secularization would merely be a process of disintegration and destruction which has always been the fate of the world as such. It would be meaningless to attempt to reverse it. Examples for both of these views are two men who might be regarded as the most profound analysts of the modern world: Kierkegaard and Nietzsche.

The other answer to the question about the relationship between secularization and the Christian faith would contend that the former is germane to the latter and that the value of the Christian faith can only be properly understood by recognizing secularization as an intrinsic part of it. Admittedly the phenomenon was present at first only in its potential, and only later resulted in the historical developments which today can be observed by almost all the disciplines of research. This would mean that a proper view of and proper attitude toward secularization can be gained only by perceiving its root in the Christian faith. In this case, however, one would have to assume that secularization exists in two different modes. It may contradict the Christian faith and become the fateful phenomenon familiar to us only when it is not recognized as a part of the Christian faith and when, therefore, the wrong consequences are drawn from it.

The Christian Understanding of the World

In order to answer the question of the relationship of secularization to the Christian faith we need to clarify the latter's understanding of the world. For the very word "secularization" implies the world and its relation to the Christian faith.

Therefore, the starting point for our understanding of secularization must not be the world, that is the history of general philosophical thought, but Christian faith. Otherwise secularization simply means the secularizing of the Christian faith. If general philosophical thought had the last word about secularization, the secularizing process of the Christian faith would also mean its historical demise, regardless of the acknowledgment of its influence upon Western civilization and regardless of the fact that the rise of the modern world is unthinkable without the Christian faith. For in this kind of secularization, revelation and faith become meaningless. Christian faith without revelation, however, is like a fish out of water, a king without a crown. Revelation and faith would become paradoxical features which might lend a certain "divine" glow to the secular. If, however, secularization can and should be understood theologically in terms of its root in the Christian faith and as its legitimate outgrowth, it cannot mean secularization of the Christian faith but it means the secularization of the world. It means that the world is and remains what it is under all circumstances and in every respect in all that belongs to it: the world.

The first and foremost statement about the meaning of the Christian faith for the world is the freedom from the world it offers man. This freedom is of the essence of Christian faith. Without it faith would not be what it is: faith is God and knowledge of him. This freedom sets faith apart from all pre-Christian religiosity, both of the pagan and the Jewish variety. If we are to grasp this meaning, we must steer clear of the concept of the world as it is commonly used in popular speech. "World" does not stand for—at least not primarily—something like sensuality or distraction. Rather, we should think of "world" in terms of the orderly cosmos of the Greek or the all-embracing divine principalities and powers which in pre-Christian understanding determined the life of men. What is meant by "world" becomes abundantly clear when the close ties between the "world" and what theology calls "law" are recognized. It is therefore the orderly world, anchored in the law, from which Christian faith frees us. The apostle Paul, proclaiming freedom from the law as freedom from the *stoicheia*, the legalistic powers of the world, could not be more explicit. In his view, these *stoicheia* are powers which possess divine and all-permeating force. However—and this is the knowledge gained by Paul through faith in Christ—since they belong to the created world, they are not in essence (*physei*) gods and therefore are no gods at all.

This second statement—that the *stoicheia* belong to the created world, are creatures and no real gods—should not overshadow the first, namely, that they are of prime significance in the world. Because they are powers of the law, they preserve the world as world. This has two implications, corresponding to the peculiar double meaning which Paul ascribes to the term "world." First, these powers keep the world in its worldly order without which it would not be the world, would not be an ordered entity. Second, they accomplish this by attempting to enclose the world so that the world seeks its basis and its meaning in itself. In the first instance, the *stoicheia*, as do all other powers of which Paul speaks, fulfill their task as creatures. In the second, however, they turn into powers that are hostile to God. For inasmuch as the world together with them becomes enclosed in itself, it shuts itself up against its creator and against its own creatureliness.

It is extremely important to see that these powers, as Paul understands them, are not in essence hostile to God. This is so—although it is not easily grasped—because the concepts of these powers stem from the cosmological dualism of gnosticism where they, together with the law, represent the antidivine principle. Paul, on the other hand, does not recognize a cosmic dualism. Whatever else he may have to say about the world, it is and remains for him God's creation, and is not—as is the case in gnosticism—the work of a countergod. True, Paul knows of dualism and he develops his thinking within a dualistic framework. But it is a dualism of a quite different kind, as we shall see later. His dualistic sayings, if only on account of Gnostic connotations, closely resemble the cosmic dualism of God and world in gnosticism; yet they may never be taken in this sense, but only in the sense of an opposition between sinful man and holy God. Likewise, the hostility of the powers toward God must be understood from man's viewpoint. These powers pervade the world and close it off from God. Their hostility toward God, according to Paul, is not cosmic fate in which man is caught, but it is man's guilt. Man's sin enables the powers to engulf the world. And for Paul sin means that man who lives in the world as God's creation and who is thus placed between God and the world, has decided in favor of the world against God.

To have worshiped and served the creature rather than the Creator, this is according to the first chapter of Romans the ungodliness and wickedness by which men have suppressed the truth. By worshiping the world and its powers man enables them to turn the world against God. Furthermore, the powers gain control over man and he cannot extricate himself from them. We must not overlook the basis from which Paul speaks of man and his sin in this way. This is the concept of man's greatness and glory. This greatness somehow still attaches to him. He no longer possesses it, but it is still demanded of him. He has lost it not through an external fate but through his own fault. The reason for the fact that man is under the power of the world without possibility of escape is not, in the last analysis, to be found in the overpowering strength of the world but in his own greatness, his responsibility for the world and himself which he has forfeited. Paul's argument reveals its full weight and its revolutionary meaning when it is realized that he is not simply opposing piety to ungodliness. When he calls sin the worship of the creature instead of the creator he opposes a fundamentally new piety to the "pagan" worship. Therefore, we must try to understand what Paul is saying in its implications for this "pagan" piety. The central meaning of this piety is envisioned in what Paul attacks as "the ungodliness and wickedness of men." For in this piety man worships the powers which pervade the world as a divine reality. For such a piety Paul's argument is bound to appear as a horrible blasphemy. It elevates man above the divine power of the world. In the view of "pagan" thought (we could also say ancient thought) it entails an intolerable profanization of the

111

world and of the powers which pervade it. When this happens, nothing can be divine anymore for man; his life falls prey to an inevitable arbitrariness and becomes totally meaningless.

There is a Gnostic answer to the accusation of "pagan" piety and it has often been confused with the Christian faith while in fact, gnosticism was the most dangerous Christian heresy during the first centuries. If Paul had been a Gnostic, he would have answered that there was indeed nothing divine about the world since it was the creation of a demiurge, an antigod. The powers which pervade it as well as the law which sustains it are in the service of the rebellious lord and creator. The world and everything worldly keeps man away from the true God and from his own true human life. Therefore, the Gnostic would continue, man can only be liberated from the prison of the world through a radical break by extricating himself from its law, either by way of asceticism or by way of libertinism which despises all worldly ties.

Paul says nothing of this sort, he cannot subscribe to this answer. For him the evil which befell man and the world is the result of man's guilt and not of a cosmic mishap. Man's sin in which he serves and worships the creature instead of the creator causes the unfortunate transformation of the cosmos. God's creation in which everything created by God is good and nothing is to be rejected if it is received with thanksgiving (1 Tim. 4:4), has been transformed through man's sin into the world which is in the power of the evil one (1 John 5:19). Sin affects God and the world, it perverts the fundamental order of all existence, the relation between the creation and the creator; therefore, it becomes indeed something like a fate which man cannot reverse.

The Christian faith and gnosticism are similar in maintaining man's superiority over the world. In this both are in sharp opposition to previous ancient thought, and in both, therefore, the world is turned around in the true sense of the word. For both, man's superiority over the world is ontological. In opposition to all previous thought, both gnosticism and the Christian faith understand man as a being which is not from the world, which owes its existence not to the fact that it is enclosed by the world and embedded in its orders, but to its not-being-from-the-world. However, both understand man's ontological superiority over the world in fundamentally different ways. For man to be called out of the world does not mean the same here and there.

Gnosticism understands this calling in terms of cosmic dualism. Its thought is determined by a view of the cosmos in the light of the discovery of "the radical difference between human and extra-human, worldly, existence." In contrast to previous thought, gnosticism represents the breakthrough of the insight into the basic foreignness of everything worldly to everything human, causing a "tremendous insecurity, a world anxiety, fear of the world and of oneself." This insight and anxiety is the driving force of gnosticism: it defines its attitude toward the world and hence to everything else. Therefore, it can content itself with negative statements concerning man who stands in opposition to the world, and concerning the god in whom man finds his salvation. Their negative character is their positive value, for it expresses the ontological foreignness of human existence over against the world and hence his superiority. This superiority has only the negative meaning that human existence is not worldly, not "of" the world. In this way gnosticism is the pioneer in discovering man's selfhood, a consciousness over against everything worldly which is rooted in itself, and is no longer enclosed by the world. But since the discovery of this self only helps man to retreat from the world, it can and needs to be described only in negative terms; it remains the "paradoxical subject of constant self-elimination." Gnosticism is also the first to discover the otherworldly God. But this "otherworldly," too, has only the negative meaning of "non- and antiworldly." The hiddenness and novelty of this God, therefore, again indicates nothing else than his being opposed to the world.

The superiority of man over the world as it is opened up by the Christian faith is of a very different sort. Admittedly it, too, has a negative meaning which scarcely can be stated too radically. Christians are admonished to return to their senses and escape from the trap of the devil who had caught them and made them obey his will (2 Tim. 2:26), to rise from sleep (Rom. 13:11), and to be awake because they belong to the day and not to the night (1 Thess. 5:5 ff.). As in gnosticism which likes to use the same expressions, this means that they are being called out of the world. Here, too, the world is called evil and hostile to God; it is the realm of the lord of this eon (1 Cor. 2:6, 8), its wisdom is folly in God's sight (1 Cor. 3:19). What gnosticism says of the law which belongs to the world is true here as well: It does not bring life, as man is wont to believe in his worldly captivity; on the contrary, it brings death (Rom. 7:10). But at this point, with regard to the law, it becomes evident that all these statements have a fundamentally different meaning for the Christian faith. For while Paul says that the law brings death to man, he says at the same time that this law has been given to bring life. For "the law is holy . . . and just and good." The reason for the fact that it causes death for man who deals with it and seeks life in it, is not the law itself but man's sin. It is not the law which has become death for him, but sin which through the law caused death in order that its true nature as sin might be revealed, that by means of the law sin might become ever more terribly sinful (Rom. 7:12). Hence it is man who has caused this evil. Through him this world has become—and this is emphatically stated in the New Testament—"this world," the world of sin and hostility toward God.

This is the way in which the Christian faith understands man's superiority over the world. Through sin man has forfeited this superiority and also his salvation. If man is addressed as sinner, he must be addressed as one who has lost his superiority over the world. Obviously, the superiority as discovered by the Christian faith is of a fundamentally different kind from that of gnosticism. The primary difference is that the Christian view of superiority has its basis in man's responsibility for the world. This difference makes all the apparent similarities meaningless between gnosticism and Christianity.

Everything depends now on the correct understanding of this responsibility for the world. Since man's superiority over the world is ontological (as in gnosticism), this responsibility must be of the same sort. It would therefore be missing the main point, if the responsibility were only to be understood in a moral sense. This also corresponds to the Christian understanding of sin. When we said above that man has perverted the basic order of all being, that is, the order between creator and creature, this is correctly understood only when it is recognized that herein man has forfeited his own being. Worshiping and serving the creature instead of the creator is not an act which, once done, can freely be reversed; it transforms man: from being-out-of-God to being-out-of-the-world. For to worship God means nothing less than to receive one's being from him. When this happens to me in my worship, where this becomes its basis, I worship and thank God as a *God* (Rom. 1:21). In such worship I recognize (which, in biblical terms means to actually experience) what is known to God and revealed to me by him. Paul characterizes this knowledge with an infinite paradox: I recognize "his invisible nature, namely, his eternal power and deity, has been clearly perceived in the things that have been made" (Rom. 1:20). God cannot be recognized in creation as it immediately confronts us. Whoever wants to recognize him in the immediacy of the visible creation will inevitably miss him; he will ascribe to the creature the honor which is due the creator. The creature cannot as such be recognized in what it visibly is, but only in that it is nothing *in and of itself*. When the "works of creation" are perceived in terms of their own nothingness and therefore in correspondence with their meaning as creatures as well as the power and deity of God, then God's invisible nature is recognized in them. In other words, the creature cannot be recognized out of itself but only on the basis of God being the creator. Such recognition is possible only in worship in which I receive my being from God and recognize myself as God's creature. Once I recognize in worship God as God, I can perceive the things of the world as God's creatures.

5

The New Hermeneutics

Hermeneutics became one of the vogue words, along with others like *paradox, demythologizing,* and *secularization,* of twentieth-century theology. The etymological origin of the word in Greek is disputed, one theory being that it is related to the god Hermes, the messenger of the other gods, in Greek mythology. Whatever the merit of this suggestion, the word does mean to bring to speech, to clarify meanings, or to translate into another medium.

In traditional theology, hermeneutics was simply the science or art of expounding and interpreting the Holy Scriptures. In contemporary theology, particularly under the influence of Rudolf Bultmann (1884–1976), Gerhard Ebeling (1912–), and Ernst Fuchs (1903–), hermeneutics has acquired a broader meaning. Going beyond the methodological rules governing the interpretation of historical texts, it includes as well a fundamental inquiry into the epistemological conditions of historical understanding. This shift in the scope of hermeneutics from mere rules of textual analysis to the art of interpretation in a deeper sense can be traced back to Friedrich Schleiermacher's (1768–1834) psychological theory of interpretation and Wilhelm Dilthey's (1833–1911) call for a "critique of historical reason," reminiscent of Kant's "critique of pure reason" or his "critique of judgment."

Schleiermacher realized that we today cannot understand the ancient biblical texts simply by using the objective methods of literary and historical criticism. The interpreter must intuitively penetrate a written work as the life-expression of the author, that is, by imaginatively recapitulating the creative act by which the work was originally produced. The presupposition of this psychological approach is that the author and the interpreter share the potential for similar experiences by virtue of their common human nature. The limitation of the psychological method of retrieving past meanings is that it cannot take adequate account of the differences between the historical situations of the ancient texts and present-day interpretation. Furthermore, it shifts the focus of understanding from the truth content of the text to the process by which the text came to expression from the author's religious experiences.

Wilhelm Dilthey carried further Schleiermacher's psychological hermeneutics. He agreed that the interpreter must re-experience the original creative moment in which an author gives expression to a profound dimension of life. He grasped more clearly, however, that texts do not merely express personal experience but are subject to history. Yet the historian of today is able to interpret the past because all historical events are somehow effects of the human spirit in whose structures and capacities the historian also participates. The person who interprets history is the same kind of being as the one who makes history—otherwise, historical knowledge and understanding would be impossible. Dilthey's approach, applied to Scripture, implies that the historian of today will never succeed in discovering anything—such as divine revelation—mediated through historical events that transcends universally human possibilities of experience. It is as if looking into history one can see only the reflection of a human face in the bottom of a well. The study of history then functions merely as a reflection of human possibility and not also as a medium of divinely revealed truth.

I

Rudolf Bultmann's theory of hermeneutics retained continuity with Schleiermacher and Dilthey. They had properly focused on the presupposition of all historical interpretation, namely, the basic experiential consanguinity of the author of a text and its interpreter. Bultmann wanted to explore that presupposition more closely. He too approached the text with a prior concept of the structure of human existence and its possibilities. An essential element of this structure is the prior understanding an interpreter brings to a particular text, ready to put an appropriate question and to be addressed by it. In Bultmann's own formula, "Exegesis without presuppositions is impossible."

The theological question arises, "What kind of preunderstanding is appropriate in the interpretation of the Bible?" Bultmann's answer to this question appears in the essay chosen for this volume, "The interpretation of biblical writings is not subject to conditions different from those applying to all other kinds of literature." Therewith the older distinction between sacred and profane hermeneutics was erased, with the result that the historical critical method is applied without regard to the church's traditional interpretations of Scripture. The risk here is that biblical exegesis and church dogmatics head off in different directions, never to connect up again.

Hans Georg Gadamer (1900–), the Heidelberg philosopher, pointed out that, although Bultmann claimed general validity for his preunderstanding on the grounds of existentialist philosophy, he nevertheless actually operated with a preunderstanding shaped by theological assumptions. Bultmann

116

in fact approached the texts of Scripture with existential questions prepared to be addressed by its message, which he may hear as the Word of God calling him to a decision of faith, granting a new possibility of authentic existence.

II

Gerhard Ebeling and Ernst Fuchs became the leaders of the post-Bultmannian school of theology that came to be known as "the new hermeneutic." They latched on to Bultmann's idea that the subject matter of a text also makes a claim, a demand, on us and calls us to decision, but were critical of his notion that the aim of exegesis is to search for the understanding of existence underlying the language of the text. Thus, in the hermeneutical writings of Ebeling and Fuchs, the catchword is not "existential understanding" but "linguistic event." Fuchs used the term *"Sprachereignis"* (language event) while Ebeling preferred the term *"Wortgeschehen"* (word event). The difference between Bultmann, on the one hand, and Ebeling and Fuchs, on the other hand, parallels the shift in Martin Heidegger's thinking from his earlier to his later period. The turn in Heidegger's thought was away from the analysis of existence (*Dasein*) provided in his *Being and Time,* which viewed language as a secondary objectification of the understanding given with existence, to an understanding of human language as the primal nonobjectifying voice of Being. Thus, with the aid of Heidegger, Fuchs and Ebeling rediscovered the hermeneutical import of language.

The hermeneutical issue for Fuchs and Ebeling is: How can the Word of God, which once took the form of human speech in a given time and place, be understood and translated without losing any of its power and meaning in a different time and place? No attempt will be made here to discern fine points of difference in the positions of Ebeling and Fuchs. We agree with James Robinson's statement that there grew up between them "not only a unique personal friendship but also a material unity of position that has made of the new hermeneutic a single school of thought with a shared leadership."

Whereas Bultmann interrogates the New Testament texts for expressions of inauthentic and authentic existence—a merely anthropological version of the Lutheran law/gospel dialectic—Fuchs finds in them utterances of inauthentic or authentic language. Humans are by nature linguistic beings, answering the call of being, and thereby constituting their existence. This call comes through history, for history is basically the history of language, of being coming to expression through language. The coming of the Word of God is the coming of true language, the language of love, especially in Jesus' language of love. As such, Jesus can be called the "language event," creating a new language tradition, the language of faith. For this reason, theology can no longer abide Bultmann's refusal of theological interest in the historical Jesus (though as a historian Bultmann retained some degree of historical interest); theology must go behind the linguistic expressions of faith to the "language event" as such, that is, behind the christological kerygma of the early church to the historical Jesus in the Gospels.

Ebeling answered Ernst Käsemann's (1906–) call for a new quest of the historical Jesus. Ebeling asked, "Would it not be significant if it could be historically shown that Jesus and faith are inseparably joined together, so that whoever has to do with the historical Jesus has to do with him from whom and in view of whom faith comes?"

For Fuchs, too, the Christology of the early church must be legitimized by tracing its roots back into the historical Jesus. Christian faith would lose its ground if faith could be shown to be a misunderstanding of the significance of Jesus' ministry and message. This drive to get back to the historical Jesus is motivated by the conviction that Jesus is the source of faith in God. We receive God only through our relation to Jesus, for God comes near in Jesus' offer of salvation to humanity.

The hermeneutics of Ebeling and Fuchs does not only reach back to the original speech of Jesus but also forward into the "world come of age," meeting Bonhoeffer's demand for a "nonreligious interpretation of biblical concepts." The hermeneutical problem includes the unfinished task of translation, not in the superficial sense of reduplicating the words of one language into more or less equivalent words of another language, but in the sense of a radical transference of meaning, a transculturation of the Word in new words. Ebeling and Fuchs agreed with Heidegger that we are living in a time of counterfeit language, of inauthentic speech, when the language of the Western tradition has degenerated into the corruptible, objectifying language of a technical society which turns humans into objects to be controlled and manipulated like other things.

III

Critics of "the new hermeneutic" pointed out that this massive concentration on the word and the language of faith tends to depreciate the meaning of history mediated by the language of facts. The crucifixion and resurrection of Jesus were historic events creative of language, and reveal God only when the historic action and kerygmatic word are kept indissolubly together. Biblical revelation contains a rich and varied content that can hardly be reduced to a personal existential exchange between Word and faith. The Bible as a book of history contains a lengthy narrative about Israel and the church that can hardly be fully accounted for in terms of an I–Thou relationship bracketed by language and faith.

Modern hermeneutical thinking has suffered from the divorce between the historical and theological approaches to the Bible. The new hermeneutics tried to build a bridge that spans the wide chasm that separates the biblical message of salvation and contemporary history. Bultmann, Ebeling, and Fuchs explored language and faith to find the formative power to bridge the vertical gap between time and eternity and the horizontal gap between past and present. A new attempt was soon to follow, that of eschatological theology: going beyond language and faith to history and hope, with their orientation to the future and the kingdom of God.

11. Rudolf Bultmann, *The Problem of Hermeneutics*

According to Wilhelm Dilthey, hermeneutics as the "art of understanding expressions of life fixed in writing" always draws attention to itself only "during a great historical movement." Such a movement makes "understanding unique historical existence," or "scientific knowledge of individual persons, in fact, of the great forms of unique human existence in general," an urgent concern of science. If we today are in the midst of a "great historical movement," there is reason to consider the problem of hermeneutics. And in point of fact, discussion with the historical tradition forms an essential part of contemporary self-reflection, which is simultaneously reflection on "the great forms of unique human existence."

The problem with which hermeneutics is concerned, according to Dilthey, arises from the question, "Is such a knowledge [namely, of the great forms of unique human existence] possible, and what means do we have for attaining it?" More specifically it is the question "whether understanding the unique can be raised to the level of general validity." "How can one individual come to an objective, generally valid understanding of another individual's expression of life as given through the senses?" Thus, it is the question of the possibility of achieving objectivity in understanding unique historical existence of the past. In principle, it is a question of the possibility of understanding historical phenomena in general insofar as they are witnesses to unique human existence, in which case hermeneutics would be the science of understanding history in general. In fact, Dilthey restricts hermeneutics to the interpretation of "expressions of life that are enduringly fixed," namely, monuments of culture, and so primarily literary documents, although works of art, also, are of essential importance.

II

Ever since Aristotle hermeneutical rules have been developed for the interpretation of literary texts, and these rules have become traditional and are usually followed as a matter of course. As Aristotle himself saw, the first requirement is for a formal analysis of a literary work with respect to its structure and style. Interpretation has to analyze the composition of the work, understanding the parts in light of the whole and the whole in light of the parts. This yields the insight that any interpretation moves in a "hermeneutical circle." As soon as one undertakes to interpret texts in an ancient or foreign language, one becomes aware of the further requirement that the interpretation must be done in accordance with the rules of grammar. Already with the Alexandrians this demand for a grammatical knowledge of the language was supplemented by the demand for a knowledge of the individual author's usage, so that, for example, a criterion was acquired by means of which to decide questions of authenticity in the interpretation of Homer. With the development of historical work during the Enlightenment, the question about the individual author's usage was expanded into the question about the use of language in the particular period in which the text was written. But hand in hand with insight into the historical development of language went knowledge of historical development in general, and hence of the fact that all literary documents are historically conditioned by circumstances of time and place, which henceforth must be known if there is to be any appropriate interpretation.

The science that has as its object the interpretation of literary texts and that makes use of hermeneutics to this end is philology. In the course of its development, however, it becomes clear that hermeneutics as the art of scientific understanding is by no means adequately defined by these traditional hermeneutical rules. Harald Patzer has recently shown how philology, which began by using the science of history for the purpose of interpretation, gradually came to be used by history, or itself became the branch of history for which texts are only "witnesses" or "sources" for projecting a historical picture by reconstructing some past time. This is certainly an understandable development, since there is also naturally a circle between philosogical and historical knowledge. But the upshot was that philology lost its real object in the interpretation of texts for the sake of understanding them. The deeper reason for this development, however, is that the task of understanding was not understood profoundly enough and thus seemed to have already been accomplished simply by following the hermeneutical rules. In other words, the insight into the process of understanding for which Friedrich Schleiermacher had once striven had been lost.

Schleiermacher had already seen that a genuine understanding cannot be achieved simply by following the hermeneutical rules. In addition to the interpretation that they serve to guide, which in his terminology is called "grammatical," there must also be "psychological" interpretation. Schleiermacher recognized that the composition and unity of a work cannot be grasped solely by the categories of a formal logical and stylistic analysis. Rather, the work must be understood as a moment in the life of a certain human being. In addition to grasping the "outer form," one must grasp the "inner form," which is a matter not of objective but of subjective, "divinatory" interpretation. Thus, interpretation is a matter of "reproduction" or "reconstruction" that takes place in living relation to the process of literary production itself. Understanding becomes "one's own recreation of the living nexus of thoughts." Such "recreation" is possible because "the individuality of the interpreter and that of the author do not stand over against one another as two incomparable facts." Rather, "both have been formed on the basis of universal human nature, whereby the community of human beings with one another in speech and understanding is made possible." Dilthey appropriates these ideas of Schleiermacher and seeks to explain them further. "All distinctions between individuals are ultimately conditioned not by qualitative differences between one person and another but by differences of degree between their psychical processes. If as interpreters, then, we transpose our own life experimentally, as it were, into another historical milieu, we are able for the time being to stress or strengthen one psychical process, even while allowing another to recede, and thus to reproduce another alien life in ourselves." The condition of understanding "lies in the fact that nothing can appear in the expression of another individual that is not also contained in the life of the interpreter." Thus, it can be said that "interpretation is a work of personal art whose consummate exercise is conditioned by the genius of the interpreter; it rests on congeniality, intensified by living closely with the author by constant study."

Schleiermacher's view of understanding is naturally connected historically with J. J. Winckelmann's "interpretation of works of art" and with J. G. von Herder's "congenial empathy with the souls of epochs and races." It is oriented to the interpretation of philosophical and poetic texts. But is it also valid for other texts? Does the interpretation of a text in mathematics or medicine, say, grow out of reenacting the psychical processes that took place in the author? Or what about the inscriptions of Egyptian kings reporting their deeds in war, or the historical and chronological texts of ancient Babylonia and Assyria, or the grave inscription of Antiochus of Commagene, or the *Res Gestae Divi Augusti*? Are they, too, understandable only insofar as one transposes oneself into the inner creative process out of which they emerged?

No, it would not appear so. And in point of fact, it is not in this way that they must be understood insofar as the interpretation has to do with what they directly communicate—thus, for example, their mathematical or medical knowledge or their report of the facts and processes of world history. But this, of course, is the primary interest of those who read such texts. To be sure, even they may be read with another interest, as is shown, for example, by Georg Misch's interpretation of the inscriptions in question as "expressions of life" or "forms of unique human existence," whether of individual persons or as expressing the "feeling for life," or understanding of existence, of certain epochs. It thus becomes clear that the view of Schleiermacher and Dilthey is one-sided insofar as it is guided by a certain way of asking questions.

The upshot, then, is that any understanding or interpretation is always oriented to a certain way of asking questions or to a certain objective. This means that it is never without presuppositions; more exactly, it is always guided by a preunderstanding of the subject matter about which it questions the text. Only on the basis of such a preunderstanding is a way of asking questions and an interpretation at all possible.

The subject matter about which Dilthey questions texts is "life," namely, the personal, historical life that has taken shape in the texts as "expressions of life that are enduringly fixed"; it is the "psychical life" that is to be objectively known by interpretation of "expressions that are given and perceptible through the senses." But this is not the only subject matter with which interpretation can have to do; therefore, the process of understanding characterized by this interest is not the only such process that can be enacted in an interpretation. Rather, in each case the process of understanding will be different, depending on how the objective of interpretation is determined.

It is evidently not enough to say "depending on the kind of text," that is, on the subject matter that is directly expressed in the text or the interest by which it itself is guided. For all texts can in fact be interpreted in the way in which Dilthey asks questions, that is, as documents of personal, historical life. Of course, in the first instance questioning of the text is oriented to the subject matter that is talked about in the text and mediated by it. Thus, I interpret a text in the history of music by asking what it contributes to my understanding of music and its history, and so on.

III

A way of asking questions, however, grows out of an interest that is grounded in the life of the questioner; and the presupposition of all understanding interpretation is that this interest is also alive in some way in the text to be interpreted and establishes communication between the text and the interpreter. Insofar as Dilthey designates kinship between the author and the interpreter as the condition of the possibility of understanding, he does in fact discover the presupposition of all understanding interpretation. For this condition holds good not only for the special way of asking questions distinctive of Schleiermacher and Dilthey but also for any other interpretation that can never be accomplished simply by following the traditional "hermeneutical rules." All that is necessary is that this presupposition be more exactly defined. What is required instead of reflection on the individuality of the author and of the interpreter, on their psychical processes, and on the interpreter's genius or congeniality is reflection on the simple fact that the presupposition of understanding is the life relation of the interpreter to the subject matter that is—directly or indirectly—expressed in the text.

Interpretation does not come about simply because "the individuality of the interpreter and that of the author do not stand over against one another as two incomparable facts" but because or insofar as both have the same life relation to the subject matter under discussion or in question. And this they have because or insofar as they both stand in the same context of life. This relation to the subject matter with which the text is concerned, or about which it is questioned, is the presupposition of understanding. For this reason it is also understandable that every interpretation is guided by a certain objective, for a question that is oriented somehow is possible only because of the conditions of a context of life. It is likewise understandable for the same reason that every interpretation includes a certain preunderstanding, namely, the one growing out of the context of life to which the subject matter belongs.

The fact that underlying any interpretation there is a life relation to the subject matter with which the text is concerned, or about which it is questioned, can be readily illustrated by reflecting on the process of translating from a foreign language. The nature of this process is as a rule obscured because knowledge of ancient languages in our cultural sphere is mediated to us by tradition and does not have to be acquired anew. Knowledge of a foreign language can be acquired anew (provided there are no texts in more than one language) only when the subject matters designated by the words (things, modes of conduct, etc.) are familiar from use and association in life. An object or a way of acting that is simply meaningless in my context of life, in my environment, or in my way of living is also unintelligible and untranslatable when it is designated in language, unless a word is chosen for it that describes its outer appearance—as, for example, when the *churunga* of the Australian aborigines is rendered in German by *Schwirrholz* (literally, whirring wood). Observing use, insofar as it is understandable, can lead to further description, so that a *churunga* can be described as a "powerful instrument of magic," assuming that the idea of instruments of magic is intelligible to me in my own context of life. In principle, the same process is involved whenever texts are given in or with pictorial presentations that for their part can be understood in terms of my life context. In fact, a child's understanding language and learning how to speak take place together with its becoming familiar with the environment and with human associations, in short, with the context of life.

Therefore, interpretation always presupposes a life relation to the different subject matters that—directly or indirectly—come to expression in texts. I understand a text that treats of music only if and insofar as I have a relation to music, which explains why many parts of Thomas Mann's *Doktor Faustus* are unintelligible to many readers. Likewise, I understand a mathematical text only if I have a relation to mathematics or a historical account only insofar as I am familiar with life in history and know from my own life what is involved, for example, in love and friendship, family and vocation, and so on. It is for just this reason that many pieces of literature are closed to many persons, depending on their age or education.

Naturally, my life relation to the subject matter can be utterly naive and unreflective, and in the process of understanding, in the interpretation, it can be raised to the level of consciousness and clarified. It can also be superficial and ordinary, and through understanding of the text it can be deepened and enriched, modified and corrected. In any case, a life relation to the subject matter in question is presupposed, and recognizing this eliminates certain false problems right from the outset—like, for example, the question about the possibility of understanding an "alien soul." The possibility of such understanding is given simply in the common relation of author and interpreter alike to the particular subject matter. If Dilthey affirms that the condition of the possibility of understanding is a "basis of universal human nature," or the fact that "nothing can appear in the expression of another individual that is not also contained in the life of the interpreter," this can be put more precisely by saying that the condition of interpretation is the fact that interpreter and author are human beings who live in the same historical world in which human existence takes place as existence in an environment in understanding association with objects and other persons. Naturally, it belongs to such understanding that it should also include questions and problems, struggle and suffering, joy as well as resigned withdrawal . . . .

IV

Let us now summarize the preceding discussion.

The presupposition of any understanding interpretation is a prior life relation to the subject matter that is directly or indirectly expressed in the text and that provides the objective in questioning it. Without such a life relation in which text and interpreter are bound together, questioning the text and understanding it are impossible, and questioning it is not even motivated. This is also to say that any interpretation is necessarily sustained by a certain preunderstanding of the subject matter that is expressed or asked about.

It is out of interest in the subject matter that there emerges some way of asking questions, some objective in questioning the text, some particular hermeneutical principle. The objective of questioning can be identical with the intention of the text, in which case the text mediates the subject matter asked about directly. But the objective can also grow out of interest in matters that appear in any possible phenomena of human life and, accordingly, in any possible text. In this case, the objective of questioning does not coincide with the intention of the text, and the text mediates the subject matter asked about indirectly.

Thus, for example, the objective of interpretation can be given by an interest in reconstructing the continuum of past history—whether political history, the history of the forms and problems of social life, intellectual history, or the history of culture in the broadest sense. In this case the interpretation will always be determined by the understanding that the interpreter has of history in general.

The objective of interpretation can also be given by a psychological interest, which subjects the texts to some way of asking about psychology, whether individual, social, or religious—for instance, by asking about the psychology of literature or of technology, and so on. In all such cases the interpretation is guided by some presupposed preunderstanding of psychological phenomena.

Or again the objective can be given by an aesthetic interest which subjects the text to a formal analysis and questions a work of art about its structure, its "outer" and "inner" form. This aesthetic interest may be combined with the romantic-religious interest, or it may remain simply in the sphere of stylistic analysis.

Finally, the objective of interpretation can be given by an interest in history as the sphere of life in which human existence takes place, in which we acquire and develop our possibilities, and in which, by reflecting on these possibilities, we each come to an understanding of ourselves and of our own possibilities. In other words, the objective can be given by the question about human existence and one's own existence. The texts that most nearly lend themselves to such questioning are the texts of philosophy and religion and literature. But in principle all texts (like history in general) can be subjected to it. Such questioning is always guided by some prior understanding, some particular understanding of human existence, which can be quite naive, but out of which the categories first emerge that alone make the questioning possible—as when one asks, for example, about "salvation," or about the "meaning" of one's personal life or of history, or about the norms of moral action and of order in human community, and the like. Without such a preunderstanding and the questions guided by it, the texts are dumb. The point, then, is not to eliminate the preunderstanding but to risk it, to raise it to the level of consciousness, and to test it critically in understanding the text. In short, in questioning the text one must allow oneself to be questioned by the text and to give heed to its claim.

With this insight we also find the answer to the skeptical question whether we can achieve objectivity in interpretation and in the knowledge of historical phenomena. If the concept of objective knowledge is taken over from natural science (where, by the way, its traditional meaning has also become problematic today), it is not valid for the understanding of historical phenomena, which are of a different kind from the phenomena of nature. As historical phenomena they do not exist at all without a historical subject who understands them. For facts of the past become historical phenomena only when they become meaningful for a subject who exists in history and participates in it. They become historical phenomena only when they speak, and this they do only for the subject who understands them. This is not to say, of course, that the subject simply attaches a meaning to them by arbitrary preference; it is to say, rather, that they acquire a meaning for anyone who is bound together with them in historical life. Thus, in a certain sense, it belongs to a historical phenomenon that it should have its own future in which it alone shows itself for what it is.

It would be misleading to express this by saying that every historical phenomenon is ambiguous. For even if it is indeed vulnerable to arbitrary interpretation according to preference, it is nevertheless in principle unambiguous for scientific understanding. On the other hand, every historical phenomenon is complex and many-sided; it is open to different ways of asking quetions, whether the way of intellectual history, psychology, sociology, or what have you, provided only that it arise out of the historical bond between the interpreter and the phenomenon. Any such way of asking questions leads to objective, unambiguous understanding if the interpretation is carried through in a methodical way. And, naturally, there is no reason to object that real understanding is developed only by discussion and the conflict of opinions; the simple fact that every interpreter is limited in his or her subjective capacity is in principle irrelevant.

Knowledge acquired in a methodical way is "objective," which can only mean "appropriate to the object once it comes within a certain way of asking questions." To call the way of asking questions as such "subjective" is pointless. It may indeed be so called if one considers that it naturally has to be chosen in each case by some subject. But what does "choosing" mean here? The way of asking questions as such does not grow out of individual preference but out of history itself, in which every phenomenon, in keeping with its complex nature, offers different aspects, that is, acquires—or, better, claims—significance in different directions. And it is in this same history that every interpreter, in keeping with the motives present in the variety of historical life, acquires the way of asking questions within which the phenomenon begins to speak.

Thus, the demand that the interpreter has to silence his or her subjectivity and quench any individuality in order to achieve objective knowledge could not be more absurd. It makes sense and is justified only insofar as it means that the interpreter must silence his or her personal wishes with respect to the results of interpretation—such as a wish, say, that the text should confirm a certain (dogmatic) opinion or provide useful guidelines for praxis. Often enough, such wishes have been present in exegesis past and present; and, of course, being without presuppositions with respect to results is as unalterably required in the case of interpretation as in any other scientific research. For the rest, however, this demand completely misjudges the nature of genuine understanding, which presupposes the utmost liveliness of the understanding subject and the richest possible unfolding of his or her individuality. Just as we can succeed in interpreting a work of art or literature only by allowing it to grip us, so we can understand a political or sociological text only insofar as we ourselves are concerned with the problems of political and social life. The same holds good, finally, of the kind of understanding to which Schleiermacher and Dilthey orient their hermeneutical theory and which can be said to be understanding of historical phenomena in the ultimate and highest sense, namely, the interpretation that questions texts about the possibilities of human existence as one's own. Here the "most subjective" interpretation is the "most objective," because the only person who is able to hear the claim of the text is the person who is moved by the question of his or her own existence. The monuments of history "speak to us out of the depth of reality that has produced them only when we ourselves, out of our own readiness for experience, are aware of the problem, the finally insurmountable need and threat, that constitute the ground and the abyss of our being-in-the-world."

VII

Interpretation of the biblical writings is not subject to different conditions of understanding from those applying to any other literature. Beyond question, it is subject first of all to the old hermeneutical rules of grammatical interpretation, formal analysis, and explanation in terms of contemporary conditions. But then it is clear that here, also, the presupposition of understanding is the bond between the text and the interpreter, which is established by the interpreter's prior relation to the subject matter mediated by the text. Here, too, the presupposition of understanding is a preunderstanding of the subject matter.

This assertion is contested today by the claim that the subject matter of holy scripture, especially of the New Testament, is the act of God. Of this act there simply cannot be any preunderstanding because we human beings do not naturally have any prior relation to God but rather can know of God only through God's revelation, and thus through God's act.

This counterclaim is only apparently right. It is indeed true that one can no more have a preunderstanding of God's act as a real event than one can have of other events as events. Before I learn from tradition about the death of Socrates I can know nothing about it, anymore than I can know about the assassination of Julius Caesar or Martin Luther's posting of his Ninety-Five Theses. But in order to understand these events as historical events and not merely as arbitrary happenings, I have to have a preunderstanding of the historical possibilities within which they acquire their significance and therewith their character as historical events. I have to know what it means to lead a life of philosophical inquiry, what makes happenings into political events, or what Catholic and Protestant self-understandings are as possibilities open to human beings who must decide who they are to be. (It is hardly necessary to observe that such knowledge naturally need not be explicit.)

Likewise, understanding reports of events as the act of God presupposes a preunderstanding of what in general can be called God's act—as distinct, say, from the acts of human beings or from natural events. And if it is objected that we human beings cannot know who God is and hence also cannot know what God's act means prior to God's revelation, the proper reply is that we can very well know who God is in the question about God. Unless our existence were moved (consciously or unconsciously) by the question about God in the sense of Augustine's "Thou hast made us for thyself, and our heart is restless until it rests in thee," we would not be able to recognize God as God in any revelation. There is an existential knowledge of God present and alive in human existence in the question about "happiness" or "salvation" or about the meaning of the world and of history, insofar as this is the question about the authenticity of our own existence. If the right to describe this question as the question about God is first acquired by faith in God's revelation, still the phenomenon as such is a relation to the subject matter of revelation.

This existential knowledge of God is always somehow interpreted wherever it is consciously present. If it becomes conscious, for example, in the question, "What must I do to be saved?" (Acts 16:30), some idea of "salvation" is necessarily presupposed. Any question directed to the New Testament must be prepared to have the idea that it brings with it corrected by hearing the word of the New Testament itself, and yet it can receive such correction only if the basic intention of the question interpreted by the concept of "salvation" concurs with the intention of the answer given in the New Testament.

So far at least as the scientific exegesis of theology is concerned, everything turns on the appropriate interpretation of the question, and this means at the same time the appropriate interpretation of what it means to be a human being. To work this out is a matter of human reflection, and concretely it is the task of a philosophical, existentialist analysis of human existence. Of course, this kind of work is not a presupposition of a simple hearing of the word of the New Testament, which is addressed directly to existential self-understanding and not to existentialist knowledge. But it is otherwise in the case of a scientific interpretation of scripture. It finds its objective by asking about the understanding of human existence that scripture brings to expression. Consequently, it has to concern itself with the appropriate concepts for talking about human existence.

These are grounded in the exegete's life relation to the subject matter expressed in scripture and include a preunderstanding of it. It is an illusion to think that one can do without such a preunderstanding, and the concepts flowing from it, and understand a single word of the New Testament as word of God. The interpreter is in need of critical reflection on the appropriate concepts precisely when he or she seeks to let scripture itself speak to the present as a power addressing our own existence, and thus does not treat the biblical writings as a compendium of dogmatic statements, or as "sources" for reconstructing a bit of past history, or for studying some particular religious phenomenon or the essence of religion in general, or for learning about the psychological development and objectification of religious experiences. If the objective of interpretation is said to be the question about God, or about God's revelation, this means that it is the question about the truth of human existence. But then interpretation has to concern itself with the conceptuality of an existentialist understanding of existence.

VIII

Karl Barth rejects the opinion that a theological statement can be valid only if it can be shown to be a genuine element in the Christian understanding of human existence. This is relevant to the present discussion only insofar as theological statements are interpretations of the assertions of scripture, and thus only insofar as Barth disputes my existentialist interpretation of scripture. This he does in the following passage (which in context has to do with the chief statements of the Christian confession): "They [sc. these statements] are indeed all related to human existence. They ground and make possible a Christian understanding of it, and so—inflected—also become determinations of human existence. But this is not what they are to begin with. To begin with, they determine the being and action of the God who is other than us human beings and who encounters us: Father, Son, and Holy Spirit. For this reason they are not to be reduced to statements about the inner life of a human being."

The last sentence betrays a complete misunderstanding of existentialist interpretation and of what it means by human existence. This is in no way "the inner life of a human being," which can be understood apart from all that is other than it and encounters it (whether the environment, fellow human beings, or God). This may indeed be how psychology of religion, say, considers human existence, but it is not the way of existentialist analysis. For such analysis seeks to grasp and understand the actual (historical) existence of human beings, who exist only in a context of life with "others," and thus in encounters. Existentialist analysis endeavors to develop an appropriate conceptuality for just such an understanding. But Barth evidently orients his notion of it to a concept of anthropology derived from Ludwig Feuerbach, which he even attributes to Wilhelm Herrmann, instead of seeing that Herrmann was struggling to understand human existence as historical (even if in an inadequate conceptuality).

The demand to make of Barth is that he give an account of his own conceptuality. He grants my claim, for example, that the resurrection of Jesus is not a historical fact that could be established as such by means of the science of history. But it does not follow from this, he thinks, that the resurrection did not occur: "Is it not possible for a story to have really happened and for an acknowledgment of the story to be legitimate even in a case where, simply for reason of good taste, one would not speak of 'historical fact' and where the 'historian' may very well prefer to speak of 'saga' or 'legend' because the story does indeed elude the means and methods, together with the tacit presupposition of this historian?"

I ask, What does Barth understand here by "story" and "happened"? What kind of an event is it of which one can say that "it far more certainly really happened in time than all the things that the historians as such can establish"? It is perfectly clear that Barth interprets the statement of scripture by means of a conceptuality that he brings with him. But what is the source and meaning of this conceptuality?

Furthermore, what way of "believing" is it if credence is to be given to the assertion of events that are supposed to have happened in time and history and yet cannot be established by the means and methods of historical science? How do such events come within the purview of the believer? And how is such faith to be distinguished from a blind acceptance by means of a *sacrificium intellectus?* In what sense does Barth appeal to a demand for honesty that is of another or higher kind than the demand for honesty that requires me to hold nothing to be true that contradicts the truths which are the factual presuppositions of the understanding of the world that guides everything I do? What elements are contained in the mythical world picture to which we do not have to commit ourselves as a whole, but from which we can appropriate certain things eclectically? To ask about a valid meaning of the mythical world picture is precisely the intention of my existentialist interpretation of myth, in which I attempt to proceed methodically, even while all I can find in Barth are arbitrary assertions. What is *his* principle of selection?

It is clearly in Barth's sense that Walter Klaas confronts me with the statement: "One interprets scripture who allows it alone to be the rule and guide of proclamation [where do I dispute this?], who knows the word of prophets and apostles to be foreordained and repeats it as one has responsibly heard it." Such a statement shows only that the person making it still does not see the problem of interpreting scripture. The exegete is supposed to "interpret" scripture after he or she has responsibly "heard" its word. But how is one to hear without understanding? The problem of interpretation is precisely the problem of understanding.

12. Gerhard Ebeling, *The Word of God and Hermeneutics*

Whatever precise theological definition may be given to the *concept of the Word of God*, at all events it points us to something that happens, *viz.*, to the movement which leads from the text of holy scripture to the sermon ("sermon" of course taken in the pregnant sense of proclamation in general). As a first definition of the concept of the Word of God the reference to this movement from text to proclamation may suffice. For this is in fact according to Christian tradition the primary place of the concept of the Word of God. We here set aside questions that probe behind that—why the holy scripture that presses for proclamation or the proclamation that takes its stand on holy scripture should be marked out in particular above other things as Word of God; or what form of the Word of God to some extent precedes scripture; and whether the Word of God is not found also outside the relation of text and sermon. For according to Christian conviction the answers to all these questions can be truly known only in connexion with that movement from the text to the sermon. But it is of decisive importance to choose this movement as the starting-point for the definition of the concept of the Word of God.

The criticism usually made of the orthodox doctrine is, that it identifies scripture and the Word of God without distinction. And the correction then made is to say instead of "Scripture is the Word of God" something like, "Scripture *contains or witnesses to* the Word of God"—in other words, to refer to a factor distinct from scripture which has to be sought within or behind it. There is no doubt some truth in that. Yet the decisive shortcoming of the orthodox position lies in the fact that holy scripture is spoken of as the Word of God without any eye to the proclamation, and thus without expression being given also to the future to which holy scripture points forward as its own future. On closer inspection the concept of the Word of God certainly seeks to be interpreted in a still more comprehensive sense in terms of event. Yet that results from the basic starting-point in the process of the text becoming proclamation. The question as to the real nature of this event must therefore be at least one essential element in the doctrine of the Word of God.

And now, whatever the precise definition that may be given to *"hermeneutics,"* at all events as the theory of understanding it has to do with the word-event. And indeed, like every science, ultimately with a practical aim, as an aid to the word-event, *viz.*, as guidance on how a word that has taken place comes to be understood. That is not intended by any means to simplify hermeneutics by reducing it to a collection of rules. But even when the hermeneutic problem is entered into radically, teaching about understanding must give proof of itself by serving the understanding, be it only in providing a critical indication of its limits.

Now if in the Word of God we have a case of the word-event that leads from the text of holy scripture to the proclamation, then the question is, whether hermeneutics can be expected to help towards that happening rightly. Here doubts arise at once. Can the event of the Word of God be served at all by scientific methods? Must the hermeneutic approach as such not at once have a destructive effect on the concept of the Word of God, as also on the corresponding concept of the Holy Spirit? But doubts, too, of a less radical kind also call in question the service of hermeneutics here. Can hermeneutics not deal only with an exposition which is subject to scientific criteria? Even then there are, as is well known, already great methodological difficulties. Now in so far as the sermon is preceded by a scientific exposition of the text, hermeneutics may also have significance for it. But then the question remains what the scientific exposition contributes to the sermon and what distinguishes it from the exposition that takes place in the sermon itself; whether it is appropriate to contrast the latter as "practical" exposition with the scientific kind and so withdraw it from the strict standpoint of hermeneutics, or to distinguish it as *applicatio* from the *explicatio* and thereby deny that the sermon in its essential nature is exposition at all, however much it may contain textual exposition. Yet is it not bringing the event of the Word of God into dangerous isolation from word-events in general, if we withdraw it from the reach of hermeneutics? Indeed, is it not the case that the concept of the Word of God can be used at all only when hermeneutic justification can be given for it? But what does "hermeneutics" then mean? Let us therefore attempt first of all a more precise clarification of the concept hermeneutics.

According to the common view there is a sharp distinction between exegesis as the process of exposition itself and hermeneutics as the theory of exposition. And here indeed it is assumed that verbal statements are the object of exposition, i.e.

the thing requiring exposition. According to the several kinds of verbal statement, general hermeneutics may be differentiated into various special hermeneutics, though of course without departing from the comprehensive framework of general hermeneutics.

This customary view of hermeneutics requires correction in various respects.

1. On the threshold of the Enlightenment the *distinction of general and special hermeneutics* had taken the place of the very different articulated orthodox distinction of *hermeneutica sacra* and *hermeneutica profana*. The basic proposition that holy scripture is not to be differently interpreted from other books seemed, it is true, now to allow of only one single science of hermeneutics and to relieve theology of any special discussion of the hermeneutic problem, indeed even to forbid it. But owing to the colourlessness and abstractness of the proposition of a general hermeneutics, it did not exclude the introduction of various special hermeneutics applied and related to concrete subjects, as long as these various special hermeneutics remained subject to and derived from general hermeneutic criteria. Indeed, modern hermeneutics developed at first almost entirely in the form of special hermeneutics of such kinds, in the construction of which theology played an outstanding part along with classical philology and jurisprudence. It can even be said that the principle of a single science of hermeneutics worked itself out in practice as the principle of an increasing hermeneutic specialization.

For theology this meant in the first instance that, although specifically theological hermeneutics disappeared, there arose within theology various hermeneutics in different degrees of specialization, such as biblical, Old Testament or New Testament hermeneutics, or (the demand for this at all events has already been made) in such a way that each biblical book requires a special hermeneutics. We must not let ourselves be deceived abou the real nature of this state of affairs by, say, the fact that such extreme specialization was never realized, and that biblical or Old or New Testament hermeneutics owing to the theological dignity of these books at once gives the impression of theological hermeneutics. Strictly, however, the basic conception is, that there is no such thing as theological hermeneutics. For the differentiation in hermeneutics is held to be justified indeed from the standpoint of different literary complexes, but not on the basis of particular, non-universal epistemological principles such as those of theology. Thus hermeneutics in theology became the methodology of definite individual disciplines—*viz.* the biblical ones—and therewith at once the boundary separating them from dogmatics, which as such had nothing to do with hermeneutics.

The fact that in contrast to this, historical and systematic theology today join hands in the hermeneutic problem and hermeneutics has expanded to become the methodology no longer merely of individual theological disciplines but of theology as a whole, is to a great extent a distant result of *Schleiermacher.* For his pioneer view of hermeneutics as the theory of the conditions on which understanding is possible modified the relation of general and special hermeneutics in a twofold way.

First: a special hermeneutics must now take strict account of what can here be *differentia specifica*. The view which Schleiermacher himself here put forward in detail is doubtless obsolete. His basic demand, however, is still valid. The view emphatically advanced today by Bultmann that the difference as to what one is after in the interrogation *(Woraufhin der Befragung)* has differentiating character in the hermeneutic sphere is a first step towards further clarification of this side of the hermeneutic problem—a step that is capable of being developed and certainly also stands in need of further development. This provides, without relapsing into an alleged *hermeneutica sacra*, the possibility of speaking of a hermeneutics related to theology as a whole, which on the basis of the specifically theological approach works out structures and criteria of theological understanding that apply in theology not only to the exegetical but also to the dogmatic understanding. It is absolutely necessary that this should then be done in demonstrable connexion with a general theory of understanding. The nature of the connexion, however, raises difficult problems.

The other impulse which Schleiermacher gave to the further history of hermeneutics is today discernible above all in a surprisingly *extended use of the word hermeneutics.* It is not only that hermeneutics can now be spoken of in sciences in which it was not possible before and which do not have to do with texts at all but with phenomena—for example, psychology. Rather, the development from Schleiermacher via Dilthey to Heidegger shows that the idea of a theory of understanding is on the move towards laying the foundation of the humanities, indeed even becomes the essence of philosophy, that hermeneutics now takes the place of the classical epistemological theory, and indeed that fundamental ontology appears as hermeneutics.

Thus outside of theology, too, hermeneutics today is breaking through the old, narrow bounds of philological or historiographical hermeneutics, or is plumbing their depths. For theology the hermeneutic problem is therefore today becoming the place of meeting with philosophy. And that always involves at the same time both community and contrast. This confirms once again that in an approach so radical as this there is point in speaking of theological hermeneutics without in any way refurbishing the division into *hermeneutica sacra* and *profana*.

2. The customary view that *hermeneutics is the theory of the exposition of texts* already seemed a moment ago to have undergone correction in that phenemona can also be objects of exposition. If we followed that further, then we should doubtless have to limit it to phenomena in so far as they have to do with the linguisticality of existence, and are thus "texts" in the wider sense. Hermeneutics would then also remain related to the word-event. But what is now to be held against the usual view is something other than that.

It is usually taken for granted that the reason why hermeneutics has to do with the word-event is, that verbal statements pose the problem of understanding. Now however much the need for hermeneutics does in fact arise primarily from difficulties of understanding in the word-event, it is nevertheless completely false to take this situation as the point of orientation for one's basic grasp of the relation between word and understanding and of what is ultimately constitutive for hermeneutics. The superficial view of understanding turns matters upside down and must therefore be completely reversed. *The primary phenomenon in the realm of understanding is not understanding of language, but understanding through language.* The word is not really the object of understanding, and thus the thing that poses the problem of understanding, the solution of which requires exposition and therefore also hermeneutics as the theory of understanding. Rather, the word is what opens up and mediates understanding, i.e. brings something to understanding. *The word itself has a hermeneutic function.* If the word-event takes place normally, i.e. according to its appointed purpose, then there is no need of any aid to understanding, but it is itself an aid to understandning. It is to my mind not unimportant for the proper grasp of the hermeneutic problem whether we set out from the idea that a verbal statement in itself is something obscure into which the light of the understanding must be introduced from elsewhere, or whether, on the contrary, we set out from the fact that the situation in terms of which and into which the verbal statement is made is something obscure which is then illumined by the verbal statement. This starting-point opens up three important perspectives for the question of hermeneutics.

First: interpretation, and therefore also *hermeneutics,* is *requisite* only in the case *where the word-event is hindered* for some reason or other. But for that reason also the hermeneutic aid can only consist in removing hindrances in order to let the word perform its own hermeneutic function. And the removing of hindrances to understanding can usually likewise take place only by word. For hermeneutics is of course not a departure from the linguistic realm in order to understand language, but a deeper penetration into the linguistic realm in order to understand by means of language.

From the point of view that it is a question of removing hindrances, we can now also grasp that the scope of the hermeneutic task can vary in extent. There is relative justification for restricting ourselves to what immediately concerns the grammatical and philological understanding of a text. We can include in the realm of the hermeneutic task also the very much wider problem of historical understanding. We can extend hermeneutics also to the understanding of what confronts us with the task of understanding by encountering us in the present. And we can thus, moving ever further afield, relate hermeneutics to the problem of understanding as such, i.e. to the problem of the ultimate conditions under which it is possible for understanding to take place at all. We are not, of course, left to choose at will. How radically we have to consider the hermeneutic problem depends on the extent to which lack of understanding arises.

Secondly, because hermeneutics can only make room for the word's own hermeneutic function, and thus because, as we could also say, hermeneutics only serves the word's own intelligibility, the content and *object of hermeneutics is the word-event as such*. For where a word happens, understanding is made possible. If hermeneutics, in order to be an aid to understanding is possible, then it has to reflect on the nature of words. *Hermeneutics as the theory of understanding must therefore be the theory of words*.

If that is formulated with the help of Greek by saying that hermeneutics is the theory of the Logos, then within the limits of Greek thinking that would doubtless seem very reasonable. For the Logos which holds equal sway alike in things and in the knowing subject himself is the condition of the possibility of understanding. The Logos is for the Greek a hermeneutic principle. It is a question, of course, what relation responsible hermeneutics today could adopt towards this Greek conception of hermeneutics. However little explication we have as yet given to our references so far to word-event and linguistic event, there is nevertheless obviously a considerable difference from the Greek Logos concept. Yet for all that, wherever the subject of hermeneutics is taken up, contact with the problems of Greek thinking is surely *conditio sine qua non*. For the taking up of the hermeneutic problem has its origin in Greek thinking. And however far we may diverge in our view of the word-event, hermeneutics will never be able to enter into complete opposition to the Greek Logos. Otherwise it would have to be denied altogether that hermeneutics is an undertaking which makes sense.

And lastly, if what is constitutive for hermeneutics is the word that does not require to be made understandable but itself opens up understanding, just because it has to do with the word-event, has always to do at once with the thing that is to be brought to understanding by means of the word-event. For that reason it is false to hold that hermeneutics is restricted to pure matters of form. For in that hermeneutics addresses itself directly to the word, it addresses itself directly to the reality that comes to understanding through the word. True, to speak of the formal character of hermeneutics is right enough in a way, if it is borne in mind that "formal" is the designation of a relation, so that the selfsame thing which in one regard is a definition of content can in another respect be a formal definition.

That hermeneutics must always in some way or other have a bearing on actualities, is a thing I now merely indicate by mentioning a few symptoms in a disconnected list: —We can get to the root of understanding only when we encounter what is not understood and what cannot be understood. We can know about the nature of words only when we come upon what is underivably given and is beyond the reach of words. Words produce understanding only by appealing to experience and leading to experience. Only where word has already taken place can word take place. Only where there is already previous understanding can understanding take place. Only a man who is already concerned with the matter in question can be claimed for it.

The significance of this for the grasp of the hermeneutic relationships is, that the hearer's relation to the verbal statement must always be coupled with a corresponding relation to reality (to which incidentally there is added a third, at least potential relation to his fellow men, in order to verify his understanding by joint understanding). It follows for the hermeneutic removal of hindrances to understanding that apart from difficulties of understanding that can be removed by the manifold means of philological and historical interpretation, there are also difficulties of a kind that their ground in the relation to the matter in question and to overcome which we must therefore also begin with that relation.

3. A third correction of the common view relates to the seemingly so straightforward and sensible distinction between exegesis or interpretation and hermeneutics. It is true that this distinction brings us into certain difficulties with the wide use in Greek of ἑρμηνεύειν which of course is really a synonym of ἐξηγεῖσθαι and *interpretari*. But why should a terminology of somewhat arbitrary coining, such as appeared in the seventeenth century with the concept hermeneutics, not be as valid?

Now I think all the same that the basic meaning of ἑρμηνεύειν, "to bring to understanding," which combines the various meanings "state," "expound," and "translate," accords very well with the real sense of hermeneutics. Indeed, I hold it moreover to be in the nature of the case that the words "interpretation" and "hermeneutics" at bottom mean the same. True, it is at first sight one thing to interpret and another to reflect on the method of interpretation. We do not expect the same of New Testament exegesis as of New Testament hermeneutics. Yet how is hermeneutic insight actually acquired? Where does hermeneutics itself find the basis of its knowledge? If hermeneutics is the theory of understanding, then how, we must surely ask, does understanding itself come to understanding? If hermeneutics as the theory of understanding is the theory of words, how then does "word" itself come to expression so that there can be a theory of words? If hermeneutics is to be an aid to understanding, an auxiliary in the word-event, then where is understanding opened up in such a way that aid to understanding is to be expected from that quarter? Where do words so encounter us, where do words so take place, that therein the word-event itself comes into view? If, as we have made clear, "word" itself is a hermeneutic principle, i.e. is that from which understanding proceeds and in which it has its origin, then hermeneutics as the theory of words must thus arise from the word-event itself. Hermeneutics therefore, in order to be an aid to interpretation, must itself be interpretation. Here we have the famous hermeneutic circle in its methodological significance for hermeneutics itself.

The question which is now constitutive for hermeneutics—the question where we are encountered by the word-event which becomes the source of the understanding of word-events, which is thus of relevance for fundamental ontology, and which we have to hold to in order to achieve hermeneutic insight—is a question which obviously calls for ultimate decisions and therefore also, as we must suppose, gives rise to ultimate differences. For although hermeneutics is meant to serve understanding, and therefore assuredly also agreement, yet it is also part of the phenomenon of understanding that the ground of the understanding, being a point beyond which no further questioning is possible, confronts us with a decision. Comprehensive differences of understanding, such as those for example between the confessions, are therefore of a hermeneutic kind and by their antithetical character point the ultimate limits of the possibility of agreement, just because they touch upon ultimate mysteries of the ground of understanding. This much, however, can be said in general terms on the question of what has to be the guiding light of hermeneutics: it must be a word-event in the comprehensive sense that it embraces both linguistic tradition and encounter with reality. Only by facing up to both of these together can hermeneutic knowledge be acquired. . . .

The central point in our deliberation on hermeneutics—*viz.* that "word" itself has a hermeneutic character and hermeneutics is the theory of "word"—now suggests as a corresponding proposition: theological hermeneutics is the theory or doctrine of the Word of God. . . .

If the concept of the Word of God is to be taken strictly, then of course the Word of God must be ascribed hermeneutic relevance for theology, i.e. the Word of God must then in itself be a source of theological understanding; and the structure of the understanding peculiar to theology must result from the essential structure of the Word of God. . . .

That Christian faith has adopted the hermeneutic approach is indeed identical with its having assented to the possibility and necessity of theology. . . .

When John 1:14 says that the Word became flesh, that surely means (interpreted of course in very abbreviated terms) that here word became event in a sense so complete that being word and being man became one. But that does not allow of any analogical transference to the relation of two kinds of word—let us say for the moment, in order to lay bare the metaphysical misunderstanding it contains, of heavenly word and earthly word. When the Bible speaks of God's Word, then it means here unreservedly word as word—word that as far as its word-character is concerned is completely normal, let us not hesitate to say: natural, oral word taking place between man and man. . . .

This word-event takes place, Christian's confess, in the Gospel. It is savingly related to the word-event which always proceeds from God and strikes the foolish man as the law which kills. But for that reason, too, it is only in the light of the Gospel that we can grasp what God's Word really means and how far the law is God's Word. For God's Word must not on any account be reduced to a formal concept which would be indifferent towards any intrinsic definition of the Word of God. For God's Word is not various things, but one single thing—the Word that makes man human by making him a believer, i.e. a man who confesses to God as his future and therefore does not fail his fellowmen in the one absolutely necessary and salutary thing, *viz.* true word. . . .

The real rub in the hermeneutic problem, as it presents itself for theology, consists in the connexion between exposition of the text as proclamation that has taken place and execution of the text in proclamation in the present. The concept of existentialist interpretation has been employed to characterize this fundamental hermeneutic problem. The efforts towards a closer definition of it are still going on. I think the concept can be meaningful and helpful if it brings out the fact that existence is existence through word and in word. Then existentialist interpretation would mean interpretation of the text with regard to the word-event. There, in my opinion, lies the decisive starting point from which to direct historical exposition towards the utmost fulfillment of its task, and presisely in so doing to gain criteria for the inner hermeneutic connection between text and sermon.

The hermeneutic principle would then, in accord with what we said earlier, be the word-event itself. For hermeneutics, we said, is the theory of words. And we can now designate as identical with that, because merely the radicalization of it, the fact that theological hermeneutics is the doctrine of the Word of God, but that for that very reason there can also be doctrine of the Word of God only as theological hermeneutics. In view of that the hermeneutic principle could be given various precise definitions. With an eye to the real sphere of the word-event I suggest for consideration the formula: The hermeneutic principle is *man* as conscience. I refrain here from further attempt to ground and elucidate that. For a principle should surely be something that is obvious of itself, or at all events gives clear guidance and proves its fitness in use. . . .

13. Ernst Fuchs, *The Essence of the "Language Event" and Christology*

The Problem

In the last few years our enquiries have again been directed to the historical Jesus. Rudolf Bultmann, who in 1926 himself published a book about Jesus which remains the best up to the present day, has rejected the new quest as theologically irrelevant. At least it is in his opinion not in keeping with the essence of faith in Jesus Christ. His main argument is that the enquiry into the historical Jesus cannot and indeed should not contribute to faith in Jesus Christ. The enquiry should not contribute anything to faith, because faith in Jesus Christ dispenses with every security or support; and it cannot contribute anything, because the certainty peculiar to faith is not to be mixed up with the uncertainty and relativity of historical research. The basis and content of faith are identical. For faith in Jesus Christ is obedient rendering up of the self. Such rendering up of the self is obedient response to the paradoxical truth that the historical event of Jesus Christ is the eschatological event. This means that the believer is aware of being asked whether he will recognize that the crucified Jesus is to be proclaimed as the resurrected Christ; and whether he is therefore willing to recognize that Jesus becomes present for us as the word of God only through this proclamation. If then Jesus is present only in this marvelous manner, he is present for us in no other way, not even through historical research.

I am not quite sure if I have done justice to Bultmann's view in this presentation of it. And I openly admit that it is not clear to me whether in this matter Bultmann has a firm view at all, or whether he wavers about how he should make up his mind. Is he giving up his book on *Jesus?* In my own opinion it must, in fact, be stated that faith responds to the proclamation of the word of God in this way, that he who is questioned and grasped by the proclamation confesses for his part—Jesus is God's word. Without a confession of this kind the hearer of the proclamation would not become a "partner" of the proclamation. The proclamation, however, is intended to have or win its hearer as a "partner." All of us, and not just the apostles of long ago, can become partners of the Christian proclamation.

In the word which is to be proclaimed there is therefore contained a question which is addressed to the hearer. The hearer is, however, not simply asked if he will accept and hand on a list of doctrinal points which is presented to him. Otherwise the Church of the word of God would simply be a union of theologians imposing their will on the world. What the hearer is asked is if he will, through his own decision, give precision to the proclamation. The proclamation then consists not simply in the recital of doctrinal points, nor even in the repetition of facts which have at some time taken place. Instead, the proclamation poses the question which the hearer has to answer by his faith. This means that only the faith of the hearer makes evident as the word of God the word that is proclaimed to him. For this reason the proclamation is consummated in the confession of faith, and it is a contradiction of the free nature of the word which is to be proclaimed when in worship we come forward with the confession of faith before the proclamation takes place. The dynamic circle which links proclamation and confession of faith must include the active attitude of the hearer. The hearer should not be constrained to limp into place behind a previously established unity of preaching and confession. For the word of God sets free. But it only sets free the man who, having heard, is able himself to acknowledge the proclamation as the liberating word of God. The word of God is certainly not made into the word of God by the hearer. But the word of God does not reveal itself as such, it does not appear as the word of God, unless it is believed as the word of God. This only happens when the hearer realizes that he is placed in the position of answering the proclamation with his own confession. The confession of faith should not then be forestalled by the preaching. However, the question now arises, why the believer continually needs preaching, although the issue was always the further confession of faith.

What, then, is proclaimed when the resurrection of Jesus is proclaimed? There meets us in the proclamation of the resurrection of Jesus the stumbling-block of his cross. This stumbling-block has always to be overcome anew, and therefore it keeps reappearing. In actual fact our reason refuses to believe things that cannot be conceived. Does reason know what sin is? How are we to conceive of a man without sin? As an angel perhaps? But what is an angel? In mythological language is there not also a fallen angel? Obviously reason and its criteria by-pass what we actually have in mind when we speak of sin. Nor is sin simply immorality, though it may lead to immorality. Probably we only really recognize sin when we are freed from it. Sin is then a mark of the "whole" man. What the "whole" man is—one who can be not only sinful but also free from sin—first appears in the moment of self-confrontation. Something like this happens too in a secular judgment. But it also happens in the Christian proclamation, as soon as it is recognized that the stumbling-block of the proclamation of the resurrection of Christ is, in fact, the proclamation of the stumbling-block of his crucifixion. We reject the crucified Jesus as the word of God, if we maintain that his being proclaimed as the resurrected Christ is senseless. But the crucified Jesus *must* be proclaimed as the resurrected Christ, because he is not to be swallowed up in death, but is to remain present as the word of God. In terms of this apostolic insight, are we to attribute only one meaning or significance to Jesus (in the way that all historical phenomena can become meaningful)? What, for example, is the difference between Leonidas, who fell fighting for his fatherland, and the crucified Jesus? Leonidas gains his significance from the fact that he did what perhaps anyone else should have done, as soon as the battle had been joined. From the start we are in agreement with Leonidas, for we see in him one of us, and the result is that Leonidas has necessarily to become a prototype. In the case of Jesus it is quite different. His death on the cross is not an example, but a stumbling-block. The proclamation therefore asks us if we are prepared to let the stumbling-block of Jesus' crucifixion become a judgment on our own existence. The question shows that, as soon as our life is at stake, we reckon not with the defeat but with the victory. When we sacrifice ourselves for others we hope that they will be victorious as the result of our sacrifice. We want to be victorious, because we understand ourselves as being worthy of life. But Jesus' crucifixion shatters our worthiness.

If we submit to that, then the proclamation tells us that this judgment emanates from God. In this judgment God intends to demonstrate his graciousness towards us. We must let it come to this, then—the message thrusts us right into the "nothingness" of our existence, in order to declare God as the sole saving power. As this power is in Jesus, so it extends to us. That is to say, it is "for us" for Jesus' sake. God bestows life through bringing death (1 Cor: 15–36). Consequently God has revealed himself in Jesus as the paradox of our correctly understood existence, an existence received through obedience which is the rendering up of ourselves. If someone inquires after God, then the Christian believer must say to him: God is the paradox of our existence. The paradox is in the first instance the expression of an *"existentiell"* antithesis between spirit and flesh, between surrender and self-assertion. But within this contrast God is the power of any one life, a power which is beyond the realm of our disposal, and which only encounters the man who, in response to its bidding, repeatedly accepts and recognizes that his personal being *(Dasein)* is, in fact, under the power of death; a man therefore who wills to exist in faith in this word or bidding of God. That is, authentic existence, which can already be comprehended by the philosopher, can be realized only in faith. I am asked how I understand myself, if I want to have a future. My relation to the future decides whether or not I exist authentically. . . .

So the *problem* arises: How is the proclamation, required by faith, to be provided? In my opinion this problem can be resolved by an understanding of the connexion between the essence of the "language-event" and Christology. We can now pose the question: Why does the preaching of faith have a text?

The Hermeneutical Significance of the "Situation"

The question why the preaching of faith should have a text can indeed be answered simply thus: because the preaching of faith is the preaching of the gospel. And the preaching of the gospel, as in the case of Paul, is relatively easily paraphrased as the proclamation of grace, in terms of the contrast between faith and the works of the law. Indeed, this procedure leads also to the concept to which I shall be referring in what follows: the concept of the "situation." This procedure has, however, the disadvantage that it is dogmatically weighted, because we assume we know that the situation of man before God is the being of man under the law. As a result of this assumption one becomes involved in the discussion of the usage or *usus*, of the law, which is also variously applied exegetically; in the light of faith in the gospel the law appears other than it does apart from faith.

Is there, however, for the question which investigates the text of preaching, any other procedure than that of the distinction between law and gospel? From the exegetical point of view, some other is to be expected. For the Pauline antithesis between faith and the works of the law is not dominant, for example, in the Synoptic Gospels (although it is taken into consideration in the Fourth Gospel; compare John 1:17 with 6:28). The Synoptic Gospels still preserve for us some insight into Jesus' own proclamation. Jesus' proclamation shows us that he understood himself as the one who "brought into language" the call of God in the final hour. "Leave the dead to bury their dead" (Luke 9:60). "Whoever would save his life will lose it" (Mark 8:31). "Whoever gives heed to Jesus will find in God a father" (Luke 15:11 ff). "Blessed is he who takes no offence at me" (Luke 7:23 par. Matt. 11:6). One could take offense at Jesus. For in his attitude to those publicans and sinners who were prepared to hear him he portrayed God's rule, and thereby excluded from God's saving word the representatives of the law of Moses, who rejected him (so the Sermon on the Mount). We must try to see this conduct of Jesus in harmony with the keen accent of his language.

I understand Jesus' proclamation as a "language-event." That is not to say that Jesus created new concepts. It is his parables which are typical of Jesus. These parables certainly contain the same proclamation as the "logia" quoted above. But they go further than the "logia" in this respect at least, that in the parables Jesus' understanding of his situation "enters language" in a special way. The special characteristic of the parables becomes clear as soon as we try to "objectify" them. Matthew has already done this by relating the parables directly to the rule of God. He probably provides in this way the correct exposition, so long as we hold simply to his key-word, and not to his occasional commentaries and additions (as, for example, his explanations of the parables of the wheat and the tares, and of the net, Matt. 13:36–43, 49 f). Without doubt Jesus' parables summon to decision, just as his "logia" do. Like the man who found treasure, or the pearl merchant who found the one pearl of great price, the hearer must stake all on one thing—that he win the future which Jesus proclaims to him. But this "all" is not restricted to external possessions. What is meant is that one must allow oneself to be laid hold of. This can happen in no other way than that the man who is addressed understands himself anew, in that he receives himself from God as a new creature, who is able to love even his enemy (Luke 6:27 f; Matt. 5:44 f). It is clear that this kind of conduct simply corresponds to Jesus' conduct to obvious sinners. Thereby it is also made clear that the rule of God already begins to be effective in the presence of Jesus, so that one can speak of "blessed eyewitnesses" (Matt. 13:16 f par. Luke 10:23 f). . . .

The "language-event" of this proclamation is thereby already described. We notice that every "speaking" has a content. What is the presupposition for being able to speak in terms of content? The statement that all speaking is related to our conceptions of the subjects spoken of would hardly be sufficient. For our conceptions come not only from our own observations, but also from the stock of conceptions which has accumulated both unnoticed and openly in our consciousness. In relation to our current observations we bring also a preunderstanding, upon which our language capacity has extensively played. However, it cannot be denied that current observations continually bring a fresh impetus to our language. Hence a new observation can throw all our previous conceptions into confusion, or rearrange them completely; as, for example, our observing the slaughter of an animal, and the way this is done. What has been observed in other ways and preserved in conceptions comes into conflict with that which is newly observed, and so demands a comparison. This comparison requires from us a decision. Only when the decision is made can I speak further. My language is therefore never solely the expression of single conceptions, but is always at the same time the expression of a decision. In this decision there takes place the adjustment which supersedes the differences in my conceptions. This power of language which creates unity is what I call the "language-event." For in language I do not remain self-contained as I do in thinking. In language I expose those conceptions which I have unified to the agreement or contradiction of others. That is by no means to say that we live dialectically. Our language moves rather in a being which, as that decision concerning the unity of our conceptions, is indeed always my being; but in that it is always my being it reveals the situation, in which the being of others strives after an adjustment with my being. This means that we have a common understanding, whether friendly or hostile, of how we conceive ourselves, *because* we speak with each other. The real content of language, that which is an event not only in language but also precisely as language among men, is therefore being itself. But because being itself discloses in language something like our situation, as that which is ever and again understood between us, I term being itself *situation*. Situation is the essence of the "language-event."

The Christological Reference of the "Language-Event"

The concept of the situation, which is understood as the essence of the "language-event," is able to reveal that Jesus' person belongs to the content of his proclamation. This makes it possible to answer the question of how Jesus' person belongs to his proclamation and to the proclamation of faith in Jesus. Then it will also be clear why the preaching of faith has a text.

Whoever speaks of God as Jesus does alters and fixes the situation of man, and thereby of being, as the content of language. Unless his hearers were firmly determined to listen to him, Jesus' proclamation, just like Paul's, had necessarily to throw their traditional conceptions into confusion. This can be seen from the antitheses of the Sermon on the Mount in Matt: 5. Had, then, the word of the law of Moses, delivered to those of old, been invalid? No, it had become invalid. Under what condition? At the point when the situation of man before God had changed. This is just what Jesus said: "But I say to you . . . " We can therefore speak of a claim of Jesus, which met and meets everyone's situation. . . .

Jesus' claim was radical, for he conceived the situation of man before God as "presence." Only he who gave heed to Jesus could, according to Jesus' claim, be certain that he found himself *within* a saving relationship to God. This proclamation was a direct challenge to the Jewish cult and to the ruling operation of the law, because Jesus claimed to bring God himself decisively "into language," while offering to each of his hearers a new self-understanding before God, because it was a "being to God."

Whoever made the decision for this new self-understanding had given heed to God, in that he believed in Jesus' proclamation (cf. Mark 1.15). However, Jesus had not in any way made special claims for his own person. Obviously he fully accepted the offense of his person (Matt. 11:6 par.). It will then be correct for us to set out from some point other than Jesus' authority. This concept is better suited to the critique of opponents, and to the proclamation of the early Church. The Church awaited the crucified Jesus as the messianic Son of Man coming to judgment; just as Paul, too, could proclaim him as the Lord and the Son of God at God's judgment seat (2 Cor. 5:10; cf. Rom. 1:4). In the case of the historical Jesus himself one has solely to hold fast to the fact that he was conscious of the scandal of his claim, and wanted therefore to justify himself purely on the grounds of his proclamation. But the legitimation of Jesus' proclamation lay completely in the future; and that remained so, however near this future may have approached (cf. Luke 11:20 par. Matt. 12:28). This is why Jesus demanded decision in regard to his own person—this much at least can be gathered from those sayings of disputed authenticity which tell of the judgment of the coming Son of Man (Luke 12:8 f; Mark 8:38). For Jesus' conduct towards those publicans and sinners who were prepared to hear him (Matt. 11:19 par. Luke 7:34; cf. also Mark 2:14 f par.) cannot be separated from his parables which summon to decision, any more than it can from the "logia" which summon to decision, and from his calls of woe.

As his conduct shows, Jesus clearly did not want to be understood apart from his proclamation, but rather in it. His whole proclamation is one single self-testimony, not as witness for his possible messianic consciousness (for in my opinion Jesus spoke definitely of the future Son of Man), but because this proclamation presupposes a new being of man, in which God speaks with the individual; and as a result, the individual also is able to speak freely of God, as the parables of the laborers in the vineyard and the prodigal son do. (The early Christian formula *Maranatha*—1 Cor. 16:22—could quite conceivably also have been used by Jesus, when it is understood as an appeal to God.) Jesus did not claim for himself a special position before God. He understood himself as the *witness of a new situation*, as the authentic witness for the exposition of the future of the rule of God. . . .

Therefore the criterion for Jesus' understanding of his being and for his self-understanding is solely the *"language-power" of his proclamation*. Especially in the parable form, this "language-power" expresses the obedience of Jesus in relation to God. For in his proclamation Jesus preserves God's liberating freedom. Only then can we correctly assess Jesus' conduct in terms of Jesus' own intention, when on the strength of this we are able to bring God himself "into language." That happened, for example, with the conception of the Son of Man, which was transferred to Jesus himself.

Without doubt the early Christian proclamation also intended to bring God "into language." The attempts to do this have become the *text* for the entire subsequent Christian preaching of faith. It was thereby decisive that Jesus' own person moved definitely into the centre of the proclamation. That was, on the one hand, the consequence of Jesus' crucifixion, which raised the question of his authority. But what was conclusive was that the early Christian proclamation for its part expressed in God's name its conviction about Jesus, by believing in the crucified Jesus as him who had been exalted to the position of the Son of Man; as the resurrected Christ; as the lord over sin and death, who had been made into the word of God decisive for all men (Acts 2:36). God had spoken in Jesus; or as Paul says, God had in Christ reconciled the world to himself and established the preaching of reconciliation (2 Cor. 5:19). The being between God and man, the situation before God, would in the future be determined by the Spirit of God as the Spirit of Christ. Whoever understood himself out of this situation would bring Jesus Christ "into language." Jesus would in the future speak to his community as its Lord. From the *witness* of faith in God there had arisen the *basis* of this faith. Why? Because in the future also Jesus would place himself before God, though now as he who intercedes for us before God (Rom. 8:34; Heb. 7:25); as he whom we understand in our faith in God, as the Fourth Gospel shows. The historical Jesus had become the Jesus whom we understand.

Thereby it was, in fact, stated that no one can talk of God, if he intends somehow to do this and still bypass Jesus. Jesus therefore became the text of the proclamation. But the written word does not replace the proclamation. It simply preserves the situation in which we have to speak of God. We have to speak of God in that Jesus himself is proclaimed as the word of God; in such a way that faith in God sets free the "language-power" which is presented to it, and with this power faith is able to speak of Jesus, because it has understood him. Through this freedom in its character as an event, it becomes ever and again clear that faith in God speaks out of that self-understanding to which Jesus once summoned his hearers. The text of preaching has therefore a hermeneutical task, namely to lead us to that point in the proclamation where it is ever anew decided whether we are at one with Jesus; whether we therefore, like Jesus, speak the language of faith. This is the language which for its part presupposes the being of man before God, just as Jesus did, and thereby is the cause of Jesus' relationship to God becoming an event for us also. The time of the parable has now been superseded by the time of confession to Jesus, just as in worship the text makes way for preaching. This is because Jesus' obedience preceded faith in Jesus. The Church of faith then moves towards a future which ever anew confirms the Church's unity with Jesus, when the Church through its own obedience is able to invoke God as the Father of Jesus Christ and through Jesus Christ as our Father. Therefore the Church prays for the Holy Spirit as the power of her word, too. The being which Jesus revealed is fulfilled as being before God, by means of the word which, in the name of Jesus, is spoken as our word in faith.

What situation has now become central? The situation in which the historical Jesus himself appears delivered over to God's mortal judgment on all our lives? Or the one in which Jesus opposes this judgment, because something entirely new, the rule of God, will come? Jesus' proclamation says that he considers the time of God's rule to have come. His words and actions are said and done for the sake of his hearers—those who listen to him because they understand him. Therefore, we have to speak of Jesus' love. But this love means not just to continue, but to be believed in as the power which is stronger than God's judgment.

It is brought into language so that it might be believed in, so that we might believe that its hour has come. This faith will then always be its first part. If God holds fast to this love, he will then have held fast to Jesus. If God has held fast to Jesus, then he wants to have our faith in the time for love—our faith, not only the faith of the Apostles. God's word will then for Jesus' sake be that "yes" to Jesus which for us means faith in the time for love. This is the situation in which the language of faith becomes confession, even though this confession may love in silence. The situation certainly does not become an ideal scene; it remains the situation of Jesus, the situation of proclamation by which Jesus himself appealed to God, the temporal announcement of God's rule, of the rule of love. Through the time of Jesus time itself becomes the content of faith and therefore of proclamation. In the world the final hour will always have struck.

The quest of the historical Jesus then reveals to us our own time as a time conditioned by the situation of the preaching of faith. Who has asked us the question about the historical Jesus? And what is it about time, if our own time is itself to become the content of faith? Where will theology derive her understanding of time? In terms of a history? But how can this be, if faith is directly opposed to history, since, in regard to history's inexorability, faith submits to no further deception? Has our future begun to speak in the historical Jesus? Jesus' resurrection could then become a word to us only through our future entering language in this word. And this would mean—our death.

6

Eschatological Theology

In his *Critique of Pure Reason,* Immanuel Kant (1724–1804) stated: "The whole interest of reason, speculative as well as practical, is centered in the three following questions:

1. What can I know?
2. What ought I to do?
3. What may I hope?"

Much of modern theology has been preoccupied with the first question, the epistemological question, and, to a lesser extent, with the second, the ethical question. One strand of twentieth-century theology has engaged in vigorous debate over the Christian answer to Kant's third question, spurred by intensive investigations into the New Testament and the eschatological beliefs of Jesus and the early church. A new school of eschatological theology emerged under the leadership of Wolfhart Pannenberg (1928–), Jürgen Moltmann (1926–), and Johannes B. Metz (1928–). For these theologians it was not sufficient to establish what Jesus or Paul or John or any of the early Christians believed about the eschatological future—the so-called "last things," such as the final judgment, the end of the world, and the general resurrection. That in itself could be merely a matter of historical interest. Rather, as theologians, they aimed to show that hope is a structural dimension of human existence, and that therefore biblical eschatology may provide a true answer to the universally human question of hope, providing the ground and goal of human hoping.

I

Karl Barth, as the young pastor-theologian of crisis, had already sounded the eschatological note in his earliest commentary on Paul's Epistle to the Romans. He made the striking claim: "Christianity that is not entirely and altogether eschatology has entirely and altogether nothing to do with Christ." The Bultmann school also accentuated the theme of eschatology as a matter of existential decision. But from the perspective of Pannenberg and Moltmann, the future horizon of eschatology was absorbed into the "existential moment" (Bultmann) or the "eternal present" (Barth). Eschatology without futurity loses sight of the oncoming future of God in relation to temporal experience and world history; it is reduced somehow to a hidden dimension of the present.

In 1961, Wolfhart Pannenberg edited a volume of essays, *Revelation as History*, written by a circle of his friends at the University of Heidelberg, to which he contributed the programmatic essay. In 1964, Jürgen Moltmann published his *Theology of Hope*, which succeeded in synthesizing certain of Pannenberg's pioneering ideas on eschatology and revelation, hope and the future, hermeneutics and universal history, and on Jewish apocalypticism and the resurrection of Jesus Christ.

The little word *as* in *Revelation as History* is most significant. It intends to convey that the revelation of God comes not merely in or through history but as history. Pannenberg is thus signaling a break with prevailing interpretations of revelation in relation to history, among *Heilsgeschichte* theologians (e.g., Oscar Cullmann), Barthians, and Bultmannians. For these schools of thought, in Pannenberg's view, revelation and history mix like oil and water, since they locate revelation somewhere else, either above history (*Übergeschichte*), before history (*Urgeschichte*), or in a moment of existential encounter (*Geschichtlichkeit*).

Pannenberg's theses on revelation expounded in the essay selected for this volume advance the idea that only the totality of reality as history mediates the self-revelation of God. This notion of universal history as comprising the self-communication of the divine is one of Hegelian provenance. However, to make it useful for Christian theology, Pannenberg had to solve a problem that bedeviled the Hegelian schools to the left and right. The problem is, if history as a whole is the revelation of God, how can one particular historical event—the Christ event—claim absolute revelatory meaning? It would seem that God's revelation in Jesus Christ could be superseded in the future, could be perhaps only one among many significant stages in the history of religion. Pannenberg's solution to this problem is to play the eschatological card. Only the end of history can provide the ultimate perspective from which to understand the totality of history, and it is precisely this end that has occurred ahead of time, so to speak, in the resurrection of Jesus from the dead.

For Pannenberg, Jewish apocalypticism provides the indispensable background to the eschatology of Jesus and the early Christian communities. Jesus shared the apocalyptic hope of Judaism for the coming of God's kingdom. Jesus reshaped that hope first by his message and ministry, then by his death and resurrection. Pannenberg asserts: "This resounding motif of Jesus' message—the imminent kingdom of God—must be recovered as a key to the whole of Christian theology. . . . Our starting point then is the kingdom of God understood as the eschatological future brought about by God himself."

II

Pannenberg's attempt to breathe new life into the eschatological beliefs of the early church found resounding affirmation and elaboration in the classic text of eschatological theology, Jürgen Moltmann's *Theology of Hope.* There had been no lack of talk about eschatology, on account of the research of Johannes Weiss and Albert Schweitzer on the origins of Christian belief on the one side, and the attempt of Bultmann to make eschatology existentially relevant on the other side, but often such talk seemed sterile and detached from reality. Having second thoughts about so much eschatological rhetoric, just prior to the arrival of the new eschatological theology, Barth advised, "The time has surely come when we should awaken from this pan-eschatological dream."

Moltmann's wake-up call took the dramatic form of claiming that eschatology lies at the beginning of all Christian theology, adapting an aphoristic statement from Ernst Bloch's *Das Prinzip Hoffnung* (1959), "The real genesis is not at the beginning, but at the end." Never in the history of Christian theology have the themes of hope and the future been singled out for such colorful highlighting as they received by Moltmann. Since Christian faith lives absolutely from the resurrection of the crucified Christ, it is directed as hope toward the universal future promised in Christ. The future, says Moltmann, is the real problem of Christian theology, not just any future, but the future of Jesus Christ.

But how is it possible to speak of the future when by definition it has not yet happened? In a certain sense there can be no eschatology, no logos of the eschaton, for the Greek *logos* concept presupposes that human reason can grasp only the truth about reality that is always and already there. In Greek ontology, reality is not open-ended. Since it has no real future, there is no need for hope and no problem of history. In Christian eschatology, by contrast, the future of Christian hope is not a recurrence of the past or extension of the present; hope looks forward to a real future of new things that have never occurred before.

Christian eschatology speaks of the future in utterances of hope based on the history of promise. Such statements of hope do not express our given experiences of reality; they stand over against experience, contradicting it, driven by a promise for real change, as the condition for the possibility of new experience. The element of contradiction is essential in the language of hope, as the "negation of the negative." Thus there can be no empirical verification of hope, for it is of the nature of hope to press towards that which cannot yet be seen. "Now hope that is seen is not hope.

For who hopes for what he sees?" (Rom. 8:24). Christian hope itself, says Moltmann, is born from contradiction, from the resurrection's negation of death, its putting of death to death, as it were.

Christian faith acknowledges that the eschatological future which overcomes the discrepancies between righteousness and sin, joy and suffering, peace and war, good and evil, life and death, has already arrived in history in Jesus Christ. Without faith's knowledge and experience of Christ, hope would become merely utopian, a leap into the empty air. Because the limits of finitude, sin, and death have been transgressed by the resurrection of Christ, hope becomes a confidence that all the promises of God for humanity and the world will reach an ultimate fulfillment.

The deepest ontological basis of eschatological theology is the idea of God as the power of the future. The biblical God is the God of promises who leads history forward to its universal and final future in God. The future is not to be thought of only as a predicate of history striving forward or human subjective longing for fulfillment, but as ontologically grounded in God's own mode of being. God has not only the power to determine the future of our present, but has determined the future of all past times on their way to becoming present, a notion that leads to a concept of creation oriented not as traditionally to a primeval event at the start of time but to the eschatological future.

In the thinking of Pannenberg and Moltmann, the futurity of God transforms the notion of God's eternity. In other systems, eternity has been thought of as timelessness or as an endless continuation of something in existence; in the view of eschatological theology, eternity is the power of the future over every past, over every present, as ontologically prior to every event and epoch at the remotest distance from us. Thus, eternity is not an attribute of an absolutely immutable being, but expresses the primacy of the future of the God of the kingdom, the future for which humanity is destined by the electing grace of God.

III

The work of Johannes B. Metz applied the insights of eschatological theology to the field of political ethics, envisioning a new relation of the church to the world. Metz criticized the "trend toward the private" in Protestant existentialist theology and Roman Catholic transcendental Thomism. Metz became the leading exponent of political theology which he understood as the praxis of eschatological hope. Both Metz and Moltmann appropriated and revised the Marxist concept of praxis, laying the foundations for the distinctive methodology of Latin American liberation theology. Moltmann stated, "The new criterion of theology and of faith is to be found in praxis."

Metz's political theology placed in circulation an entire vocabulary of now familiar new terms and themes—privatization, oppression, ideology, liberation, bourgeois religion, dangerous memory—later popularized by various types of liberation theology. Metz criticized the bourgeois consciousness that ignores the special relation of God to those who suffer in history, the poor and the oppressed. He called the church to a critical witness in society, using symbols from the apocalyptic tradition to subvert the consciousness of modernity and to enter into solidarity with those who suffer through the dangerous memory of the passion, death, and resurrection of Jesus Christ.

The political grounding of eschatology aimed to correct the tendency to let the gospel fall into the realm of private concerns, into the personalistic sphere of I–Thou relationships. The vision of salvation includes the ongoing transformation of the social, political, and ecological conditions of the world, for the sake of a new future for all people. As a political force in history the church is called to the front lines of struggle, in pursuit of the politics of hope in society.

14. Wolfhart Pannenberg, *Revelation as History*

Thesis 2: Revelation is not Comprehended Completely in the Beginning, But at the End of the Revealing Story. . . .

The linking of revelation with the end of history is related to its indirect character. It follows directly out of the indirectness of the divine self-vindication, and without this presupposition revelation cannot be understood.

We have seen that the revelation of God is the defined goal of the present events of history. And only after their occurrence is God's deity perceived. Thus, placing revelation at the close of history is grounded in the indirectness of revelation.

This proves to be valuable knowledge if one is not involved with single revelatory events, but with a series of occurrences. We have already seen that the Old Testament's understanding of revelation tended in this direction. In the development from the Jahwistic tradition to the apocalyptic literature, it is not just the extent of events proving the deity of God that is increasing, but also the content of revelation that is continually revising itself. What had previously been the final vindication of God is now seen as only one step in the ever-increasing context of revelation. . . .

The history that demonstrates the deity of God is broadened to include the totality of all events. This corresponds completely to the universality of Israel's God, who is not only the God of Israel, but will be the God of all men. This broadening of the *Heilsgeschichte* (salvation history) to a universal history is in essence already accomplished in the major prophets of Israel in that they treat the kingdoms of the world as responsible to God's commands. With the exception of the lists in Chronicles, this point of view is first carried through systematically in apocalyptic literature. Since the time of the Deuteronomist and the prophets of the exile, the God of Israel was known as the Lord of all. Correspondingly, the apocalyptic viewpoint conceived of Jahweh's Law as the ground of the totality of world events. It is at the end of this chain of world events that God can for the first time be revealed with finality as the one true God. . . .

Placing the manifestation of God at the end of history means that the biblical God has, so to speak, his own history. That is, the historical event of revelation cannot be thought of in an outward way as revealing the essence of God. It is not so much the course of history as it is the end of history that is at one with the essence of God. But insofar as the end presupposes the course of history, because it is the perfection of it, then also the course of history belongs in essence to the revelation of God, for history receives its unity from its goal. Although the essence of God is from everlasting to everlasting the same, it does have a history in time. Thus it is that Jahweh first becomes the God of all mankind in the course of the history that he has brought to be. . . .

It is only in the course of this history brought about by Jahweh that this tribal God proves himself to be the one true God. This proof will be made in the strict and ultimate sense only at the end of all history. However, in the fate of Jesus, the end of history is experienced in advance as an anticipation. As we now conceptualize more precisely—it is only in view of the end that we can say God has proved himself in the fate of Jesus as the one true God. It is not by chance that the salvation now is for the Gentile also. This is a necessity because in the fate of Jesus as the anticipation of the end of all history, God is revealed as the one God of all mankind who had been expected since the times of the prophets. The inclusion of the heathen belonged to the universality of the eschatological revelation of God. Thus, it is appropriate that the proclamation of the God who raised Jesus would be tested by means of Greek philosophy and its questions about God, for philosophy is that discipline that raises the question of the true form of God for all men. Where the eschatological self-revelation of the God of Israel was proclaimed as the one God of all men, this question could not be overlooked, although it would be answered in a way that could not have been foreseen by any Greek. It is from this perspective, namely, the explication of the Christ event as an event for all peoples, that it becomes clear that the father of Jesus Christ has always been the one God from the very beginnings of Israel and, indeed, from the beginning of the world.

Thesis 3: In Distinction from Special Manifestations of the Deity, the Historical Revelation is Open to Anyone Who Has Eyes to See. It Has a Universal Character. . . .

We are ordinarily urged to think of revelation as an occurrence that man cannot perceive with natural eyes and that is made known only through a secret mediation. The revelation, however, of the biblical God in his activity is no secret or mysterious happening. An understanding that puts revelation into contrast to, or even conflict with, natural knowledge is in danger of distorting the historical revelation into a gnostic knowledge of secrets. . . .

To say that the knowledge of revelation is not supernatural does not mean that man is only confirming what he already knows through the force of his own intellect. In this respect, no one comes to the knowledge of God by his own reason or strength. This is not only true about the knowledge of God, but about other experiences that we have. The divinely revealed events and the message that reports these events brings man to a knowledge he would not have by himself. And these events do have transforming power. When these are taken seriously for what they are, and in the historical context to which they belong, then they speak their own language, the language of facts. God has proved his deity in this language of facts. Naturally, these experiences are not to be treated as naked facts, but are to be seen in their traditio-historical context. If we are to take these facts seriously, nothing ought to be inserted so as to allow them to be seen in a way different from what would naturally emerge. That these and also other events are veiled from many men, indeed, from most men, does not mean that this truth is too high for them, so that their reason must be supplemented by other means of knowing. Rather, it means that they must use their reason in order to see correctly. If the problem is not thought of in this way, then the Christian truth is made into a truth for the in group, and the church becomes a gnostic community.

The history of Israel all the way to the resurrection is a series of very special events. Thus they communicate something that could not be gotten out of other events. The special aspect is the event itself, not the attitude with which one confronts the event. A person does not bring faith with him to the event as though faith were the basis for finding the revelation of God in the history of Israel and of Jesus Christ. Rather, it is through an open appropriation of these events that true faith is sparked.

This is not to say that faith is made superfluous by the knowledge of God's revelation in the events that demonstrate his deity. Faith has to do with the future. This is the essence of trust. Trust primarily directs itself toward the future, and the future justifies, or disappoints. Thus a person does not come to faith blindly, but by means of an event that can be appropriated as something that can be considered reliable. True faith is not a state of blissful gullibility. The prophets could call Israel to faith in Jahweh's promises and proclaim his prophecy because Israel had experienced the dependability of their God in the course of a long history. The Christian risks his trust, life, and future on the fact of God's having been revealed in the fate of Jesus. This presupposition must be as certain as possible to him. Otherwise who could expect to obtain a participation in the life that has been manifested in Jesus, if such a presupposition were not oriented to the future?

There is a consequence for the Christian proclamation from this point. The proclamation of Christ presents, for those who hear it, a fact (taken to be reasonably and reliably true) that in the fate of Jesus of Nazareth, God has been revealed to all men. The proclamation of the gospel cannot assert that the facts are in doubt and that the leap of faith must be made in order to achieve certainty. If this sort of assertion were allowed to stand, then one would have to cease being a theologian and Christian. The proclamation must assert that the facts are reliable and that you can therefore place your faith, life, and future on them.

The knowledge of God's revelation in the history demonstrating his deity must also be the basis of faith. Faith does not need to worry that this knowledge has been altered because of shifts in historical research, just as long as this current image of the facts of history allows him to reassess and to participate in the events that are fundamental to it. This far-reaching independence of faith from the particular form of historical knowledge out of which it has come is founded on the fact that, in the act of trust, faith transcends its own picture of the event. The event has its own foundation in that it relies on the God who reveals himself in it. In the trusting surrender of his existence, the faithful man is thrust beyond his own theological formulations and open to new and better understandings of history, which are the basis for his life. It is through such faith that the patriarchs of Israel had a part in the fulfillment, in Jesus Christ, of the promises given to them, a fulfillment very different from anything that they might have been able to imagine. Through such faith, men have a part in the same history of God even though their ideological formulations of the history of God are irreconcilable. Such men are not only reciprocally bound to each other through faithful participation in the one history, but are also bound to those men who have no understanding of what the two are arguing about. Nevertheless, only the knowledge of God's revelation can be the foundation of faith, no matter how confused or mixed with doubt such knowledge might be. It should also be emphasized that it is not knowledge, but the resulting faith in God that secures participation in salvation.

Thesis 4: The Universal Revelation of the Deity of God Is Not Yet Realized in the History of Israel, but First in the Fate of Jesus of Nazareth, Insofar as the End of All Events Is Anticipated in His Fate.

In the history of Israel, Jahweh had not proved himself to be a God for all men. He had only established himself as the God of Israel. This came about in a way that is quite understandable, although it is hardly applicable to us as non-Israelites. Jahweh had proved himself to be a powerful God in the eyes of Israel by delivering the land promised to Israel. And as long as Israel remained in possession of the land, the knowledge of being under the protection of his might enabled Israel to acknowledge the one to whom it was obligated for such possession. This kind of thinking is clearly understandable, and only the greatest superficiality would ignore the evidence of this complex. It would be a superficiality of a type that would see all earthly developments as nothing but human arrangements and involvements. In any event, the occupancy of the land is not proof for us of the deity of Jahweh in its fullest sense, since we are heirs of the Greek philosophical tradition and can give the name God in an unqualified way only to the one God of all men, and can understand the gods of the religions as at best representations and analogies of the one god. From this point of view, to understand the deity of Jahweh in any other way would be to allow the divine figure of a religion to surpass the concept of God in philosophy. Israel's or Judah's faith in Jahweh was matured in crisis through the loss of the land in the destruction of the year 587. Only because the prophets had for a long time been sounding the warning about just such a catastrophe could it later be understood as the self-vindication of Jahweh. Thus, the faith of Israel survived the collapse of its own national identity and the temporary loss of the gifts of salvation and pointed to Jahweh's new proof of salvation. This understanding had been remarkably substantiated by the prophets through the course of events that had already been proclaimed. . . .

If we allow the apocalyptic expectation of the end of the world to be linked with the general resurrection of the dead, then in these events the God of Israel has proved himself to be the one God of all men. More can be said about this in the context of the following thesis. Let us remember: The one and only God can be revealed in his deity, but only indirectly out of a totality of all events. This was also the lead thought regarding the true form of the divine in Greek philosophy. It is only that this philosophy did not understand the totality of reality as a history always open to the new contingency, but rather took it to be a world with unchangeable structures of order. In this way, one could make inferences about the true form of the divine on the basis of the totality of phenomena that are known to every period of time. But, in the context of the history of thought, the Greek cosmos offered only a narrow conception of reality that was open to man's experience. The biblical experience of reality as history is more inclusive, since the contingency of the real event is included in this conception. Experience of the reality of history is superior to that connected with the contemplation of the cosmos. This is true both then and now because history can accept cosmic reflection as an element within it and make the regularity expressed in this cosmic reflection more realistic in structure and movement by providing it with a broader base of presuppositions. In such a situation, the God who is revealed out of the totality of history in this indirect way would also be the dominant answer to the philosophical question about God.

Now the history of the whole is only visible when one stands at its end. Until then, the future always remains as something beyond calculation. And, only in the sense that the perfection of history has already been inaugurated in Jesus Christ is God finally and fully revealed in the fate of Jesus. With the resurrection of Jesus, the end of history has already occurred, although it does not strike us in this way. It is through the resurrection that the God of Israel has substantiated his deity in an ultimate way and is now manifest as the God of all men. It is only the eschatological character of the Christ event that establishes that there will be no further self-manifestation of God beyond this event. Thus, the end of the world will be on a cosmic scale what has already happened in Jesus. It is the eschatological character of the Christ event as the anticipation of the end of all things that alone can establish this development so that from now on the non-Jew can acknowledge the God of Israel as the one true God, the one whom Greek philosophy sought and the only one who could be acknowledged as the one true God from that time on. This is a point of view quite distinct from the self-vindication of Jahweh through the giving of the promised land to Israel. This acknowledgment, and the accompanying ratification of the universal revelation of God in the fate of Jesus, is itself a fact that became a part of world history through the absorption of the classical world into the ancient church.

In the fate of Jesus the God of Israel was the hidden God. The hiddenness and transcendence of the God who is revealed in the crucified Jesus surpassed the canon of the incomprehensibility of the philosophical concept of God. On the basis of the above-mentioned reasons, one can really know that the resurrection of the crucified one is the eschatological self-revelation of God. However, no one person can see everything or exhaust what is specifically contained in this self-manifestation of God. There are many concrete things that can be said about him, but at the same time there is an incomprehensible future that stands before us in the "then" and "there" of the Jesus event. We can speak of the resurrection, but we are not able to exhaust all the implications of what we say with that term, although what we appropriate from the event of the resurrection of Jesus, namely, our life's reality in the light of the final decision, does place us in a position to speak about the self-revelation of God and justifies such language even now. From the point of view of our comprehension, the inexhaustibility of the event of revelation as an eschatological event is very important. Otherwise one would easily misunderstand what has previously been said about the knowledge of the self-disclosure of God as a claim to knowing everything.

In the fate of Jesus, the God of Israel is revealed as the triune God. The event of revelation should not be separated from the being of God himself. The being of God does not belong just to the Father, but also to the Son. The Holy Spirit also shares in the being of God by virtue of his participation in the glory of God that comes to life in the eschatological congregation. Hegel and Barth are correct in the principle of grounding the doctrine of the Trinity in revelation. In all periods of history, one can experience with special force the incomprehensibility of God in that the dualism of the one and the many, which always guided Greek conceptualization of God, is here overcome. All of this is connected with the fact that the doctrine of the Trinity formulates the concept of God as a historically experienced revelation.

If the fate of Jesus Christ is the anticipation of the end, and thus the revelation of God, then no further revelation of God can happen. Of course, God is active even in the events after Christ, and he also discloses himself in that time, but not in any fundamentally new way, but rather as the one who has already been revealed in the fate of Jesus. This does not mean that nothing new happens after Christ. The history after Christ bears his mark. Its special motifs seem to become noticeable for the first time in the thrust that is contained in the Christ event. The history after Christ is determined in essence by the proclamation of the revelation in Christ. In the effects of this proclamation, new facts are created in the history of the world. . . .

Thesis 5: The Christ Event Does Not Reveal the Deity of the God of Israel as an Isolated Event, but rather Insofar as It Is a Part of the History of God with Israel.

The way of Jesus of Nazareth and the revelational meaning of his fate is first understood from the viewpoint of the history and traditions of Israel. The Father of Jesus Christ was the God of the Old Testament, the God of the prophets, and of the Law that Jesus interpreted. It is precisely the incomparably full authority of the interpretation of the Law by Jesus as well as his whole manner of action that is understandable only from the background of the Israelitic spirit, namely, as a special form of the proleptic unveiling of the eschatological event that the apocalyptic writers claimed for themselves (or their pseudonyms). This was a link between Jesus and the self-understanding of the prophets. The peculiarity of Jesus' consciousness of authority, which distinguished him from the apocalyptic writers, ought to be connected with his conviction of the immediate nearness of the end. However, this distinction must still be seen as having arisen out of the soil of prophetic and apocalyptic traditions. This conviction links Jesus also with John the Baptist. What distinguishes Jesus from John, and what makes his activity a claim exceeding John's, is that Jesus proclaimed the impending end, not just as a judgment calling for repentance, but in a manner that presented himself as the eschatological salvation. It is for this reason—quite apart from the Jewish presuppositions—that the question about his authority must be put to him with such urgency. As Ulrich Wilkens has shown, it is from this perspective that the journey of Jesus to Jerusalem and his conduct there is understandable. The appearance and the fate of Jesus is thus decisively defined by means of the prophetic-apocalyptic expectation of the end, no matter how much this is recast in the proclamation of the presence of salvation. This connection is even clearer, if that is possible, in the primitive Christian message about the resurrection of Jesus. The resurrection of Jesus first assumed the meaning of being the anticipation of the end in connection with the understanding of history in the apocalyptic literature. It was only within the horizon of the apocalyptic expectation that the disciples of Jesus would designate as "resurrection" all experiences of the Living One who is distinct from earthly life on the other side of death. In these experiences, the Jesus whom they trusted is again acknowledged. In the sphere of this expectation, the appearance of the risen Jesus had its own language. The resurrection of Jesus is not just the divine authentication of the pre-Easter claim of Jesus concerning an authority reaching beyond any earthly authority. It also means the end has broken in with the fate of Jesus and that God is manifest in him. The story of the conversion of Paul shows how in the horizon of the apocalyptic expectation the fact of the resurrection of Jesus has a ready-made eschatological meaning. In the light of this it would be possible to connect, in a very particular way, the promises of Israel to the fate of Jesus, just as the primitive Christian proof from scripture has done.

Thesis 6: In the Formulation of the Non-Jewish Conceptions of Revelation in the Gentile Christian Church, the Universality of the Eschatological Self-Vindication of God in the Fate of Jesus Comes to Actual Expression.

The eschatological character of the revelation of Israel's God demanded the turn to the whole human community. Thus, in the same way, the gospel to the Gentiles came to be seen as a necessary consequence of the eschatological character of the Christ event. It has already been mentioned that the proclamation in the Gentile world of the universal deity of the God of Israel could not bypass the philosophical question regarding the true form of the divine. This question and its postulate was already taken into service in the time of the early church's mission, as a criterion from which the universality of the God revealed in Jesus was proved. . . .

Thesis 7: The Word Relates Itself to Revelation as Foretelling, Forthtelling, and Report.

The inclusive designation of revelation in history as "Word" of God in the gnostic understanding of a direct divine self-manifestation is not to be confused with God's manifold and many-pronged involvement in the concrete execution of the history of revelation by means of his authorized word.

History is not composed of raw or so-called brute facts. As the history of man, the history of revelation is always bound up with understanding, in hope and remembrance. The development of understanding is itself an event in history. In their fundamental givenness, these elements are not to be separated from history; history is also the history of the transmission of history. The natural events that are involved in the history of a people have no meaning apart from the connection with the traditions and expectations in which men live. The events of history speak their own language, the language of facts; however, this language is understandable only in the context of the traditions and the expectations in which the given events occur. We have an implication of this in the case of the resurrection of Jesus.

The biblical traditions are to be related to the same God who brings the events of history into being. Our question is: To what extent are the words, authorized by the God of Israel and Jesus of Nazareth, to be related to the history that he activates? The three words in the history of revelation that are used in connection with the functions of God do not exhaust this question. However, they take care of the most important aspects of the relation of word and revelation.

1. *The Word of God as promise:* Israel experienced the self-vindication of Jahweh in the given events of its history largely as a confirmation of words of promise or threat that are still in the future. Nevertheless, the prophetic word is the vehicle of proclamation and thus is not of itself the self-vindication of God. If it is to be found in visions and auditions, these were not understood as the direct self-disclosure of God. One gains a revelation of God's deity in seeing the way in which he fulfills promises. There is a circularity in this. The prophetic word precedes the acts of history, and these acts are understandable as acts of Jahweh only because a statement coming in the name of Jahweh interprets them this way. Then, as deutero-Isaiah often stressed, "establishment" of it is needed before it becomes revelation. The word of the prophets that announces history is still continued in the proclamation of the apocalyptic literature and of Jesus about the nearness of the impending kingdom of God.

2. *The Word of God as forthtelling:* The Old Testament essay has already shown that the Israelite Law of God presupposed the knowledge of the deity of Jahweh and also his self-vindication as demonstrated. Law and commandment follow as a result of the divine self-vindication. They do not themselves have the character of revelation. They could be this only insofar as the acts that established Jahweh's Law indirectly showed who he was, just as his other acts did. This usage was also continued in primitive Christianity in that it was not just the Old Testament Law, but also the declarations of Jesus that were characterized as the Word of God. The authority of Jesus as the bearer of the authority of God himself is thus already presupposed.

3. *The Word of God as kerygma:* Because the first two functions of the Word of God within the history that revealed God penetrated into primitive Christianity out of the usage of the Old Testament, a third function emerges for the first time in the New Testament. This is most significant. It is a question here of the word that comes from the eschatological revelation of God. . . .

The issuing of the kerygma, as the report of the revelation of God in the fate of Jesus, is itself an element in the accomplishment of the revelation event. The self-vindication of God before all men cannot be thought of apart from the universal notification. However, the kerygma is not by itself a revelatory speech by virtue of its formal characteristic, that is, as a challenge or call. The kerygma is to be understood solely on the basis of its content, on the basis of the event that it reports and explicates. In this sense, the kerygma is not to be thought of as bringing something to the event. The events in which God demonstrates his deity are self-evident as they stand within the framework of their own history. It does not require any kind of inspired interpretation to make these events recognizable as revelation. . . .

15. Jürgen Moltmann, *Theology of Hope*

What Is the "Logos" of Christian Eschatology?

Eschatology was long called the "doctrine of the last things" or the "doctrine of the end." By these last things were meant events which will one day break upon man, history, and the world at the end of time. They included the return of Christ in universal glory, the judgment of the world and the consummation of the kingdom, the general resurrection of the dead and the new creation of all things. These end events were to break into this world from somewhere beyond history, and to put an end to the history in which all things here live and move. But the relegating of these events to the "last day" robbed them of their directive, uplifting, and critical significance for all the days which are spent here, this side of the end, in history. Thus these teachings about the end led a peculiarly barren existence at the end of Christian dogmatics. They were like a loosely attached appendix that wandered off into obscure irrelevancies. They bore no relation to the doctrines of the cross and resurrection, the exaltation and sovereignty of Christ, and did not derive from these by any logical necessity. They were as far removed from them as All Souls' Day sermons are from Easter. The more Christianity became an organization for discipleship under the auspices of the Roman state religion and persistently upheld the claims of that religion, the more eschato-logy and its mobilizing, revolutionizing, and critical effects upon history as it has now to be lived were left to fanatical sects and revolutionary groups. Owing to the fact that Christian faith banished from its life the future hope by which it is upheld, and relegated the future to a beyond, or to eternity, whereas the biblical testimonies which it handed on are yet full to the brim with future hope of a messianic kind for the world—owing to this, hope emigrated as it were from the church and turned in one distorted form or another against the church.

In actual fact, however, eschatology means the doctrine of the Christian hope, which embraces both the object hoped for and also the hope inspired by it. From first to last, and not merely in the epilogue, Christianity is eschatology, is hope, forward looking and forward moving, and therefore also revolutionizing and transforming the present. The eschatological is not one element *of* Christianity, but it is the medium of Christian faith as such, the key in which everything in it is set, the glow that suffuses everything here in the dawn of an expected new day. For Christian faith lives from the raising of the crucified Christ, and strains after the promises of the universal future of Christ. Eschatology is the passionate suffering and passionate longing kindled by the Messiah.

Hence eschatology cannot really be only a part of Christian doctrine. Rather, the eschatological outlook is characteristic of all Christian proclamation, of every Christian existence and of the whole church. There is therefore only one real problem in Christian theology which its own object forces upon it and which it in turn forces on mankind and on human thought: the problem of the future. For the element of otherness that encounters us in the hope of the Old and New Testaments—the thing we cannot already think out and picture for ourselves on the basis of the given world and of the experiences we already have of that world—is one that confronts us with a promise of something new and with the hope of a future given by God. The God spoken of here is no intra-worldly or extra-worldly God, but the "God of hope" (Rom. 15:13), a God with "future as his essential nature" (as E. Bloch puts it), as made known in Exodus and in Israelite prophecy, the God whom we therefore cannot really have in us or over us but always only before us, who encounters us in his promises for the future, and whom we therefore cannot "have" either, but can only await in active hope. A proper theology would therefore have to be constructed in the light of its future goal. Eschatology should not be its end, but its beginning.

But how can anyone speak of the future, which is not yet here, and of coming events in which he has not as yet had any part? Are these not dreams, speculations, longings, and fears, which must all remain vague and indefinite because no one can verify them? The term "eschato-logy" is wrong. There can be no "doctrine" of the last things, if by "doctrine" we mean a collection of theses which can be understood on the basis of experiences that constantly recur and are open to anyone. The Greek term *logos* refers to a reality which is there, now and always, and is given true expression in the word appropriate to it. In this sense there can be no *logos* of the future, unless the future is the continuation or regular recurrence of the present. If, however, the future were to bring something startlingly new, we have nothing to say of that, and nothing meaningful can be said of it either, for it is not in what is new and accidental, but only in things of an abiding and regularly recurring character that there can be log-ical truth. Aristotle, it is true, can call hope a "waking dream," but for the Greeks it is nevertheless an evil out of Pandora's box.

But how, then, can Christian eschatology give expression to the future? Christian eschatology does not speak of the future as such. It sets out from a definite reality in history and announces the future of that reality, its future possibilities and its power over the future. Christian eschatology speaks of Jesus Christ and *his* future. It recognizes the reality of the raising of Jesus and proclaims the future of the risen Lord. Hence the question whether all statements about the future are grounded in the person and history of Jesus Christ provides it with the touchstone by which to distinguish the spirit of eschatology from that of utopia.

If, however, the crucified Christ has a future because of his resurrection, then that means on the other hand that all statements and judgments about him must at once imply something about the future which is to be expected from him.

Hence the form in which Christian theology speaks of Christ cannot be the form of the Greek *logos* or of doctrinal statements based on experience, but only the form of statements of hope and of promises for the future. All predicates of Christ not only say who he was and is, but imply statements as to who he will be and what is to be expected from him. They all say: "He is our hope" (Col. 1:27). In thus announcing his future in the world in terms of promise, they point believers in him towards the hope of his still outstanding future. Hope's statements of promise anticipate the future. In the promises, the hidden future already announces itself and exerts its influence on the present through the hope it awakens.

The truth of doctrinal statements is found in the fact that they can be shown to agree with the existing reality which we can all experience. Hope's statements of promise, however, must stand in contradiction to the reality which can at present be experienced. They do not result from experiences, but are the condition for the possibility of new experiences. They do not seek to illuminate the reality which exists, but the reality which is coming. They do not seek to make a mental picture of existing reality, but to lead existing reality towards the promised and hoped-for transformation. They do not seek to bear the train of reality, but to carry the torch before it. In so doing they give reality a historic character. But if reality is perceived in terms of history, then we have to ask with J. G. Hamann: "Who would form proper concepts of the present without knowing the future?"

Present and future, experience and hope, stand in contradiction to each other in Christian eschatology, with the result that man is not brought into harmony and agreement with the given situation, but is drawn into the conflict between hope and experience. "We are saved by hope. But hope that is seen is not hope; for what a man seeth, why doth he yet hope for? But if we hope for that we see not, then do we with patience wait for it" (Rom. 8:24, 25). Everywhere in the New Testament the Christian hope is directed towards what is not yet visible; it is consequently a "hoping against hope" and thereby brands the visible realm of present experience as a god-forsaken, transient reality that is to be left behind. The contradiction to the existing reality of himself and his world in which man is placed by hope is the very contradiction out of which this hope itself is born—it is the contradiction between the resurrection and the cross. Christian hope is resurrection hope, and it proves its truth in the contradiction of the future prospects offered and guaranteed for righteousness as opposed to sin, life as opposed to death, glory as opposed to suffering, peace as opposed to dissension. Calvin perceived very plainly the discrepancy involved in the resurrection hope: "To us is given the promise of eternal life—but to us, the dead. A blessed resurrection proclaimed to us—meantime we are surrounded by decay. We are called righteous—and yet sin lives in us. We hear of ineffable blessedness—but meantime we are here oppressed by infinite misery. We are promised abundance of all good things—yet we are rich only in hunger and thirst. What would become of us if we did not take our stand on hope, and if our heart did not hasten beyond this world through the midst of the darkness upon the path illumined by the word and Spirit of God!" (on Heb. 2:1).

It is in this contradiction that hope must prove its power. Hence eschatology, too, is forbidden to ramble, and must formulate its statements of hope in contradiction to our present experience of suffering, evil, and death. For that reason it will hardly ever be possible to develop an eschatology on its own. It is much more important to present hope as the foundation and the mainspring of theological thinking as such, and to introduce the eschatological perspective into our statements on divine revelation, on the resurrection of Christ, on the mission of faith, and on history.

The Believing Hope

In the contradiction between the word of promise and the experiential reality of suffering and death, faith takes its stand on hope and "hastens beyond this world," said Calvin. He did not mean by this that Christian faith flees the world, but he did mean that it strains after the future. To believe does in fact mean to cross and transcend bounds, to be engaged in an exodus. Yet this happens in a way that does not suppress or skip the unpleasant realities. Death is real death, and decay is putrefying decay. Guilt remains guilt and suffering remains, even for the believer, a cry to which there is no ready-made answer. Faith does not overstep these realities into a heavenly utopia, does not dream itself into a reality of a different kind. It can overstep the bounds of life, with their closed wall of suffering, guilt, and death, only at the point where they have in actual fact been broken through. It is only in following the Christ—who was raised from suffering, from a god-forsaken death, and from the grave—that it gains an open prospect in which there is nothing more to oppress us, a view of the realm of freedom and of joy. Where the bounds that mark the end of all human hopes are broken through in the raising of the crucified one, there faith can and must expand into hope. There it becomes παρρησία and μακροθυμία. There its hope becomes a "passion for what is possible" (Kierkegaard), because it can be a passion for what has been made possible. There the *extensio animi ad magna*, as it was called in the Middle Ages, takes place in hope. Faith recognizes the dawning of this future of openness and freedom in the Christ event. The hope thereby kindled spans the horizons which then open over a closed existence. Faith binds man to Christ. Hope sets this faith open to the comprehensive future of Christ. Hope is therefore the "inseparable companion" of faith. . . . Thus in the Christian life faith has the priority, but hope the primacy. Without faith's knowledge of Christ, hope becomes a utopia and remains hanging in the air. But without hope, faith falls to pieces, becomes a fainthearted and ultimately a dead faith. It is through faith that man finds the path of true life, but it is only hope that keeps him on that path. Thus it is that faith in Christ gives hope its assurance. Thus it is that hope gives faith in Christ its breadth and leads it into life.

To believe means to cross in hope and anticipation the bounds that have been penetrated by the raising of the crucified. If we bear that in mind, then this faith can have nothing to do with fleeing the world, with resignation, and with escapism. In this hope the soul does not soar above our vale of tears to some imagined heavenly bliss, nor does it sever itself from the earth. For, in the words of Ludwig Feuerbach, it puts "in place of the beyond that lies above our grave in heaven the beyond that lies above our grave on earth, the *historic future*, the *future of mankind*." It sees in the resurrection of Christ not the eternity of heaven, but the future of the very earth on which his cross stands. It sees in him the future of the very humanity for which he died. That is why it finds the cross the hope of the earth. This hope struggles for the obedience of the body, because it awaits the quickening of the body. It espouses in all meekness the cause of the devastated earth and of harassed humanity, because it is promised possession of the earth. *Ave crux—unica spes!*

But on the other hand, all this must inevitably mean that the man who thus hopes will never be able to reconcile himself with the laws and constraints of this earth, neither with the inevitability of death nor with the evil that constantly bears further evil. The raising of Christ is not merely a consolation to him in a life that is full of distress and doomed to die, but it is also God's contradiction of suffering and death, of humiliation and offense, and of the wickedness of evil. Hope finds in Christ not only a consolation *in* suffering, but also the protest of the divine promise *against* suffering. If Paul calls death the "last enemy" (1 Cor. 15:26), then the opposite is also true: that the risen Christ, and with him the resurrection hope, must be declared to be the enemy of death and of a world that puts up with death. Faith takes up this contradiction and thus becomes itself a contradiction to the world of death. That is why faith, wherever it develops into hope, causes not rest but unrest, not patience but impatience. It does not calm the unquiet heart, but is itself this unquiet heart in man. Those who hope in Christ can no longer put up with reality as it is, but begin to suffer under it, to contradict it. Peace with God means conflict with the world, for the goad of the promised future stabs inexorably into the flesh of every unfulfilled present. If we had before our eyes only what we see, then we should cheerfully or reluctantly reconcile ourselves with things as they happen to be. That we do not reconcile ourselves, that there is no pleasant harmony between us and reality, is due to our unquenchable hope. This hope keeps man unreconciled, until the great day of the fulfillment of all the promises of God. It keeps him in *statu viatoris*—in that unresolved openness to world questions which has its origin in the promise of God in the resurrection of Christ and can therefore be resolved only when the same God fulfills his promise. This hope makes the Christian Church a constant disturbance in human society, seeking as the latter does to stabilize itself into a "continuing city." It makes the church the source of continual new impulses towards the realization of righteousness, freedom, and humanity here in the light of the promised future that is to come. This church is committed to "answer for the hope" that is in it (1 Pet. 3:15). It is called in question "on account of the hope and resurrection of the dead" (Acts 23:6). Wherever that happens, Christianity embraces its true nature and becomes a witness of the future of Christ.

The Sin of Despair

If faith thus depends on hope for its life, then the sin of unbelief is manifestly grounded in hopelessness. To be sure, it is usually said that sin in its original form is man's wanting to be as God. But that is only the one side of sin. The other side of such pride is hopelessness, resignation, inertia, and melancholy. From this arise the *tristesse* and frustration which fill all living things with the seeds of a sweet decay. Among the sinners whose future is eternal death in Rev. 21:8, the "fearful" are mentioned before unbelievers, idolaters, murderers, and the rest. For the Epistle to the Hebrews, falling away from the living hope, in the sense of being disobedient to the promise in time of oppression, or of being carried away from God's pilgrim people as by a flood, is the great sin which threatens the hopeful on their way. Temptation then consists not so much in the titanic desire to be as God, but in weakness, timidity, weariness, not wanting to be what God requires of us.

God has exalted man and given him the prospect of a life that is wide and free, but man hangs back and lets himself down. God promises a new creation of all things in righteousness and peace, but man acts as if everything were as before and remained as before. God honours him with his promises, but man does not believe himself capable of what is required of him. That is the sin which most profoundly threatens the believer. It is not the evil he does, but the good he does not do, not his misdeeds but his omissions, that accuse him. They accuse him of lack of hope. For these so-called sins of omission all have their ground in hopelessness and weakness of faith. "It is not so much sin that plunges us into disaster, as rather despair," said Chrysostom. That is why the Middle Ages reckoned *acedia* or *tristitia* among the sins against the Holy Spirit which lead to death.

Joseph Pieper, in his treatise *Über die Hoffnung* (1949), has very neatly shown how this hopelessness can assume two forms: it can be presumption, *praesumptio*, and it can be despair, *desperatio*. Both are forms of the sin against hope. Presumption is a premature, self-willed anticipation of the fulfillment of what we hope for from God. Despair is the premature, arbitrary anticipation of the nonfulfillment of what we hope for from God. Both forms of hopelessness, by anticipating the fulfillment or by giving up hope, cancel the wayfaring character of hope. They rebel against the patience in which hope trusts in the God of the promise. They demand impatiently either fulfillment "now already" or "absolutely no" hope. "In despair and presumption alike we have the rigidifying and freezing of the truly human element, which hope alone can keep flowing and free." Thus despair, too, presupposes hope. "What we do not long for, can be the object neither of our hope nor of our despair" (Augustine). The pain of despair surely lies in the fact that a hope is there, but no way opens up towards its fulfillment. Thus the kindled hope turns against the one who hopes and consumes him. "Living means burying hopes," says Fontane in one of his novels, and it is these "dead hopes" that he portrays in it. Our hopes are bereft of faith and confidence. Hence despair would seek to preserve the soul from disappointments. "Hope as a rule makes many a fool." Hence we try to remain on the solid ground of reality, "to think clearly and not hope any more" (Camus), and yet in adopting this so-called realism dictated by the facts we fall victim to the worst of all utopias—the utopia of the *status quo*, as R. Musil has called this kind of realism.

The despairing surrender of hope does not even need to have a desperate appearance. It can also be the mere tacit absence of meaning, prospects, future, and purpose. It can wear the face of smiling resignation: *bonjour tristesse!* All that remains is a certain smile on the part of those who have tried out the full range of their possibilities and found nothing in them that could give cause for hope. All that remains is a *taedium vitae*, a life that has little further interest in itself. Of all the attitudes produced by the decay of a noneschatological, bourgeois Christianity, and then consequently found in a no-longer-Christian world, there is hardly any which is so general as *acedia, tristesse*, the cultivation and dandling manipulation of faded hopes. But where hope does not find its way to the source of new, unknown possibilities, there the trifling, ironical play with the existing possibilities ends in boredom, or in outbreaks of absurdity.

At the beginning of the nineteenth century the figure of presumption is found at many points in German idealism. For Goethe, Schiller, Ranke, Karl Marx and many others, Prometheus became the great saint of the modern age. Prometheus, who stole fire from the gods, stood in contrast to the figure of the obedient servant of God. It was possible to transform even Christ into a Promethean figure. Along with that there frequently went a philosophical, revolutionary millenarianism which set itself to build at last that realm of freedom and human dignity which had been hoped for in vain from the God of the divine servant.

In the middle of the twentieth century we find in the literary writings of the existentialists the other form of apostasy from hope. Thus the patron saint that was Prometheus now assumes the form of Sisyphus, who certainly knows the pilgrim way, and is fully acquainted with struggle and decision and with patient toil, yet without any prospect of fulfillment. Here the obedient servant of God can be transformed into the figure of the honest failure. There is no hope and no God any more. There is only Camus's "thinking clearly and hoping no more," and the honest love and fellow-feeling exemplified in Jesus. As if thinking could gain clarity without hope! As if there could be love without hope for the beloved!

Neither in presumption nor in despair does there lie the power to renew life, but only in the hope that is enduring and sure. Presumption and despair live off this hope and regale themselves at its expense. "He who does not hope for the unexpected, will not find it," runs a saying of Heraclitus. "The uniform of the

day is patience and its only decoration the pale star of hope over its heart"
(I. Bachmann).

Hope alone is to be called "realistic," because it alone takes seriously the possibilities with which all reality is fraught. It does not take things as they happen to
stand or to lie, but as progressing, moving things with possibilities of change.
Only as long as the world and the people in it are in a fragmented and experimental state which is not yet resolved, is there any sense in earthly hopes. The
latter anticipate what is possible to reality, historic and moving as it is, and use
their influence to decide the processes of history. Thus hopes and anticipations
of the future are not a transfiguring glow superimposed upon a darkened existence, but are realistic ways of perceiving the scope of our real possibilities, and
as such they set everything in motion and keep it in a state of change. Hope and
the kind of thinking that goes with it consequently cannot submit to the reproach
of being utopian, for they do not strive after things that have "no place," but after
things that have "no place *as yet*" but can acquire one. On the other hand, the
celebrated realism of the stark facts, of established objects and laws, the attitude
that despairs of its possibilities and clings to reality as it is, is inevitably much
more open to the charge of being utopian, for in its eyes there is "no place" for
possibilities, for future novelty, and consequently for the historic character of reality. Thus the despair which imagines it has reached the end of its tether proves
to be illusory, as long as nothing has yet come to an end but everything is still full
of possibilities. Thus positivistic realism also proves to be illusory, so long as the
world is not a fixed body of facts but a network of paths and processes, so long as
the world does not only run according to laws but these laws themselves are also
flexible, so long as it is a realm in which necessity means the possible, but not the
unalterable.

Statements of hope in Christian eschatology must also assert themselves
against the rigidified utopia of realism, if they would keep faith alive and would
guide obedience in love on to the path towards earthly, corporeal, social reality.
In its eyes the world is full of all kinds of possibilities, namely all the possibilities
of the God of hope. It sees reality and mankind in the hand of him whose voice
calls into history from its end, saying, "Behold, I make all things new," and from
hearing this word of promise it acquires the freedom to renew life here and to
change the face of the world.

Does Hope Cheat Man of the Happiness of the Present?

The most serious objection to a theology of hope springs not from presumption
or despair, for these two basic attitudes of human existence presuppose hope, but
the objection to hope arises from the religion of humble acquiescence in the
present. Is it not always in the present alone that man is truly existent, real, contemporary with himself, acquiescent and certain? Memory binds him to the past
that no longer is. Hope casts him upon the future that is not yet. He remembers

having lived, but he does not live. He remembers having loved, but he does not love. He remembers the thoughts of others, but he does not think. It seems to be much the same with him in hope. He hopes to live, but he does not live. He expects to be happy one day, and this expectation causes him to pass over the happiness of the present. He is never, in memory and hope, wholly himself and wholly in his present. Always he either limps behind it or hastens ahead of it. Memories and hopes appear to cheat him of the happiness of being undividedly present. They rob him of his present and drag him into times that no longer exist or do not yet exist. They surrender him to the nonexistent and abandon him to vanity. For these times subject him to the stream of transience—the stream that sweeps him to annihilation. Pascal lamented this deceitful aspect of hope: "We do not rest satisfied with the present. We anticipate the future as too slow in coming, as if in order to hasten its course; or we recall the past, to stop its too rapid flight. So imprudent are we that we wander in times which are not ours, and do not think of the only one which belongs to us; and so idle are we that we dream of those times which are no more, and thoughtlessly overlook that which alone exists. . . . We scarcely ever think of the present; and if we think of it, it is only to take light from it to arrange the future. The present is never our end. The past and the present. . . ."

16. Johannes Metz, *The Church and the World in Light of "Political Theology"*

The notion of political theology is ambiguous, hence exposed to misunderstanding, because it has been burdened with specific historical connotations. However, in view of the space at my disposal, I must refrain from historical clarifications here. May I then ask you to understand this paper on political theology in the way I shall use this notion in what follows; in using it, I shall attempt to elucidate its meaning. I understand political theology, first of all, to be a critical correction of present-day theology inasmuch as this theology shows an extreme privatizing tendency (a tendency, that is, to center upon the private person rather than "public," "political" society). At the same time, I understand this political theology to be a positive attempt to formulate the eschatological message under the conditions of our present society.

1. Let me first explain the function of political theology as a *critical corrective* of modern theology. I shall begin with a few *historical reflections.*

The unity and coordination of religion and society, of religious and societal existence, in former times acknowledged as an unquestionable reality, shattered as early as the beginning of the Enlightenment in France. This was the first time that the Christian religion appeared to be a particular phenomenon within a pluralistic milieu. Thus its absolute claim to universality seemed to be historically conditioned. This problematic situation is also the immediate foundation of the critique developed by the Enlightenment and, later, by Marxism. From the beginning, this critique took on the shape in which it still appears today. It approaches religion as an ideology, seeking to unmask it as a function, as the ideological superstructure of definite societal usages and power structures. The religious subject is being denounced as a false consciousness, that is, it is viewed as an element of society which has not yet become aware of itself. If a theology seeks to meet such a critique, it must uncover the sociopolitical implications of its ideas and notions. Now—and here I am conscious of daring simplification—classic metaphysical theology failed to discharge its responsibilities in this quarrel. The reason is that its notions and categories were all founded upon the supposition that there is no problem between religion and society, between faith and societal practice. As long as this supposition was true, it was indeed possible for a purely metaphysical interpretation of religion to be socially relevant, such as was the case, for instance, in the Middle Ages with its great theologians. However, when this unity was broken, this metaphysical theology got itself into a radical crisis as the theoretical attorney in the pending case between the Christian message of salvation and sociopolitical reality.

The prevailing theology of recent years, a theology of transcendental, existential personalist orientation is well aware of the problematic situation created by the Enlightenment. We might even say that, in a certain sense, it originated as a reaction against this situation. Still this reaction was not direct and sustained: the societal dimension of the Christian message was not given its proper importance but, implicitly or explicitly, treated as a secondary matter. In short, the message was "privatized" and the practice of faith reduced to the timeless decision of the person. This theology sought to solve its problem, a problem born of the Enlightenment, by eliminating it. It did not pass through the Enlightenment, but jumped over it and thought thus to be done with it. The religious consciousness formed by this theology attributes but a shadowy existence to the sociopolitical reality. The categories most prominent in this theology are the categories of the intimate, the private, the apolitical sphere. It is true that these theologians strongly emphasize charity and all that belongs to the field of interpersonal relations; yet, from the beginning, and as though there were no questions, they regard charity only as a private virtue with no political relevance; it is a virtue of the I–Thou relation, extending to the field of interpersonal encounter, or at best to charity on the scale of the neighborhood. The category of encounter is predominant; the proper religious way of speaking is the interpersonal address; the dimension of proper religious experience is the apex of free subjectivity, of the individual or the indisposable, the silent center of the I–Thou relation. It seems clear then that the forms of transcendental existential and personalist theology, currently predominant, have one thing in common: a trend towards the private.

I should like to cast further light on this tendency which I have called a privatizing tendency. Let us look at the result of modern *Formgeschichte* and the way they are interpreted by modern theology. It is well known that the Gospels' intention is not to present a biography of Jesus in the current sense of the word; their account of Jesus does not belong to the genus of private biography, but to the genus of public proclamation—of kerygma—which is the form in which the Christian message of salvation couches its assertions. The exegetical studies in so-called *Formgeschichte* have shown that the Gospels are a multilayered text in which the message is proclaimed in the aforesaid way. Now it seems to me that it was, in a certain sense, a fateful event when the discoveries and conclusions of *Formgeschichte* were at once interpreted in the categories of theological existentialism and personalism. This meant that the understanding of the kerygma was immediately limited to the intimate sphere of the person; briefly, it was privatized. Its word was taken merely as a word addressed to the person, as God's personal self-communication, not as a promise given to men, to society. The hermeneutics of the existential interpretation of the New Testament proceeds within the closed circuit of the I–Thou relation. Hence the necessity to deprivatize critically the understanding of the datum of our theology. *The deprivatizing of theology is the primary critical task of political theology.*

This deprivatizing, it seems to me, is in a way as important as the program of demythologizing. At least it should have a place with a legitimate demythologizing. Otherwise there is a danger of relating God and salvation to the existential problem of the person, of reducing them to the scale of the person, and so of downgrading the eschatological kerygma to a symbolic paraphrase of the metaphysical questionableness of man and his personal private decisions.

No doubt there is an emphasis on the individual in the message of the New Testament. We might even say that it is the gist of this message—especially in its Pauline expression—to place the individual before God. When we insist on deprivatizing, we do not in the least object to this orientation. On the contrary, for it is our contention that theology, precisely because of its privatizing tendency, is apt to miss the individual in his real existence. Today this existence is to a very great extent entangled in societal vicissitudes; so any existential and personal theology that does not understand existence as a political problem in the widest sense of the word, must inevitably restrict its considerations to an abstraction. A further danger of such a theology is that, failing to exercise its critical and controlling function, it delivers faith up to modern ideologies in the area of societal and political theory. Finally, an ecclesiastical religion, formed in the light of such a privatizing theology, will tend more and more to be a "rule without ruling power, a decision without deciding power. It will be a rule for those who are willing to accept it, so long as no one gives it a knock; it will not be a rule inasmuch as no other impulse will proceed from it but on the impulse to self-reproduction."

2. With this, the *positive task* of political theology comes to light. It is, to determine anew the relation between religion and society, between church and

societal "publicness," between eschatological faith and societal life; and, it should be added, "determine" is not used here in a "pre-critical" sense—that is, with the intention of *a priori* identifying these two realities—but "post-critically" in the sense of a *"second reflection."* Theology, insofar as it is political theology, is obliged to establish this "second degree reflection," when it comes to formulate the eschatological message under the conditions of the present situation of society. Hence let me briefly describe the characteristics both of this situation, that is, how it should be understood, and of the biblical message, which is the determining factor of this theological political reflection.

(a) I shall explain the situation from which today's theological reflection takes its *starting point*, by referring to a problem raised by the Enlightenment and which, at least since Marx, has became unavoidable. This problem may, in an abbreviated formula, be presented thus: according to Kant, a man is enlightened only when he has the freedom to make public use of his reason in all affairs. Hence the realization of this enlightenment is never a merely theoretical problem, but essentially a political one, a problem of societal conduct. In other words, it is linked with such sociopolitical suppositions as render enlightenment possible. Only he is enlightened who, *at the same time*, fights to realize those sociopolitical presuppositions that offer the possibility of publicly using reason. When, therefore, reason aims at political freedom and, consequently, theoretical transcendental reason appears within practical reason, rather than the reverse, a deprivatization of reason is absolutely necessary. Every "pure" theory, whether it be stressed or even overstressed, is nothing but a relapse into a pre-critical consciousness. For it is clear that the subject's critical claims cannot be sustained as "mere" theory. A new relation between theory and practice, between knowledge and morality, between reflection and revolution, will have to be worked out, and it will have to determine theological thought, if theological thought is not to be left at a pre-critical stage. Henceforth, practical and, in the widest sense of the word, political reason must take part in all critical reflections in theology. More and more, practical political reason will be the center of the classical discussion of the relation between *fides* and *ratio,* and the problem of the responsibility of faith will find the key to its solution, again, in practical public reason. Properly speaking, the so-called fundamental hermeneutic theology stands in relation to historical theology, how dogma stands in relation to history, but what is the relation between theory and practice, between understanding the faith and social practice? If the task of political reflection in theology, as emerging from the present situation, is to be characterized summarily, it might best be done in the way we have just indicated. This also shows that our intention is not, once again, to mix faith and "politics" in a reactionary manner. Rather, it is to actualize the critical potential of faith in regard to society.

(b) *Biblical tradition*, in its turn, obliges us to undertake this "second reflection" on the relation between eschatological faith and societal action. Why? Because salvation, the object of the Christian faith in hope, is not private salvation.

Its proclamation forced Jesus into a moral conflict with the public powers of his time. His cross is not found in the intimacy of the individual, personal heart, not in the sanctuary of a purely religious devotion. It is erected beyond these protected and separated precincts, "outside," as the theology of the Epistle to the Hebrews tells us. The curtain of the temple is torn forever. The scandal and the promise of this salvation are public matters. This "publicness" cannot be retracted nor dissolved, nor can it be attenuated. It is a recognizable fact attending the message of salvation as it moves through history. In the service of this message, Christian religion has been charged with a public responsibility to criticize and to liberate. "All the authors of the New Testament"—I am quoting the well-known biblical scholar, H. Schlier—"are convinced Christ is not a private person and the church is not a private association. They tell us of Christ's and his witnesses' encounter with the political world and its authorities. None of them has given more fundamental importance to this aspect of the history of Jesus than the apostle John. To him it is a lawsuit, which the world, represented by the Jews, brings against Jesus and his witnesses. This suit was brought to its public judicial conclusion before Pontius Pilate, the representative of the Roman Empire and the holder of the political power." Provided it is not read with the eyes of Bultmann, John's account of the passion is organized around this scene. The scene before Pilate is heavy with symbolism.

Political theology seeks to make contemporary theologians aware that a trial is pending between the eschatological message of Jesus and the sociopolitical reality. It insists on the permanent relation to the world inherent in the salvation merited by Jesus, a relation not to be understood in a natural–cosmological but in a sociopolitical sense; that is, as a critical, liberating force in regard to the social world and its historical process.

It is impossible to privatize the eschatological promises of biblical tradition: liberty, peace, justice, reconciliation. Again and again they force us to assume our responsibilities towards society. No doubt, these promises cannot simply be identified with any condition of society, however we may determine and describe it from our point of view. The history of Christianity has had enough experience of such direct identification and direct "politifications" of the Christian promises. In such cases, however, the "eschatological proviso," which makes every historically real status of society appear to be provisional, was being abandoned. Note that I say "provisional," not "arbitrary." This eschatological proviso does not mean that the present condition of society is not valid. It *is* valid, but in the "eschatological meanwhile." It does not bring about a negative but a critical attitude to the societal present. Its promises are not an empty horizon of religious expectations; neither are they only a regulative idea. They are, rather, a critical liberating imperative for our present times. These promises stimulate and appeal to us to make them a reality in the present historical condition and, in this way, to verify them—for we must "verify" them. The New Testament community knew at once that it was called to live out the coming promise under the conditions of what was their "now," and so to overcome the world. Living in accord with the promise of peace and justice implies an ever-renewed, ever-changing work in the "now" of our historical existence. This brings us, forces us, to an ever-renewed, critical, liberating position in face of the extant conditions of the society in which we live. Jesus' parables—to mention another biblical detail in this context—are parables of the kingdom of God but, *at the same time,* they instruct us in a renewed critical relationship to our world. *Every eschatological theology, therefore, must become a political theology, that is, a (socio)critical theology.* . . .

If the church is tentatively so defined, then two objections come immediately to the fore.

(a) There is, first, the question of *principle:* Can an institution as such have the task of criticism? After all, would not "institutionalized criticism" be like squaring the circle? Is not institution by its nature something anticritical? Hence is it not going to utopian limits to postulate this "second order institution," which is not only the object but also the subject of critical liberty and which, therefore, has to make possible and to secure this criticism? In this context, I can only answer briefly by posing a question in reply. Is it not, on the contrary, the specific note of the religious institution of the church to be, and even to have to be, the subject of this critical liberty? As institution the church herself lives under the eschatological proviso. She is not for herself; she does not serve her own self-affirmation, but the historical affirmation of the salvation of all men. The hope she announces is not a hope for herself but for the kingdom of God. As institution, the church truly lives on the proclamation of her own proviso. And she must realize this eschatological stipulation in that she establishes herself as the institution of critical liberty, in the face of society and its absolute and self-sufficient claims.

(b) But, granted that in this way our first objection is answered, there is still one additional critical question addressed to the church: What is the *historical and social basis of her critical task?* When was the church truly an institution of critical liberty? When was she in fact critically revolutionary? When was she not simply counterrevolutionary, resentful, and nagging in her relation to the societal world? Did not the church often neglect to speak her critical word, or come out with it too late? Did she not again and again appear to others as the ideological superstructure of societal relations and power constellation, and has she, indeed, always been able, with her own strength, to confound such accusation? Take recent centuries: is it not true that, more and more, religious institution and critical reflection have become incompatible things, so much so that, today, there is a theological reflection that ignores institution and an institution that ignores reflection? Where, then, is the historical and social basis of the claim made when defining the church as a critical institution in the face of society? This objection is valid. There is hardly one idea of critical societal importance in our history—take Revolution, Enlightenment, Reason, or again, Love, Liberty—which was not at least once disavowed by historical Christianity and its institutions. No theory, no retrospective reinterpretation is of any help. If anything is to help here, it will be new ways of thinking and acting in the church. May we hope for this? I think we may. All that follows is supported by this confidence.

3. In what does the *critical liberating function of the church*, in view of our society and its historical process, now consist? Which are the elements of that creative negation which make the progress of society to be progress at all? I should like, without pretending to either a systematic or a complete presentation, to specify a few of these critical tasks of the church.

(a) In virtue of its eschatological proviso in the face of every abstract idea of progress and of humanity, the church protects the individual man, living here and now, from being considered exclusively as matter and means for the building of a completely rationalized technological future. The church contradicts the practice that would see individuality only as the function of society's progress technically directed. It is true that even our societal utopias may contain a positive notion of the individual; still he is of value only inasmuch as he is the first to inaugurate new societal possibilities, in other words, inasmuch as he in himself anticipates the revolutionary social change that is to come, and inasmuch as he now is what everybody will have to be later. But then what about the poor and the oppressed? Are they not poor because they are unable to be first in the sense just explained? In this case, it is the church's task in virtue of the eschatological proviso and with all her institutionalized, sociocritical power, to protect the individual against being taken as a number on a human-progress-computer-card.

(b) It seems to me that a further point in this criticism is the following: today more than ever, when the church is faced with the modern political systems, she must emphasize her critical, liberating function again and again, to make it clear that man's history as a whole stands under God's eschatological proviso. She must stress the truth that history as a whole can never be a political notion in the strict sense of the word, that for this reason, it can never be made the object of a particular political action. There is no subject of universal history one can point to in this world, and whenever a party, a group, a nation, or a class sought to see itself as such a subject, thereby making the whole of history to be the scope of its political action, it inevitably grew into a totalitarian ideology.

(c) Lastly, it seems to me that, especially in this day, the church must mobilize that critical potency that lies in her central tradition of Christian love. Indeed it is not permissible to restrict love to the interpersonal sphere of the I–Thou. Nor is it enough to understand love as charitable work within a neighborhood. We must interpret love, and make it effective, in its societal dimension. This means that love should be the unconditional determination to bring justice, liberty, and peace *to the others*. Thus understood, love contains a sociocritical dynamism that can be viewed in two ways.

First: Love postulates a determined criticism of pure power. It does not allow us to think in the categories of "friend–enemy," for it obliges us to love our enemies and even to include them within the universal orbit of hope. Of course the church, which calls herself the church of love, will be able to express credible and efficient criticism of pure power only if, and to the extent that, she herself does not appear in the accoutrements of power. The church cannot and must not desire to press her point by means of political power. After all, she does not work for the affirmation of herself, but for the historical affirmation of salvation for all. She has no power prior to the power of her promises; this is an eminently critical proposition! It urges the church on, again and again, to a passionate criticism of pure power; it points an accusing finger at her when—and how often this has been the case in history—her criticism of the powerful of this world was too weak, or came too late, or when she was hesitant in protecting all those, without distinction of persons, who were persecuted or threatened, and when she did not passionately stand up and fight whenever and wherever man was being treated contemptuously by man. This criticism of power would not oblige Christians to withdraw from the exercise of political power in every case. Such a withdrawal, if it were a matter of principle, could be a sin against love, for Christians possess in their very faith and its tradition, a principle of criticism of power.

Second: The sociocritical dynamism of love points in yet another direction. If love is actualized as the unconditional determination to freedom and justice for the others, there might be circumstances where love itself could demand actions of a revolutionary character. If the status quo of a society contains as much injustice as would probably be caused by a revolutionary upheaval, a revolution in favor of freedom and justice for the sake of "the least of our brothers" would be permissible even in the name of love. Therefore, we should not underestimate the seriousness of Merleau-Ponty's remark that no church has ever been seen supporting a revolution for the sole reason that it appeared to be just. At this point it becomes more clear once more, that the sociocritical task of the church becomes the task of criticizing religion and church as well. The two go together like the two faces of a coin.

4. The sociocritical function brings about a change in the church herself. Ultimately, indeed, its objective is a *new self-understanding of the church* and *a transformation of her institutional attitudes towards modern society.* Let me say a few words about this point of political theology. We started by considering that, not only the individual, but the church as institution is the subject of a critical attitude with regard to society. There are several reasons for this. One of these springs from the general philosophy and sociology of modern critical consciousness. It points to the aporiae in which the critical individual finds himself when faced with this society and its anonymous structures. Criticism, therefore, must be institutionalized and a "second order institution," which can be bearer and guardian of critical freedom, is necessary. But there is a question: Is the church such a "second order institution"? In her present form, she is not: but I dare to say,

she is *not yet*. How, then, and under what conditions will she be such an institution? Are there signs that she will be such? I shall add a few remarks on this point.

(a) What happens—this is our first question—when the church today makes a concrete sociocritical assertion? She has attempted to do so, for instance, in some passages of the pastoral constitution of the last Council and, even more clearly and decidedly, in the encyclical *Populorum Progressio*. What exactly did happen when these assertions were made? At this point, the church was obliged to take into account and to elaborate data which did not simply result from inner ecclesiastical theological reflection. Hence, these sociopolitical pronouncements bring to life new nontheological resources. The church must receive such data in order to fulfill her mission to the world, which is not merely, not simply, to reproduce herself. All this will not fail to dissolve an uncritical, monolithic consciousness within the ecclesiastical institution. Moreover, the novelty of these data, which indeed are the foundation of new ecclesiastical pronouncements, requires *a new mode of speaking in the church*. Assertions founded on such data cannot be expressed simply as a doctrine. The courage is needed to formulate hypotheses suitable to contingent situations. Directives have to be issued which are neither weak and vague suggestions nor doctrinal-dogmatic teachings. This necessity of today's church to speak out concretely and critically brings about, at the same time, a sort of demythologizing and deritualizing in her speech and conduct. For it is evident that the ecclesiastical institution is now undergoing a new experience; it must bear contradiction. Its decisions cannot avoid taking one side and therefore being provisional and risky. If this institution learns the new language, it will no longer encumber the societal initiative of individual Christians with doctrinal rigidity; although, on the other hand, it will also remove arbitrariness from their initiative.

(b) A *further* point comes to mind immediately. Ecclesiastical criticism of society can ultimately be credible and efficient only if it is supported more and more by a *critical public opinion within the church* herself. If not this public opinion, what else is to be on guard, lest the church, as institution, become an illustration of the very conditions which she criticizes in others? It should be noted, however, that, because of lack of data, it is difficult today to give a detailed account of this critical public opinion. I shall at least enumerate some of its tasks. One of them is to interpose a veto, whenever the ecclesiastical institution oversteps the boundaries of its competence. Here I have in mind the case where the authorities attempt by institutional measures to carry through their own decisions in a matter of sociopolitical or economic relevance. Another of these tasks is the criticism of the inner ecclesiastical milieu: I am thinking of the fact that, within the church, certain mentalities prevail—usually, middle-class mentality—while others are thought to be irrelevant and, as it were, pushed to the background, out of the glare of the spotlight. A criticism of these uncontrolled yet powerful prejudices should be the object of public opinion. A further critical task is to show the historical conditioning and the change of the societal notions in the church herself; the change of ideas is not always synchronous with the facts, it is less easy to see but nonetheless real. It is also important—this is still another example of public criticism—to denounce the church's struggle on wrong battle fronts, if necessary. The skill sometimes spent in the defense of certain social positions would, indeed, be sufficient for radical and courageous change. And again, why is it that Christianity seems to have relatively little to say in matters of reconciliation and toleration? Finally, why is it that the church does not appear unmistakenly and effectively as the one institution in which certain sociological prejudices are not admitted: for instance, racism, nationalism, and whatever ways there are to express contempt for other men? These indications may suffice here. The courage to build up such a critical public opinion can, no doubt, be drawn only from the confident hope that there will be a certain change of the institutional customs of the church. But this confidence is perhaps one of the most important concrete features of membership in the church today.

(c) One last remark: In the pluralistic society, it cannot be the sociocritical attitude of the church to proclaim one positive societal order as an absolute norm. It can only consist in effecting within this society a critical, liberating freedom. The church's task here is not the elaboration of a system of social doctrine, but of social criticism. The church is a particular institution in society, yet presents a universal claim; if this claim is not to be an ideology, it can only be formulated and urged as *criticism*. Two important aspects may be pointed out on this basis. In the first place, it is clear now why the church, being a sociocritical institution, will not, in the end, come out with a political ideology. No political party can establish itself merely as such a criticism; no political party can take as its object of political action that which is the scope of the ecclesiastical criticism of society, namely, the whole of history standing under God's eschatological proviso. And in the second place, one can see now, again on the basis of the church's critical function with regard to society, how cooperation with other non-Christian institutions and groups is possible in principle. The basis of such a cooperation between Christians and non-Christians, between men and groups of even the widest ideological differences, cannot primarily be a positive determination of the societal progress or a definite objective opinion of what the future free society of men will be. In the realm of these positive ideas, there will always be differences and pluralism.

This pluralism, in the positive design of society, cannot be abolished within the conditions of our history if complete manipulation is not to replace its free realization. In view, therefore, of the aforementioned cooperation, there is a negative, critical attitude and experience to which we should pay our chief attention: the experience of the threat to humanity, that is, the experience of freedom, justice, and peace being threatened. We should not underestimate this negative experience. There is to it an elementary positive power of mediation. Even if we cannot directly and immediately agree as to the positive content of freedom, peace, and justice, yet we have a long and common experience with their contraries, the lack of freedom, justice, and peace. This negative experience offers us a chance for consensus, less in regard to the positive aspect of the freedom and justice we are seeking, than in regard to our critical resistance against the dread and terror of no freedom and no justice. The solidarity which grows out of this experience offers the possibility of a common front of protest. This must be grasped; this must be exploited. The danger of new wards is too close. The irrationalities of our actions in the social and political field are too manifest. There is still with us the possibility that "collective darkness" will descend upon us. The danger of losing freedom, justice, and peace is, indeed, so great that indifference in these matters would be a crime.

7

Trinitarian Theology

A major theological enterprise of the later twentieth century, which continues to gather momentum at the time this volume is prepared, is the restoration of the doctrine of Trinity to its original role in the structure of theology, and to that end the further development of the doctrine itself. Key writings of this enterprise are dated after the chronological cutoff established for inclusion in our collection—our limitation is perhaps especially arbitrary in this particular connection. We are, however, able to present three writings that can, each in its way, be regarded as foundational for the movement.

In the ancient church, Christian teaching and the doctrine of Trinity coincided. To think theologically, and to meditate on the relation of the Son to the Father in the Spirit, were understood to be much the same thing. It was perhaps Neo-Protestantism's deepest alienation from classical theology that, with one or two exceptions in the line of Hegel, Neo-Protestantism instead found the Trinity doctrine an embarrassment, and either passed it over with a historical mention or so freely interpreted it as to replace its meaning and function.

In this, Neo-Protestantism merely completed a development that had long been in progress. The doctrine of Trinity, hammered out through the first centuries of the church's history, interpreted the very being of God by the biblical story of his history in and with his people. God, said the Fathers of Nicea and Constantinople, *is* the life lived in the Spirit between Jesus and the God of Israel whom he called Father. Father, Son, and Spirit are the mutual actors of a history that is God's own life. But Western theology from Augustine (354–430) on so understood the "simplicity" and "changelessness" of God that such an interpretation of God's being, as action and personal community, became incomprehensible.

Western theology indeed for the most part continued to assert: God is in himself somehow Father, Son, and Holy Spirit. This was, after all, church dogma. But the reality of this differentiation in God was held to be strictly unthinkable, since, it was thought, any complexity or history in God himself is incompatible with the very notion of deity. Thereby the doctrine of Trinity became dysfunctional in the total body of the church's thinking, for what itself cannot be thought cannot of course be used in thinking through other matters.

Thus, the doctrine of Trinity became for the run of Western theology a dogmatically imposed conundrum about one and three. The Enlightenment freed theologians from responsibility for dogma merely as dogma. Neo-Protestantism took advantage of the permission, and openly dispensed with what had long been unused. A remarkable feature of the twentieth century's theology is that this development is being reversed.

I

Uniquely among works excerpted in this volume, Karl Barth's *Church Dogmatics* is twice represented. We have not used our space in this fashion without powerful reason: the trinitarian renewal was pioneered by this work above all.

The *Church Dogmatics* reinitiates for modernity three sorts of trinitarian reflection. First, Barth so locates the doctrine of Trinity systematically, as "prolegomena" to the whole work, as to make it *identify* the God whose ways the work will seek to trace. It is the God identified by the biblical narratives, and of whom these narratives are therefore true in a way that specifies his being, of whom all following assertions are to be made. Barth's observation—so easy to make once he had made it—that the doctrine of Trinity is Christianity's identification of which God it worships, would be an epochal theological contribution had he made no other.

Second, Barth developed the Trinity doctrine itself in a way integral to his theological project, so that the doctrine no longer appeared as a mere dogmatic carryover. At each step, Barth achieved the next trinitarian proposition by asking what must be true if God is indeed to *be* in himself exactly the same God as he is in *revealing* himself. And that God in himself is just as he is in his revelation is, of course, one way of stating the entire project of Barth's latter theology.

Third, through the *Church Dogmatics,* Barth *uses* the church's and his insight into God's triunity. Whatever the *locus,* Barth explores its questions by pointing to features of God's life as Father, Son, and Spirit. Thus, for example, Barth's doctrine of creation describes the creation as a whole and each of those features to which he turns his attention as deriving from the decision before all time by which the love between the Father and the Son is the love between the Father and a human creature-to-be.

II

No selection from foundational writings of the trinitarian revival could omit *The Trinity* by Karl Rahner. Several features of this small book or big pamphlet demand its inclusion.

First, although the movement of trinitarian theology is fully ecumenical, Catholic participation in the movement has its own basis in the inner history of Catholic theology. Karl Rahner was first among several theologians who set out in the years around the Second Vatican Council to rejoin Catholic theology to the theological history begun by the Enlightenment, by deliberately melding Thomist positions with Neo-Protestant patterns of thought. This strategy made disciples of many younger Catholic theologians. Thus, Rahner's own brief but classic exposition became foundational for renewed trinitarian reflection where it occurs within Catholicism.

Second, the form and tone of *The Trinity* have made it an exceptional educational tool. A generation of students in *all* confessions learned from this book most of what it knows about the possibility of thinking in trinitarian fashion.

Finally, Rahner lays down a thesis that has become a sort of rallying slogan for trinitarian thinkers, again of all confessions: that the "economic Trinity" and the "immanent Trinity" are the same. In the tradition, the "economic Trinity" is Father, Son, and Holy Spirit as these together are the actors of God's saving history with us; the "immanent Trinity" is Father, Son, and Holy Spirit as realities in "God himself." A form of the Western paralysis of trinitarianism has been a tendency to talk as if these were two metaphysically different things. Not so, said Rahner; the whole point of the doctrine is that as God is "economically," in his saving history, so he is "immanently," in himself. To be sure, it is not clear that Rahner would always approve what others have made from this slogan.

III

The Doctrine of the Trinity by Eberhard Jüngel (1933–), originally and much better titled *Gottes Sein ist im Werden,* has had one role in common with Rahner's similarly sized book: it has been much used in instruction. It has probably, however, not been so well understood in this use.

Jüngel's book is an interpretation of Karl Barth's doctrine of Trinity, in all the aspects discussed above. But it is an interpretation of a very special sort.

Jüngel transposes Barth's doctrine into a thought-world very different from Barth's, the thought-world of "hermeneutic" reflection. This sort of reflection derives from certain of the dialectical theologians, notably Bultmann. It is characteristic of this theology to be directly concerned for ontological interpretation in theology; thus the original German title of the present book, which one may perhaps translate, "With God, the Being is in the Becoming."

In this discourse, "interpretation"—such as Jüngel here offers!—is thus itself an ontological category. God *becomes* and therein *is* in that he interprets himself to himself and to us. The doctrine of Trinity, itself an interpretation, has as its matter precisely this divine self-interpretation. God interprets himself to us and, because this interpretation is true, to himself, by the Son in their Spirit. He *is* the event, the *"werden,"* of this interpreting.

17. Karl Barth, *The Doctrine of the Trinity*

God's word is God himself in his revelation. For God reveals himself as the Lord and that according to Scripture signifies for the concept of revelation that God himself in unimpaired difference is Revealer, Revelation, and Revealedness. . . .

The Root of the Doctrine of the Trinity

According to Scripture God's revelation is God's own immediate speaking, not to be distinguished from the act of this speaking, therefore not to be distinguished from God himself, from the divine I which confronts man in this act in which it addresses him as "thou." Revelation is *Dei loquentis persona.*

From the standpoint of the comprehensive concept of the Word of God we must say that here, in God's revelation, God's Word is identical with God himself. Among the three forms of the Word of God that can be said unconditionally and with strictest proprietary only of revelation, not with the same unreservedness and directness of Holy Scripture and of church proclamation as well. For if the same may and must also be said of them, it must at all events be added that their identity with God is an indirect one. . . .

According to Holy Scripture God's revelation is a ground which has no sort of higher or deeper ground above or behind it, but is simply a ground in itself, and therefore as regards man an authority from which no appeal to a higher authority is possible. Its reality and likewise its truth do not rest upon a superior reality and truth, are under no need of an initial actualization or legitimation as a reality from any other such point, and so are also not measured by reality and truth such as might be found at such another point, are not to be compared with such, nor to be judged and regarded as reality and truth in the light of such. On the contrary, God's revelation has its reality and truth wholly and in every respect—i.e. ontically and noetically—within itself. Only by denying it can we wish to ascribe to it a higher or deeper ground different from itself, or regard, adopt, or reject it from the vantage of such a higher or deeper ground. Obviously the adoption of revelation from the point of view of such a ground, differing from it and presumably superior to it—e.g. an affirmation of revelation, in which a man previously set up his conscience to be the judge of it—can only be achieved by denying revelation. Revelation is not real and true from the standpoint of anything else, either in itself or for us. It is so in itself, and for us through itself. . . .

All that we sum up in the statement, God reveals himself as the Lord. This statement is to be regarded as an analytical judgment. The distinction between form and content cannot be applied to the biblical concept of revelation. Hence, where according to the Bible revelation is an event, there is no second inquiry as to what its content might be. And its content could not become manifest in some other event just as well as in this. But here revelation as such is, of course, in accordance with the riches of God, never one time like another but always new, yet, as revelation, invariably the announcement of the βασιλεία τοῦ θεοῦ, the lordship of God. And how otherwise could the announcement of this βασιλεία follow than just by means of what is here called revelation? To be Lord means to be what God in his revelation is towards man. To act as Lord means to act as God in his revelation acts on man. And to acquire a Lord is what man acquires in God by receiving his revelation—revelation here always being regarded in the unconditional sense in which we meet it in the witness of Scripture. All else we know as "lordship" must be a copy, and is in reality a sad caricature of this Lordship. Without revelation man is unaware that there is a Lord, that he, man, has a Lord, and that God is this Lord. He is aware of it through revelation. Revelation is the revelation of lordship, and at the same time of the Lordship of God. For that is the godhead of God, it is that of which man is unaware and which God must reveal to him and does reveal according to the witness of Scripture—lordship. Lordship is present in revelation, just because its reality and truth are so utterly grounded in itself, because it need be actualized and legitimated in no other way than by the fact of its occurrence, because it is not in any relation to anything else, but is revelation by its own agency, because it is the self-contained novum we spoke of. Lordship means freedom. . . .

Godhead in the Bible means freedom, ontic and noetic independence. In the decisions taken in this freedom of God the divinely good becomes an event; truth, righteousness, holiness, mercy, deserve to be called what their names declare, because they really are so in the freedom of God. In this way, as this Free, the alone Free, the God of the Bible has lordship. In this way, too, he reveals it. It is precisely that self-sufficiency or immediacy, so characteristic of Bible revelation, which characterizes this revelation on the one hand as the revelation of lordship. But that does not become completely characteristic until we notice that it is not an abstract matter of the revelation of lordship but a concrete one of the revelation of the Lord, not of godhead (even were it godhead regarded as freedom), but of God himself, who in this freedom speaks as I and addresses by Thou. The happening of this is called in the Bible revelation and therefore revelation of his lordship. Because this I speaks and addresses by Thou, God announces his kingdom and he distinguishes this announcement from all speculations upon freedom, lordship, godhead, as man might perhaps set them up without revelation. As freedom, lordship, godhead are real and true in God himself and only in God himself, and so inaccessible and unknown unless this I speaks and addresses by Thou—so, in God himself, they are the meaning of the event which the Bible calls revelation. "God reveals himself as the Lord" means that he reveals what only he himself can reveal, himself. And so, precisely as himself he possesses and exercises his freedom and lordship. He is God, he is the ground without grounds, with whose word and will man can but begin without asking Why, in order therein and thereby to receive everything worthy the name of true and good. It becomes and is true and good because we receive it from him, because God as himself is with us, with us as only a man who says I and addresses us as Thou is with another man, yet with us as him whom he is, as the Lord who is the Free. God's being with us in this way is according to the Bible the event of revelation.

The statement, "God reveals himself as the Lord," understood in this sense, i.e. the meaning intended by statement, and therefore the revelation itself attested by Scripture we call "the root of the doctrine of the Trinity."

We mean by the doctrine of the Trinity, in a general and preliminary way, the proposition that he whom the Christian church calls God and proclaims as God, therefore the God who has revealed himself according to the witness of Scripture, is the same in unimpaired unity, yet also the same in unimpaired variety thrice in a different way. Or, in the phraseology of the dogma of the Trinity in the church, the Father, the Son, and the Holy Spirit in the Bible's witness to revelation are the one God in the unity of their essence, and the one God in the Bible's witness to revelation is in the variety of his Persons the Father, the Son, and Holy Spirit.

When we designate the statement, God reveals himself as the Lord, i.e. the actual revelation designated by this statement and attested by the Scripture, as the root of the doctrine of the Trinity, two things are involved:

First (negatively): the statement or statements about the Trinity of God can not claim to be directly identical with the statement about revelation, or with revelation itself. The doctrine of the Trinity is an analysis of this statement, i.e. of what it designates. The doctrine of the Trinity is a work of the church, a document of how she regards that statement, or its object, a document of how she knows God, i.e. how she struggles against error and for the relevancy of her proclamation, a document of her theology and to that extent a document of her faith and only to that extent, only indirectly, a document of revelation itself. The text of the doctrine of the Trinity, whether we are thinking of one of its ecclesiastically dogmatic formulations or of our own or another theological-dogmatic explication of the church dogma, is therefore not identical with a bit of the text of the Bible witness to revelation. The text of the doctrine of the Trinity is throughout connected with texts in the Bible witness to revelation, it includes also certain concepts taken from that text, but it does so just as an interpretation does, i.e. it translates and expounds that text, and that involves its availing itself of other concepts than those contained in the text before it. That means that it not only repeats what is there, but it confronts what is there with something new, to explain what is there. . . .

Second (positively): By describing revelation as the root of the doctrine of the Trinity, we assert that the proposition or propositions about the Trinity of God, of course, claim to be, not directly but indirectly, identical with the proposition about revelation. . . .

But let us come to our point, namely, that the ground, the root, of the doctrine of the Trinity, if it has one and so has the right to be a dogma—and it has one, it has the right to be a dogma—lies in revelation.

By that we do not assert that the doctrine of the Trinity is merely the interpretation of revelation and not also an interpretation of the God who reveals himself in revelation. That would be meaningless, because after all revelation is the self-interpretation of this God. If we have to do with his revelation, we have to do with himself and not, as modalists of all periods have thought, with an entity distinct from himself. And it is as the answer to the question about the God who reveals himself in revelation that the doctrine of the Trinity interests us. Which means that it is a part, in fact the decisive part of the doctrine of God, which at this point is not yet under discussion. We here anticipate the discussion of this part of the doctrine of God and shall later build up all that remains to be developed in this context upon this very presupposition, the Triunity of God. In a dogmatics of the Christian church we cannot speak correctly of the nature and attributes of God without presupposing that it is God the Father, Son, and Holy Spirit of whom we are speaking. But this fact, that the doctrine of the Trinity is the basic presupposition of the doctrine of God as such also, does not in any way prevent it from being regarded also and at this early stage as the interpretation of revelation as such. Not as an exhaustive interpretation; to give such a one we could not only speak of God who reveals himself, but we should also have to speak of the way in which and of man to whom he reveals himself, and for that we should require further anticipations from the realm of the so-called special dogmas; there are definite parts of Christology and Pneumatology of which we should have to take account. But from the doctrine of the Trinity we actually gather who the God is who reveals himself and therefore we let it find expression here as the interpretation of revelation. By that then we do not mean that revelation is the ground of the Trinity, as if God were the Three-in-one only in his revelation and for the sake of his revelation. But, of course, we say that revelation is the ground of the doctrine of the Trinity; the doctrine of the Trinity has no other ground than this. We come to the doctrine of the Trinity by no other way than by that of an analysis of the concept of revelation. And *vice versa*, revelation, to be rightly interpreted, must be interpreted as the ground of the doctrine of the Trinity. The question, decisive for the concept of revelation, about the self-revealing God cannot be answered by ignoring the answer given in the doctrine of the Trinity to this very question, but the doctrine of the Trinity itself is the answer to be given here. Our assertion then is that we designate the doctrine of the Trinity as the interpretation of revelation, or revelation as the ground of the doctrine of the Trinity; we find revelation itself so attested in Holy Scripture that our understanding of revelation (which is related to this testimony), i.e. of the self-revealing God, must be this very doctrine of the Trinity. . . .

Revelation in the Bible means the *self-unveiling*, imparted to men, of the God who according to his nature cannot be unveiled to man. The element of self-unveiling in this definition may be described not as the logically material, but as the historical centre of the biblical concept of revelation. When the Bible speaks of revelation it does so in the form of narrating a story or a series of stories. But the content of the story and of each one of these stories is just the self-unveiling of God referred to. When it gives us this narrative, our experience, of course, also is that it is the God who according to his nature cannot be unveiled to man who unveils himself there, and that this self-unveiling is imparted to particular men. Logically and substantially that is at once just as important as the self-unveiling in the narrative. Historically the latter constitutes the centre. But what is the meaning here of self-unveiling? Since it is the God who according to his nature cannot be unveiled to man, who unveils himself there, self-unveiling means that God does what man himself cannot do in any sense or in any way; he makes himself present, known, and significant to them as God. In the historical life of men he moves into a place and a very definite place at that, and makes himself the object of human contemplation, human experience, human thought, human speech. He makes himself an authority and an agent, and a concrete authority, an historical agent at that, an element in their human existence, significant and effective in time and in temporal relations. He exists himself, he exists as God for them exactly as quite other things or persons exist for them — as Esau existed for Jacob, as Mount Horeb or the ark of the covenant for the people of Israel, as John for Peter or Paul for his church — naturally in his own special form, not to be confused with any other, but really and concretely exists in definite form, so much so that the men specially involved could say, without the slightest speculation or metaphor, Immanuel, God with us! so that without the slightest fiction or self-deception they could say Thou to him, could pray to him. That is what self-unveiling is, that is the thing man cannot supply himself with, what only God can give him, but what he actually does give him in his revelation. It is the concept of form which he must single out from what has been said as the decisive one. Whoever and whatever the self-revealing God may be otherwise, that is certain that in his revelation, according to the witness of the Bible, he takes form, and that this taking form is his self-unveiling. For him it is not impossible and for him it is not too petty a thing, to be his own double in his revelation, double so far as his self-unveiling, his taking form is obviously not a thing that goes without saying but an event, and an event at that which can be explained by or derived from neither the will and act of man nor the rest of the world's course, so far as a move on his part is necessary to this event, and so far as this move obviously means something novel in God, God's distinguishing himself from himself, a being of God in a mode of existence, not subordinate as compared with his first, hidden mode of being as God, but just different, one in which he can also be existent for us. He who reveals himself here as God is able to reveal himself; already the fact of his revelation declares that it is his property to distinguish himself from himself, i.e. in himself and hiddenly to be God and yet at the same time in quite another way, manifestly, i.e. in the form of something he himself is not, to be God a second time. . . .

That God is capable of what the Bible ascribes to him in its narratives of what happened from the patriarchs through Moses and the prophets, past Golgotha and up to Easter and Whitsunday, namely that God can become manifest to men in the strictly real sense in which that becomes conclusively visible in the Jesus-revelation, i.e. that God can become so unlike himself that he is God in such a way as not to be bound to his secret eternity and eternal secrecy, but also can and will and really does assume temporal form — this ability, desire, and real action of God we might now regard as a first confirmation of our sentence, God reveals himself as the Lord. . . .

The Lordship which becomes visible in the biblical revelation consists in God's freedom to distinguish himself from himself, to become other than himself, and yet to remain as he was: in fact more, to be the one God equal to himself and to exist as the one sole God by the very fact that he thus, so inconceivably deeply, distinguishes himself from himself, that he is not only God the Father but also — in this direction this is the comprehensive meaning of the entire biblical witness — God the Son. That he reveals himself as the Son is what is primarily meant by saying that he reveals himself as the Lord. Actually this Sonship is God's lordship in his revelation.

Revelation in the Bible means the self-unveiling, imparted to men, *of the God who according to his nature cannot be unveiled to man.* By emphasizing this element we return to the Subject of the revelation. The revelation attested in the Bible is the revelation of the God who according to his nature cannot be unveiled to man. There are other things, there are also other gods, who also cannot be unveiled to man, i.e. of which in fact he has actually no experience and no conception but of which he might very well have experience and a conception, whose inscrutability is only factual and might some day be removed by some other fact, because it is not based upon the nature of the thing or of the god in question. Inscrutability, however, hiddenness, belongs to the nature of him who is called God in the Bible. As Creator, this God is distinct from the world, i.e. as the person he is, he does not belong to the realm of what man as a creature can know directly about God. Nor can he be unveilable to him even indirectly, in the created world, because he is the Holy One, whom to see, even to see indirectly, would require other eyes than ours which are corrupted by sin. And finally this God by his grace, i.e. by his self-unveiling, says to every one to whom it is imparted, that of himself he cannot do what is done for him and to him. Thus it is the nature of this God to be inscrutable to man. Of course, inscrutable in his revealed nature. It is the *Deus revelatus* who is the *Deus absconditus,* the God to whom there is no way and no bridge, of whom we could not say or have to say one single word, had he not of his own initiative met us as *Deus revelatus.* Only when we have grasped this as the meaning of the Bible do we take in the bearing of its pronouncement that God reveals himself, i.e. that he has assumed a form for our benefit. We cannot withdraw one iota from our previously given interpretation of revelation, that it consists in God having assumed a form. If we deny that, we deny revelation itself. But that it is the God who according to his nature cannot be unveiled to men, who there reveals himself, is a fact with its own very definite significance for understanding his unveiling. It must signify that even in the form which he assumes by revealing himself, God is free to reveal himself or not to reveal himself. In other words, we can regard his self-unveiling in each separate instance only as his act in which to a man who has no power to unveil him he himself unveils himself, which means, shows himself in a definite form, but himself reveals himself. Revelation always means to reveal, even in the form, even in the means of revelation. The form as such, the means, does not take the place of God. It is not the form that reveals, speaks, comforts, works, helps but God in the form. The result therefore of God assuming a form is not a medium or a third thing between God and man, nor a reality different from God, which as such would be the subject of revelation. That would mean that God could be unveiled to man after all, that there was no longer any need of God for his revelation, or rather that God was given into the hands of the man who, by God's form being given to him, could more or less dispose of God as of other realities. God's assumption of form means that he disposes of the form in which he meets man, just as he disposes of man. God's presence is always God's decision to be present. The divine Word is the divine speaking, the divine gift is the divine giving. God's self-unveiling remains the act of sovereign divine freedom. . . .

And now we repeat that the God of the biblical revelation is also able for what is ascribed to him in this respect by the biblical witnesses: that his revelation does not in the least betoken a loss of his mystery, that, true, he assumes a form, but without any form compassing him, that in gifting himself he remains free to give himself afresh or to refuse to, so that it is always his new self-giving that remains man's sole hope, that his "second time in quite another way" really does not prevent him from remaining quite equal to himself—in the fact that this is so we hear confirmation for the second time, obviously in a very different way compared with the first, that God reveals himself as the Lord. . . .

God reveals himself as the Father, that is to say the Father of the Son in whom he assumes form for our benefit. God the Father is God who even in assuming form in the Son always does not assume form, God as the free ground and the free power of his being God in the Son. It were no revelation within the bounds of the biblical witness in which God would not also be manifest thus as the Father, his doing this is the other thing—it is really something else, the same and yet not to be brought to the same denominator as the first—that is meant when we say that he reveals himself as Lord. God's Fatherhood, too, is God's lordship in his revelation.

Revelation in the Bible means the self-unveiling, imparted to men, of the God who according to his nature cannot be unveiled to man. We inquired previously about the source of the revelation. And now we ask where it goes to. . . .

It belongs to the concept of biblically attested revelation, to be an historical event. . . .

God in his inconceivability and God in the act of his revelation—that is not the formula of an abstract metaphysics of God, the World, or religion, claiming to hold good always and everywhere. It is rather the narrative about an event which took place uniquely, i.e. in a place and at a time always more or less exactly determined. That this place and time lie for us, historically, to a large extent in obscurity, that the separate data provided by the Bible about them are to historical criticism, is obvious in the case of documents of a date and civilization which had no knowledge at all of a historical question in our sense, quite apart from the fact that no serious part, even in the sense possible in that time and in that civilization, could be played by historical interest in the composition of those documents which did in fact claim to be documents of revelation. But that makes no difference to the fact that by the thing it calls revelation the Bible always means a unique event, one occurring in that place and at that time. . . .

The Bible lays such extraordinary weight upon the historicity of the revelation it recounts, because by revelation it does not mean a creation by man. It declares so emphatically that revelation was imparted to such and such men in such and such a situation, because thereby it describes it as a thing that is being imparted to men. This is what is overlooked or denied in applying to the Bible not, so far, the concept of saga but the concept of myth. The revelations attested in the Bible do not claim to be the naturally special phenomena of a universal, an idea, which man might then be comfortably in the position of comparing with this idea and regarding and estimating in its specialty. . . .

If the goodness and the holiness of god are themselves neither experiences which we could manufacture, nor concepts which we could construct for ourselves, but divine modes of existence to which human experiences and concepts can at all events respond, so far as they are asked the appropriate question, then at last their togetherness, their dialectic, i.e. one achievable by ourselves, but merely one that can be ascertained and acknowledged is actually taking place. It is this factual circumstantiality, its becoming ascertainable and acknowledgeable, that constitutes the historicity of revelation. By such a concept we mean that in the Bible revelation is the matter of God's being imparted, of a revealedness in God, by which the existence of definite men in a definite situation was so signalized that their experiences as well as their concepts were able, not to grasp God in his unveiling and God in his veiling and God in the dialectic of unveiling and veiling, but to follow him, to respond to him. . . .

Without this historical revealedness of God, revelation would not be revelation. God's revealedness makes it a relationship between God and man, the effective meeting between God and man. But it is God's own revealedness that makes it that. In this respect, too, and therefore with respect to its aim, our statement that God reveals himself as the Lord is confirmed. God's power to do what the biblical witnesses ascribe to him, not only to assume form, not only to remain free in this form, but in this form and this freedom of his to become the God of such and such men, Eternity in a moment, this is the third sense in which he is Lord in his revelation. . . .

God reveals himself as the Spirit, not as any spirit, not as the discoverable and arousable subsoil of man's spiritual life, but as the Spirit of the Father and of the Son, and so as the same one God, but this time as the same one God in this way as well, namely, in this unity, nay, in this self-disclosing unity, disclosing itself to men, unity with the Father and the Son. The fact of his doing this, this third thing also—which does not follow obviously from the first and second, as surely as there is nothing, absolutely nothing, obvious in their existence and co-existence either—that there is such a manifestation of the Father, and the Son, is what we mean when we say that he reveals himself as the Lord. The fact, too, that according to John 4:24 God is a Spirit is God's lordship in his revelation.

18. Karl Rahner, *The Trinity*

The Isolation of Trinitarian Doctrine in Piety and Textbook Theology

Despite their orthodox confession of the Trinity, Christians are, in their practical life, almost mere "monotheists." We must be willing to admit that, should the doctrine of the Trinity have to be dropped as false, the major part of religious literature could well remain virtually unchanged. Nor does it help to remark that the doctrine of the incarnation is theologically and religiously so central for the Christian that, through it, the Trinity is always and everywhere inseparably "present" in his religious life. Nowadays when we speak of God's incarnation, the theological and religious emphasis lies only on the fact that "God" became man, that "one" of the divine persons (of the Trinity) took on the flesh, and not on the fact that this person is precisely the person of the Logos. One has the feeling that, for the catechism of head and heart (as contrasted with the printed catechism), the Christian's idea of the incarnation would not have to change at all if there were no Trinity. For God would still, as (the one) person, have become man, which is in fact about all the average Christian explicitly grasps when he confesses the incarnation. There must surely be more than one voluminous modern scientific Christology which never makes it very clear exactly which divine hypostasis has assumed human nature. Today's average textbook doctrine of the incarnation uses practically only the abstract concept of a divine hypostasis, despite this concept's merely analogical and precarious unity. It makes no use of the precise concept of the second divine hypostasis as such. It wishes to find out what we mean when we say that God became man, not, more specifically, what it means for the Logos, precisely as Logos, as distinct from the other divine persons, to have become man. No wonder, since starting from Augustine, and as opposed to the older tradition, it has been among theologians a more or less foregone conclusion that each of the divine persons (if God freely so decided) could have become man, so that the incarnation of precisely this person can tell us nothing about the peculiar features of this person within the divinity.

It is not surprising, then, that Christian piety practically remembers from the doctrine of the incarnation only that "God" has become man, without deriving from this truth any clear message about the Trinity. Thus solid faith in the incarnation does not imply that the Trinity means something in normal Christian piety. We might mention other examples which show how the present climate of piety affects dogmatic theology, despite the faint opposition deriving from the frozen hieratic formulas of ancient liturgy. Thus theology considers it almost a matter of course that the "Our Father" is addressed in the same way, with equal appositeness, indifferently to the Holy Trinity, to the three divine persons; that the sacrifice of the Mass is offered in the same manner to the three divine persons. The current doctrine of satisfaction, hence also of redemption, with its theory of a double moral subject in Christ, regards the redemptive activity as offered indifferently to the three divine persons. Such a doctrine does not give sufficient attention to the fact that satisfaction comes from the incarnate Word, not simply from the God-man. It supposes that another person could, as man, have offered to the triune God a *satisfaction condigna* (adequate satisfaction). It is willing to admit that such a satisfaction would be perfectly conceivable without the presupposition of the Trinity as a condition of its possibility.

Accordingly, the doctrine of grace, even if it is entitled "On the Grace of Christ," is in fact monotheistic, not trinitarian: a participation in the divine nature leading to a blessed vision of the divine essence. We are told that this grace has been "merited" by Christ. But this grace of Christ is, at best, presented as the grace of the "God"-man, not as the grace of the incarnate Word as Logos. It is conceived as the recovery of a grace which, in its supralapsarian essence, is usually considered merely the grace of God, not the grace of the Word, much less of the "Word who is to become man." Thus the treatise of grace too is not much of a theological or religious introduction into the mystery of the triune God.

With notable exceptions, which only confirm the rule, this same anti-trinitarian timidity has induced theologians to conceive the relation brought about by grace between man and the three divine persons as one based upon "created grace," a product of God's efficient causality, merely "appropriated" differently to the single persons. The same remark applies, of course, to the treatises on the sacraments and on eschatology. Unlike the great theology of the past, as we find it in Bonaventure, today's theology hardly ever sees any connection between the Trinity and the doctrine of creation. This isolation is considered legitimate, since the "outward" divine operations are "common" to the three divine persons, so that the world as creation cannot tell us anything about the inner life of the Trinity. The venerable classical doctrine of the "vestiges" and the "image of the Trinity" in the world is thought to be—although one would never explicitly say so—a collection of pious speculations, unobjectionable once the doctrine has been established, but telling us nothing, either about the Trinity itself or about created reality, which we did not already know from other sources.

Thus the treatise on the Trinity occupies a rather isolated position in the total dogmatic system. To put it crassly, and not without exaggeration, when the treatise is concluded, its subject is never brought up again. Its function in the whole dogmatic construction is not clearly perceived. It is as though this mystery has been revealed for its own sake, and that even after it has been made known to us, it remains, as a reality, locked up within itself. We make statements about it, but as a reality it has nothing to do with us at all. Average theology cannot reject all these assertions as exaggerations. In Christology it acknowledges only a hypostatic function of "one" divine person, which might as well have been exercised by any other divine person; practically it considers as important for us in Christ only that he is "one" divine person. Which divine person does not matter. It sees in divine grace only the appropriated relations of the divine persons to man, the effect of an efficient causality of the one God. In final analysis, all these statements say explicitly in cold print that we ourselves have nothing to do with the mystery of the Holy Trinity except to know something "about it" through revelation. Someone might reply that our future happiness will consist precisely in face-to-face vision of this triune God, a vision which "introduces" us into the inner life of the divinity and constitutes our most authentic perfection, and that this is the reason why we are already told this mystery during this life. But then we must inquire how this could be true, if between man and each one of the three divine persons there is no real ontological relation, something more than mere appropriation. How can the contemplation of any reality, even of the loftiest reality, beatify us if intrinsically it is absolutely unrelated to us in any way? He who appeals to the beatific vision is therefore invited to draw the conclusions implied in his position. Or is our awareness of this mystery merely the knowledge of something purely extrinsic, which, as such, remains as isolated from all existential knowledge about ourselves as in our present theology the treatise on the Trinity is isolated from other dogmatic treatises telling us something about ourselves conducive to our real salvation?

The Problem of the Relation between the Treatises "On the One God" and "On the Triune God"

The above remarks shed light on other facts as well, especially on the separation immemorially taken for granted between the two treatises "On the One God" and "On the Triune God," and on the sequence in which they are taught. Not a few authors have explicitly defended both as being quite essential, and theologians such as Schmaus and Stolz constitute the remarkable exception. Yet it is impossible to use tradition as a cogent argument in behalf of the usual separation and sequence of these two treatises. For they became customary only after the *Sentences* of Peter Lombard were superseded by the *Summa* of St. Thomas.

If, with Scripture and the Greeks, we mean by ὁ Θεός in the first place the Father
. . . then the trinitarian structure of the Apostles' Creed, in line with Greek theology of the Trinity, would lead us to treat first of the Father and to consider also,
in this first chapter of the doctrine of God, the "essence" of God, the Father's
godhead. Thus the Master of the *Sentences* subsumed the general doctrine of
God under a doctrine of the Trinity (a fact which Grabman considered one of
Lombard's "main weaknesses"). Likewise in the *Summa Alexandri* there is yet no
clear separation between the two treatises. As we said above, this separation took
place for the first time in St. Thomas, for reasons which have not yet been fully
explained. Here the first topic under study is not God the Father as the unoriginate origin of divinity and reality, but as the essence common to all three persons. Such is the method which has prevailed ever since. Thus the treatise of the
Trinity locks itself in even more splendid isolation, with the ensuing danger that
the religious mind finds it devoid of interest. It looks as if everything which matters for us in God has already been said in the treatise "On the One God." This
separation of the two treatises and the sequence in which they are explained
probably derives from the Augustinian-Western conception of the Trinity, as contrasted with the Greek conception, even though the Augustinian conception had
not, in the High Middle Ages, developed the kind of monopoly it would later
enjoy. It begins with the one God, the one divine essence as a whole, and only *afterwards* does it see God as three in persons. Of course, great care is then taken
and must be taken, not to set up this divine "essence" itself as a "fourth" reality
pre-existing in the three persons. The Bible and the Greeks would have us start
from the one unoriginate God, who is already *Father* even when nothing is
known as yet about generations and spiration. He is known as the one unoriginate hypostasis which is not *positively* conceived as "absolute" even before it is
explicitly known as relative.

But the medieval-Latin starting point happens to be different. And thus one
may believe that Christian theology too may and should put a treatise on the one
God *before* the treatise on the triune God. But since this approach is justified by
the unicity of the divine essence, the only treatise which one writes, or can write,
is "on the one divinity." As a result, the treatise becomes quite philosophical and
abstract and refers hardly at all to salvation history. It speaks of the necessary
metaphysical properties of God, and not very explicitly of God as experienced in
salvation history in his free relations to his creatures. For should one make use of
salvation history, it would soon become apparent that one speaks always of him
whom Scripture and Jesus himself calls the Father, *Jesus'* Father, who sends the
Son and who gives himself to us in the Spirit, in his Spirit. On the other hand, if
one starts from the basic Augustinian-Western conception, an a-trinitarian treatise
"on the one God" comes as a matter of course before the treatise on the Trinity. In
this event, however, the theology of the Trinity must produce the impression that
it can make only purely formal statements about the three divine persons, with
the help of concepts about the two processions and about the relations. Even

these statements, however, refer only to a Trinity which is absolutely locked within itself—one which is not, in its reality, open to anything distinct from it; one, further, from which we are excluded, of which we happen to know something only through a strange paradox. It is true that, in an Augustinian, "psychological" theology of the Trinity efforts are made to give real content to such formal concepts as procession, communication of the divine essence, relation, and relative subsistence. But honesty forces us to admit that this does not lead very far. We do not mean that a psychological doctrine of the Trinity is a pure or even unsuccessful theological speculation. The hints given in Scripture show that the two divine processions, whose reality is assured by revelation, have certainly something to do with the two basic spiritual activities of knowing and loving. Thus the starting point of an Augustinian theology of the Trinity is undeniable. Yet if, unlike scholastic theology, we wish to avoid an artificial "eisegesis" into scriptural theology, we shall have to remember that this inner conception is indicated in Scripture only insofar as, in the economy of salvation, this intra-divine knowledge is seen as self-revealing, and this intra-divine love as self-communicating. When the theologian mentions this connection, as pointed out in the Scriptures, his Augustinian-psychological speculations on the Trinity result in that well-known quandary which makes all of his marvelous profundity look so utterly vacuous: for he begins from a human philosophical concept of knowledge and love, and from this concept develops a concept of the word and "inclination" of love; and now, after having speculatively applied these concepts to the Trinity, he must admit this application fails, because he has clung to the "essential" concept of knowledge and love, because a "personal," "notional" concept of the word and "inclination" of love cannot be derived from human experience. For should he try so to derive it, the knowing Word and the loving Spirit themselves must in their turn have a word and a love as persons proceeding from them.

Things do not necessarily have to be this way every time the two treatises "On the One God" and "On the Triune God" are separated and studied in the usual sequence. Although it is certainly incorrect to claim that this separation and sequence follow the course of revelation, which would also have progressed from a revelation of the divine essence to a revelation of the three persons, this separation and sequence may be considered more a didactic than a fundamental problem. The important question is: what is said in both treatises and how well are they related to each other, when thus separated in the usual way? What we wish to emphasize here is that, in the customary separation and sequence, the unity and the connection of the two treatises are too easily overlooked, as evidenced by the very fact that this separation and sequence are considered quite naturally as necessary and obvious.

Something else follows also from this encapsulation and isolation of the doctrine of the Trinity: the timid rejection of all attempts to discover, outside of Christendom or in the Old Testament, analogies, hints, or preparations pointing towards such a doctrine. We would hardly exaggerate and oversimplify if we stated that ancient apologetics against the pagans and the Jews was mainly interested in trying to discover at least some traces of the Trinity even before the New Testament, and outside of Christendom, in a few privileged minds. The patriarchs of the Old Testament were supposed to know something about the Trinity through their faith, and the liberality with which Augustine credited the great philosophers with the knowledge of this mystery would scandalize us nowadays. More recent Catholic apologetics is strongly opposed to all such attempts, and no wonder, since this kind of trinitarian theology has no integral place in the world and in salvation history. When the question arises whether such vestiges can really be discovered (we should not, of course, assert a priori that they can), the answer is already more or less tacitly presupposed: there are no such vestiges, because there can not be any. At any rate, there is little desire in such attempts to attribute any positive value to trinitarian allusions or analogies in the history of religions or in the Old Testament. The only point which is almost always emphasized is the incommensurability of these doctrines within and outside of Christianity.

The Axiomatic Unity of the "Economic" and "Immanent" Trinity

The isolation of the treatise of the Trinity *has* to be wrong. There *must* be a connection between Trinity and man. The Trinity is a mystery of *salvation*, otherwise it would never have been revealed. We should show why it is such a mystery. We must point out in every dogmatic treatise that what it says about salvation does not make sense without referring to this primordial mystery of Christianity. Wherever this permanent perichoresis between the treatises is overlooked, we have a clear indication that either the treatise on the Trinity or the other treatises have not clearly explained connections which show how the mystery of the Trinity is for us a mystery of salvation, and why we meet it wherever our salvation is considered, even in the other dogmatic treatises.

The *basic thesis* which establishes this connection between the treatises and presents the Trinity *as* a mystery of salvation (in its reality and not merely as a doctrine) might be formulated as follows: *The "economic" Trinity is the "immanent" Trinity and the "immanent" Trinity is the "economic" Trinity.*

Of course, the correctness of this statement can, strictly speaking, be established only by what will have to be said in the third section. If we succeed at that point, with the help of this axiom, to develop systematically a doctrine of the Trinity which *first* takes into account the really binding data of the doctrine of the Trinity as presented by the magisterium; *next* can more naturally do justice to the biblical statements concerning the economy of salvation and its threefold structure, and to the explicit biblical statements concerning the Father, the Son, and the Spirit, so that we are no longer embarrassed by the simple fact that in reality the Scriptures do *not explicitly* present a doctrine of the "immanent"

Trinity (even St. John's prologue is no such doctrine); *finally* helps us to understand that in the Christian's act of faith, as *salutary* faith, and in the Christian's life the Trinity is present and has to be present; *then* we shall have justified our axiom. Of course, this justification presupposes not only parts of Christology, but also some truths which must be more explicitly explained and demonstrated in the doctrine of grace — for instance, that the true and authentic concept of grace interprets grace (hence also salvation history) as a *self*-communication of God (not primarily as "created grace") in Christ and in his Spirit. Grace should not be reduced to a "relation" (a purely mental relation at that) of the one God to the elected creature, nor to a relation which is merely "appropriated" to the other divine persons. In the recipient himself grace is not some created sanctifying "quality" produced in a merely causal way by the one God. All this is presupposed. Yet in order to justify the basic axiom of our doctrine of the Trinity, we must at once propose a few remarks about it.

The "economic" Trinity *is* the immanent Trinity, according to the statement which interests us. In one way this statement is a defined doctrine of the faith. Jesus is not simply God in general, but the Son. The second divine person, God's Logos, is man, and only he is man. Hence there is at least one "mission," one presence in the world, one reality of salvation history which is not merely appropriated to some divine person, but which is proper to him. Here we are not merely *speaking* "about" this person in the world. Here something occurs "outside" the intra-divine life in the world itself, something which is not a mere effect of the efficient causality of the triune God acting as one in the world, but something which belongs to the Logos alone, which is the history of one divine person, in contrast to the other divine persons. This remains true even if we admit that this hypostatic union which belongs exclusively to the Logos is causally effected by the whole trinity. There has occurred in salvation history something which can be predicted only of one divine person. At any rate, this *one* case shows up as *false* the statement that there is nothing in salvation history, in the economy of salvation, which cannot equally be said of the triune God as a whole and of each person in particular. On the other hand, the following statement too is *false:* that a doctrine of the Trinity treating of the divine persons in general and of each person in particular can speak only of that which occurs within the divinity itself. And we are sure that the following statement is true: that no adequate distinction can be made between the doctrine of the Trinity and doctrine of the economy of salvation.

19. Eberhard Jüngel, *The Doctrine of the Trinity*

At the end of this paraphrase we shall briefly confront Barth's exposition of God's being with Gollwitzer's exposition of God's existence as confessed by faith. On the one hand the confrontation will be restricted to the difficulty in Gollwitzer's book which remained unsolved and which may be formulated in the following question: How is God's being-in-and-for-itself, maintained by Gollwitzer, related to God's being-in-and-for-us which is also maintained by Gollwitzer and which provided the basis for the assertion of God's being-in-and-for-itself? On the other hand the confrontation will be in the form of a summary—certainly a rather sketchy one—of the preceding paraphrase. Thereby the same problem will be discussed in its various aspects, so that there will necessarily be repetitions.

Gollwitzer maintained that we must not "evade or shrink from saying: 'God is in-and-for-himself.' This proposition should be understood not 'as a speculative proposition' but rather as the expression for 'an indispensable element in the knowledge of faith.' For the aim of the proposition is to prevent the being of God being identified with God's being-for-us, so that this fact shall be firmly established: 'in God's being-for-us man receives a free, unmerited gift . . . which is not based upon anything that is necessary to God. . . ."

Expressed in the concepts of classical ontology this means that God, as he who exists concretely, is a first substance. For it is a characteristic of the so-called first substances that as such they are not necessarily related to something other. First substances are as such no relation towards something and certainly they are to be comprehended as relational being neither as wholes, nor with respect to their parts. . . . If on the other hand one would wish to comprehend God in his being as relational being, then the being of the other to which God in his being were to be related would necessarily be connoted with the being of God. For all relational being so far as it is specified according to its own peculiarity demands the other to which it is related, reciprocally. . . . Thus if one would wish to comprehend God's being as such under the category of relational being and if one would have to regard man as the something other to which God as God is related, then God without man could not be comprehended as God; likewise, but conversely, God would then also have to be always connoted with the concept of man. Gollwitzer wants to prevent just that. Now it shall certainly not be denied that God has turned himself towards man, that he is really for us. That God's being is also relational being is for Gollwitzer not in question. But this relationship of God to man is not a necessary attribute of God's being. Rather is God's relationship to man a contingent relation which must not make God's being-in-and-for-itself into a problem. God in his determining as God is not then related necessarily to man but only . . . contingently. And just for this reason God and man do not make demands on each other reciprocally, for if it refers to what is contingent—not to what is necessary—the relationship is not reciprocal.

Gollwitzer thus comprehends God's being completely in the sense of the classical concept of substance. However, he does not consciously make use of this concept. For Gollwitzer the essential thing is to comprehend God's being as person-being. "The personal way of speaking is unsurpassable for Christian talk of God." But: "Personal being means being in relationship!" And: "It must therefore be emphatically maintained that person is a concept expressing relationship, or at any rate it may be used theologically only (!) as a concept of relationship and not as a concept of substance expressing the nature of *a magnitude existing for itself.*" On the other hand, however, "we must not evade or shrink from saying: God is in-and-for-himself."

The dilemma which originates here is plain. Gollwitzer resists it "through the distinction between a God's being-for-us which flows from the freedom of his being-for-himself, and a being-for-our-sake in which God is only thought of in a functional sense, since he cannot like worldly entities be demonstrated in objective independence." Thus God is not to be thought of only in a functional sense, although God's being can be comprehended only as personal being, and personal being according to Gollwitzer may be used, at any rate theologically, only as a concept of relationship. Gollwitzer's explications compel a clarification of the relation-concept with whose help it is supposed to be possible for God's being to be formulated adequately.

If God's being-for-us is not to be a being-for-our-sake then it must be asked how God's being-for-us can be thought of as a relation without God being thought of only in a functional sense. If one concedes the necessity of this distinction then the inquiry into the *relation* between God's being-for-us and the freedom of his being-for-himself becomes even more pressing. One should not be deceived: if this relation is not comprehended, then revelation as revelation remains uncomprehended. The reference to God's groundless mercy can here, therefore, not be the last word, because it has significance theologically only in so far as it excludes a ground for God's mercy external to God himself. However, if God's unfathomable mercy must not have its ground in God's *being,* then the concept of mercy is no longer a concept of God. Gollwitzer has no inkling of this consequence. But does he avoid it when he clings to his distinction between God's essence and God's will?

It is clear that this distinction of Gollwitzer's is also meant in an anti-metaphysical sense. But is not a metaphysical background introduced into God's being precisely through this distinction, which will permit as theologically legitimate only speech about the essence of the will of God? Is not Gollwitzer prevented from thinking of God's being in a consistent historical way precisely because of this distinction and demarcation? Must not the very *freedom* of God's being-for-himself be *formulated* starting from the *grace* of God's being-for-us which has been revealed, and indeed, so that God's being can become event in the grace of God's being-for-us because God's being in the freedom of his being-for-himself is originally event?

Whoever, like Gollwitzer, wants to maintain and think of God's independence cannot avoid the task of conceiving God's independence (*Selbständigkeit*) *out of* God's own subsistence (*Selbstand*) and thus also of thinking of *this subsistence.* God's subsistence is certainly to be thought of *only* out of God's revelation, thus out of an event in which God's being has become manifest as being-for-us. But then one will not be able to think of God's being as subsistence in the sense

198

in which Plato conceives essence (οὐσία), to which he ascribes the definition of being (λόγος τοῦ εἶναι): are these essences . . . always what they are, having the same simple self-existent and unchanging forms, not admitting of variation at all, or in any way, or at any time? Such a being as subsistence excludes the event out of itself, so that such an independent being cannot reveal itself. The subsistence of being as idea excludes the event of revelation because it excludes the event of being as subsistence. God is in-and-for-himself therefore remains an extremely mistaken statement so long as the independence of God which is maintained in this statement is not formulated out of the event of revelation, such that thereby God's being as subsistence allows the event of revelation to be formulated from this being.

But if God's being as subsistence is so thought of, that this being makes the event of revelation not impossible, but first and foremost possible, then the being of God as subsistence which is deduced from the event of God's revelation is itself thought of as event. And, indeed, as an event *granting* the event of revelation. God's independent being must thus be understood from the event of revelation as an event granting this event of revelation. God's being as subsistence is self-movement. As self-movement God's independent being makes revelation possible. Revelation as God's interpretation of himself is the expression of this self-movement of the being of God. Formulated differently: The grace of God's being-for-us must be able to be a copy (*Abbild*) of the freedom of God's being-for-himself, so that this freedom as the original (*Urbild*) of that grace becomes visible in that grace as the copy of this freedom. If revelation as God's *being*-for-us is to be taken seriously, then in Jesus Christ God's being must *become* visible and *be able* to become visible. This means, however, that both this becoming as well as this being-able-to-become must be understood from God's being itself, if indeed it is really true that *God* has revealed *himself*. Thus the historicality of God must be formulated *from God*. And on the other side, God's being must be formulated in view of this becoming and of this being-able-to-become if indeed it is really true that God has *revealed* himself. Thus at all cost we must formulate God's *historicality*.

Yet what help is the assurance that one must speak of God's being historically, when one *cannot* speak historically of God's being? It is still not achieved by ascribing historical predicates to the concept of God. History and the being of God are then again all too easily caused to be divided from one another. God's being is first then and only then really formulated historically when God's being as such is comprehended as historical being.

In such comprehension, however, the all important thing is that history does not in any way become a general concept for the being of God. ('God's being is historical' is and must remain a proposition of revelation.) As a proposition of revelation this proposition is itself certainly a historical proposition. For revelation is a historical event or it is just not revelation. But revelation is just that historical event in which God's being shows itself as being which is not only able to bear historical predicates, but demands them! In the historical event of revelation God's being is itself event, and indeed with the result that human language (and thus anthropomorphic language also; for human language even as the most abstract language—certainly hidden from itself—is anthropomorphic) about God becomes not only appropriate, but necessary.

This necessity does not veil the fact, but makes it first and foremost manifest, that human speech as such is not suited to speak about God. The demand made by God's being for historical predicates does not cover, but first and foremost uncovers, the fact that historical predicates are as such not suited to predicate the being of God. But if, however, it is true that the being of God must not only be spoken about historically, but also can be spoken about, then God's being must be historical in a more original way than historical predicates are historical.

Barth's understanding of revelation as God's self-interpretation is the systematic attempt to think of God's being-in-itself as event in such a way that God's being is capable of possessing historical predicates, although these as such are not capable of predicating the being of God. In that God in revelation *interprets* himself, God's being is *reiterated* with the help of historical predicates. Since, however, this self-interpretation is a reiteration *of the being of God through God*, God's being as such is a being capable of reiteration. As being capable of reiteration, God's being is *event*. For being which is no event can only reiterate itself as tautological identity. God's revelation, however, is not tautological identity, but indeed *self-interpretation*.

At this point a further reflection is indispensable: this first enables us to comprehend fully that God's being is not only able to bear historical predicates—in spite of their unqualified nature—but also demands them. For if it is true that God's being on the basis of the reiteration of this being which has taken place as revelation is a being capable of reiteration, then it will also have to be true that God's being on the basis of the self-interpretation of this being which has taken place as revelation is a being capable of interpretation. Take note: capable of being reiterated and interpreted by God alone. But just this, too, must be understood—that from eternity God is capable of interpreting himself through himself. The ability to possess predicates must belong constitutively to God's historicality. The *ability* to possess predicates, however, is the *event of the word* which is there before all predications and which makes all predications possible. In this sense it will have to be true that God's being, which has been formulated from the event of revelation, is in himself *verbal (wörtlich)* and precisely in this same measure also historical. That the logos is in the beginning with God—if this logos is supposed to be the subject of the historical predicate Jesus of Nazareth—is of intratrinitarian relevance.

How are we to understand the assertion that God's being is verbal in himself? God's being is verbal in himself in so far as God says "Yes" to himself. This "Yes" of God to himself constitutes his being as God the Father, God the Son, and God the Holy Spirit. And at the same time, from the beginning, this constitutes the historicality of God's being, in which all history has its basis. This "Yes" of God to himself is the *mystery* of God's being and as such one cannot go behind it. For in God's saying "Yes" to himself, God's being *corresponds* to itself as Father, as Son, and as Holy Spirit. This correspondence is an absolute mystery and cannot be surpassed by any paradox.

In this correspondence the being of God takes place as the history of the divine life in the Spirit. And in the history which is constituted through this correspondence God *makes space* within himself for *time.* This making-space-for-time within God is a continuing event. This space of time which is so comprehended as a continuing event we call eternity. God has time, because and as he has eternity. We know eternity primarily and properly not by the negation of the concept of time. . . . The theological concept of eternity must be set free from Babylonian captivity of an abstract opposite to the concept of time. This takes place when eternity is comprehended as the continuing event of the making-space-for-time, and thus as God's space of time. God *is* in this space of time in that he *goes his* ways. To say that God moves in certain directions is not a mere figure of speech, nor is it a reality only in his relation to what he has created. It is an eternal reality in himself.

The eternity in which God goes his ways, is, as the space of time for which God continually makes space within himself, not a-historical but in an eminent sense historical. And because God's being in eternity, which is constituted through the correspondence of Father, Son, and Spirit, is historical, revelation is therefore possible as "eternity in a single moment." The mystery of the correspondence of his being which takes place in God's self-affirmation makes revelation as historical event possible, and in this event it becomes manifest as mystery.

Single moments do not tarry but single moments can make history. Revelation as eternity in a single moment makes history, in that revelation brings human being into correspondence with the being of God which corresponds to itself. And in just this way human speech about God becomes possible in the "freedom for the word" (Ernst Fuchs) which is granted by God. It owes its being to revelation in which God himself—and that means his being!—manifested himself in human language. The historical predicate by which God manifested his being in human language is called Jesus of Nazareth. This predicate, too, is as such not suited to act as a predicate of God's being. It is as such not the predicate of an analytical proposition. What the patristic doctrine of the *anhypostasis* had to say of the human nature of Jesus Christ is true of this predicate as such. "Jesus of Nazareth" as such cannot be regarded as a predicate of revelation. But this predicate is *true* as substantial to the word of God. In order that this predicate might be true, God elected it from eternity. Is it too much to assert with Barth that the Word, in which "Jesus of Nazareth" alone can be the predicate of revelation, was already with God in the beginning as the subject of this historical predicate and thus the *"locum tenens* for Jesus"? With his teaching of the being of the man Jesus in the beginning with God, Barth has taught us to understand the relation of the historicality of God's being to the historical predicates Christologically. One will have to prize this theological pronouncement as something valuable so long as one has nothing better to set in its place.

In the attempt to overcome the difficulty to which we were led by Gollwitzer's book we have passed over to the interpretation of Barth's own statements. We will now have to clarify what meaning these statements have for the formal task set us by Gollwitzer's book, the task of thinking out God's being as a relationship.

The fact that God *becomes manifest* means that God's being is relational being. But if the dilemma sketched above is now to be avoided, if God's being is to be comprehended as *in relation to something* and yet to remain protected from being dependent on every *other thing* without on the other hand the relation becoming the *accidens* of a substance existing in and for itself, then one will have to understand God's being essentially as *double* relational being. This means that God can enter into relationship *(ad extra)* with another being (and just in this relationship his being can exist ontically *without* thereby being ontologically dependent on this other being), because God's being *(ad intra)* is a being *related to itself.* The doctrine of the Trinity is an attempt to think out the self-relatedness of God's being. It attempts to think out the self-relatedness of the being of God as Father, Son, and Spirit, but it can only do this appropriately when it understands God's self-relatedness in his modes of being (not at all as a kind of ontological egoism of God, but rather) as the *power* of God's being to *become* the God of another. It must not be made a condition that God's becoming must first take place through something other than God perhaps even in the sense of a transcendental condition positing the possibility of God being our God. God's self-relatedness must rather be understood as a *becoming, peculiar* to his *own* being, a becoming which allows us to comprehend God's being as a being-in-act. Only when God's self-relatedness is understood as a becoming peculiar to his own being is God's being-for-us also adequately considered. God's self-relatedness, his power to be in relation to himself, would then be the power of his being in relation to another. God's eternal love in which Father, Son, and Holy Spirit become eternally one would then be the ground (with respect to all that is not God) of groundless mercy. God's being in relation to another is thus no farewell to himself. God's being-for-us is just as little farewell to himself as it is God's coming-to-himself.

Thus it is not enough to formulate God's being simply as a being in relationship. A conscious or unconscious natural theology certainly does not become Protestant by making the relation the basic category of its statements. And the relation as pure relationship is still not formulated adequately enough so long as this its purity is not formulated theologically.

Protestant theology cannot formulate the purity of the relationship without an origin of relationship, which as the origin of relationship *is*, in that it *sets itself in relation.* Such setting-itself-in-relation is, understood theologically, pure relationship. And in the sense of such a setting-itself-in-relation God's being is *essentially relational;* God's being is "pure relationship."

Pure relationship thus means relationship as a becoming of itself but not from itself. But then from what does it become? God's self-relatedness is based on God's "Yes" to himself. In this "Yes" of God to himself God sets himself in relation to himself, in order so to be he who he is. In this sense God's being is in becoming. Pure relationship can thus be only the predicate, but never the subject of a proposition related to God. But this predicate can be the predicate of an analytical and a synthetic proposition. With respect to God's Trinitarian self-relatedness this predicate is to be understood as that of an analytical proposition. With respect to God's revelation this predicate is to be understood as that of a synthetic proposition. The synthetic proposition nevertheless *corresponds* to the analytical proposition. This correspondence signifies that God's being as self-relatedness is a being in becoming, which possesses the peculiarity of being able to *reiterate itself.*

The reiteration, however, is nothing without that which is to be reiterated. That means in Gollwitzer's sense that God's being-for-us is nothing without God's being-for-himself. The *ratio essendi* of the reiteration is that which is to be reiterated. The problems which become thematic in this context must be considered as a counterpart to the doctrines of *enhypostasis* and *anhypostasis* in a doctrine of the reiteration of his being for himself. Such a doctrine of reiteration would have to bring to its rightful place with respect to the relations, that which the doctrines of *enhypostasis* and *anhypostasis* seek to validate christologically for the poles of the relation (God—man). Thereby the doctrine of *enhypostasis* would now be formulated together with that of *enhypostasis* by opposing the two doctrines to each other: God's being *ad extra* would be anhypostatic if in this relation an *enhypostasis* of the being of God as Father, as Son, and as Spirit was not fulfilled. But in that God in his revelation reiterates his being as Father, as Son, and as Spirit as being for us, this reiteration also possesses being. This would mean that God in his revelation *imparts* himself to his concrete relational existence as Father, Son, and Spirit by reiterating himself. The reiteration as God's relation to us is the correspondence to God's self-relatedness: *analogia relationis.* Revelation, so understood, is really God's self-interpretation. And so understood, God in his revelation can *be πρὸς ἕτερον* [related to something] without being dependent upon this *ἕτερον.* But conversely, man and his world owe their being to the being of God *πρὸς ἕτερον.* In the irreversibility of this ontological relatedness of God and the world lies the ontological difference between God and the world. Hence God can be the God of man without being defined as God by a relation to man. Yet at the same time, if the proposition concerning the reiteration of God's being in the correspondence of the relations *ad extra* and *ad intra* is really true, the proposition "God is in-and-for-himself" *in concreto* is just as false as the proposition "God is God only as the God of man."

What has been said may be summed as follows:

1. What may be known and said about God's being may only be known and stated from God's being-for-us.
2. The fact that what is to be known about God's being is made known to us from God's being, is based on the fact that God's being-for-us is event in Jesus Christ. This event is called revelation and as such is God's interpretation of himself.
3. God's being-for-us does not define God's being but certainly God in his being-for-us interprets his being.
4. Interpretation lives from that which is to be interpreted. As relational being God's being-for-us is the reiteration of God's self-relatedness in his being as Father, as Son, and as Holy Spirit.
5. In reiteration that which is to be reiterated lets itself be known. In God's being-for-us God's being-for-himself makes itself known to us as a being which grounds and makes possible God's being-for-us.
6. God's being corresponds to itself:
    (a) in the event of God's self-relatedness; as the relation of Father, Son, and Holy Spirit.
    (b) in the event of revelation: as the relation of God's being-for-us to God's being in the event of his self-relatedness.

    The correspondence-relation *(b)* derives its ontological power from the correspondence-relation *(a)*. The correspondence-relation *(a)* constitutes the correspondence-relation *(b)*.
7. This constituting is itself to be thought of as the power which is proper to the correspondence-relation *(a)*, in which the *hidden* God is the God who *reveals* himself. God's being hidden and God's being revealed, is as relational being, a being in the power of becoming.

It only remains to consider one last reflection. In that we called God's being a being in becoming we understood that God can reveal himself. But that God does what he can, that he has reiterated himself in his revelation, this rests on no necessity: That is much more grace. Yet this grace is not strange to God's being. How otherwise would it be distinguished from necessity? God's grace is rather the reiteration of God's Yes to himself (which constitutes God's being) in relation to something other. In so far as this Yes in relation to something other than God first calls this something other into being, God's gracious Yes sets his being in relationship to the nothing. But in so far as this Yes of grace frees the creation which has been called into being from the threatening which comes through the nothing, last resort, therefore, God's grace signifies God's own self-surrender. But if God's self-surrender is not also God's abandoning of himself, then

God's self-relatedness wanted to provide itself precisely in God's relation to the nothing.

God's self-relatedness thus springs from the becoming in which God's being is. The becoming in which God's being is is a becoming out of the word in which God says Yes to himself. But to God's affirmation of himself there corresponds the affirmation of the creature through God. In the affirmation of his creature, as this affirmation becomes event in the incarnation of God, God reiterates his self-relatedness in his relation to the creature, as revealer, as becoming revealed and as being revealed. This Christological relation to the creature is also a becoming in which God's being is. But in that God in Jesus Christ became man, he is as creature exposed to perishing. Is God's being in becoming, here, a being unto death?

The witness of the New Testament answers this question with the message of the death and resurrection of Jesus Christ. This message witnesses that there, where God's being-in-becoming was swallowed up in perishing, the perishing was swallowed up in the becoming. Therewith it was settled that God's being remains a being in becoming. With his "Yes" to man God remains in the event of the death of Jesus Christ true to himself as the triune God. In the death of Jesus Christ God's "Yes," which constitutes all being, exposed itself to the "No" of the nothing. In the resurrection of Jesus Christ this "Yes" prevailed over the "No" of the nothing. And precisely with this victory it was graciously settled why there is being at all, and not rather nothing. For:

> Were he not raised,
> Then the world would have perished;
> But since he is raised,
> Then praise we the Father of Jesus Christ.
> *Kyrie eleison!*

PART TWO

ALTERNATIVE PARADIGMS IN THEOLOGY

8

Theology of Religions

Most of the theological debates we have covered to this point have dealt with the internal crises of Christian faith in the context of modern culture. In the course of the colonial experience of Western nations, the Christian missionary encounter with people of other faiths, and the massive migrations of people to Europe and America from the Orient, the place of Christianity among the world religions has become an inescapable issue in twentieth-century theology. Ernst Troeltsch (1865–1923), both a theologian and a historian of religions, was the first to call for new thinking about the relation of Christianity to other religions, and is widely acknowledged by friend and foe as the father of the pluralist paradigm so much in vogue in current academic discussions.

Ernst Troeltsch was the systematic theologian of the history-of-religions school. He advocated a view of Christianity that would leave behind all dogmatism, supernaturalism, absolutism, and exclusivism. Studying all the religions strictly from a historical point of view, Troeltsch held that God's revelation in the Bible and through Jesus Christ represents only one stage in the universal history of divine revelation in the religions. In his book, *The Absoluteness of Christianity and the History of Religions,* Troeltsch argued that there can be no absolute religion in the midst of the relativities of history, because the absolute can be thought to lie only at the end of history. Even though Christianity does not represent a category different from other religions, it can be shown, also on purely historical grounds, to be relatively superior to all others through its cultural success, spiritual power, and rationality. Every religion is on the road to the Absolute in a way appropriate to its own cultural situation. For Troeltsch, Christianity is the religion of Europe and America, not a faith with universal validity for all other nations. The traditional aim of the Christian mission to convert persons of whatever religious background is therefore wrongheaded; at best, its aim should be a cross-fertilization of ideas in which Christianity might play a leading role in helping others to reach a greater fulfillment of their own potential. The historical relativity of Christianity implies that it must abandon its claim to possess the only saving revelation of God to the world. The revelation of God in Christ is but one slice of the loaf of God's revelation in the history of religions, and this Christian portion cannot claim to be the whole of universal revelation and salvation.

I

Karl Barth attacked the liberal theology of Troeltsch along with the entire stream of modern Protestant theology, though he himself never set out to write an alternative theology of the history of religions as such. It fell to Hendrik Kraemer (1888–1965), a Dutch missionary deeply influenced by the theology of Karl Barth and Emil Brunner, to work out a christocentric theology of religions, informed not only by his experience on the mission field in Indonesia but also by the pioneering Dutch phenomenology of religion, e.g., that of Gerardus van der Leeuw. If Troeltsch most clearly typifies the pluralist paradigm, now touted by John Hick and Paul Knitter, the twin leaders of today's pluralistic theory of religions, the Barth–Kraemer position represents with like distinctiveness the exclusivist paradigm. Kraemer wrote *The Christian Message in a Non-Christian World,* from which we have selected part of a chapter that expresses his understanding of the Christian approach to the world religions, as a study document for the International Missionary Council that met in Tambaram, India, in 1938. The core of this classic of missiology is the basic evangelical belief that "God has revealed the Way and the Life and the Truth in Jesus Christ and wills this to be known through all the world." For Troeltsch and the pluralists, Christ is *a* way, just one among many; for Barth, Kraemer, and evangelical exclusivists, he is *the* way, the only way that God has revealed for the salvation of humanity. A world of theological difference lies between the two little particles of speech.

Kraemer wrote many books and articles on the relation of Christianity to other religions, but he never modified his firm belief that salvation is a reality only on account of God's grace revealed in Jesus Christ: "I propose to set the religions, including Christianity, in the light of the Person of Jesus Christ, who is the Revelation of God and alone has the authority to criticize . . . every religion and everything that is in man or proceeds from him."

For this reason, Kraemer has no interest in searching for points of contact or continuity in religious experience, in the world religions, or in natural theology. In the light of Christ's judgment, these are all misdirected and irrelevant because they render the incarnation of God's only Son unnecessary.

The radical exclusivity of the Barth–Kraemer line paradoxically contains within itself an inclusive vision of the totality of humankind, based on divine grace rather than human religion. Neither Barth nor Kraemer saw any need for the religions to generate salvation—though it was admittedly their business to try—because God had already accomplished the world's salvation in Christ.

II

A third view beyond Troeltsch's pluralism and Kraemer's exclusivism is the inclusivist paradigm of Karl Rahner (1904–1984), the Jesuit theologian who more than any other revolutionized Roman Catholic thinking after Vatican II on the place of the non-Christian religions in God's universal plan of salvation. The traditional axiom, "no salvation outside the church," was reinterpreted by Rahner to mean that persons of other faiths who neither believe in Christ nor belong to his church may nevertheless be saved by observing their own religious rites and duties. In a highly controversial phrase, Rahner called such persons, not intending to be insulting, "anonymous Christians."

Rahner tries to hold together two seemingly incompatible propositions. With the pluralists, he affirms that an all-loving God would not consign people of other religions to everlasting hell through no fault of their own; with the exclusivists, he maintains that salvation is wrought by the grace of God through Christ alone as mediated by his church. How is it possible that the grace of God in Christ is savingly present in the non-Christian religions, through no awareness on their part? Rahner states that if we are to take seriously that God wills that all be saved, we must believe that somehow God offers his grace not only to the few who have heard and responded in faith to the gospel but to all human beings not in spite of but through their own concrete religions. Non-Christians who have truly accepted God's grace in the depths of their being may be regarded in some sense as fellow Christians, though unbeknown to them.

III

At the end of his career, Paul Tillich (1886–1965) was beginning to sketch the elements of a new theology of the history of religions. He did not get far because he realized that "we need a longer, more intensive period of interpenetration of systematic theological study and religious historical studies." Then he added that this was his hope for the future of theology.

Tillich's position parallels that of Rahner in some ways in that he also attempted to find a middle way between the pluralism of Troeltsch and the exclusivism of Barth and Kraemer. In place of Rahner's notion of "anonymous Christianity," Tillich offered the idea of the "latent church," to which persons might belong without believing in Christ or belonging to his church through baptism.

Tillich's positive estimate of the non-Christian religions was based on certain assumptions. First, there is divine revelation in all religions. Second, this revelation is always received in limited and distorted ways, also in Christianity. Third, it is necessary to subject the religions to theological criticism to discover what is of revelatory significance in them. Fourth, there is one event that unifies the multiplicity of revelatory experiences within the religions, and that event is the appearance of the New Being in Jesus as the Christ.

On the basis of these assumptions, Christian theology can enter into dialogue with representatives of other religions with an open and inquiring attitude, seeking to identify elements of value in their traditions. The New Testament itself, as the Old Testament before, clothed divine revelation and salvation in symbols and myths drawn from the religious traditions of the Mediterranean area. The figure of Jesus was placed in the context of a long preparation in religious history; God's revelation is always incarnate in concrete religious expressions. In Tillich's view, the whole history of revelation in the religions is a preparation for what he calls "the Religion of the Concrete Spirit." This religion cannot be identified with any particular religion, not even with Christianity as a religion. The inner aim of the history of religions is to be realized in such a Religion of the Concrete Spirit, yet not in the sense that is wholly future. We could say that all the religions contain authentic elements that point to this Religion of the Concrete Spirit. In addition to the christological criterion, the New Being in Jesus as the Christ, Tillich applied a prophetic criterion of the fight going on in the religions against the demonic. This fight is most clearly discernible in prophetic religion, sometimes in mysticism, but also in the secular critique that attacks demonic perversions of religion.

IV

The three models we have described as pluralist, exclusivist, and inclusivist are three distinctly possible ways of negotiating the relations between Christianity and the world religions. The plethora of books on this topic, however, indicate that this threefold scheme makes the available options seem much more neat and tidy than they actually are. Most theologians combine elements of strength—and sometimes also weaknesses—from all three positions. None of the theologians whose views we have highlighted can be so simply comprised by a label.

The theological problem that concerns all three positions is how God's universal salvific will can be accomplished and what role the religions plays as vehicles of divine revelation and salvation. How is a universal goal achieved by particular means? In the history of Christianity, there has always been a tension between those who stress the universality of God's will unto salvation and those who stress the particularity of the means chosen by God to realize his will. Both Catholics and Protestants have stressed the historical particularity of Christianity, Catholics with their belief in the indispensability of the one holy catholic church and Protestants with their belief in the necessity of personal faith in Jesus Christ. The particularists see that God has elected particular historical means to reveal and accomplish his mission in world history; the universalists with equal zeal tend to expand the definition of salvation to somehow include all the religions. This struggle continues to our day.

20. Paul Tillich, *The Significance of the History of Religions for the Systematic Theologian*

In this lecture, I wish to deal with three basic considerations. I call the first one "two basic decisions." A theologian who accepts the subject, "The Significance of the History of Religions for the Systematic Theologian," and takes this subject seriously, has already made, explicitly or implicitly, two basic decisions. On the one hand he has separated himself from a theology which rejects all religions other than that of which he is a theologian. On the other hand if one accepts the subject affirmatively and seriously, he has rejected the paradox of a religion of nonreligion, or a theology without *theos*, also called a theology of the secular.

Both of these attitudes have a long history. The former has been renewed in our century by Karl Barth. The latter is now most sharply expressed in the so-called theology-without-God language. For the former attitude, either the one religion is *vera religio*, true religion, against all others which are *religiones falsae*, false religions, or as it is expressed in modern terms, one's own religion is revelation, but the other religion is only a futile human attempt to reach God. This becomes the definition of all religion—a futile human attempt to reach God.

Therefore, from this point of view it is not worthwhile to go into the concrete differences of the religions. I remember the half-hearted way in which, for instance, Emil Brunner did it. I recall the theological isolation of historians of religion like my very highly esteemed friend, the late Rudolf Otto, and even today the similar situation of a man like Friedrich Heiler. Also one recalls the bitter attacks on Schleiermacher for his use of the concept of religion for Christianity. I remember the attacks on my views when for the first time (forty years ago) I gave a seminar on Schleiermacher at Marburg. Such an approach was considered a crime at that time.

In order to reject both this old and new orthodox attitude, one must accept the following systematic presuppositions. First, one must say that revelatory experiences are universally human. Religions are based on something that is given to a man wherever he lives. He is given a revelation, a particular kind of experience which always implies saving powers. One never can separate revelation and salvation. There are revealing and saving powers in all religions. God has not left himself unwitnessed. This is the first presupposition.

The second assumption states that revelation is received by man in terms of his finite human situation. Man is biologically, psychologically, and sociologically limited. Revelation is received under the conditions of man's estranged character. It is received always in a distorted form, especially if religion is used as a means to an end and not as an end in itself.

There is a third presupposition that one must accept. When systematic theologians assume the significance of the history of religions, it involves the belief that there are not only particular revelatory experiences throughout human history, but that there is a revelatory process in which the limits of adaptation and the failures of distortion are subjected to criticism. Such criticism takes three forms: the mystical, the prophetic, and the secular.

A fourth assumption is that there may be—and I stress this, there *may* be—a central event in the history of religions which unites the positive results of these critical developments in the history of religion in and under which revelatory experiences are going on—an event which, therefore, makes possible a concrete theology that has universalistic significance.

There is also a fifth presupposition. The history of religions in its essential nature does not exist alongside the history of culture. The sacred does not lie beside the secular, but it is its depths. The sacred is the creative ground and at the same time a critical judgment of the secular. But the religious can be this only if it is at the same time a judgment on itself, a judgment which must use the secular as a tool of one's own religious self-criticism.

Only if the theologian is willing to accept these five presuppositions can he seriously and fully affirm the significance of the history of religions for theology against those who reject such significance in the name of a new or of an old absolutism.

On the other hand, he who accepts the significance of the history of religion must stand against the no-God-language theology. He must reject also the exclusive emphasis on the secular or the idea that the sacred has, so to speak, been fully absorbed by the secular.

The last of the five points, the point about the relation of the sacred and the secular, has already reduced the threat of the "God is dead" oracle. Religion must use the secular as a critical tool against itself, but the decisive question is: *Why any religions at all?* Here one means religions in the sense of a realm of symbols, rites, and institutions. Can they not be neglected by a secular theologian in the same way he probably neglects the history of magic or of astrology? If he has no use for the idea of God, what can bring him to attribute high significance to the history of religion?

In order to affirm religion against the attack from this side, the theologian must have one basic presupposition. He must assume that religion as a structure of symbols of intuition and action—that means myths and rites within a social group—has lasting necessity for any, even the most secularized culture and the most demythologized theology. I derive this necessity, the lasting necessity of religion, from the fact that spirit requires embodiment in order to become real and effective. It is quite well to say that the Holy, or the Ultimate, or the Word is within the secular realm and I myself have done so innumerable times. But in order to say that something is *in* something, it must have at least a possibility to be *outside* of it. In other words, that which is *in* and that *in* which it is, must be distinguishable. In some way their manifestations must differ. And this is the question: *In what does the merely secular differ from that secular which would be the object of a secular theology?*

Let me say the same thing in a well-known, popular form. The reformers were right when they said that every day is the Lord's Day and, therefore, they devaluated the sacredness of the seventh day. But in order to say this, there must have been a Lord's Day, and that not only once upon a time but continuously in counterbalance against the overwhelming weight of the secular. This is what makes God-language necessary, however untraditional that language may be. This makes a serious affirmation of the history of religion possible.

Therefore, as theologians, we have to break through two barriers against a free approach to the history of religions: the orthodox-exclusive one and the secular-rejective one. The mere term "religion" still produces a flood of problems for the systematic theologian, and this is increased by the fact that the two fronts of resistance, though coming from opposite sides, involve an alliance. This has happened and *still* happens.

Both sides are reductionistic, and both are inclined to eliminate everything from Christianity except the figure of Jesus of Nazareth. The neo-orthodox group does this by making him the exclusive place where the word of revelation can be heard. The secular group does the same things by making him the representative of a theologically relevant secularity. But this can be done only if the picture and message of Jesus is itself drastically reduced. He must be limited to an embodiment of the ethical call, especially in the social direction, and this is then the only thing which is left of the whole message of the Christ. In *this* case, of course, history of religion is not needed any longer, not even the Jewish and Christian. Therefore, in order to have a valued, evaluated, and significant understanding of the history of religions, one has to break through the Jesus-centered alliance of the opposite poles, the orthodox as well as the secular.

Now I come to my second consideration: a theology of the history of religions. The traditional view of the history of religions is limited to that history as it is told in the Old and New Testament, and enlarged to include church history as the continuity of that history. Other religions are not qualitatively distinguished from each other. They all are perversions of a kind of original revelation but without particular revelatory experiences of any value for Christian theology. They are pagan religions, religions of the nations, but they are not bearers of revelation and salvation. Actually, this principle was never fully carried through. Jews and

Christians were both influenced religiously by the religions of conquered and conquering nations, and frequently these religions almost suffocated Judaism and Christianity and led to explosive reactions in both of them.

Therefore, what we need, if we want to accept the title of this lecture, "The Significance of the History of Religions for the Systematic Theologian," is a theology of the history of religions in which the positive valuation of universal revelation balances the critical one. Both are necessary. This theology of the history of religions can help systematic theologians to understand the present moment and the nature of our own historical place, both in the particular character of Christianity and in its universal claim.

I am still grateful, looking back to my own formative period of study and the time after it, to what in German is called the *religionsgeschichtliche Schule*, the School of History of Religions, in biblical and church historical studies. These studies opened our eyes and demonstrated the degree to which the biblical tradition participates in the Asia Minor and Mediterranean traditions. I remember the liberating effect of the understanding of universal, human motives in the stories of Genesis, or in Hellenistic existentialism and in Persian eschatology as they appeared in the late periods of the Old and New Testament.

From this point of view, all the history of religions produced symbols for savior figures which then supplied the framework for the New Testament understanding of Jesus and his work. This was liberating. These things did not fall from heaven like stones, but there was a long preparatory revelatory history which finally, in the *kairos*, in the right time, in the fulfilled time, made possible the appearance of Jesus as the Christ. All this was done without hurting the uniqueness of the prophetic attack on religion in the Old Testament and of the unique power of Jesus in the New Testament. Later on, in my own development, as in that of many other theologians, the significance was made clear both of the religions which surrounded the Old and New Testament situation, and the importance of religions farther removed from Biblical history.

The first question confronting a theology of the history of Israel and of the Christian Church is the history of salvation, but the history of salvation is something within the history. It is expressed in great symbolic moments, in *kairoi* such as the various efforts at reform in the history of the Church. In the same way, nobody would identify history of religions and history of salvation, or revelation, but one searches for symbolic moments. If the history of religions is taken seriously, are there *kairoi* in the general history of religions? Attempts have been made to find such *kairoi*. There was the enlightenment of the eighteenth century. Everything for these theologians was a preparation for the great *kairos*, the great moment, in which mature reason is reached in mankind. There are still religious elements in this reason: God, freedom, immortality. Kant developed it in his famous book, *Religion Within the Limits of Pure Reason*.

Another attempt was the romanticist understanding of history which led to Hegel's famous effort. From his point of view, there is a progressive history of religion. It progresses according to the basic philosophical categories which give the structure of all reality. Christianity is the highest and last point, and it is called "revealed religion," but this Christianity is philosophically demythologized. Such a view is a combination of Kantian philosophy and the message of the New Testament.

All earlier religions in Hegel's construction of the history of religions are *aufgehoben*, which can only be translated by two English words, namely, "taken in" and "removed." In this way, therefore, that which is past in the history of religion has lost its meaning. It is only an element in the later development. This means, for instance, that for Hegel the Indian religions are long, long past, long ago finished, and have no contemporary meaning. They belong to an early stage of history. Hegel's attempt to develop a theology of the history of religion resulted in the experiential theology which was very strong in America about thirty years ago. It was based on the idea of remaining open to new experiences of religious character in the future. Today men like Toynbee point in this direction—or perhaps look for that in religious experience which leads to a union of the great religions. In any case, it is a post-Christian era that is looking for such a construction.

It is necessary to mention also Teilhard de Chardin who stresses the development of a universal, divine-centered consciousness which is basically Christian. Christianity takes in all spiritual elements of the future. I am dissatisfied with such an attempt, I am also dissatisfied with my own, but I will give it in order to induce you to try yourself because that is what one should do if he takes the history of religions seriously.

My approach is dynamic-typological. There is no progressive development which goes on and on, but there are elements in the experience of the Holy which are always there, if the Holy is experienced. These elements, if they are predominant in one religion, create a particular religious type. It is necessary to go into greater depth, but I will only mention a tentative scheme which would appear this way. The universal religious base is the experience of the Holy within the finite. Universally in everything finite and particular, or in this and that finite, the Holy appears in a special way. I could call this the sacramental basis of all religions—the Holy here and now which can be seen, heard, dealt with, in spite of its mysterious character. We still have remnants of this in the highest religions, in their sacraments, and I believe that without it, a religious group would become an association of moral clubs, as much of Protestantism is, because it has lost the sacramental basis.

Then, there is a second element, namely a critical movement against the demonization of the sacramental, making it into an object which can be handled. This element is embodied in various critical ways. The first of these critical movements is mystical. This mystical movement means that one is not satisfied with any of the concrete expressions of the Ultimate, of the Holy. One goes beyond them. Man goes to the one beyond any manifoldness. The Holy as the

Ultimate lies beyond any of its embodiments. The embodiments are justified. They are accepted but they are secondary. One must go beyond them in order to reach the highest, the Ultimate itself. The particular is denied for the Ultimate One. The concrete is devaluated.

Another element, or the third element in the religious experience, is the element of "ought to be." This is the ethical or prophetic element. Here the sacramental is criticized because of demonic consequences like the denial of justice in the name of holiness. This is the whole fight of the Jewish prophets against sacramental religion. In some of the words of Amos and Hosea this is carried so far that the whole cult is abrogated. This criticism of the sacramental basis is decisive for Judaism and is one element in Christianity. But again I would say, if this is without the sacramental and the mystical element, then it becomes moralistic and finally secular.

I would like to describe the unity of these three elements in a religion which one could call—I hesitate to do so, but I don't know a better word—"The Religion of the Concrete Spirit." And it might well be that one can say the inner *telos*, which means the inner aim of a thing, such as the *telos* of the acorn is to become a tree—the inner aim of the history of religions is to become a Religion of the Concrete Spirit. But we cannot identify this Religion of the Concrete Spirit with any actual religion, not even Christianity as a religion. But I would dare to say, of course, dare as a Protestant theologian, that I believe that there is no higher expression for what I call the synthesis of these three elements than in Paul's doctrine of the Spirit. There we have the two fundamental elements: the ecstatic and the rational element united. There is ecstasy but the highest creation of the ecstasy is love in the sense of *agape*. There is ecstasy but the other creation of ecstasy is *gnosis*, the knowledge of God. It is knowledge, and it is not disorder and chaos.

The positive and negative relation of these elements or motives now gives the history of religions its dynamic character. The inner *telos* of which I spoke, the Religion of the Concrete Spirit, is, so to speak, that toward which everything drives. But we cannot say that this is a merely futuristic expectation. It appears everywhere in the struggle against the demonic resistance of the sacramental basis and the demonic and secularistic distortion of the critics of the sacramental basis. It appears in a fragmentary way in many moments in the history of religions. Therefore, we have to absorb the past history of religions, and annihilate it in this way, but we have a genuine living tradition consisting in the moments in which this great synthesis became, in a fragmentary way, reality. We can see the whole history of religions in this sense as a fight for the Religion of the Concrete Spirit, a fight of God against religion within religion. And this phrase, the fight of God within religion against religion, could become the key for understanding the otherwise extremely chaotic, or at least seemingly chaotic, history of religions.

Now, as Christians we see in the appearance of Jesus as the Christ the decisive victory in this struggle. There is an old symbol for the Christ, Christus Victor, and this can be used again in this view of the history of religions. And so it is already connected in the New Testament with the victory over the demonic powers and the astrological forces. It points to the victory on the cross as a negation of any demonic claim. And I believe we see here immediately that this can give us a Christological approach which could liberate us from many of the dead ends into which the discussion of the Christological dogma has led the Christian churches from the very beginning. In this way, the continuation of critical moments in history, of moments of *kairoi* in which the Religion of the Concrete Spirit is actualized fragmentarily can happen here and there.

The criterion for us as Christians is the event of the cross. That which has happened there in a symbolic way, which gives the criterion, also happens fragmentarily in other places, in other moments, has happened and will happen even though they are not historically or empirically connected with the cross.

Now I come to a question which was very much in the center of this whole conference, namely, how these dynamics of the history of religions are related to the relationship of the religious and of the secular. The holy is not only open to demonization and to the fight of God against religion as a fight against the demonic implications of religion. But the holy is also open to secularization. And these two, demonization and secularization, are related to each other insofar as secularization is the third and most radical form of dedemonization. Now, this is a very important systematic idea.

You know the meaning of the term, profane, "to be before the doors of the sanctuary," and the meaning of secular, "belonging to the world." In both cases, somebody leaves the ecstatic, mysterious fear of the Holy for the world of ordinary rational structures. It would be easy to fight against this, to keep the people in the sanctuary if the secular had not been given critical religious function by itself. And this makes the problem so serious. The secular is the rational and the rational must judge the irrationality of the Holy. It must judge its demonization.

The rational structure of which I am speaking implies the moral, the legal, the cognitive and the aesthetic. The consecration of life which the Holy gives is at the same time the domination of life by the ecstatic forms of the Holy, and the repression of the intrinsic demands of goodness, of justice, of truth and of beauty. Secularization occurring in such a context is liberation.

In this sense, both the prophets and the mystics were predecessors of the secular. The Holy became slowly the morally good, or the philosophically true, and later the scientifically true, or the aesthetically expressive. But then, a profound dialectic appears. The secular shows its inability to live by itself. The secular which is right in fighting against the domination by the Holy, becomes empty and becomes victim of what I call "quasi-religions." And these "quasi-religions" imply an oppressiveness like the demonic elements of the religions. But they are worse, as we have seen in our century, because they are without the depths and the richness of the genuine religious traditions.

And here, another *telos*, the inner aim of the history of religions, appears. I call it *theonomy* from *theos*—God and *nomos*—law. If the autonomous forces of knowledge, of aesthetics, of law and morals point to the ultimate meaning of life, then we have theonomy. Then they are not dominated, but in their inner being they point beyond themselves to the Ultimate. In reality, there takes place another dynamic struggle, namely, between a consecration of life, which becomes heteronomous and a self-actualization of all the cultural functions, which becomes autonomous and empty.

Theonomy appears in what I called "the Religion of the Concrete Spirit" in fragments, never fully. Its fulfillment is eschatological, its end is expectation which goes beyond time to eternity. This theonomous element in the relation of the sacred and the secular is an element in the structure of the Religion of the Concrete Spirit. It is certainly progressive, as every action is. Even to give a lecture has in itself the tendency to make progress in some direction, but it is not progressivistic—it doesn't imagine a temporal fulfillment once upon a time. And here I differ from Teilhard de Chardin to whom I feel very near in so many respects.

And now my third and last consideration: the interpretation of the theological tradition in the light of religious phenomena. Let me tell you about a great colleague, a much older colleague at the University of Berlin, Adolph Harnack. He once said that Christianity in its history embraces all elements of the history of religions. This was a partially true insight, but he did not follow it through. He did not see that if this is so, then there must be a much more positive relationship between the whole history of religion and the history of the Christian Church. And so, he narrowed down his own constructive theology to a kind of high bourgeois, individualistic, moralistic theology.

I now want to return my thanks on this point to my friend Professor Eliade for the two years of seminars and the cooperation we had in them. In these seminars I experienced that every individual doctrinal statement or ritual expression of Christianity receives a new intensity of meaning. And, in terms of a kind of an apologia yet also a self-accusation, I must say that my own *Systematic Theology* was written before these seminars and had another intention, namely, the apologetic discussion against and with the secular. Its purpose was the discussion or the answering of questions coming from the scientific and philosophical criticism of Christianity. But perhaps we need a longer, more intensive period of interpenetration of systematic theological study and religious historical studies. Under such circumstances the structure of religious thought might develop in connection with another or different fragmentary manifestation of theonomy or of the Religion of the Concrete Spirit. This is my hope for the future of theology.

To see this possibility one should look to the example of the emphasis on the particular which the method of the history of religions gives to the systematic theologian. It is to be seen in two negations: against a supranatural and against a natural theology. First, one sees this in supranatural theology which was the way classical Protestant orthodoxy formulated the idea of God in systematic theology. This concept of God appears in revelatory documents which are inspired but were not prepared for in history. For orthodoxy these views are found in the biblical books, or for Islam in the Koran. From there, dogmatic statements are prepared out of the material of the holy books by the Church, usually in connection with doctrinal struggles, formulated in creeds or official collections of doctrines, and theologically explained with the help of philosophy. All this was done without looking beyond the revelatory circle which one calls one's own religion or faith. This is the predominant method in all Christian churches.

Then there is the method of natural theology, the philosophical derivation of religious concepts from an analysis of reality encountered as a whole, and especially from an analysis of the structure of the human mind. Often these concepts, God and others, are then related to traditional doctrines; sometimes they are not related.

These are the two main methods traditionally used. The method of the history of religions takes the following steps: first, it uses the material of the tradition as existentially experienced by those who work theologically. But since one works theologically, he must also have the detachment which is necessary to observe any reality. This is the first step.

In the second step, the historian of religions takes over from the naturalistic methodology the analysis of mind and reality to show where the religious question is situated in human experiences both within ourselves and within our world. For instance, the experience of finitude, the experience of concern about the meaning of our being, the experience of the Holy as Holy, and so on.

Then the third step is to present a phenomenology of religion, showing the phenomena, especially that which shows itself in the history of religion—the symbols, the rites, the ideas, and the various activities. Then the fourth step consists in the attempt to point out the relation of these phenomena—their relatedness, their difference, their contradictions—to the traditional concepts and to the problems that emerge from this. Finally, the historian of religions tries to place the reinterpreted concepts into the framework of the dynamics of religious and of secular history and especially into the framework of our present religious and cultural situation. Now these five steps include part of the earlier methods but they introduce that which was done by the earlier methods into the context of the history of the human race and into the experiences of mankind as expressed in the great symbols of religious history.

The last point, namely, putting everything into the present situation leads to another advantage, or if you wish to call it so, to a new element of truth. This provides the possibility of understanding religious symbols in relation to the social matrix within which they have grown and into which we have to reintroduce them today. This is an exceedingly important step. Religious symbols are not stones falling from heaven. They have their roots in the totality of human experience including local surroundings, in all their ramifications, both political and economic. And these symbols then can be understood partly as in revolt against them. And in both cases, this is very important for our way of using symbols and reintroducing them.

A second positive consequence of this method is that we can use religious symbolism as a language of the doctrine of man, as the language of anthropology, not in the empirical sense of this word, but in the sense of doctrine of man — man in his true nature. The religious symbols say something to us about the way in which men have understood themselves in their very nature. The discussion about the emphasis on sin in Christianity and the lack of such emphasis in Islam is a good example. This shows a fundamental difference in the self-interpretation of two great religions and cultures, of men as men. And in this way, we enlarge our understanding of the nature of man in a way which is more embracing than any particular technical psychology.

But now my last word. What does this mean for our relationship to the religion of which one is a theologian? Such a theology remains rooted in its experiential basis. Without this, no theology at all is possible. But it tries to formulate the basic experiences which are universally valid in universally valid statements. The universality of a religious statement does not lie in an all-embracing abstraction which would destroy religion as such, but it lies in the depths of every concrete religion. Above all it lies in the openness to spiritual freedom both from one's own foundation and for one's own foundation.

21. Hendrik Kraemer, *Christian Attitudes toward Non-Christian Religions*

The Christian religion in its real sense, that is, as the revelation in Christ with all that that involves as to faith and ethics, revolves around two poles.

The first pole is knowledge of God of a very special kind that upsets all other conceptions of God or of the Divine. The God revealed and active in Christ is the holy, reconciling God. He is the God who, in his act of reconciling the world and man unto himself, manifested his holiness as well as his love. He set a new course so as to re-establish his rightful dominion of men on the foundation of a new relation of "love which has no dread in it."

The second pole is a knowledge of man, also of a very special kind and revolutionary in comparison with any other conception of man. Man, in the light of the revelation in Christ, is God's creature, destined to be his child and coworker, hence of great worth and great qualities. His nature and condition, however, have become perverted by a radical self-centeredness, explained in the Bible as the will to be "like God, knowing good and evil," the root of sin and death in the world. Man's God-rooted origin and end, and his splendid God-given qualities, assert themselves still in the ways in which he tries to master and regulate life, as manifested in his great achievements in the field of culture, art, science, political, social, and economic life. The perversion of sin, which permeates all his achievements with the will that makes for god-likeness, causes that in all things, not excepting the greatest and sublimest in any sphere of life, man is trying to evade his fundamental problem, namely, this perversion of sin. Yet at the same time, in these evasions he is trying to overcome and conquer—though unsuccessfully—by his own devices this his fundamental problem. Therefore human life in all its manifestations, abject as well as sublime, lies under the judgment of God and can only be redeemed and fundamentally renewed by recognizing wholeheartedly this judgment and the love and faith of God which are embodied therein. The wholehearted recognition and acceptance of God's judgment and love by man is called faith, and the life built on that kind of faith is called the new life of the Spirit. . . .

It is our task to determine against this background our attitude towards the non-Christian religions.

The problem of this attitude is, for various reasons, one of the greatest and gravest which the Christian Church all over the world and the missionary cause have to face at the present time. Properly speaking, it is part of the root-problem which occupies us through our whole discussion—that is, the Christian Church and the Christian religion in their relation to the world and its spheres of life. The question behind this root-problem is always in some form or another: What do you think about man, his nature, his possibilities, his achievements? It is very pertinent to remind ourselves of this, for two reasons.

First, the non-Christian religions are not merely sets of speculative ideas about the eternal destiny of man. The departmentalization of religion in the modern world as a result of the secularist differentiation of life-spheres strongly forces this erroneous conception of religion on the general mind. These non-Christian religions, however, are all-inclusive systems and theories of life, rooted in a religious basis, and therefore at the same time embrace a system of culture and civilization and a definite structure of society and state. To pronounce from the standpoint of the Christian faith upon our attitude towards the non-Christian religions necessarily means to pronounce upon the relation of the Christian faith to culture, state, society—in short, to the world and its spheres of life.

Secondly, the course usually followed—and which we shall follow too—when discussing the attitude of Christianity towards the non-Christian religions is that of expressing the whole problem in terms of the problems of general revelation and natural theology. This theological limitation of the discussion is all to the good, because it concentrates thought on the fundamental religious problems, effecting thereby a greater clarity of insight. It ought, however, constantly to be kept in mind that it is embedded in the all-embracing problem of the Christian religion or the Christian Church in its relation to the world. The great advantage that is to be derived from sticking to this commanding view is that the burning missionary problem of the attitude towards the non-Christian religions is a specimen of the great problem with which the Christian Church all over the world in different ways is inescapably confronted. In the condition of universal transition and revolutionary revision of culture, structure of state, society and economic order in which the world of to-day finds itself, the Church has to state anew its position in the obligation towards these spheres of life and their *present* presuppositions, pretensions, tendencies and values.

The confusion left behind in many minds from the discussion in the Jerusalem Meeting of the I.M.C. [International Missionary Council] in 1928 of the papers on the values of the different religions was due to the fact that the value of those religions was discussed in a too-isolated way and the religions were not therefore given their appropriate setting. The questions that, from the Christian point of view, i.e. the viewpoint of revelation, lie at the back of such terms as general revelation and natural theology may be expressed as follows. Are nature, reason and history sources of revelation in the Christian sense of the word? If so, what is the relation of the Christian revelation and its implications to the body of human self-unfolding which takes place in philosophy, religion, culture, art, and other domains of life? Whether the answer of the Christian Church is in the terms of a resolute renunciation of the world, as in the first centuries, or in those of a form of cooperation as in the Middle Ages, or is still different, depends wholly on the concrete circumstances of a given period and which aspect of its obligation as a Church, which lives by only one supreme loyalty, has to be operative in this given period.

There are, however, two conditions never to be lost sight of. In the first place, Christianity, under all circumstances, must always be aware that it is built on the prophetic and apostolic witness to a divine, transcendental order of life that transcends and judges by virtue of its inherent authority the whole range of historical human life in every period.

In the second place, whether the attitude is one of renunciation, of reserve or of intimate relation, it has to be essentially a *positive* attitude, because the world remains the domain of God who created it. After its rebellion against him, he did not let it go but held it fast in his new initiative of reconciliation. It must be a positive attitude also because the Christian Church, as the witness to and representative of the new order of salvation and reconciliation, has been set by God *in* this world in order to be and work for the sake of this world. Jesus taught us to pray, "God's will be done on earth as it is in heaven," and this petition will always be the Magna Charta of the Church's obligation to occupy itself strenuously and positively with the world and its spheres of life, including the non-Christian religions.

The two conditions just mentioned indicate clearly the dialectical relation in which Christianity, if true to its nature and mission, ought to stand to the world—the combination of a fierce "yes" and at the same time a fierce "no" to the world: the *human* and *broken* reflection of the divine "no" and "yes" of the holy God of reconciliation, who held the world under his absolute judgment and at the same time claimed it for his love.

Such are the perennial terms of the problem of the relation of Christianity to the world, which in every period of history require their peculiar expression and application. Now in turning to the great missionary problem of the attitude towards the non-Christian religions as a part of this all-inclusive problem, there are some considerations that ought to be continuously present in our mind when discussing it. The reason why we stand so badly in need of clarification about this problem is that the spiritual atmosphere of the present world makes it for the Christian Churches "at home" and in the non-Christian countries and for the vitality of the missionary cause a question of life or death. The "younger Churches" are living in a numerically overwhelming non-Christian world and in a not less overwhelming non-Christian atmosphere. To define their attitude towards these non-Christian religions is, on one hand, an indispensable necessity to them in order to develop the right sense of direction and certitude; on the other hand, it implies a judgment and evaluation not only of the *religious* life and heritage of their own people in the restricted sense of the word, but also of the whole cultural, social and political structure and heritage of the people of whom they physically and spiritually are a living part. At least, if they want to penetrate into the real meaning of the Christian religion and become conscious of its implications for their task in their environment, they need light as to their attitude. But even if they did not feel this desire, the present state of the non-Christian world with its social, political and cultural upheaval presses the problem in this all-inclusive form very urgently on their minds.

In addition—and this applies not alone to the Younger Churches but as much to the Christian Church in general and the missionary enterprise as such—the problem of the attitude towards the non-Christian religions as representative and massive structures of religious life has a setting quite of its own in the modern world in which we live, and a tone of particular gravity. A few centuries ago the attitude all over the world was to assume, as a matter of course, the unquestionable and unquestioned superiority and validity of one's own religion. The increasing contact which the different civilizations and religions have with each other, and the accompanying rise and development of the scientific study and comparison of religions, has radically changed this atmosphere and has made this attitude impossible. By painstaking research, by efforts to get an insight into the historical and psychological development of the different religions, we have today a knowledge of these religions more accurate and extensive than ever before. Amazing similarities and not less amazing dissimilarities in them have come to the light, and the result has been that the religious uncertainty and lack of a sense of direction, already flowing from other sources, have enormously increased. The question, "What is truth in religion?" is more urgent and more obscure than ever. This question is particularly urgent for Christianity, because it claims as its source and basis a divine revelation which at the same time is claimed to be the standard of reference for all truth and all religion. "I am the Way, the Truth and the Life. No one comes to the Father except through me" (John 14:6). "There is no salvation by anyone else, nor even a second Name under heaven appointed, for us men and our salvation" (Acts 4:12). This question of truth is particularly urgent for the missionary cause, because missions inevitably must love their vital impetus if this conviction becomes thin or turns out to be invalid, or is held with an uneasy conscience and a confused intellect. The psychological, cultural, social and moral value of Christianity may be rich and impressive; yea, it may even be still richer than can be demonstrated by historical research and clear reasoning, but this argument carries us only to the point that Christianity is an extraordinarily valuable asset of historic human life, and in all probability will continue in the future to be so. From the standpoint of human history and culture this is highly important, but it ignores entirely the claim for truth which is the core of all real religious life and especially of Christianity, the religion of God's sole incarnation in Jesus Christ.

The argument of value does not coincide in any way whatever with that of truth. The non-Christian religions can just as well as Christianity show up an impressive record of psychological, cultural and other values, and it is wholly dependent on one's fundamental axioms of life whether one considers these non-Christian achievements of higher value for mankind than the Christian. The weakness of the value-argument in relation to the problem of ultimate and authoritative truth is still more patent if one remembers that, from the standpoint of relative culture value, fictions and even lies have been extraordinarily valuable and successful. Today we are taught unforgettable lessons on this score. Learned, ingenious, enthusiastic apologies for Christianity or religion, which shun the problem of truth because of its difficulty and satisfy themselves with important secondary motivations, are bred in ambiguity. A pragmatist position means ultimate scepticism or agnosticism and involves the surrender of the problem of truth. At the end the problem of truth stares us always sternly in the face, because man's deepest and noblest instincts refuse to extinguish the mark of his divine origin, namely, his thirst for and want of imperishable truth. The subjectively motivated superiority of religious truths, experiences, and values can never substantiate the claim for truth or justify and keep alive a missionary movement. The only possible basis is the faith that God has revealed *the* Way and *the* Life and *the* Truth in Jesus Christ and wills this to be known through all the world. A missionary movement and obligation so founded is alone able to remain unshaken and undiscouraged, even when it is without visible result as, for example, is so largely true in the case of Islam.

And how are we to justify this faith? The only valid answer, which is at the same time according to the character and nature of faith, is that it will become justified in the end when God will fulfill his purpose. For "Faith is a well-grounded assurance of that for which we *hope*, and a conviction of the reality of

HENDRIK KRAEMER

things which we do *not* see" (Heb. 11:1). To demand a rational argument for faith is to make reason, that is, man, the standard of reference for faith, and ends in a vicious circle. Ultimate convictions never rest on a universally lucid and rational argument, in any philosophy and in any religion, and they never will. To adhere to a certain view of life and of the world has always meant a choice and a decision; not a rational step in the sense of being universally demonstrable as a mathematical truth. Religion and philosophy deal with different things from mathematics and physical science. They deal with man and his desires, his passions and aspirations; or—to put it more adequately—loving, hating, coveting, aspiring man tries to deal with himself in religion and philosophy, and this involves every moment ethical and religious choices and decisions. The Christian's ultimate ground of faith is: "The Spirit bears witness along with our own spirits that we are children of God" (Rom. 8:16); and he can die for that.

It has to be emphatically stated that the science of comparative religion, which brought and brings this confusion and anxiety, has exercised in many respects a highly salutary influence on religious life and our notions of it. Many fruits of the great humanistic movements of the last few centuries have made for a noble quest for truth, and for the liberation and widening of the human mind. So the science of comparative religion has effected in many directions a beneficent purification of religious insight. This remains true notwithstanding the many misguided notions and aberrations that it naturally entertained as being an occupation of human beings. In God's Hand it has become a means to unveil the stupendous richness of the religious life of mankind, in the good sense of the word as well as in the bad; to foster a spirit of openness and honesty towards this alien religious life; to undermine the unchristian intellectualistic and narrow-minded arrogance towards these other religions; to open the eyes to the often all-too-human element in Christianity in its historical development and reality, often as degrading as the basic elements in the other religions; to make aware of the petrification of faith and church-life into which the Christian Church slips as easily as other religions fall short of their original stimuli. Whosoever has learnt, with the aid of the science of comparative religion, to look honestly in the face the empirical reality of Christianity—I am not now speaking about the Christian revelation and its reality—and of the other religions, and has understood that Christianity as an historical religious body is thoroughly human, that is, a combination of sublime and abject and tolerable elements, will feel deeply that to speak glibly of the superiority of Christianity is offensive. Of course, there are many traits in which Christianity in its historical manifestation is superior to other religions; but of other traits the same can be said in regard to the non-Christian religions. The truly remarkable thing about Christianity as an historic and empirical reality, which differentiates it from all other religions, is rather that radical self-criticism is one of its chief characteristics, because the revelation in Christ to which it testifies erects the absolute

227

superiority of God's holy Will and judgment over *all* life, historical Christianity included.

The feeling of superiority is essentially a cultural, and not at all a religious, product; and decidedly not a Christian one. A feeling of superiority can only thrive on a definite consciousness of achievement. The famous student of religion, Troeltsch, who declined the Christian claim of representing the ultimate, exclusive truth as revealed in Jesus Christ, yet who nevertheless maintained a so-called relative absoluteness for Christianity, was virtually giving expression to his innate feeling of Western cultural achievement. There is no reason why a Hindu or a Chinese, being nurtured in his particular atmosphere, should not claim, after a comparative survey of the cultures and religions of the world, the same relative absoluteness with regard to his religion.

In the light of the Christian revelation, however, it is impossible and unnatural to think in terms of achievement, whether ethical or religious; for the heart of the Gospel is that we live by divine grace and forgiveness, and that God has *made* Jesus Christ for us "wisdom from God," "righteousness," "sanctification" and "redemption" in order that "he who boasts, let his boast be in the lord" (1 Cor. 1:30, 31) and not in any achievement of his own. Speaking strictly as a Christian, the feeling of superiority is the denial of what God meant and did through the Gospel. That in Christianity and in the mission field the superiority-feeling has so many victims indicates the intellectualist distortion of the Gospel into which pious Christians can lapse, by forgetting that to be a Christian means always and in all circumstances to be a forgiven sinner and never the *beatus possidens* of ready-made truth. In one of the preparatory papers for the Oxford Conference, Niebuhr makes the acute observation, which is pertinent to this attitude: "The final symbol of the perennial character of human sin is in the fact that the theologies, which preach humility and contrition, can nevertheless be vehicles of human pride."

Three points of crucial importance have now become clear. In the first place, the attitude towards the non-Christian religions is to be seen in the context of the general problem of the relation of Christianity to the world and its spheres of life. To define our attitude towards these religions virtually means to affirm our conception of man and his faculties, to pass judgment on our fellow-man and his aspirations, attainments and aberrations.

Secondly, it confronts us with the question of normative truth. In both cases it is clear that for a Christian the only standard of reference can be the new and incommensurable world which has been revealed and made real by God in Jesus Christ and his life and work, and which is accessible to faith alone, that is, the free affirmative answer of man to God's "wonderful deeds." Christ, as the ultimate standard of reference, is the crisis of all religions, of the non-Christian religions and of empirical Christianity too. This implies that the most fruitful and legitimate way to analyse and evaluate all religions is to investigate them in the light of the revelation of Christ.

In the third place, the character of this faith and the nature of the divine truth of revelation consists not in general ideas but in fundamental conditions and relations between God, man and the world. Strengthened by the liberating work of the science of comparative religion, it excludes all feeling of superiority, requiring an honest recognition of our common humanity with adherents of other religions, as well in religious attainments as in religious defects. A missionary or a Christian who harbours the tiniest spark of spiritual arrogance and boasts of "his" superiority by being a Christian and "having" the truth, grieves the Spirit of Christ and obscures his message, because the foundation of the Christian life is to "boast in the Lord" and to rejoice gratefully and humbly in *his* mercy.

We must, however, go still further. From the standpoint of the Christian revelation, what answer can be given to the question: Does God—and if so, how and where does God—reveal himself in the religious life as present in the non-Christian religions?

This question is more difficult than it appears. Surveying human endeavor towards spiritual expression over the whole range of life, the obvious statement to be made is that all religions, the so-called "higher" as well as the so-called "lower" ones, all philosophies and world-views, are the various efforts of man to apprehend the totality of existence, often stirring in their sublimity and as often pathetic or revolting in their ineffectiveness. So philosophy is this effort towards apprehension by way of knowledge; religion is the same effort by way of the heart; theology, as, for example, Moslem theology or Ramanuja's bhakti-theology, is an effort to reflect in a system of coherent thinking the religious apprehension of existence. This universal effort towards the apprehension of the totality of existence being the effort of man, it is quite natural that there should be an amazing amount of concurrence as to the aspirations, ideas, institutions, symbols and intuitions in all the religions and philosophies of mankind, despite their great variations caused by differences of environment, mental structure and historical development. There is a universal religious consciousness amongst men of all ages and climes and races, which evidently produces in very different forms and concatenations many similar data and symbols of religious and ethical insight. Hence the well-known fact that, whether we live with peoples of "higher" or of "lower" religions, we so often recognize our own religious or ethical aspirations or insight, and that many a religious handbook, which has fame and authority with the followers of the religion which produced it, is equally valued by followers of other religions. Take, for example, the *Tao Teh King*, the *Bhagavadgita*, the *Kural* of Tiruvalluvar, the *Imitatio*, and some Moslem handbooks of religion and ethics. Another well-known fact is that again and again people arise who try to construe out of these concurring religious and ethical evidences the "normal," "natural" religion of mankind. This endeavour, although quite intelligible on account of the mentioned similarities, is false. It confuses concurrent but widely scattered, unevenly distributed, differently graded and differently motivated religious and ethical notions, with a supposedly coherent system, governed by some leading general ideas which the creators of this "natural" religion arbitrarily put upon it. As scientific research and critical thinking both teach, there is no "natural" religion; there is only a universal religious consciousness in man, which produces many similarities. Besides that, there are concrete religions, each with its peculiar structure and character.

Man's dangerous condition is that he is a dual being. He is a divine origin, and he is corrupted by sin and constantly prone to assert his self-centered and disordered will against the divine will. In a magnificent way Pascal has expressed this in his *Pensées*. He says: "*Quelle chimére est-ce donc quel'homme! Quelle nouveauté! quel monstre, quel chaos, quel sujet de contradiction, quel prodige! Juge de toutes choses, imbécile ver de terre, dépositaire du vrai, cloaque d'incertitude et d'erreur, gloire et rebut de l'univers.*" (What a chimera man is! What a novelty, what a monster, how chaotic, how full of contradictions, what a marvel! Judge of all things, a stupid earthworm, a depository of truth, a heap of uncertainty and error, the glory and refuse of the universe.) This fundamental disharmony is also manifested in all the spheres of life in which man moves, and in his cultural and religious achievements. His divine origin and his great gifts make him a creature that masters and regulates life in many ways, and that develops great cultures and civilizations. The development and progress which can be traced in their history are the manifestation of the deep urge of his splendid faculties and of his destiny "to subdue and master the earth and all that is in it" (Gen. 1:28).

In the domain of the religious consciousness man's possibilities and abilities shine in the lofty religions and the ethical systems that he has produced and tried to live by. The non-Christian world in the past and the present offers many illustrious examples. His sin and his subjection to evil and to satanic forces, however, corrupt all his creations and achievements, even the sublimest, in the most vicious way. The mystic, who triumphantly realizes his essential one-ness with God or the Divine, knowing himself in serene equanimity the supreme master of the universe and of destiny, and who by his marvelous feats of moral self-restraint and spiritual self-discipline offers a fascinating example of splendid humanity, commits in this sublime way the root-sin of mankind, "to be like God" (Gen. 3:5). The splendid results of human mastery of the laws of nature and of human inventiveness become the instruments of the most barbarous and monstrous violations of elementary humanity. The world of development and progress is at the same time the world of degeneration, decay and destruction. The doom of death, corruption and demonic self-destruction is always hovering over this splendid world of man and nature. Hence the universal religious consciousness of man has everywhere produced also the most abhorrent and degrading filth that perverted human imagination and lust can beget. This fundamental and horrid disharmony, this dialectical condition of man is called by the Christian revelation, as contained in Biblical realism, sin, guilt, lostness past recovery except by God himself; and no other religion does this in such unmistakable and consistent terms. The universal religious consciousness of man itself nowhere speaks this clear language, because it is confused and blinded by its inherent disharmony.

The Christian revelation places itself over against the many efforts to apprehend the totality of existence. It asserts itself as the record of God's self-disclosing and recreating revelation in Jesus Christ, as an apprehension of existence that revolves around the poles of divine judgment and divine salvation, giving the divine answer to this demonic and guilty disharmony of man and the world.

22. Karl Rahner, *Christianity and the Non-Christian Religions*

"Open Catholicism" involves two things. It signifies the fact that the Catholic Church is opposed by historical forces which she herself cannot disregard as if they were purely worldly forces and a matter of indifference to her but which, on the contrary, although they do not stand in a positive relationship of peace and mutual recognition to the Church, do have a significance for her. "Open Catholicism" means also the task of becoming related to these forces in order to understand their existence (since this cannot be simply acknowledged), in order to bear with and overcome the annoyance of their opposition and in order to form the Church in such a way that she will be able to overcome as much of this pluralism as should not exist, by understanding herself as the higher unity of this opposition. "Open Catholicism" means therefore a certain attitude towards the present-day pluralism of powers with different outlooks on the world. We do not, of course, refer to pluralism merely as a fact which one simply acknowledges without explaining it. Pluralism is meant here as a fact which ought to be thought about and one which, without denying that—in part at least—it should not exist at all, should be incorporated once more from a more elevated viewpoint into the totality and unity of the Christian understanding of human existence. For Christianity, one of the gravest elements of this pluralism in which we live and with which we must come to terms, and indeed the element most difficult to incorporate, is the pluralism of religions. We do not refer by this to the pluralism of Christian denominations. This pluralism too is a fact, and a challenge and task for Christians. But we are not concerned with it here.

Our subject is the more serious problem, at least in its ultimate and basic form, of the different religions which still exist even in Christian times, and this after a history and mission of Christianity which has already lasted two thousand years. It is true, certainly, that all these religions together, including Christianity, are faced today with an enemy which did not exist for them in the past. We refer to the decided lack of religion and the denial of religion in general. This denial, in a sense, takes the stage with the ardour of a religion and of an absolute and sacred system which is the basis and the yard-stick of all further thought. This denial, organized on the basis of a State, represents itself as the religion of the future — as the decided, absolute secularization of human existence excluding all mystery. No matter how paradoxical this may sound, it does remain true that precisely this state of siege in which religion in general finds itself, finds one of its most important weapons and opportunities for success in the fact that humanity is so torn in its religious adherence. But quite apart from this, this pluralism is a greater threat and a reason for greater unrest for Christianity than for any other religion. For no other religion — not even Islam — maintains so absolutely that it is the religion, the one and only valid revelation of the one living God, as does the Christian religion.

The fact of the pluralism of religions, which endures and still from time to time becomes virulent anew even after a history of two thousand years, must therefore be the greatest scandal and the greatest vexation for Christianity. And the threat of this vexation is also greater for the individual Christian today than ever before. For in the past, the other religion was in practice the religions of a completely different cultural environment. It belonged to a history with which the individual only communicated very much on the periphery of his own history; it was the religion of those who were even in every other respect alien to oneself. It is not surprising, therefore, that people did not wonder at the fact that these "others" and "strangers" had also a different religion. No wonder that in general people could not seriously consider these other religions as a challenge posed to themselves or even as a possibility for themselves. Today things have changed. The West is no longer shut up in itself; it can longer regard itself simply as the centre of the history of this world and as the centre of culture, with a religion which even from this point of view (i.e. from a point of view which has really nothing to do with a decision of faith but which simply carries the weight of something quite self-evident) could appear as the obvious and indeed sole way of honouring God to be thought of for a European. Today everybody is the next-door neighbor and spiritual neighbor of everyone else in the world. And so everybody today is determined by the intercommunication of all those situations of life which affect the whole world. Every religion which exists in the world is — just like all cultural possibilities and actualities of other people — a question posed, and a possibility offered, to every person. And just as one experiences someone else's culture in practice as something relative to one's own and as something existentially demanding, so it is also involuntarily with alien religions. They have become part of one's own existential situation — no longer merely theoretically but in the concrete — and we experience them therefore as something which puts the absolute claim of our own Christian faith into question. Hence, the question about the understanding of and the continuing existence of religious pluralism as a factor of our immediate Christian existence is an urgent one and part of the question as to how we are to deal with today's pluralism.

This problem could be tackled from different angles. In the present context we simply wish to try to describe a few of those basic traits of a Catholic dogmatic interpretation of the non-Christian religions which may help us to come closer to a solution of the question about the Christian position in regard to the religious pluralism in the world of today. Since it cannot be said, unfortunately, that Catholic theology—as practiced in more recent times—has really paid sufficient attention to the questions to be posed here, it will also be impossible to maintain that what we will have to say here can be taken as the common thought of Catholic theology. What we have to say carries, therefore, only as much weight as the reasons we can adduce, which reasons can again only be briefly indicated. Whenever the propositions to be mentioned carry a greater weight than this in theology, anyone trained in theology will realize it quite clearly from what is said. When we say that it is a question here of a *Catholic* dogmatic interpretation of the non-Christian religions, this is not meant to indicate that it is necessarily a question also of theories controverted among Christians themselves. It simply means that we will not be able to enter explicitly into the question as to whether the theses to be stated here can also hope to prove acceptable to Protestant theology. We say too that we are going to give a dogmatic interpretation, since we will pose our question not as empirical historians of religion but out of the self-understanding of Christianity itself, i.e., as dogmatic theologians.

First Thesis: We must begin with the thesis which follows, because it certainly represents the basis in the Christian faith of the theological understanding of other religions. This thesis states that Christianity understands itself as the absolute religion, intended for all men, which cannot recognize any other religion beside itself as of equal right. This proposition is self-evident and basic for Christianity's understanding of itself. There is no need here to prove it or to develop its meaning. After all, Christianity does not take valid and lawful religion to mean primarily that relationship of man to God which man himself institutes on his own authority. Valid and lawful religion does not mean man's own interpretation of human existence. It is not the reflection and objectification of the experience which man has of himself and by himself.

Valid and lawful religion for Christianity is rather God's action on men, God's free self-revelation by communicating himself to man. It is God's relationship to men, freely instituted by God himself and revealed by God in this institution. *This* relationship of God to man is basically the same for all men, because it rests on the Incarnation, death and resurrection of the one Word of God become flesh. Christianity is God's own interpretation in his Word of this relationship of God to man founded in Christ by God himself. And so Christianity can recognize itself as the true and lawful religion for all men only where and when it enters with existential power and demanding force into the realm of another religion and—judging it by itself—puts it in question. Since the time of Christ's coming—ever since he came in the flesh as the Word of God in absoluteness and reconciled, i.e. united the world with God by his death and resurrection, not merely theoretically but really-Christ and his continuing historical presence in the World (which we call "Church") is *the* religion which binds man to God.

Already we must, however, make one point clear as regards this first thesis (which cannot be further developed and proved here). It is true that the Christian religion itself has its own pre-history which traces this religion back to the beginning of the history of humanity—even though it does this by many basic steps. it is also true that this fact of having a pre-history is of much greater importance, according to the evidence of the New Testament, for the theoretical and practical proof of the claim to absolute truth made by the Christian religion than our current fundamental theology is aware of. Nevertheless, the Christian religion as such has a beginning in history; it did not always exist but began at some point in time. It has not always and everywhere been *the* way of salvation for men—at least not in its historically tangible ecclesio-sociological constitution and in the reflex fruition of God's saving activity in, and in view of, Christ. As a historical quantity Christianity has, therefore, a temporal and spatial starting point in Jesus of Nazareth and in the saving event of the unique Cross and the empty tomb in Jerusalem. It follows from this, however, that this absolute religion—even when it begins to be this for practically all men—must come in a historical way to men, facing them as the only legitimate and demanding religion for them. It is therefore a question of whether this moment, when the existentially real demand is made by the absolute religion in its historically tangible form, takes place really at the same chronological moment for all people, or whether the occurrence of this moment has itself a history and thus is not chronologically simultaneous for all people, cultures and spaces of history. (This is a question which up until now Catholic theology has not thought through with sufficient clarity and reflection by really confronting it with the length and intricacy of real human time and history.) Normally the beginning of the objective obligation of the Christian message for all men—in other words, the abolition of the validity of the Mosaic religion *and* of all other religions which (as we will see later) may also have a period of validity and of being-willed-by-God—is thought to occur in the apostolic age. Normally, therefore, one regards the time between this beginning and the actual acceptance of the personally guilty refusal of Christianity in a non-Jewish world and history as the span between the already given promulgation of the law and the moment when the one to whom the law refers takes cognizance of it.

It is not just an idle academic question to ask whether such a conception is correct or whether, as we maintain, there could be a different opinion in this matter, i.e. whether one could hold that the beginning of Christianity for actual periods of history, for cultures and religions, could be postponed to those moments in time when Christianity became a real historical factor in an individual history and culture—a real historical moment in a particular culture. For instance, one concludes from the first, usual answer that *everywhere* in the world, since the first Pentecost, baptism of children dying before reaching the use of reason is necessary for their supernatural salvation, although this was not necessary before that time. For other questions, too, a correct and considered solution of the present question could be of great importance, as for instance for the avoidance of immature conversions, for the justification and importance of "indirect" missionary work, etc. One will have to ask oneself whether one can still agree today with the first opinion mentioned above, in view of the history of the missions which has already lasted two thousand years and yet is still to a great extent in its beginnings—for even Suarez himself, for instance, had already seen (at least with regard to the Jews) that the *promulgatio* and *obligatio* of the Christian religion, and not merely the *divulgatio* and *notitia promulgationis*, take place in historical sequence. We cannot really answer this question here, but it may at least be pointed out as an open question; in practice, the correctness of the second theory may be presupposed since it alone corresponds to the real historicity of Christianity and salvation-history.

From this there follows a delicately differentiated understanding of our first thesis: we maintain positively only that, as regards destination, Christianity is the absolute and hence the only religion for all men. We leave it, however, an open question (at least in principle) at what exact point in time the absolute obligation of the Christian religion has in fact come into effect for every man and culture, even in the sense of the *objective* obligation of such a demand. Nevertheless— and this leaves the thesis formulated still sufficiently exciting—wherever in practice Christianity reaches man in the real urgency and rigour of his actual existence, Christianity—once understood—presents itself as the only still valid religion for this man, a necessary means for his salvation and not merely an obligation with the necessity of a precept. It should be noted that this is a question of the necessity of a social form for salvation. Even though this is Christianity and not some other religion, it may surely still be said without hesitation that this thesis contains implicitly another thesis which states that in concrete human existence as such, the nature of religion itself must include a social constitution—which means that religion can exist only in a social form. This means, therefore, that man, who is commanded to have a religion, is also commanded to seek and accept a social form of religion. It will soon become clear what this reflection implies for the estimation of non-Christian religions.

Finally, we may mention one further point in this connection. What is vital in the *notion* of *paganism* and hence also of the non-Christian pagan religions (taking "pagan" here as a theological concept without any disparaging intent) is not the actual refusal to accept the Christian religion but the absence of any sufficient historical encounter with Christianity which would have enough historical power to render the Christian religion really present in this pagan society and in the history of the people concerned. If this is so, then paganism ceases to exist in this sense by reason of what is happening today. For the Western world is opening out into a universal world history in which every people and every cultural sector becomes an inner factor of every other people and every other cultural sector. Or rather, paganism is slowly entering a new phase: there is *one* history of the world, and in this *one* history both the Christians and the non-Christians (i.e. the old and new pagans together) live in one and the same situation and face each other in dialogue, and thus the question of the theological meaning of the other religions arises once more and with even greater urgency.

Second Thesis: Until the moment when the Gospel really enters into the historical situation of an individual, a non-Christian religion (even outside the Mosaic religion) does not merely contain elements of a natural knowledge of God, elements, moreover, mixed up with human depravity which is the result of original sin and later aberrations. It contains also supernatural elements arising out of the grace which is given to men as a gratuitous gift on account of Christ. For this reason a non-Christian religion can be recognized as a *lawful* religion (although only in different degrees) without thereby denying the error and depravity contained in it. This thesis requires a more extensive explanation.

We must first of all note the point up to which this evaluation of the non-Christian religions is valid. This is the point in time when the Christian religion becomes a historically real factor for those who are of this religion. Whether this point is the same, theologically speaking, as the first Pentecost, or whether it is different in chronological time for individual peoples and religions, is something which even at this point will have to be left to a certain extent an open question. We have, however, chosen our formulation in such a way that it points more in the direction of the opinion which seems to us the more correct one in the matter although the *criteria* for a more exact determination of this moment in time must again be left an open question.

The thesis itself is divided into two parts. It means first of all that it is *a priori* quite possible to suppose that there are supernatural, grace-filled elements in non-Christian religions. Let us first of all deal with this statement. It does not mean, of course, that all the elements of a polytheistic conception of the divine, and all the other religious, ethical and metaphysical aberrations contained in the non-Christian religions, are to be or may be treated as harmless either in theory or in practice. There have been constant protests against such elements throughout the history of Christianity and throughout the history of the Christian interpretation of the non-Christian religions, starting with the Epistle to the Romans and following on the Old Testament polemics against the religion of the "heathens." Every one of these protests is still valid in what was really meant and expressed by them. Every such protest remains a part of the message which Christianity and the Church has to give to the peoples who profess such religions. Furthermore, we are not concerned here with an *a posteriori* history of religions. Consequently, we also cannot describe empirically what should not exist and what is opposed to God's will in these non-Christian religions, nor can we represent these things in

236

their many forms and degrees. We are here concerned with dogmatic theology and so can merely repeat the universal and unqualified verdict as to the unlawfulness of the non-Christian religions right from the moment when they came into real and historically powerful contact with Christianity (and at first only thus!). It is clear, however, that this condemnation does not mean to deny the very basic differences within the non-Christian religions especially since the pious, God-pleasing pagan was already a theme of the Old Testament, and especially since this God-pleasing pagan cannot simply be thought of as living absolutely outside the concrete socially constituted religion and constructing his own religion on his native foundations—just as St. Paul in his speech on the Areopagus did not simply exclude a positive and basic view of the pagan religion.

The decisive reason for the first part of our thesis is basically a theological consideration. This consideration (prescinding from certain more precise qualifications) rests ultimately on the fact that, if we wish to be Christians, we must profess belief in the universal and serious salvific purpose of God towards all men, which is true even within the post-paradisean phase of salvation dominated by original sin. We know, to be sure, that this proposition of faith does not say anything certain about the *individual* salvation of man understood as something which has in fact been reached. But God desires the salvation of everyone. And this salvation willed by God is the salvation won by Christ, the salvation of supernatural grace which divinizes man, the salvation of the beatific vision. It is a salvation really intended for all those millions upon millions of people who lived perhaps a million years before Christ—and also for those who have lived after Christ—in nations, cultures and epochs of a very wide range which were still completely shut off from the viewpoint of those living in the light of the New Testament. If, on the one hand, we conceive salvation as something specifically *Christian*, if there is no salvation apart from Christ, if according to Catholic teaching the supernatural divinization of mankind can never be replaced merely by good will on the part of man but is necessary as something itself given in this earthly life; and if, on the other hand, God has really, truly and seriously intended this salvation for all men—then these two aspects cannot be reconciled in any other way than by stating that every human being is really and truly exposed to the influence of divine, supernatural grace which offers an interior union with God and by means of which God communicates himself whether the individual takes up an attitude of acceptance or of refusal towards this grace. It is senseless to suppose cruelly—and without any hope of acceptance by the man of today, in view of the enormous extent of the extra-Christian history of salvation and damnation—that nearly all men living outside the official and public Christianity are so evil and stubborn that the offer of supernatural grace ought not even to be made in fact in most cases, since these individuals have already rendered themselves unworthy of such an offer by previous, subjectively grave offenses against the natural moral law.

If one gives more exact theological thought to this matter, then one cannot regard nature and grace as two phases in the life of the individual which follow each other in time. It is furthermore impossible to think that this offer of supernatural, divinizing grace made to all men on account of the universal salvific purpose of God, should in general (prescinding from the relatively few exceptions) remain ineffective in most cases on account of the personal guilt of the individual. For, as far as the Gospel is concerned, we have no really conclusive reason for thinking so pessimistically of men. On the other hand, and contrary to every merely human experience, we do have every reason for thinking optimistically of God and his salvific will which is more powerful than the extremely limited stupidity and evil-mindedness of men. However little we can say with certitude about the final lot of an individual inside or outside the officially constituted Christian religion, we have every reason to think optimistically—i.e. truly hopefully and confidently in a Christian sense—of God who has certainly the last word and who has revealed to us that he has spoken his powerful word of reconciliation and forgiveness into the world. If it is true that the eternal Word of God has become flesh and has died the death of sin for the sake of our salvation and in spite of our guilt, then the Christian has no right to suppose that the fate of the world—having regard to the whole of the world—takes the same course on account of man's refusal as it would have taken if Christ had not come. Christ and his salvation are not simply one of two possibilities offering themselves to man's free choice; they are the need of God which bursts open and redeems the false choice of man by overtaking it. In Christ God not only gives the *possibility* of salvation, which in that case would still have to be effected by man himself, but the actual salvation itself, however much this includes also the right decision of human freedom which is itself a gift from God. Where sin already existed, grace came in superabundance. And hence we have every right to suppose that grace has not only been offered even outside the Christian Church (to deny this would be the error of Jansenism) but also that, in a great many cases at least, grace gains the victory in man's free acceptance of it, this being again the result of grace.

Of course, we would have to show more explicitly than the shortness of time permits that the empirical picture of human beings, their life, their religion and their individual and universal history does not disprove this optimism of a faith which knows the whole world to be subjected to the salvation won by Christ. But we must remember that the theoretical and ritualistic factors in good and evil are only a very inadequate expression of what man actually accomplishes in practice. We must remember that the same transcendence of man (even the transcendence elevated and liberated by God's grace) can be exercised in many different ways and under the most varied labels. We must take into consideration that whenever the religious person acts really religiously, he makes use of, or omits unthinkingly, the manifold forms of religious institutions by making a consciously critical choice among and between them. We must consider the immeasurable difference—which it seems right to suppose to exist even in the Christian sphere—between what is objectively wrong in moral life and the extent to which this is really realized with subjectively grave guilt. Once we take all this into consideration, we will not hold it to be impossible that grace is at work, and is even being accepted, in the spiritual, personal life of the individual, no matter how primitive, unenlightened, apathetic and earth-bound such a life may at first sight appear to be. We can say quite simply that, wherever, and in so far as, the individual makes a moral decision in his life (and where could this be declared to be in any way absolutely impossible — except in precisely "pathological" cases?), this moral decision can also be thought to measure up to the character of a supernaturally elevated, believing and thus saving act, and hence to be more in actual fact than merely "natural morality." Hence, if one believes seriously in the universal salvific purpose of God towards all men in Christ, it need not and cannot really be doubted that gratuitous influences of properly Christian supernatural grace are conceivable in the life of all men (provided they are first of all regarded as individuals) and that these influences can be presumed to be accepted in spite of the sinful state of men and in spite of their apparent estrangement from God.

Our second thesis goes even further than this, however, and states in its second part that, from what has been said, the actual religions of "pre-Christian" humanity too must not be regarded as simply illegitimate from the very start, but must be seen as quite capable of having a positive significance. This statement must naturally be taken in a very different sense which we cannot examine here for the various particular religions. This means that the different religions will be able to lay claim to being lawful religions only in very different senses and to very different degrees. But precisely this variability is not at all excluded by the notion of a "lawful religion," as we will have to show in a moment. A lawful religion means here an institutional religion whose "use" by man at a certain period can be regarded on the whole as a positive means of gaining the right relationship to God and thus for the attaining of salvation, a means which is therefore positively included in God's plan of salvation.

That such a notion and the reality to which it refers can exist even where such a religion shows many theoretical and practical errors in its concrete form becomes clear in a theological analysis of the structure of the Old Covenant. We must first of all remember in this connection that only in the New Testament — in the Church of Christ understood as something which is eschatologically final and *hence* (and only for this reason) "indefectible" and infallible — is there realized the notion of a Church which, because it is instituted by God in some way or other, already contains the permanent norm of differentiation between what is right (i.e. willed by God) and what is wrong in the religious sphere, and contains it both as a permanent institution and as an intrinsic element of this religion. There was nothing like this in the Old Testament, although it must undoubtedly be recognized as a lawful religion. The Old Covenant — understood as a concrete, historical and religious manifestation — contained what is right, willed by God, and what is false, erroneous, wrongly developed and depraved. But there was no permanent, continuing and institutional court of appeal in the Old

Covenant which could have differentiated authoritatively, always and with certainty for the conscience of the individual between what was willed by God and what was due to human corruption in the actual religion. Of course, there were the prophets. They were not a permanent institution, however, but a conscience which had always to assert itself anew on behalf of the people in order to protest against the corruption of the religion as it existed at the time, thus—incidentally—confirming the existence of this corruption. The official, institutional forms known as the "kingdom" and the priesthood were so little proof against this God-offending corruption that they could bring about the ruin of the Israelitic religion itself. And since there were also pseudo-prophets, and no infallible "institutional" court of appeal for distinguishing genuine and false prophecy, it was—in the last analysis—left to the conscience of the individual Israelite himself to differentiate between what in the concrete appearance of the Israelitic religion was the true covenant with God and what was a humanly free, and so in certain cases falsifying, interpretation and corruption of this God-instituted religion. There might have been objective criteria for such a distinction of spirits, but their application could not simply be left to an "ecclesiastical" court—not even in the most decisive questions—since official judgments could be wrong even about these questions and in fact were completely wrong about them.

This and nothing more—complete with its distinction between what was willed by God and what was human, all too human, a distinction which was ultimately left to be decided by the individual—was the concrete Israelitic religion. The Holy Scriptures do indeed give us the official and valid deposit to help us differentiate among the spirits which moved the history of the Old Testament religion. But since the infallible delimitation of the canon of the Old Testament is again to be found only in the New Testament, the exact and final differentiation between the lawful and the unlawful in the Old Testament religion is again possible only by making use of the New Testament as something eschatologically final. The unity of the concrete religion of the Old Testament, which (ultimately) could be distinguished only gropingly and at one's own risk, was however the unity willed by God, providential for the Israelites in the order of salvation and indeed the lawful religion for them. In this connection it must furthermore be taken into consideration that it was meant to be this only for the Israelites and for no one else; the institution of those belonging to the Jewish religion without being of the Jewish race (i.e. of the proselytes) was a very much later phenomenon. Hence it cannot be a part of the notion of a lawful religion in the above sense that it should be free from corruption, error and objective moral wrong in the concrete form of its appearance, or that it should contain a clear objective and permanent final court of appeal for the conscience of the individual to enable the individual to differentiate clearly and with certainty between the elements willed and instituted by God and those which are merely human and corrupt.

We must therefore rid ourselves of the prejudice that we can face a non-Christian religion with the dilemma that it must either come from God in everything it contains and thus correspond to God's will and positive providence, or be simply a purely human construction. If man is under God's grace even in these religions—and to deny this is certainly absolutely wrong—then the possession of this supernatural grace cannot but show itself, and cannot but become a formative factor of life in the concrete, even where (though not only where) this life turns the relationship to the absolute into an explicit theme, viz; in religion. It would perhaps be possible to say in theory that where a certain religion is not only accompanied in its concrete appearance by something false and humanly corrupted but also makes this an explicitly and consciously adopted element—an explicitly declared condition of this nature—this religion is wrong in its deepest and most specific being and hence can no longer be regarded as a lawful religion—not even in the widest sense of the word. This may be quite correct in theory. But we must surely go on to ask whether there is any religion apart from the Christian religion (meaning here even only the Catholic religion) with an authority which could elevate falsehood into one of its really essential parts and which could thus face man with an alternative of either accepting this falsehood as the most real and decisive factor of the religion or leaving this religion. Even if one could perhaps say something like this of Islam as such, it would have to be denied of the majority of religions. It would have to be asked in every case to what extent the followers of such religions would actually agree with such an interpretation of their particular religion. If one considers furthermore how easily a concrete, originally religious act can be always directed in its intention towards one and the same absolute, even when it manifests itself in the most varied forms, then it will not even be possible to say that theoretical polytheism, however deplorable and objectionable it may be objectively, must always and everywhere be an absolute obstacle to the performance in such a religion of genuinely religious acts directed to the one true God. This is particularly true since it cannot be proved that the practical religious life of the ancient Israelites, in so far as it manifested itself in popular theory, was always more than mere henotheism.

Furthermore, it must be borne in mind that the individual ought to and must have the possibility in his life of partaking in a genuine saving relationship to God, and this at all times and in all situations of the history of the human race. otherwise there could be no question of a serious and also actually effective salvific design of God for all men, in all ages and places. In view of the social nature of man and the previously even more radical social solidarity of men, however, it is quite unthinkable that man, being what he is, could actually achieve this relationship to God—which he must have and which if he is to be saved, is and must be made possible for him by God—in an absolutely private interior reality and this outside of the actual religious bodies which offer themselves to him in the environment in which he lives. If man had to be and could always and everywhere be a *homo religiosus* in order to be able to save himself as such, then he was this *homo religiosus* in the concrete religion in which "people" lived and had to live at that time. He could not escape this religion, however much he may have and did take up a critical and selective attitude towards this religion on individual matters, and however much he may have and did put different stresses in practice on certain things which were at variance with the official theory of this religion. If, however, man can always have a positive, saving relationship to God, and if he always had to have it, then he has always had it within *that* religion which in practice was at his disposal by being a factor in his sphere of existence. As already stated above, the inherence of the individual exercise of religion in a social religious order is one of the essential traits of true religion as it exists in practice. Hence, if one were to expect from someone who lives outside the Christian religion that he should have exercised his genuine, saving relationship to God absolutely outside the religion which society offered him, then such a conception would turn religion into something intangibly interior, into something which is always and everywhere performed only indirectly, a merely transcendental religion without anything which could become tangible in categories. Such a conception would annul the above-mentioned principle regarding the necessarily social nature of all religion in the concrete, so that even the Christian Church would then no longer have the necessary presupposition of general human and natural law as proof of her necessity. And since it does not at all belong to the notion of a lawful religion intended by God for man as something positively salvific that it should be pure and positively willed by God in all its elements, such a religion can be called an absolutely legitimate religion for the person concerned. That which God has intended as salvation for him reached him, in accordance with God's will and by his permission (no longer adequately separable in practice), in the *concrete* religion of his actual realm of existence and historical condition, but this fact did not deprive him of the right and the limited possibility to criticize and to heed impulses of religious reform which by God's providence kept on recurring within such a religion. For a still better and simpler understanding of this, one has only to think of the natural and socially constituted morality of a people and culture. Such a morality is never pure but is always also corrupted, as Jesus confirmed even in the case of the Old Testament. It can always be disputed and corrected, therefore, by the individual in accordance with his conscience. Yet, taken in its totality, it is *the* way in which the individual encounters the natural divine law according to God's will, and the way in which the natural law is given real, actual power in the life of the individual who cannot reconstruct these tablets of the divine law anew on his own responsibility and as a private metaphysician.

The morality of a people and of an age, taken in its totality, is therefore the legitimate and concrete form of the divine law (even though, of course, it can and may have to be corrected), so that it was not until the New Testament that the institution guaranteeing the purity of this form became (with the necessary reservations) an element of this form itself. Hence, if there existed a divine moral law and religion in the life of man *before* this moment, then its absolute purity (i.e. its constitution by divinely willed elements alone) must not be made the condition of the lawfulness of its existence. In fact, if every man who comes into the world is pursued by God's grace—and if one of the effects of this grace, even in its supernatural and salvifically elevating form, is to cause changes in consciousness (as is maintained by the better theory in Catholic theology) even though it cannot be simply as such a direct object of certain reflection—then it cannot be true that the actually existing religions do not bear any trace of the fact that all men are in some way affected by grace. These traces may be difficult to distinguish even to the enlightened eye of the Christian. But they must be there. And perhaps we may only have looked too superficially and with too little love at the non-Christian religions and so have not really seen them. In any case it is certainly not right to regard them as new conglomerates of natural theistic metaphysics and as a humanly incorrect interpretation and institutionalization of this "natural religion." The religions existing in the concrete must contain supernatural, gratuitous elements, and in using *these* elements the pre-Christian was able to attain God's grace: presumably, too, the pre-Christian exists even to this day, even though the possibility is gradually disappearing *today*. If we say that there were lawful religions in pre-Christian ages even outside the realm of the Old Testament, this does not mean that these religions were lawful in *all* their elements—to maintain this would be absurd. Nor does it mean that *every* religion was lawful; for in certain cases several forms, systems and institutions of a religious kind offered themselves within the historically concrete situation of the particular member of a certain people, culture, period of history, etc., so that the person concerned had to decide as to *which* of them was here and now, and on the whole, the more correct way (and hence for him *in concreto* the only correct way) of finding God.

This thesis is not meant to imply that the lawfulness of the Old Testament religion was of exactly the same kind as that which we are prepared to grant in a certain measure to the extra-Christian religions. For in the Old Testament the prophets saw to it (even though not by way of a permanent institution) that there existed a possibility of distinguishing in public salvation-history between what was lawful and what was unlawful in the history of the religion of the Israelites. This cannot be held to be true to the same extent outside this history, although this again does not mean that outside the Old testament there could be no question of any kind of divinely guided salvation-history in the realm of public history and institutions.

The main difference between such a salvation-history and that of the Old Testament will presumably lie in the fact that the historical, factual nature of the New Testament has *its* immediate pre-history in the *Old Testament* (which prehistory, in parenthesis, is insignificantly brief in comparison with the general salvation-history which counts perhaps a million years—for the former can be known with any certainty only from the time of Abraham or of Moses). Hence, the New Testament unveils *this* short span of salvation-history distinguishing its divinely willed elements and those which are contrary to God's will. It does this by a distinction which we cannot make in the same way in the history of any other religion. The second part of this second thesis, however, states two things positively. It states that even religions other than the Christian and the Old Testament religions contain quite certainly elements of a supernatural influence by grace which must make itself felt even in these objectifications. And it also states that by the fact that in practice man as he really is can live his proffered relationship to God only in society, man must have had the right and indeed the duty to live this his relationship to God within the religious and social realities offered to him in his particular historical situation.

Third Thesis: If the second thesis is correct, then Christianity does not simply confront the member of an extra-Christian religion as a mere non-Christian but as someone who can and must already be regarded in this or that respect as an anonymous Christian. It would be wrong to regard the pagan as someone who has not yet been touched in any way by God's grace and truth. If, however, he has experienced the grace of God—if, in certain circumstances, he has already accepted this grace as the ultimate, unfathomable entelechy of his existence by accepting the immeasurableness of his dying existence as opening out into infinity—then he has already been given revelation in a true sense even before he has been affected by missionary preaching from without. For this grace, understood as the a priori horizon of all his spiritual acts, accompanies his consciousness subjectively, even though it is not known objectively. And the revelation which comes to him from without is not in such a case the proclamation of something as yet absolutely unknown, in the sense in which one tells a child here in Bavaria, for the first time in school, that there is a continent called Australia. Such a revelation is then the expression in objective concepts of something which this person has already attained or could already have attained in the depth of his rational existence. It is not possible here to prove more exactly that this *fides implicita* is something which dogmatically speaking can occur in a so-called pagan. We can do no more here than to state our thesis and to indicate the direction in which the proof of this thesis might be found. But if it is true that a person who becomes the object of the church's missionary efforts is or may be already someone on the way towards his salvation, and someone who in certain circumstances finds it, without being reached by the proclamation of the church's message—and if it is at the same time true that this salvation which reaches him in this way is Christ's salvation, since there is no other salvation—then it must be possible to be not only an anonymous theist but also an anonymous Christian. And then it is quite true that in the last analysis, the proclamation of the Gospel does not simply turn someone absolutely abandoned by God and Christ into a

Christian, but turns an anonymous Christian into someone who now also knows about his Christian belief in the depths of his grace-endowed being by objective reflection and in the profession of faith which is given a social form in the church.

It is not thereby denied, but on the contrary implied, that this explicit self-realization of his previously anonymous Christianity is itself part of the development of this Christianity itself—a higher stage of development of this Christianity demanded by his being—and that it is therefore intended by God in the same way as everything else about salvation. Hence, it will not be possible in any way to draw the conclusion from this conception that, since man is already an anonymous Christian even without it, this explicit preaching of Christianity is superfluous. Such a conclusion would be just as false (and for the same reasons) as to conclude that the sacraments of baptism and penance could be dispensed with because a person can be justified by his subjective acts of faith and contrition even before the reception of these sacraments.

The reflex self-realization of a previously anonymous Christianity is demanded (1) by the incarnational and social structure of grace and of Christianity, and (2) because the individual who grasps Christianity in a clearer, purer and more reflective way has, other things being equal, a still greater chance of salvation than someone who is merely an anonymous Christian. If, however, the message of the Church is directed to someone who is a "non-Christian" only in the sense of living by an anonymous Christianity not as yet fully conscious of itself, then her missionary work must take this fact into account and must draw the necessary conclusions when deciding on its missionary strategy and tactics. We may say at a guess that this is still not the case in sufficient measure. The exact meaning of all this, however, cannot be developed further here.

Fourth Thesis: It is possibly too much to hope, on the one hand, that the religious pluralism which exists in the concrete situation of Christians will disappear in the foreseeable future. On the other hand, it is nevertheless absolutely permissible for the Christian himself to interpret this non-Christianity as Christianity of an anonymous kind which he does always still go out to meet as a missionary, seeing it as a world which is to be brought to the explicit consciousness of what already belongs to it as a divine offer or already pertains to it also over and above this as a divine gift of grace accepted unreflectedly and implicitly. If both these statements are true, then the church will not so much regard herself today as the exclusive community of those who have a claim to salvation but rather as the historically tangible vanguard and the historically and socially constituted explicit expression of what the Christian hopes is present as a hidden reality even outside the visible church.

To begin with, however much we must always work, suffer and pray anew and indefatigably for the unification of the whole human race, in the one church of Christ, we must nevertheless expect, for theological reasons and not merely by reason of a profane historical analysis, that the religious pluralism existing in the world and in our own historical sphere of existence will not disappear in the foreseeable future. We know from the gospel that the opposition to Christ and to the church will not disappear until the end of time. If anything, we must even be prepared for a heightening of this antagonism to Christian existence. If, however, this opposition to the church cannot confine itself merely to the purely private sphere of the individual but must also be of a public, historical character, and if this opposition is said to be present in a history which today, in contrast to previous ages, possesses a worldwide unity, then the continuing opposition to the church can no longer exist merely locally and outside a certain limited sector of history such as that of the West. It must be found in our vicinity and everywhere else. And this is part of what the Christian must expect and must learn to endure. The church, which is at the same time the homogenous characterization of an in itself homogenous culture (i.e. the medieval church), will no longer exist if history can no longer find any way to escape from or go back on the period of its planetary unity. In a unified world history in which everything enters into the life of everyone, the "necessary" public opposition to Christianity is a factor in the existential sphere of all Christianity. If this Christianity, thus always faced with opposition and unable to expect seriously that this will ever cease, nevertheless believes in God's universal salvific will—in other words, believes that God can be victorious by his secret grace even where the church does not win the victory but is contradicted—then this church cannot feel herself to be just *one* dialectic moment in the whole of history but has already overcome this opposition by her faith, hope and charity. In other words, the others who oppose her are merely those who have not yet recognized what they nevertheless really already are (or can be) even when, on the surface of existence, they are in opposition; they are already anonymous Christians, and the church is not the communion of those who possess God's grace as opposed to those who lack it, but is the communion of those who can explicitly confess what they *and* the others hope to be. Non-Christians may think it presumption for the Christian to judge everything which is sound or restored (by being sanctified) to be the fruit in every man of the grace of his Christ, and to interpret it as anonymous Christianity; they may think it presumption for the Christian to regard the non-Christian as a Christian who has not yet come to himself reflectively. But the Christian cannot renounce this "presumption" which is really the source of the greatest humility both for himself and for the church. For it is a profound admission of the fact that God is greater than man and the church. The church will go out to meet the non-Christian of tomorrow with the attitude expressed by St. Paul when he said: "What therefore you do not know and yet worship (and yet *worship!*) that I proclaim to you" (Acts 17:23). On such a basis one can be tolerant, humble and yet firm towards all non-Christian religions.

9

Confessional Theologies

The variety of twentieth-century theologies can be explained by their allegiance to a particular method of doing theology (e.g., dialectical theology), or their concentration on a single overriding theme (e.g., the doctrine of the Trinity), or their commitment to a particular philosophical school (e.g., process metaphysics). One additional factor is the confessional tradition in which a particular theologian stands. Some theologians take very seriously the creedal and confessional traditions of their church as their theological frame of reference and as the source material for their dogmatic and systematic constructions.

The word *confessio* originally referred to the testimony of faith that a martyr made under persecution: "Whosoever therefore shall confess me before men, him will I confess also before my Father which is in heaven" (Matt. 10:32, KJV). Its meaning expanded to refer to a document which formulates the faith of a confessing group, such as the Augsburg Confession of 1530 A.D. Some churches have a strong confessional tradition, others a very weak one or none at all. Since confessions often express the divisions among the churches, insofar as they condemn each other's teachings, some have proposed to reunify the churches simply on the basis of faith in Christ. But this is no solution because faith comes from hearing the Word of Christ *(fides ex auditu),* and responds in words of confession ("I believe . . ."). Since there is always explicit content in what the Christian community believes, it becomes necessary at times to formulate the faith in clear statements, particularly when it is challenged by contrary beliefs that some claim to be revealed by God.

As a technical term, "confessional theology" usually refers to a kind of Protestant theology that developed in nineteenth-century Europe in Reformed and Lutheran churches. The leaders of confessionalism returned to the confessional documents of the Reformation as a bulwark against pietism and rationalism, using them as hermeneutical guidelines for the interpretation of Scripture and the renewal of a churchly theology. The theological faculty of the University of Erlangen, Germany, was a stronghold of

Lutheran confessional theology in the nineteenth century, led by men of the stature of Gottfried Thomasius (1802–1879) and Johann C. K. von Hofmann (1810–1877). Their confessionalism was not merely a repristination of the Lutheran theology of the Reformation and seventeenth-century Protestant Orthodoxy, but was more like a three-legged stool, combining religious experience, biblical exegesis, and the confessions of the church.

I

The Erlangen legacy was continued in the twentieth century by a great exponent of Lutheran theology, Werner Elert (1885–1954). Like the earlier Erlangen theologians, Elert looked for the foundations of the Christian truth exclusively from within the circle of faith, and rejected all attempts of an apologetic or philosophical type to justify the Christian faith from the outside. His indefatigable efforts to reconstruct and defend the historic shape of Lutheranism earned him the title *Lutheranissimus.*

In his study of Lutheranism, Elert drew a distinction between its inner dynamic and its outer structure. The dynamic is the constant element whereas its visible structure or form is its ever-changing historical expression. The dynamic is to be found in the structure *(morphé)* and the structure is always to be judged by the dynamic. Elert's special phrase for the dynamic heart of Lutheranism was *"der evangelische Ansatz,"* which has been translated as "the impact of the gospel." The basic insight of Lutheran theology is its interpretation of human existence in terms of either the law or the gospel. To exist under the law is to be under the wrath of God and without Christ. The only God one can know apart from Christ is the hidden God, whom it is impossible to love. Elert believed that this is the fundamental human predicament that Luther experienced, and that it is no less real for people of today.

The law cannot create a bridge to the gospel; nothing can. The law does the exact opposite of the gospel; it accuses, condemns, and puts to death. The gospel brings life and salvation; only the gospel can shield us from the wrath and judgment of God which humans deserve. This contrast between law and gospel is the fulcrum of Elert's interpretation of the Christian faith. It provided the key to his criticism of the dogmatics of Karl Barth. Though he had learned much from Barth in the 1920s, Elert was destined to become Barth's most ferocious critic and leader of the German Lutheran opposition to the Barmen Declaration written by Barth. Elert believed that nothing less than the heart of Lutheran theology—the right understanding of the distinction between law and gospel—was at stake in his fight with Barth.

Elert believed that Barth's concept of the Word of God as revelation completely obscured the relation between the law and the gospel, and that is its "fundamental error," in substantial agreement with the Calvinist point of view. The law functions as the ultimate standard of God's relationship to humanity, and the gospel serves to fulfill the demands of the law. This represents the legalization of the gospel, placing the Christian life finally under the law of obedience, and thus a denial of Christian freedom. Barth said that the law is the form of the gospel, whose content is the grace of God. For Elert, law and gospel can never be so unified, for they stand in contrast exactly as death and life. Such a radical distinction between law and gospel is valid not only for dogmatics but also for ethics, for human life is experienced either under the "ethos of the law" or under the "ethos of the gospel."

Elert loved to think in terms of dualisms and dichotomies, either law or gospel, sin or grace, wrath or love, with no common ground for both, for the distinction lies not in human subjectivity, to be explained as a matter of perspective; rather, it is grounded in God's internal self-contradiction, a mystery that can never be understood by reason.

II

Our second example of confessional theology is strikingly different from Elert. Anders Nygren (1890–1978) was known around the world as a Lundensian theologian, so named because he was a professor at the University of Lund, Sweden, where other well-known theologians of this school taught, such as Gustaf Aulén and Ragnar Bring.

Nygren, like Elert, provided an alternative to the line of theology that stemmed from Karl Barth and his fellow dialectical theologians. As Elert retained continuity with the Erlangen theology of the nineteenth century, so Nygren owed much to the nineteenth-century currents of theology influenced by Immanuel Kant and Friedrich Schleiermacher. Nygren was a philosopher and a theologian; his philosophy of religion was patterned after Kant and his theology after Schleiermacher. Nevertheless, he was a confessional Lutheran theologian, a bishop of the Swedish church, and a representative of Lutheran theology in ecumenical circles.

Nygren believed that Kant's critique of metaphysics made it impossible to do theology in the manner of the older dogmaticians, Catholic or Protestant. They claimed that dogmatics was "a science of God and divine things." Kant's theory of knowledge, however, showed that it was impossible to have a "knowledge of God and divine things." This meant for Nygren that if theology was to make any sense, it would have to have a different focus for its object of inquiry, and a new starting point. What could that be?

If we start with the assumption that theology as a science can have no knowledge of the object of faith, namely God, and that therefore it must have a different task, the alternative is to switch its focus, following Schleiermacher, to the expressions of the Christian faith. Theology then becomes a positive science gathering together and examining all the given materials common to Christianity as a historical religion. The proper task of theology is to describe the content of the Christian faith as an organic whole in light of its origins and historical development. In this way, Nygren believed, theology can be critically scientific and responsibly Christian at the same time.

Nygren's type of confessional theology is a positivism of the Christian tradition critically examined. The task of dogmatics is simply to present in a systematic way the historically given expressions of the Christian faith without worrying about the truth question. What is "confessional" about this approach is that dogmatics begins with the basic contents of faith given in a particular religious community. This religio-positive method would work in principle for any religion. Every religion assumes it is the true religion; that is a matter of personal conviction. The theologian functions at a secondary level, merely reporting the factual expressions of faith, which at the same time are normative, of his or her own religious community.

Nygren knew very well that there are in fact many different historical expressions of the Christian faith. Is it possible to penetrate the multiplicity of such expressions to the very "essence of Christianity"? The answer to this question was to be found in the method of motif-research, the hallmark of Lundensian theology. For Nygren, motif-research was an objective, that is, historically scientific, way to determine the uniqueness of the Christian faith. To understand the Christian faith, or any religion, one must grasp its "fundamental motif." The basic motif of Christianity provides the answer to the universally human and religious question of how to gain communion with God. Every religion provides its own answer to the religious question of fellowship with God in terms of its own basic motif. There can be no doubt about what is the basic motif of Christianity; it is the gospel, the good news of God's love given to humanity through Jesus Christ.

Love is a notoriously slippery concept. It can mean different things, such as *"philia"* (Aristotle), *"eros"* (Plato), *"caritas"* (Augustine), *"libido"* (Freud), or it can mean *"agapé,"* the specifically Christian idea of love, rooted in the New Testament message of God's love for the world in Jesus Christ. God loves because he himself is love. God is *agapé*—that is the essence of Christianity without which it would lose its uniqueness. God's love is spontaneous and unmotivated; human love of whatever sort is not. God's love is able to love the unlovable and establish fellowship with sinners.

The nature of *agapé*-love is more clearly seen when it is compared with two conflicting motifs with which Christianity struggled in its earliest years. They were the motifs of *nomos* and *eros*. The *nomos* motif belongs to Judaism and the *eros* motif characterizes Hellenistic religion. For Nygren, Judaism is a religion of law and Hellenism is a religion based on the human desire to reach up to God as the *summum bonum*. *Eros* is the ascending love of humans reaching for heaven; *agapé* is God's descending love reaching down to meet sinners on their level. The history of Christianity shows that the pure motif of *agapé* has been amalgamated now with *nomos,* legalizing the faith, and now with *eros,* turning Christianity from its theocentrism to an anthropocentric perspective.

Nygren believed that the purest expression of the *agapé* motif can be found in the letters of the apostle Paul and the writings of Martin Luther. He developed quite elaborate philosophical and historical methods to show that the faith confessed in his Swedish Lutheran tradition, centered in the doctrine of justification by faith alone on account of Christ alone, was at one with the essence of New Testament Christianity.

III

William Temple (1881–1944), the most renowned Archbishop of Canterbury since Anselm (1033–1109), embodied the mind and spirit of Anglicanism in his comprehensive ability to combine seemingly contradictory things—liberal theology and traditional dogmas, evangelical independence and Catholic conservatism, faith and reason, philosophy and theology. Temple was a distinguished advocate and practitioner of the Anglican *via media,* looking for a middle way where others to the right or the left saw only an either/or. Temple studied under Harnack in Berlin, but he never got swept up by the heated debates among the German schools of theology. In all his writings, he seldom quoted any Continental theologians. He was more in tune with the main-stream of the classical tradition; his conversation partners were predominantly the fathers of the ancient church and medieval theologians. From Edward Caird (1835–1908) at Balliol College he learned the Hegelian system and its dialectical method of synthesizing antithetical positions, an approach that suited his Anglican style of reconciling differences between Protestantism and Catholicism.

The reading in this volume is from Temple's *Christus Veritas* on "The Person of Christ." For Temple, the incarnation of God in Christ forms the center of Christianity. In a letter to Monsignor Ronald Knox (October, 1913), Temple wrote: "The whole of my theology is an attempt to understand and verify the words: 'He that hath seen me hath seen the Father.'" The christological dogma of the ancient church that Christ is one person who is both divine and human is a true formulation of the statement at the start of John's Gospel, "The Word became flesh and lived among us" and Paul's statement, "God was in Christ reconciling the world unto himself" (2 Cor. 5:19). To modern skeptics in the Church of England who had trouble believing that Christ is God, he counseled that perhaps this is because they think they already know who God is and find Christ an enigma. The truth is that we do not already know who God is or what God is like until we find him in Christ. Just as we form our conception of God by looking to Christ, so also in Christ we find the answer to the question of true humanity. Jesus of Nazareth is the unique final self-manifestation of God, and that, to Temple, is the central affirmation of the Christian religion.

23. Werner Elert, *The Revelation of God*

The Dialectic of Revelation

Apart from the "revelations" which are received only by prophets, apostles, and charismatics, the contents of revelation in the New Testament sense of the word may be comprehended in the following categories. The first difference is this, that some relate to God, others to man. Furthermore, what is revealed of God can be subdivided into the two categories of wrath and grace. As content of the revelation of man, his sin is mentioned with particular frequency, but not exclusively. Also, works that are "done in God" are to be revealed. Likewise, the righteousness of God, which is revealed according to Rom. 1:17, is God's righteousness because he effects it, and, accordingly, it is also revelation about God; but it is simultaneously the righteousness of man "through faith," as the appended quotation attests. Paul states—not fearfully, but cheerfully—that we are revealed to God. And, above all, the announcement of man's future becoming revealed also regularly contains a reference to a separation that will take place at that time—a separation of sin from that which is not sin. And that which is not sin in man is faith alone. This faith is also mentioned as content of the becoming revealed (Gal. 3:23; cf. 2 Cor. 3:2 ff).

Thus, both chief categories of revelation-contents divide into two subcategories. Wrath and grace become revealed in God, sin and faith in man. These four subcategories correspond to each other in pairs. The revelation of God's wrath corresponds with the revelation of man's sin; the revelation of his grace, with the revelation of man's faith. That immediately leads us back to the relationship between law and gospel. The revelation of God's grace happened through Christ, who forms the declarative content of the gospel. On the other hand, his law serves the purpose of revealing sin. Thereby, however, God's wrath over sin is simultaneously revealed. That happens partly through the recorded law, thus through God's words (Rom. 3:2), partly through his works (Rom. 1:20), partly through the testimony in their "hearts" and "conscience" (Rom. 2:12 ff). In one way or another all men are under the law of God, which is imposed on all, including the unknowing; consequently, they are also under his wrath. And in that way all become revealed as sinners and as without excuse before God.

This also demonstrates the contrast between law and gospel as seen from the New Testament concept of revelation. Two things that contradict each other become manifest both in God and in man: wrath and grace in God, sin and faith in man. With regard to both, we must thus speak of a twofold revelation. But the application of the term revelation both to the law and to the gospel leads to a new specification of its reciprocal relationship.

The law is "revealed." But Paul says of those who live under it: "Whenever Moses is read a veil lies over their minds" (2 Cor. 3:15). It is entirely in accord with this when the prophet has God himself say: "In overflowing wrath for a moment I hid my face from you" (Is. 54:8). For the law and God's wrath can never be separated from each other (Rom. 4:15). But when we hear, on the other hand, that God's wrath is revealed, then law and wrath are both his revealing and his veiling. What God veils in the moment of the revelation of his wrath is identical with what he reveals in the perspective of the gospel, namely, his grace. This revelation is the "bright light of the Gospel of the glory of Christ, who is the likeness of God" (2 Cor. 4:4). In Christ "the veil is taken away" (2 Cor. 3:14). But then the entire former condition appears as darkness, despite the "revelation" of the law and the wrath of God (2 Cor. 4:6; 1 Pet. 2:9; Hebr. 12:13 ff.).

Thus, under the application of the category of revelation, law and gospel are in a dialectic relationship. When the one is revealed, the other is veiled; and when the second one shines forth, the first one is darkened. This paradox of an internally divided revelation of God cannot be dissolved by dividing its validity between two different chapters of the world's history. Apart from all else, this is out of the question already because the contrast also returns in the eschatological associations. It might be a bit more reasonable to view both in a relationship of purpose: the revelation of the law (= the veiling of grace) serves the purpose of preparing for the reception of grace (= the veiling of wrath). That is not incorrect. Paul expresses that thought when he says that "we were confined under the law, kept under restraint until faith should be revealed"; and therefore he called the law "our custodian until Christ came" (Gal. 3:23 ff.). It follows that the law, in relationship to the gospel, indeed partakes of teleological significance. However, this specification of the relationship cannot be exhaustive. If it were, we could or would have to assume that the revelation of God's wrath was not meant seriously. However, its eschatological reality already forestalls that.

Rather, the dialectic relationship between the revelation of the law and the revelation of the gospel is first understood when both are no longer only revelation, that is, a disclosure of secrets. Both are by no means only a communication of something, but rather, both bear the stamp of a validity from which we can in no wise withdraw. The gospel is valid because it is an adhortative addressed to us; the law, because it was imposed on us. Thus, even though the teleological specification of relationship is not incorrect, the causal relationship dare not be veiled by it: the gospel is valid for us, or, expressed more clearly, it makes faith necessary for us, because the law of God is valid for us. This first makes the paradox fully perceptible: it is precisely the gospel which confirms the validity of the law—of the same law whose validity is abolished by the gospel.

Thus the relationship of law and gospel is dialectical in a double sense. In the first place, because we may and must apply the term "revelation" of God to both, although this application to both is contradictory in itself. In the second place, because both are indubitably valid, although the validity of the one cancels out the validity of the other, and vice versa.

If it were only for the first contradiction, the dialectical relationship might appear only as a formal type. Applying the idealistic conception of dialectic, one might then attempt to "eliminate" the contradiction by merging the two terms "revelation" and "veiling" under a general superterm. This attempt is made, for example, when the contrast between law and gospel is to be eliminated by compressing both into the superterm of "the Word," or even when the application of this term is to render the contrast indifferent. No, law and gospel are two different words of God. Here the reciprocal relationship of revealing and of veiling consists in the fact that the one word of God confronts and opposes the other word of God. This contrast might be viewed as dissolved in the term "Word of God" only if this term is conceived of as an idea; that is, as an ideal truth which appeals to us because of its logicality. However, that would again contradict the concept of revelation.

It is just as unsatisfactory to explain the contrast in the sense of a dialectic which is construed as a mutual delimitation of its own statements, conditioned by the inadequacy of all human speech when relating to God's revelation. Law and gospel delimit each other indeed. But not because we say this or that about them, nor because the one bears this, the other that name, but because they conflict with each other in their substantive content. Therefore, to define their relationship with the concept of a mutual delimitation is already an inadmissible weakening of their true relationship. A boundary line may also mark a peaceful coexistence, an amicable territorial settlement. However, law and gospel dispute and contest each other's territory. The common territory over which they both claim sovereignty is the totality of humankind. Here they are engaged in combat with each other, as the one abrogates the validity of the other. If dialectic comprises a process of speech and rejoinder to this speech, then the contradiction to be dissolved here consists in the contradiction of the law itself with the gospel itself, and not first in the human speech about them. But since this conflict is not only a contradiction of two communications with each other, it cannot be dissolved by any theological sophistry, but only by him on whose absolute authority the validity of both the law and the gospel—and consequently, the contradiction of the validity of both—rests. That came to pass when Christ "was revealed."

The connection of the gospel with Christ's becoming revealed requires no further elaboration, because Christ is the essential content of the evangelical demonstrative "God was in Christ." But in what relationship does he stand to the law of God? The knowledge that the law cannot be understood as the aggregate of moral precepts already led to this question. That grew out of the New Testament concepts of righteousness and of sin. The relationship to Christ's becoming revealed is decisive. For the time being, we shall discuss this only in the framework of the dialectic of revelation.

The beginning of the Gospel of John (John 1:17) places Moses, the lawgiver, programmatically in contraposition to Christ, the Transmitter of grace and truth. This forestalls the error from the very beginning, to call Christ a lawgiver like Moses. Yet man lapsed into this fallacy. Perhaps the principal reason for this was the imperative form in which many of Christ's statements in the gospels are couched. Not only Paul's dogmatics forbids us to assign Christ the character of a lawgiver, but also and especially the evangelical reports. According to these, Christ's position over against the law is not that of a giver but a receiver of the law. Christ knows that the law pertains to him as it does to all men. And he bows to its validity, fulfilling it and suffering it. In particular, he also suffers death; in the opinion of his adversaries, he does this in accord with the law (John 19:7). He himself viewed his suffering as fulfillment of the writings of Moses and the prophets. Thus, the gospels, and also Paul (Gal. 4:4), teach us that Christ was under the law. And Christ acknowledged the validity of the law by his words, his acts, suffering, and death. But the very way in which this validity was demonstrated in him shows that the law is not a mere aggregate of moral precepts. A moral law is a rule of life. It only awaits the fulfillment of its precepts, and with this fulfillment it has achieved its purpose. But the law of God is the rule of death (Rom. 7:10; 8:2; cf. 2 Cor. 3:6 ff.). It reveals man's sin as it reveals the wrath of God—in both instances, it leads to death. For that very reason, it is a destiny to which everything human is forfeit, it is a curse that rests on all. And since Christ is "under the law," he also bore this curse (Gal. 3:13). Christ was the sacrifice of the law.

However, since the law could reveal no sin in Christ, this sacrifice bore a very particular meaning. It is basic for all of Christology that his obedience unto death was voluntary. That is Paul's testimony in Philippians. The very fact that he suffered the law's order of death, its doom, and its curse, and that he thereby unconditionally acknowledged its validity, emphasizes this further. On the other hand, Christ is the essential content of the gospel, because he delivered us from the curse of the law. Surely, that does not exhaust the content of the gospel, of Christ's mission, work, and significance. But at all events, the deliverance from the law's order of death is an integrative factor in this. If the gospel is valid, then also "the grace and truth that came through Jesus Christ" are valid, as we heard in that programmatic statement of John's Gospel. Then the statement is valid that he is the truth (John 14:6), but also that he is the resurrection (John 11:25), and therewith the conqueror over the law's rule of death.

Thus, the dialectical relationship between law and gospel, that is, the conflict waged between them in the form of speech and counterspeech, was adjusted in the person of Christ, in his life and in his death and—as must be elaborated later—in his resurrection. Christ's becoming revealed is the becoming revealed of the validity of the law and the validity of the gospel. Only here, only in the person of Christ, therefore, can also the adjustment of this conflict take place. The declarative of the gospel reads "God was in Christ." Consequently, he is able not only to make the voice of the law audible, as all others too can do, but he can also silence it, as no other can do. He alone can bid it be silent, because he, in contradistinction to all others, completely fulfilled and completely suffered the law. Therefore, only with him is the abrogation of the law's order of death no rebellion against God, who imposed the law. Nor does he abrogate it for himself—for he, as we know, suffered it completely—but for others. As the report of him adds this "for you," the declarative of the gospel becomes the adhortative. Therefore, for all who hear the adhortative in faith, Christ's becoming revealed signifies the becoming revealed of the grace of God and the veiling of his wrath. Accordingly, that paradoxical fact that God's wrath is both revealed and veiled can be perceived and understood only in faith in Christ, in whom it was revealed.

The Knowledge of God

Just as there is no revelation "in and of itself," but only in the dichotomy of law and gospel, there is also no knowledge of God "in and of itself," but only in the concrete being struck by law and gospel. There is a difference between knowledge and information (*"Erkennen"* and *"Kennen"*). Information may be gained without risk, that is, without the personal involvement of the subject. In this sense, there may, perhaps, be information about but never a knowledge of God. In the New Testament, knowing corresponds to being revealed.

In our discussion of the term *revelation*, we noted that the New Testament never states that God revealed himself or that he reveals himself. However, it does very definitely speak about the knowledge of God (Rom. 1:28; 11:33; 2 Cor. 10:5; Gal. 4:9; Eph. 1:17; Col. 1:11; 1 John 4:6; 2 Pet. 1:2 ff.). This knowledge is directed to the person of God himself. It is engendered by all that is revealed, whether this be about God, or about man, or in Christ. "That the God of our Lord Jesus Christ, the Father of glory, may give you a spirit of wisdom and of revelation in the knowledge of him" (Eph. 1:17).

At no point may the knowledge of God be separated from this manifold being revealed. It may not be separated because of its origin: the being revealed originates in the law and in the gospel. Consequently, without these there is also no knowledge of God. It cannot be separated because of its content; for we cannot know God without reflecting that his wrath as well as his grace, that our sin as well as our righteousness, were revealed, or will be revealed. In particular, it cannot be separated from the revelation of the Son of God—in accord with his own Word (Matt. 11:27).

The personal involvement, which is lacking in information about God, is basic presupposition for the knowledge of God. It consists in the fact that we are personally struck by the law and by the gospel, that is, that insofar as the hearer no longer confines himself to merely hearing law and gospel, but as he bares his existence to their aim at his heart. That, however, is not the only difference between information and knowledge. Whoever knows that the appeal of another is

256

addressed to him acknowledges thereby that the other already knew him prior to this. For otherwise not precisely he, the one addressed, could be meant. Therefore, Paul adds, when he speaks of our knowledge of God, that we were first known by him. Conformably, Jesus says of himself that he knows his own, as they know him. That this does not denote a mere being informed about can already be inferred from the fact that Christ threatens to say to the evildoers: "I never knew you" (Matt. 7:23; John 10:14; 1 Cor. 13:12; Gal. 4:9) (Luther uses the word *"erkennen"* here.)

That becomes perfectly clear when Paul restricts the prior knowledge by God to a definite number of men chosen by God (Rom. 8:30). The omniscient God is informed about all men. But when he knows only a segment of men, this word has another and special meaning; just as the German word *"meinen"* (to mean) has. In its original sense, it is connected with *"Minne"* (love). The old dogmaticians construed the New Testament γιγνώσκειν of God as a rendition of the Old Testament *yathah*, and thus conceived of it as a *nosse cum affectu*, as a loving knowledge directed to a definite person. That actually corresponds to the New Testament linguistic usage and also to the fact that we may know that we are "meant" by God in the adhortative of the gospel. But if this type of knowledge by God always precedes our knowledge of God, it is logical when Paul, conversely, also has the *nosse cum affectu* on our side correspond to the preceding knowledge by God: "If any one imagines that he knows something, he does not yet know as he ought to know. But if one loves God, one is known by him" (1 Cor. 8:2 f). Because our knowledge of God presupposes the knowing that we are meant, the prior being known by him, it can be no mere information. Rather, with it we enter into a personal relationship with him.

To be sure, in this sense our knowledge, conditional on God's prior knowledge, is addressed only to the God who is revealed to us in the gospel. For only with him is his preceding knowledge a loving knowledge, and his meaning a loving meaning. We are also struck solely by his law. But if we know him as the lawgiver, that is, as the one who imposed the law and decreed the sentence of death on us, we sense nothing of his loving meaning. It is his anger which faces us in the imposition of the law and of death. Here the same chasm yawns before us which separates the revelation of the law from the revelation of the gospel. Here our recognition of God seems to split in two, and we seem to lose the unity of the divine Thou. We could, indeed, not thread our way out of this cleavage and we would lose our way in the dark, if that dialectic of law and gospel had not been solved in the revelation of Christ. For the identity of the God of legislation and of the God who lovingly first knew us becomes known and certain only in Christ. For only Christ could make the voice of the law audible and, simultaneously, silence it.

It follows, in the first place, that our knowledge of God, if this is to be a loving knowledge, is borne solely by Christ's becoming revealed; furthermore, that this can never be a static possession which we recall from memory when required.

Rather, with the thought of God both always arise before us: his wrath and his grace. Here we recognize a new mark of faith. If faith is compliance with the adhortative of the gospel, it is an ever-renewed subduing of the slavish fear by the recipient of the law, by the man on whom the death sentence is imposed. It denotes a jumping across that chasm which separates the wrath of God from his grace and love.

Here the formula of "the leap" of faith, coined by Kierkegaard—and also the words usually attributed to him but actually stemming from Luther, about the "risk" of faith— gain their deeper meaning; to be sure, a meaning different from that intended by Kierkegaard. He conceives of this as a leap into the uncertain— since there can be no available knowledge of God. He here wishes to illustrate the supposed definition of faith in Hebrews 11:1: Faith addresses itself to the uncertain, because it is addressed to something invisible. However, that is not the decisive point. Of course, God is invisible. Neither his wrath nor his grace ever becomes physically visible. But also the bullet that strikes any heart is invisible to our eye. Yet it strikes us down so that there can be nothing more certain for us. The mark of faith is, rather, characterized by the fact that we are struck thus and thus, by the law and by the gospel. And the leap of faith is a risk inasmuch as it throws itself into the arms of God in defiance of his revealed wrath—with the conviction that those arms will not let us fall into the abyss, that the wrath is concealed, that sin is covered up. That is the risk of faith; and for that reason, faith pursues its course counter to appearances.

Now also the currently much discussed question regarding a "natural knowledge of God" can be answered. This question is unnecessarily obscured by its formulation as a question regarding a "natural revelation." If the question is worded thus, some believe that they must disavow it totally. For if it were affirmed, then faith's recognition that the Person of Christ alone is the revelation of God seems impaired. Others, however, believe that they have to affirm this question just as sharply, because otherwise the connection between God and earthly happenings seems lost to them. If this were the deduction made from the negation of a natural revelation of God, this negation would actually be pure atheism. All who believe in God know that they encounter him everywhere, at every place, in every event. We have every reason—especially today—constantly to hold the fact that there is no event in which God does not encounter us not only before the eyes of others, but also before our own. It may be doubtful whether we can properly call this "revelation" of God. We established earlier that this term is by no means used as consistently in the New Testament as it is in some works of dogmatics. The New Testament, as was shown, nowhere states that God reveals himself. Indeed, Rom. 1:18 declares that his wrath is "revealed" ". . . against all ungodliness and wickedness of men"; therefore, precisely against the people who refuse to believe in the gospel. Whether we call that natural revelation or supernatural revelation, we are merely quibbling about words. At all events, it is a revelation outside of or beyond the revelation of Christ.

Thus, all natural knowledge of God leads to no other result than that attained by the law of God, namely, that God reveals his wrath against all ungodly and unrighteous men. It follows also that the natural knowledge of God must be drawn into the dialectic of all revelation of God. It is like the knowledge of the order of death, like this order itself, and the wrath of God revealed therein; it is like the resistance which must be broken down through the gospel and through faith. Here the meaning of faith in the face of appearances to the contrary becomes clear. For it is appearances in the most elementary sense which reveal the order of death to us. Faith means to believe in God's grace and in the resurrection in defiance of this recognition, in defiance of this order. And, finally, this clarifies that Paul, in the Epistle to the Romans, may say of natural men that they knew God (Rom. 1:12), and, on the other hand, in the Epistle to the Galatians, that they did not know God (Gal. 4:8). For in the second passage he contraposes the knowledge of God, which is based on the prior being known by God, to the condition of not knowing God. Here it becomes evident that the knowledge of God is exactly as dichotomous in itself as is the revelation of God. What appears as the knowledge of God in the context of the Epistle to the Romans, namely, the knowledge of the revelation of God's wrath in the order of death, is covered in the knowledge of God engendered by the gospel, and expressed in the Epistle to the Galatians, just as the revelation of wrath is covered by the revelation of God's grace.

The gospel derives its name from the fact that it gives our entire existence a happy turn. This happiness-inspiring, triumphant character attaches to it, not because it reveals God to us in general, or because it mediates some pertinent knowledge of God to us, but because it overcomes the revealedness of God's wrath and, together with this, also our natural knowledge of God, which ends in fear, in defiance, in doubt, in despair, or in shame and vice. All that we know of God without the gospel, or all that we assume we know, is reality, whether this be based on the written law, or on the recognition of the "One" of the mystics, or on the fate of the Edda or the Lay of the Nibelungs. It is a real knowledge of God. But in the light of the gospel all of that appears as a hiddenness of God to us. The God who appeared in Christ is there in fact hidden.

And now, what is it that becomes "revealed" in this self-understanding of ours? Revelation, becoming revealed, implies the removal of a cover, a veil. Man's becoming revealed is always and only the reverse side of God's becoming revealed. When God is revealed as the Creator of all things, man is concurrently revealed as a creation of God. When God is revealed as the lawgiver, man is concurrently revealed as the recipient of the law. When God is revealed as sitting in judgment, we are concurrently revealed as the judged. When the veil is drawn away from man's self-understanding, that is, from the manner in which we live our life, then the fact is revealed that God himself is that power which binds us, which imposes both the ought and the must on us. We already spoke of the significance of this for our "knowledge of God." But now we have to add that on our side this reveals that our opposition, our self-asserting subjectivity is resistance and contradiction against God. And it is present in the entire gradation of possibilities open to us, between the most extreme poles of ethical and fatalistic self-understanding. Whether we persist in the questioning attitude, that is, whether we want to know about God without any risk of our own, whether we assert ourselves as ethical activists or as idealistic autonomists against the must, or whether we, conversely, divest ourselves of our own responsibility as we refer to the compulsion of fate, or whether we combine the two, acknowledge the power of fate and rebel against it in tragic defiance—there is no possibility of not finding ourselves in opposition to God.

But that is not all. The fact that God is the power which opposes us, to resist which occupies our whole existence, is not the only thing revealed of God, but also that he judges us and that his judgment is executed in the order of death imposed on us. That, in turn, reveals that we are judged and condemned by him. The law expresses that not by simply establishing our guilt, but by passing judgment on it and by condemning it as such. This sentence is in force wherever man is designated as sinner and wherever his thinking, his willing, and his acting are designated as sin. To be sure, abstractly sin and guilt are not identical. But objectively they cannot be differentiated. When we read in the New Testament that the law reveals the sin of man, this always implies the disclosure of our guilt. That gives us a first point of departure for the understanding of sin. Sin is resistance to or contradiction against God. Sin is hostility to God (Rom. 8:7; Eph. 2:16).

Thus, man's becoming revealed does not suggest a new state of affairs to us. It rather consists in the removal of the veil from the facts of our life which are known to us all. Our entire life is contradiction against God. It is the life of sinners.

To recognize the connection between sin and our entire existence was an essential aspect of the Lutheran Reformation. Being a sinner does not spring from the summation of individual feelings; but, conversely, deeds and thoughts are sins because they are characterized as deeds and thoughts of a sinner. That is the basic thought in all the elaborations on sin in the Lutheran Confessions. This is reflected, above all, in the fact that these elaborations, in the final analysis, lead to a recognition of original sin. When Luther attempts to make the essence of sin intelligible in the Smalcald Articles, he speaks only of original sin, which he calls the chief sin. The decisive point in man's becoming revealed is that original sin is not a special instance of sin among other types of sin, but that it is *the* sin, the chief sin, as Luther says, of which all the others are only the fruit.

The decisive characteristic in this concept of original sin is that it is fixed in the beginning of our existence and that it is inseparably linked with its entire course; we would be nonexistent without it. But that merely pulls the veil from the reality which cannot be excluded from our self-understanding. From the beginning of our existence, we find ourselves in contradiction to him who has free disposition over us. The contradiction is not an exceptional action, nor is it a repeated failing. We cannot exist otherwise than as subjective existence, which must uninterruptedly defend itself against that other which is not we. We are born into this compulsion to self-assertion. It is part of the substance of our life regarding which we are not asked. If we are born without being asked, then we are also born into the contradiction to God without being asked. That means that we are enemies of God by birth, thus sinners, whether we are aware of this or not, whether we want to be or not. The being revealed consists merely in the fact that this is revealed as sin, and since we are born into it, as original sin.

It is simultaneously revealed that this original sin or chief sin is guilt. For obviously the creature's resistance to his Creator renders him guilty. Nor is that guilt annulled by its inescapability. Only the very insipid wisdom of the Enlightment will dispute that. Earlier, we reminded the reader that every somewhat profound worldview intimates that we must assume guilt without being asked, and that we must bear this guilt our whole life. The ancient tragedians were aware of that as were the adherents of the doctrine of Karma. Under the execution of God's law, it becomes evident that this guilt, which is implicit in the beginning of our existence and which will accompany it to its end, is a guilt before God. If this were not so, then the law which reveals it would also be no revelation of the order of death. For it is the order of death because it says to the sinner: "Your guilt is deserving of death." In that way, the law of God strikes the very heart of man, as the adversary of God.

To be sure, now the question has to be raised again, what is revealed by the uncovering of original sins, that is, by this unasked-for becoming guilty before God? That brings us face to face with the really torturous side of the problem of original sin and, with this, of sin in general. For even if one fact here fits into the other, even if there is a logical association, and even if long familiarity with these terms in the church has made us callous—it is nonetheless something monstrous that is disclosed here. We simply cannot "understand" the connection maintained here between God and human guilt.

Surely, if we, in consequence of our sin, were arraigned before a "just" judge, that is, as we, in accord with human analogies, picture a just judge to ourselves, or as a certain theological naïveté of all times again and again declared God to be! That would be bad for us. However, we might, perhaps, be able to regulate and adjust our conduct to that type of judge. This deduction is made in the Roman and in the Rationalistic theology. But can we speak of a righteousness *here* in terms comprehensible to us? Where the law, which is to establish our sin, pursues the very aim to incite us to transgressions? Where we are so clearly and explicitly informed in the name of God that he hardens man's heart, so that man cannot at all fulfill God's will? That he makes us guilty where we, subjectively, purpose no evil? That he thrusts us into guilt, so that he may then rightfully kill us?

What we are told about the law attains its full awfulness when we apply this to ourselves. Here we can only repeat that we have to shudder before the God who, as he calls us into life, simultaneously presses a weapon into our hand, so that we *have* to fight against him, and who then throws us down, because we do fight against him, and who then, in the bargain, shouts at us: "It is your fault. You are guilty!" This is the *Deus absconditus*. Now we know that his hiddenness is not due to our slothful or feeble thinking. Paradoxically, his hiddenness is the content of his own revelation. It is unrecognizability in the most awesome sense of the word. Recognition in the deeper sense is always directed on another Thou. It is always a loving recognition. Where we recognize the Thou of another—even though afflicted with weakness, even though the face may not be beautiful, even though it may be furrowed and aged as that of our mother—our eyes beam and our heart beats joyfully. But if we try to recognize this God, then our eye darkens and heart freezes. Here we recognize no kinship with us, no love, no compassion, but above all only the reverse.

The *Deus absconditus* is no hypothesis, neither an illusion nor the destruction of an illusion. He is the direct opposite of all that we know of ourselves, that we have, think, are, will, shall do, and must do. He is the absolute Stranger with whom we cannot possibly arrive at an understanding. We only know that he is opposed to us. Over against him we are absolutely lonely. He is the One who will kill us. That is what is "revealed" by law. That had to be stated here once more very pointedly in order to render impossible every attempt to dissolve the contrast between law and gospel in the superimposed term of revelation.

24. Anders Nygren, *Agape and Christianity*

Fundamental Motifs and Motif Research

The term "fundamental motif" requires more precise definition, and two questions in particular call for an answer. First, what do we mean by describing anything as a fundamental motif? And secondly, what right have we to describe Agape as a fundamental motif of Christianity? The idea of Agape meets us as one among other characteristically Christian ideas. Have we then any grounds for ascribing to the idea of love such a special position and such a fundamental importance as is expressed by the term "fundamental motif"? Before we go on to give a definite answer to these questions, it may be well to prepare the way with some preliminary observations on the meaning of motif research.

The most important task of those engaged in the modern scientific study of religion and theological research is to reach an inner understanding of the different forms of religion in the light of their different fundamental motifs. For a long time, they have been chiefly occupied in collecting a vast mass of material drawn from different religious sources for the purposes of comparison. But when the comparison actually comes to be made, the uncertainty of it immediately becomes apparent; for it is plain that no conclusion can be drawn from the mere fact that one and the same idea or belief occurs in different religious contexts.

The idea or belief may have exactly the same form without having at all the same meaning, if in one case it is a basic conception, while in the other it is more loosely attached. Its meaning cannot be the same if—as is naturally most often the case—its setting is different in the different religions. What such an idea, or belief, or sentiment really means can only be decided in the light of its own natural context. In other words, we must try to see what is the basic idea or the driving power of the religion concerned, or what it is that gives its character as a whole and communicates to all its parts their special content and color. It is the attempt to carry out such a structural analysis, whether in the sphere of religion or elsewhere, that we describe as motif-research.

Motif-Research and Historical-Genetic Research

As distinct from historical-genetic research, motif-research is concerned less with the historical connections and origins of motifs than with their characteristic content and typical manifestations. This may suggest that in adopting the method of motif-research we are dangerously departing from the safe and solid ground of empirical fact. Does not the quest for the fundamental motif of a religion introduce an element of valuation, and therefore a subjective element, into the inquiry? When, in dealing with a spiritual phenomenon, we distinguish between "fundamental" and "non fundamental" conceptions, and regard the latter as at most a development of the former, this distinction seems not to be given in the phenomenon itself, but to be imported into it by our imaginative reconstruction of it. But is not such a procedure more akin to artistic synthesis than to scientific analysis, more a matter of intuition than of investigation? And does not motif-research expose us to the risk of arbitrary subjectivism, from which we are safe so long as we stick to the given facts and refrain from distinguishing between fundamental and more peripheral motifs? In answer to these questions there are two things to be said.

First, it is an illusion to suppose that objectivity and empirical accuracy are guaranteed by sticking to the individual data of the spiritual life. There is nothing to be gained by that except an unrealistic spiritual atomism. A mass of disconnected elements is gathered, which can be arranged in the most diverse patterns, and we can never even be sure that we have rightly understood any single one of them since their meaning depends on the context to which they belong. In order to grasp the meaning of a spiritual phenomenon, it is obviously not enough to know the elements of which it is composed, but we must also know the connection between them; and this connection, it should be noted, is no less empirically given than the elements themselves. When, therefore, motif-research concentrates on this connection—since "fundamental motif" stands for that to which the connection is due—it has in no way departed from empirical ground, but has simply directed our attention from one empirical element to another.

Secondly, the conditions of motif-research are misunderstood if we imagine that it rests on essentially unverifiable intuition and has no use for scientific analysis. It cannot, of course, be denied that the underlying idea or fundamental motif of a religion may be intuitively discerned, or that such an intuition is of inestimable value for motif-research. But intuition alone does not constitute research; and if we are to speak of research in this connection the gains of intuition must be subjected to scientific analysis and verification. The question we have to answer here, therefore, is whether it is at all possible by means of scientific analysis to determine the fundamental motif of any given form of religion. The answer can only be an unqualified affirmative. The purpose of the scientific study of religion is not merely to record the actual conceptions, attitudes, and so forth, that are found in a particular religious milieu, but more especially to find out what is characteristic and typical of them all. That is what motif-research deliberately and consistently seeks to do, and is indeed fully capable of doing. What we regard as a fundamental motif need not be a matter of subjective and arbitrary choice, for it is open to objective examination. A religion deprived of its fundamental motif would lose all coherence and meaning; and therefore we cannot rightly regard anything as a fundamental motif unless its removal would have such an effect. This gives us the basic principle on which motif-research must proceed with its analysis. It need only be added, in order to prevent a possible misunderstanding, that the fundamental motif need by no means consist of a clearly formulated idea, but can equally well consist of a general underlying sentiment.

Motif-research, then, is in no more unfavorable a position than any other empirical investigation. Sometimes it can actually produce more fully assured results than historical-genetic research. To discover the origins of a particular motif, the soil from which it has sprung, and how it has found its way into a particular religious outlook, can be extremely difficult. Hypothesis can stand against hypothesis with no possibility of an objective decision between them. But the place and importance of the motif in the outlook in question may nevertheless be unmistakably clear. This indicates a certain difference of approach between the two types of research. Both are concerned with motifs, but historical-genetic research is interested chiefly in their migrations, so to speak, and in the historically demonstrable connections between similar motifs in different places. Motif-research, as we have described it, is primarily interested in the content of the motifs, and it can show us that the same or similar motifs are to be found even in cases where there is no reason to suspect historical dependence.

Motif-Research and Value-Judgments

We have distinguished motif-research from historical-genetic research. It is still more important, though it should be unnecessary, to distinguish it clearly from every kind of valuation. We have described motif-research as a type of scientific analysis, and that alone is enough to show that there can be no question of any value-judgment. The task of science is to understand, not to appraise. This elementary fact is still far from generally recognized, however, and therefore it must be explicitly stated.

Unless this point is fully and clearly grasped, the whole of the following exposition is likely to be misconstrued. It is as easy as it is wrong, when we set the Christian idea of Agape over against the ancient idea of Eros, to suppose that we are comparing them with reference to their respective values, or even that we are assuming the superior value of the idea of Agape and making it the criterion for an unfavorable judgment on the idea of Eros. Support for such a view is given by the fact that we frequently have occasion to show how an admixture of the Eros motif has weakened the Agape motif and rendered it more or less ineffective. In order to prevent this kind of misunderstanding, it may be stated categorically at the outset that our exposition is entirely indifferent to the question of value. Admittedly we are dealing with "values," but our attitude to them is that of an observer who wishes to understand, not of a valuer assessing their worth. Agape and Eros are contrasted with one another here, not as right and wrong, nor as higher and lower, but as Christian and non-Christian fundamental motifs. We are dealing with a difference of type, not of value. It is, of course, true that Eros and Agape are still living forces which can compel us to decide our personal attitude to them; but that is something entirely outside the province of science. Such a decision is a personal affair which is determined by quite other than scientific considerations. If, finally, in our treatment of the idea of Eros we have in view primarily the solvent effects it has had on the Agape motif, that is simply due to the nature of the task we have set ourselves. Our purpose is to give an account of the Christian idea of love and the vicissitudes through which it has passed. If our purpose were to expound the idea of Eros and its vicissitudes, the emphasis of our inquiry would be correspondingly changed, and the idea of Agape would be regarded chiefly from the point of view of its solvent effects on the Eros motif. Hence even at this point there is no question of a value judgment.

It is not, however, simply in order to prevent possible misunderstanding that the indifference of this exposition to the question of value must be emphasized. The value-judgment has a habit of claiming pride of place even in scientific discussion, greatly to the detriment of theoretical clarity. It is sometimes very plain, for instance, that those who find an indispensable value in the idea of Eros as well as in that of Agape have a certain interest in glossing over and minimizing the essential difference between them. Their agreement can be put briefly as follows: both are valuable, therefore, they cannot be ultimately irreconcilable. Here a third factor, which may be termed the primacy of the practical value-judgment, joins the two already discussed—the power of language and the power of tradition—in encouraging the confusion of Eros and Agape. In opposition to the pressure of all such alien interests it will be our task to delineate as sharply as possible the characteristics of both fundamental motifs and to make clear their relation to one another.

The Place of the Idea of Agape in Christianity

We started by saying that the idea of love occupies a central place in Christianity. That is so obvious a fact that it would hardly seem to need any special investigation. But it is also a fact that the idea of Agape in Christianity constitutes the answer to certain quite definite questions; and, obviously, we can only understand the full force of an answer if we are clear about the question that is being answered. The same idea can have very different meanings, according as it represents the answer to one question or another. Hence it is by no means superfluous to inquire more closely into the question or questions to which the idea of Agape is intended as the answer. In this way the idea of Agape will be placed in its proper setting, related to its context.

We have indicated the central importance of love in Christianity by describing it as a Christian "fundamental motif"; but this term can be variously understood and we have still to define it. We raised, but did not answer, the two following questions: (1) What do we mean by describing anything as a fundamental motif? (2) What right have we to ascribe to the idea of Agape, which is after all only one among other characteristically Christian ideas, such fundamental significance as to call it a fundamental motif? These questions must now receive a definite answer.

First, then, what do we mean by calling anything a fundamental motif? The primary associations of the term are perhaps with the realm of art. The fundamental motif is that which makes a work of art into a unified whole, determines its structure, and gives it its specific character. It is the theme that constantly recurs in new variations, imparting its own tone and color to the whole. But broad and indefinite statements like these are insufficient to show the precise sense in which we are using the term "fundamental motif." For this purpose the following definition may be given: A *fundamental motif is that which forms the answer given by some particular outlook to a question of such a fundamental nature that it can be described in a categorical sense as a fundamental question.* To develop the full meaning of this statement we should have to go into the whole doctrine of the categories, for which this is naturally not the place. All we can do here is to touch on the most necessary points.

If we take the broadest possible survey of human thought, we get a lively impression of the truth of the old saying that there is nothing—or very little—new under the sun. There are a certain few themes which constantly recur in fresh variations and combinations, but in such a way that the old theme can still be recognized in the new forms. Quite early in the history of thought we find the great fundamental questions asked concerning the True, the Beautiful, the Good, and—to crown them all—the Eternal. For our Western civilization the formal statement of these questions was the work of Plato, though the materials for it were in existence long before his time. And great as the changes may be which these questions have undergone since, we can none the less say that we are still occupied ultimately with these same great questions today when we speak of the problems of Knowledge, of Esthetics, of Ethics, and of Religion. Indeed, we might very well describe the whole development of civilized thought as a constantly renewed attempt to state these questions and fix their meaning. It happens, however, from time to time in the historical process that the meaning of one or other of these questions is completely altered. This is the way in which new developments take place with respect to the great fundamental questions of humanity. It is not that a traditional question is set aside and a new question substituted for it, but rather that a new meaning is unexpectedly discovered in the old question. The form of the question remains unchanged, but its content is different; it does not mean the same; the frame is old but the picture is new.

When we speak of a fundamental motif we are moving in the realm of those comprehensive, ultimate questions which we have just mentioned. The fundamental motif is the answer given by some particular type of outlook to one or more of these questions. This answer need by no means take the form of a theoretical proposition; it can equally well be a general, underlying sentiment which involves a certain attitude towards these questions or—more passively—a certain reaction to them. There is thus a close connection between fundamental motifs and fundamental questions of the "categorical" kind we have described; but it is of the greatest importance to maintain a clear distinction between them. They differ as a question and an answer differ, and this difference cannot safely be ignored.

In all ages it has been the conscious or unconscious endeavor of metaphysics to blur this distinction. Men have believed that by philosophical analysis the answer could be deduced from the question. At this point there is an obvious difference between the metaphysical systems and every religious outlook. Even though the two types may state their answer (often for emotional reasons) in very similar language, yet the difference always remains. The metaphysician always tries in one way or another to deduce his answer as "necessary," while the religious mind firmly refuses to do so, but insists on its answer as axiomatic and thus maintains a synthetic relation between question and answer.

In the case of two of these great fundamental questions, the ethical and the religious, Christianity has brought a revolutionary change not only with regard to the answers but with regard to the questions themselves. It has so altered the way of putting both these questions that they no longer have the same meaning as before, and it has also given them both a new answer. This change, in respect both of questions and answers alike, is essentially bound up with the idea of Agape.

Agape as the Fundamental Motif of Christianity

The fundamental motif of an outlook is its answer to a fundamental question of a "categorical" nature. We have observed that human thought concentrates on a few such questions. There are a certain few great questions, first raised long ago, which recur with extraordinary persistence throughout history, demanding an answer. When men grapple with these questions their concern as a rule is simply to find an answer to them; they rarely think of the questions themselves—that is, the way in which they are stated—as a matter for investigation. The questions are simply taken over from tradition as something given and once for all established. But a question has an extraordinary power of suggestion and constraint. It directs our attention to the different possible answers and so seems to leave all the different possibilities open; yet the number of possible answers may be seriously limited by the very way in which the question is put. To a wrongly stated question there can be no right answer. The question thus indirectly influences the answer. It is in this way, above all, that a fundamental question stated in a certain way can hold the minds of men in bondage for centuries, not to say millennia. What men seek is a better way of answering the question, while the question itself is passed on unaltered. Modifications of the fundamental questions, therefore, generally take place more or less unawares, and it is only rarely that a really radical revolution occurs. When this happens it is the result of a new total attitude to life in general.

Two of these extremely rare revolutions—that which has turned the religious question from an egocentric into a theocentric question, and that which has freed the ethical question from eudaimonism and turned it into the question of "the Good-in-itself"—have resulted, as we have seen, from the contribution made by Christianity. But the creative significance of Christianity is not exhausted in the restatement of questions. It is manifested even more clearly in the answer that Christianity gives to the fundamental religious and ethical questions thus restated. Here we find also that characteristically Christian interpenetration of religion and ethics of which we spoke above, for to both these questions Christianity gives precisely the same answer. To the religious question, now stated in theocentric terms, What is God? Christianity replies with the Johannine formula: God is ἀγάπη. And to the ethical question, What is the Good, the "Good-in-itself"? the answer is similar: The Good is ἀγάπη, and the ethical demand finds summary expression in the Commandment of Love, the commandment to love God and my neighbor.

We have therefore every right to say that ἀγάπη is the center of Christianity, the Christian fundamental motif *par excellence*, the answer to both the religious and the ethical question. Agape comes to us as a quite new creation of Christianity. It sets its mark on everything in Christianity. Without it nothing that is Christian would be Christian. Agape is Christianity's own original basic conception.

25. William Temple, *The Person of Christ*

We have seen that every grade in Reality finds its own fulfillment only when it is possessed by a higher grade, and that each higher grade uses those which are lower than itself for its expression. From this it follows that humanity only reveals its true nature when it is indwelt by what is higher than itself—and supremely when it is indwelt by the Highest; and that the Highest uses what is lower to express himself and does this the more adequately as this lower approximates to likeness with himself, so that of all things known to us human nature will express him most perfectly. But if this is so, and if in Jesus Christ God lived on earth a human life, then it must be true that in Jesus Christ we shall find two things. In Jesus Christ we shall find the one adequate presentation of God—not adequate, of course, to the infinite glory of God in all his attributes, but adequate to every human need, for it shows us God in terms of our own experience. But in Jesus Christ we shall find also the one adequate presentation of man—not man as he is apart from the indwelling of God, but man as he is in his truest nature, which is only made actual when man becomes the means to the self-expression of God.

Part of the difficulty which a great teacher finds in conveying the new truth arises from the necessity of using words of which the meaning is already fixed. So the Lord Jesus was compelled to accept the title and office of the expected Messiah, because that came nearer than any other that existed to the truth about himself. The central core of meaning attached to this title was that the Messiah would inaugurate the kingdom of God; and this indeed he did; but all the existing conceptions of the kingdom and of the mode of its inauguration were so inadequate as to be misleading and productive of great difficulties in the minds of his hearers. He had to transform the meaning of the terms "Messiah" and "Kingdom" by the use which he made of them. So, later on, St. John spoke of him as the Logos, though this word too in current use had many shades of meaning that were irrelevant or misleading.

This difficulty is nowhere more apparent than in the efforts of the early church to reach some understanding of the Person of Jesus Christ. Somehow, all Christians were agreed, he is rightly called God and man. But when men began to enquire how? and became involved thereby in controversy, they were hampered by the notions of Godhead and humanity which already existed. That the same being should be both God and man in the sense in which those terms were commonly understood in the period of the church's early history was not an unintelligible mystery but a demonstrable impossibility. And yet nothing else was adequate to the fact. The church at Chalcedon virtually gave up the attempt to understand, while refusing to sacrifice either part of its apparently contradictory belief. All through the age of the Councils the whole conception of both God and man was undergoing modification, partly through the influence of the incarnation itself, partly also through the clarifying and hardening of the Greek and (in origin) heathen terminology which was alone available. The process of modification is still continuing, and presumably will continue until "the consummation of the ages." But it is at least a gain to recognize it; for as soon as we recognize it we are delivered from the futile endeavor to fit into a coherent theory of the Person of Christ conceptions of God and man which are derived wholly from elsewhere. Certainly we do not approach the problem with minds nearly blank. The conceptions of God and man derived from elsewhere—from ordinary experience, from human religion, from pre-Christian revelation—are not merely false or irrelevant. They are provisionally true, if they are adequate to the facts which give rise to them, and the truth which they contain cannot be obliterated by further revelation. But their truth is of this provisional kind; and we shall not be dismayed to find that if they are to become adequate to a fuller reality they require modification. On the contrary, we shall expect this, and deliberately assist it. Our sacramental philosophy leads at once to the supposition that nothing is fully known till it is possessed by a higher. An observer on another planet watching the nebula out of which our solar system grew might have formed a theory of matter which would have been adequate to the facts before him; but he could not have constructed the sciences of zoology, biology, or physiology; and when the data were offered on which those sciences are based, he would have had to revise his theory. Similarly, no observer knowing only animal life could anticipate human nature and human history.

Now if in Jesus Christ God lived a human life for the purpose of inaugurating his kingdom, that is an event which marks a new stage as truly as the first appearance of life or the first appearance of man. Therefore the theory or doctrine of the Person of Christ will not be found by merely stating his nature and works in terms of God and man, but will involve restating God and man in terms of the revelation given in him. . . .

When life supervenes upon Matter, it does not indeed lead to any contradiction of the "laws" of physical chemistry, but it takes direction of the physico-chemical system; it asserts priority in the sense that the explanation of the action of the living thing is sought in the requirements of its life. The physical system supplies the conditions *sine quibus non*; the life supplies the efficient causation. So when mind supervenes upon the living organism, it takes direction and becomes the cause of the agent's conduct. We shall expect, therefore, to find that when God supervenes upon humanity, we do not find a human being taken into fellowship with God, but God acting through the conditions supplied by humanity. And this is the Christian experience of Jesus Christ; he is spoken of as a Mediator, but that expression is used, not to signify one who is raised above humanity by an infusion of deity, but one in whom deity and humanity are perfectly united. This is the first point which the early theologians were concerned about in their insistence that in Christ there is only one Hypostasis and that this is not human but divine. The root of this belief is, however, the testimony of Christian experience, that fellowship with Christ is in itself fellowship with God. This testimony coincides with what we are led to expect by the analogy of the whole creation. We may say, then, without any hesitation that Christ is not a man exalted to perfect participation in the Divine Nature or Life; he is God, manifest under the conditions of humanity. The first disciples had to approach by gradual stages the realization of what lay behind the human life and was finding expression in and through it; that was the order of discovery; but it is not the order of reality. We see a man's bodily movements first and from them infer his purpose and character; but the purpose is prior and directs the movements. So we see the human life and infer the divine Person; but the Person controls and directs the life. What we find in Christian experience is witness, not to a man uniquely inspired, but to God living a human life.

Now this is exactly the culmination of that stratification which is the structure of Reality; far therefore from being incredible, it is to be expected, it is antecedently probable. Even had there been no evil in the world to be overcome, no sin to be abolished and forgiven, still the incarnation would be the natural inauguration of the final stage of evolution. In this sense, the incarnation is perfectly intelligible; that is to say, we can see that its occurrence is all of a piece with the scheme of reality as traced elsewhere.

But in another sense, it is and must remain beyond our understanding; we can understand the grades of reality subordinate to our own; we can in some degree, though perhaps not completely, understand our own. For the understanding of those above our own, or of our own as completed by the indwelling of the higher, we have not the necessary data. Our effort, therefore, to deal with the problems that arise from belief in the incarnation must start with the confession, or rather with the claim, that from the nature of the case their solution cannot be found by us. If any man says that he understands the relation of deity to humanity in Christ, he only makes it clear that he does not understand at all what is meant by an incarnation.

First there is the Nestorian difficulty: can we call a child three months old by the name of God? Or, to put the question in a modern shape, are we to say that the Infant Jesus directed from his manger at Bethlehem the affairs of Mars? This kind of difficulty has an honorable origin insofar as it is based on a determination to think things through, but it also arises from following the speculative enquiry into regions where we have no data, and forgetting the purpose of the divine act which is being considered. That purpose would seem to be twofold—revelation and atonement. For the former, what is necessary is that Jesus Christ should be truly God and truly man; for the latter what seems to be necessary is that human experience as conditioned by the sin of men should become the personal experience of God the Son—not an object of external observation but of inward feeling (to use the language of human consciousness). Neither of these requires that God the Son should be active only in Jesus of Nazareth during the days of the incarnation. "The light that lighteneth even man" did not cease to do so when he shone in full brilliance in one human Life. Jesus did not control affairs in Mars, or in China. But God the Son, who is the Word of God by whom, as agent, all things came to be and apart from whom no single thing has come to be, without ceasing his creative and sustaining work, added this to it that he became flesh and dwelt as in a tabernacle among us, so that as in the old Tabernacle there dwelt the cloud of the divine glory, so in him we saw a glory that shone through him but found in him its perfect and unique expression—"glory as of an only-be-gotten Son from a Father." He who is always God became also man—not ceasing to be God the while. For the incarnation was effected "not by Conversion of the Godhead into flesh, but by taking of manhood into God."

No doubt this position involves a difficulty with regard to the mode of the consciousness of the Eternal Son; but that is exactly where the difficulty ought most clearly to arise, for about the mode of his consciousness we can have simply no knowledge whatever. Meanwhile, if it is admissible at all it brings an im-mense alleviation of the problem which theologians have sought to solve by pressing to its furthest implications St. Paul's language about the self-emptying of himself by the pre-existent Christ in the act of his incarnation. I confess to an un-easy feeling that when this vigorous expression of a great spiritual truth is taken as precise and scientific theology, we are involved in something dangerously close to mythology. To say that God the Eternal Son at a moment of time di-vested himself of omniscience and omnipotence in order to live a human life, re-assuming these attributes at the ascension, seems to me just the kind of thing that no event occurring on this planet could ever justify. It is not of course a view that can be condemned as impossible; but it involves an assertion about the Infinite and Eternal which reverence should make us slow to make, and the evidence on which it rests is as such as, in my judgment, neither is nor could be sufficient to warrant it.

If God the Son lived the life recorded in the Gospels, then in that life we see, set forth in terms of human experience, the very reality of God the Son. The lim-itations of knowledge and power are conditions of the revelation, without which there would be no revelation *to us* at all; but the Person who lives under those limitations is the Eternal Son in whom the life of the Eternal Father goes forth in creative activity and returns in filial love. The incarnation is an episode in the life or being of God the Son; but it is not a mere episode, it is a revealing episode. There we see what he who is God's wisdom always is, even more completely than any kenotic theory allows. This view makes the humiliation and death of Christ "the measure of that love which has throbbed in the divine heart from all eter-nity." Certain attributes or functions incompatible with humanity are, in this ac-tivity of the Eternal Son, not exercised; but what we see is not any mere parable of the life of God, not an interval of humiliation between two eternities of glory. It is the divine glory itself.

As we watch that human life, we do not say: "Ah—but soon he will return to the painless joy of the glory which was his and will be his again." As we watch that life and, above all, that death we say, "We behold his glory." For God is chiefly seen in the activity of love.

In doing this, moreover, the Son of God has made our condition matter of his own experience. To the sympathy and insight of omniscient love no limit can be set, and we dare not say that after the incarnation he understood us better than before. But it is mere matter of historic fact that before the incarnation men could not say, and after the incarnation we thankfully can say, concerning the Eternal Son himself: "in that he himself hath suffered being tempted he is able to succour them that are tempted."

This human life is the very life of God. It is both human and divine in every detail. If we know what we are about we may rightly say that the unity of God and man in Christ is a unity of will, for will is the whole being of a person organized for action. But the phrase is liable to mislead, because we have to think by the analogy of our own experience, and in us will does not in fact cover the whole of our personal being, because we have not attained that perfection of personal unity which is the completedness of will. Therefore in us will is still departmental; and to say that the unity of God and man in Christ is a unity of will consequently suggests that this unity is not complete, and concerns something only adjectival. It is better then to say that in Christ God and man are personally one; the Person of the man Christ Jesus is God the Son.

Then is the humanity impersonal? or does it find its personality only in God the Son? Plainly the position indicated is that which was formulated by Leontius of Byzantium with the terms adjusted to modern usage. Indeed, the actual adjustment of terms is so slight that it may conceal the very real modification in the thought expressed. By Person we do not understand an ultimate point of reference, but the entirety of the spiritual being. As Person Jesus is both man and God.

But we must not lose what was precious in the older way of thinking, especially what was involved in the doctrine of the two wills. We cannot predicate moral progress of God the Son; we must predicate such progress, as shown above, of Jesus Christ. Therefore the will in him, while always one with, because expressive of, the will of God, is not merely identical with it. In the struggle with temptation the human will or person is at once manifesting and approximating to the will of God, until as the passion approaches and love is about to be exhibited in the perfection of sacrifice, he prays to be glorified with the eternal glory — which is the perfect sacrifice of perfect love.

Consequently, though there is only one Person, one living and energizing being, I should not hesitate to speak of the human personality of Christ. But that personality does not exist side by side with the divine personality; it is subsumed in it. Will and personality are ideally interchangeable terms; there are two wills in the Incarnate in the sense that his human nature comes through struggle and effort to an ever deeper union with the divine in completeness of self-sacrifice. And it is only because there is this real human will or personality that there is here any revelation to humanity of the divine will. Thus I do not speak of his humanity as impersonal. If we imagine the divine Word withdrawn from Jesus of Nazareth, as the Gnostics believed to have occurred before the passion, I think that there would be left, not nothing at all, but a man. Yet this human personality is actually the self-expression of the Eternal Son, so that as we watch the human life we become aware that it is the vehicle of a divine life, and that the

273

human personality of Jesus Christ is subsumed in the divine Person of the creative Word.

The doctrine of the impersonal humanity of Christ had, however, another and more practical significance than that of preserving a theoretic union of two natures in one Person; it was associated with the notion of "real universals," and implied that when Christ assumed human nature he assumed the nature of all of us, so that by his incarnation we are united, in him, to God. That is profoundly important, but it makes difficulties when so stated; for it ought to involve that all men, whether believers or not, are forthwith united to God; and experience tells us that this union is at best incomplete, while the same theologians, who state a doctrine logically involving the union of all men with God, actually limit this to members of the Christian church, who have still, moreover, to renew and deepen that unity by sacraments and lives of service.

We still believe in "real universals," but they are concrete, not abstract, universals. There is no such thing as human nature apart from all individual human beings. But there is a perfectly real thing called mankind or humanity which is a unit and not a mere agglomeration. As each man is a focusing point for Reality as seen from the place within it which he occupies, he is very largely constituted what he is by the character of his fellow-men. Influence is not an affair of external impact but of inward constitution of the person influenced. Therefore mankind or humanity is a close-knit system of mutually influencing units. In this sense, the humanity of every one of us is "impersonal"; and the greater the man, the less merely "personal" is his humanity. He is more, not less, individual than others; but he is individual by the uniqueness of his focus for the universe, not by his exclusion of all that is not himself. He more than others is humanity focused in one centre. Into this system of mutually influencing units Christ has come; but here is a unit perfectly capable, as others are only imperfectly capable, both of personal union with all other persons and of refusing to be influenced by the evil of his environment. It is this more than anything else which proves him to be more and other than his fellow-men. But thus he inaugurates a new system of influence; and as this corresponds to God's will for mankind, its appeal is to the true nature of men. So he is a second Adam; what occurred at the incarnation was not merely the addition of another unit to the system of mutually influencing units, it was the inauguration of a new system of mutual influence, destined to become, here or elsewhere, universally dominant. "By his incarnation," therefore, the Lord did indeed "raise our humanity to an entirely higher level, to a level with his own"; but this was not accomplished by the unspiritual process of an infusion of an alien "nature" but by the spiritual process of mutual influence and love that calls forth love. If this seems less than the other, it is only because we have let our pride teach us to emphasize separateness as the fundamental characteristic of our personality, so that influence only shapes but does not constitute us; this we have seen to be false. I am mankind—England—my school— my family—focused in a point of its own history. Mankind—"Adam"—has made me what I am. If similarly Christ makes me something else — the participator in his own divine freedom — then indeed "there is a new creation; the old things are passed away; behold, they are become new" (2 Cor. 5:17).

Thus in a most real sense Christ is not only a man; he is man. In Dr. Moberly's phrase, "Christ is man not generically but inclusively," just as he is "God not generically but identically." All the significance and destiny of the human race is summed up in him. He is the Head of the Body. But this is by no mechanical identification; it is by a spiritual transformation, wrought out, as is the self-manifestation of God in the incarnation, through the process of time and the course of history.

10

Transcendental Thomism

Roman Catholic theology is obviously underrepresented in this volume. This has a reason, though with unlimited space the editors might have found ways around it.

We have wanted to provide a *map* of *specifically* twentieth-century theology. We have not wanted simply to provide an anthology or even typology of theology written in the twentieth century, but to trace the course of twentieth-century theology as an identifiable period with its own characteristic branchings and bypaths. The general history within which such a twentieth-century story can be told began with the Enlightenment and continued with the nineteenth century's labor to "overcome" the Enlightenment; our twentieth-century narrative is an account of the conflicted and creative aftermath of rebellion against or persistence in the nineteenth century's thinking. But *mainline* Catholic theology, until recently, simply opposed the Enlightenment; in consequence, the history just outlined has been carried mostly by Protestant theologians.

Precisely as the Enlightenment began, Catholic and Protestant mutual condemnations had become so rigid that neither side could perceive in the other anything but an alien spirit, from which true Christianity had simply to be defended. With much justification, Catholic teaching authorities saw the Enlightenment as part and parcel of Protestantism. Thus, as Catholicism fortified itself morally and intellectually against Protestantism, it fortified itself also against the Enlightenment. Whether this strategy was well or ill advised, is perhaps not yet to be known.

Thus, from the seventeenth century until well into the twentieth, as Protestant theology underwent its modern upheavals, mainline Catholic theology instead labored at the ever greater sophistication of theological structures established in the century after the Council of Trent. This is not to say that all Catholic thinkers were occupied with this project or unaffected by the currents of modern thinking, particularly in the later nineteenth century. European "Reform Catholic" and "Modernist" movements and reactions, led by such figures as George Tyrrell (1861–1909) in England and Alfred Loisy (1857–1940) in France, ranged from mild proposals of dialogue to rejections of central Catholic positions; the "Americanism" of such leaders as Isaak Hecker (1819–1888) affirmed liberal democracy as an appropriate context of Catholic life and remains influential; and the earlier "Tübingen School" of theology represented by such figures as Johann-Sebastian Drey (1777–1853), Johann Adam Möhler (1796–1838), Johannes von Kuhn (1806–1887), *et al.*, was romantic and idealist rather than scholastic in its thinking. But only in the latter part of the period our book covers did Catholicism open her central theological life to explicit confrontation with modernity. The pressure for an opening to modern problems and habits of thought built through the first half of the century, and with the Second Vatican Council burst all remaining barriers.

It is a caricature, but for our purpose an illuminating one, to say that as Catholic theology's late-twentieth-century *"aggiornamento"* ("updating") has in fact worked out, it has been a much accelerated rerun of eighteenth- and nineteenth-century Protestant theology. And if predictions can be based on the analogy—which they probably cannot—we may expect that Catholic analogies to the theology characterized as "twentieth-century" for the concept of this book will appear only when this recapitulation is complete.

It would nevertheless be rigid indeed, on such accounts, to ignore the recent great efflorescence of Catholic theology. We must at least mention three major theologians of the Vatican II generation, whose thought will surely figure importantly in theological history: Karl Rahner (1904–1984), who is represented in an earlier chapter of this work, Bernard Lonergan (1904–1984), and Hans Urs von Balthasar (1905–1984). Von Balthasar is perhaps the giant of the three, and may also prove to have been a sort of Karl Barth of Catholicism's own "twentieth-century" theology—which will reveal his exclusion from our volume as a major blunder. It is nevertheless the work of the other two from which we here provide samples, because of their currently dominant influence in English-speaking Catholicism. And if we press our conceit one more time, we may say that Lonergan may prove to have been something like Catholic theology's Immanuel Kant—to be sure, a more orthodox Kant, though some of his followers have not been—and Rahner, its Friedrich Schleiermacher. (T. F. Torrance is said to have called *Lonergan* the Catholic Schleiermacher, but perhaps our conceit is better.)

I

Bernard Lonergan's thought is determined by a combination of post-Reformation Catholic theology's traditional presumption that theology must have a pretheological "foundation" for the plausibility of its assertions, with determination to respond to the intellectual challenges of modernity. Medieval theology founded its systematic structures by appropriating the systematics of Aristotle; now, says Lonergan, it is time—and past time—to use more modern thinking to the same purpose. Decisive for general European and North American thought from Descartes on has been, in Lonergan's judgment, "the turn to the subject." Lonergan's project is the implementation of this turn also within Catholic theology. Theology's appropriate procedures are to be discovered, and its cognition gotten underway, by self-analysis of that human subject who knows God and does theology.

Justly or unjustly, it is "the method," Lonergan's analysis of human subjectivity and his resulting methodological prescriptions, for which he is most known, rather than his more material contributions to theology. Characterization of Lonergan as Catholicism's Immanuel Kant may derive some plausibility from his own two chief slogans for "the method": it is "transcendental" and "fully critical."

The method is "transcendental" in the sense of German Kantianism and phenomenology. When we perceive or judge or choose, we are or can be simultaneously aware that we are doing these things. In such awareness, we can move back a step and inquire into the "condition of the possibility," *die Bedingung der Möglichkeit,* of our perceiving or judging or choosing. That is, we can discover structures of subjectivity itself that transcend, enable, and shape all particular acts or states of the subject. According to Lonergan, such transcendental reflection does three things for theology.

First, it discovers a set of intellectual and moral acts which are carried out by any successful effort of cognition and so must be carried out also by theology. The acts of *attention* to information, of seeking possible *explanations,* of *judging* the adequacy of proposed explanations, and of *commitment* to the results of judgment, are performed in varied modalities whenever created subjects know. Just so, modulated descriptions of these transcendentals can be prescriptions for the procedure of any particular discipline. *Method in Theology,* here excerpted, is in large part a description of the right theological curriculum.

Second, Lonergan argues that if we are fully "converted" to procedures of thought appropriate to thought's true character, then when the matter of our reflection is religion, in its generality and within the religious tradition in which we live, we will be led to affirm the plausibility of theism and indeed of Christian theism. The transcendental patterns at work in all knowing point to a transcendent Knowing, that can be shown to be in fact the God of Christianity. Thus, theology has a transcendental foundation also in the sense that transcendental reflection is itself theology's particular "condition of possibility."

Third, transcendental reflection provides the model by which Christian doctrines must themselves be understood in modernity or postmodernity. Here, Lonergan depends on the traditional Augustinian notion that the human mind and its acts are the primary created image of God. God is an unrestricted act of understanding, to which our understanding is analogous; transcendental reflection on our own capacity and action of understanding can therefore guide our knowledge of God.

All this holds, to be sure, only if our thinking is "fully critical." According to Lonergan, the Enlightenment never carried its critique of appearances all the way: modernity's various relativisms, which doubt that the "constructs" of our knowledge—for example, neutrons, past history, or God—are true *of* anything, are all survivals of the precritical supposition that "real" knowing is looking and seeing, so that what cannot be looked at cannot be a real object of knowledge. But the real simply *is*, according to Lonergan, that which is there to be grasped by actual knowing, that is, by acts that must go beyond looking and seeing to explaining, judging, and choosing. That by our explanations and judgments we *construct* history or physics or divine being does not impugn their status as real things that are known, it is the necessary condition of that status. Once this is recognized, modernity's hindrances to recognition of God and of the appropriateness of Christian teachings about God fall away.

II

Karl Rahner's program resembles Lonergan's in many ways. But Rahner is less given to laying out formulaic results of transcendental reflection itself, and is better known for material theological positions transcendentally supported and conceived. Also with Rahner, we may speak of a combination: in his case, of commitment to transcendental method with "Thomism" of a particular sort.

Through the nineteenth and early twentieth centuries, French Catholicism sometimes made an exception to the general picture of Catholicism, producing movements that challenged the notion of "fortress church." In the process, French Catholicism also nurtured more open theological enterprises. Especially relevant to our purpose are a series of Thomistic revivals, and most immediately the reinterpretation of Thomas pursued in the 1930s and 1940s by such thinkers as Joseph Maréchal (1878–1944), Henri de Lubac (1896–1991), and Henri Bouillard (1908–). For quick access to Rahner, we note one aspect of this Thomism: its understanding of "nature" and "grace."

Standard Catholic theology had tended to understand "nature" as one thing and "grace" as simply another. *Very* crudely: what we have by "nature" we have independently of what God's grace in Christ brings us; conversely, "grace" is a sheer addition to natural possibilities. De Lubac and others found a quite different conception in Thomas. The "nature" that is not yet graced is a mere—if in some conceptual contexts necessary—

abstraction from actual created human nature. This actual nature is antecedently founded on and enduringly maintained by that very same grace of God that is actual as Christ. Sharply stated: created human nature *is* openness to God in Christ.

Karl Rahner's move was to interpret Thomas's openness of human nature to divine grace by modernity's transcendental philosophy. He regards such interpretation not merely as possible but as mandatory. According to Rahner, it was classic Christian theology whose insights into the special character of personal being enabled modernity's transcendentalism in the first place; theology's appropriation of this thinking is merely reappropriation of its own inheritance.

In this interpretation, the constitutive openness of human nature to God appears as a constitutive openness of human subjectivity to a transcendent horizon of all particular discoveries of meaning. This horizon is the mystery that is God. The human spirit, precisely as reason, is "absolute transcendence," the possibility of the presence of Mystery, and at heart it is nothing but that. For we "grasp" the finite objects of our experience precisely as our intention reaches beyond and around them, and so as we grasp toward what we do not grasp. The presence to and in our subjectivity of transcending Mystery is thus the condition of all our knowing and choosing of finite objects. Nature is founded in grace.

Kant as interpreted by Martin Heidegger is Rahner's interlocutor in such reflection. Thus, perhaps Rahner's most characteristic way of founding theology is to say that *"Dasein,"* human existence in its temporal finitude, is itself a question to and about itself, and that God is what the question intends. There is a "supernatural existential"; it is natural to *Dasein* to go beyond what is natural to it.

It will be seen how close this transcendentalism is, *mutatis mutandis,* to that of Schleiermacher. A consequence that results for Schleiermacher results also for Rahner: Christian theological propositions are and must be treated as expressions of Christian religious experience. Rahner's difference from Schleiermacher—and it is a great difference—is that Rahner has the concrete church as the final subject of Christian experience, rather than the individual as such, and indeed a churchly office that distinguishes authentic from unauthentic such experience.

It is a further consequence—and a further analogy to Schleiermacher—that according to Rahner every theological topic must be treated in two ways. "Transcendental" theology must display the condition in human subjectivity of, for example, finding a Savior in the person Jesus Christ. Continuing with the example, "categorial" theology then describes the actual person Jesus Christ as this Savior. In just this fashion, Rahner wrote on nearly every traditional topic of theology, even though he never produced a *summa. Foundations of Christian Faith,* here excerpted, perhaps comes as near to a general statement of Rahner's positions as he ever wished to come.

26. Bernard J. F. Lonergan, *Method in Theology*

A Preliminary Notion

A method is a normative pattern of recurrent and related operations yielding cumulative and progressive results. There is a method, then, where there are distinct operations, where each operation is related to the others, where the set of relations forms a pattern, where the pattern is described as the right way of doing the job, where operations in accord with the pattern may be repeated indefinitely, and where the fruits of such repetition are not repetitious, but cumulative and progressive.

So in the natural sciences method inculcates a spirit of inquiry and inquiries recur. It insists on accurate observation and description: both observations and descriptions recur. It demands the formulation of discoveries in hypotheses, and hypotheses recur. It requires the deduction of the implications of hypotheses, and deductions recur. It keeps urging that experiments be devised and performed to check the implications of hypotheses against observable fact, and such processes of experimentation recur.

The Basic Pattern of Operations

Operations in the pattern are seeing, hearing, touching, smelling, tasting, inquiring, imagining, understanding, conceiving, formulating, reflecting, marshalling and weighing the evidence, judging, deliberating, evaluating, deciding, speaking, writing.

It will be assumed that everyone is familiar with some at least of these operations and that he has some notion of what the other terms mean. Our purpose is to bring to light the pattern within which these operations occur. . . .

First, then, the operations in the list are transitive. They have objects. They are transitive not merely in the grammatical sense that they are denoted by transitive verbs but also in the psychological sense that by the operation one becomes aware of the object. This psychological sense is what is meant by the verb, intend, the adjective, intentional, the noun, intentionality. To say that the operations intend objects is to refer to such facts as that by seeing there becomes present what is seen, by hearing there becomes present what is heard, by imagining there becomes present what is imagined, and so on, where in each case the presence in question is a psychological event.

Secondly, the operations in the list are operations of an operator, and the operator is named the subject. The operator is subject not merely in the grammatical sense that he is denoted by a noun that is subject of the verbs that in the active voice refer to the operations. He also is subject in the psychological sense that he operates consciously. In fact, none of the operations in the list are to be performed in dreamless sleep or in a coma. Again, whenever any of the operations are performed, the subject is aware of himself operating, present to himself operating, experiencing himself operating. Moreover, as will appear presently, the quality of consciousness changes as the subject performs different operations.

The operations then not only intend objects. There is to them a further psychological dimension. They occur consciously and by them the operating subject is conscious. Just as operations by their intentionality make objects present to the subject, so also by consciousness they make the operating subject present to himself.

I have used the adjective, present, both of the object and of the subject. But I have used it ambiguously, for the presence of the object is quite different from the presence of the subject. The object is present as what is gazed upon, attended to, intended. But the presence of the subject resides in the gazing, the attending, the intending. For this reason the subject can be conscious, as attending, and yet give his whole attention to the object as attended to.

Again, I spoke of the subject experiencing himself operating. But I do not suppose that this experiencing is another operation to be added to the list, for this experiencing is not intending but being conscious. It is not another operation over and above the operation that is experienced. It is that very operation which, besides being intrinsically intentional, also is intrinsically conscious. . . .

Different levels of consciousness and intentionality have to be distinguished. In our dream states consciousness and intentionality commonly are fragmentary and incoherent. When we awake, they take on a different hue to expand on four successive, related, but qualitatively different levels. There is the empirical level on which we sense, perceive, imagine, feel, speak, move. There is an intellectual level on which we inquire, come to understand, express what we have understood, work out the presuppositions and implications of our expression. There is the rational level on which we reflect, marshal the evidence, pass judgment on the truth or falsity, certainty or probability, of a statement. There is the responsible level on which we are concerned with ourselves, our own operations, our goals, and so deliberate about possible course of action, evaluate them, decide, and carry out our decisions.

All the operations on these four levels are intentional and conscious. Still, intentionality and consciousness differ from level to level, and within each level the many operations involve further differences. Our consciousness expands in a new dimension when from mere experiencing we turn to the effort to understand what we have experienced. A third dimension of rationality emerges when the content of our acts of understanding is regarded as, of itself, a mere bright idea and we endeavor to settle what really is so. A fourth dimension comes to the fore when judgment on the facts is followed by deliberation on what we are to do about them. On all four levels, we are aware of ourselves but, as we mount from

282

level to level, it is a fuller self of which we are aware and the awareness itself is different.

As empirically conscious, we do not seem to differ from the higher animals. But in us empirical consciousness and intentionality are only a substratum for further activities. The data of sense provoke inquiry, inquiry leads to understanding, understanding expresses itself in language. Without the data there would be nothing for us to inquire about and nothing to be understood. Yet what is sought by inquiry is never just another datum but the idea or form, the intelligible unity or relatedness, that organizes data into intelligible wholes. Again, without the effort to understand and its conflicting results, we would have no occasion to judge. But such occasions are recurrent, and then the intelligent center of experiencing reveals his reflective and critical rationality. Once more there is a fuller self of which we become aware, and once more the awareness itself is different. As intelligent, the subject seeks insight and, as insights accumulate, he reveals them in his behavior, his speech, his grasp of situations, his mastery of theoretic domains. But as reflectively and critically conscious, he incarnates detachment and disinterestedness, gives himself over to criteria of truth and certitude, makes his sole concern the determination of what is or is not so; and now, as the self, so also the awareness of self resides in that incarnation, that self-surrender, that single-minded concern for truth. There is a still further dimension to being human, and there we emerge as persons, meet one another in a common concern for values, seek to abolish the organization of human living on the basis of competing egoisms and to replace it by an organization on the basis of man's perceptiveness and intelligence, his reasonableness, and his responsible exercise of freedom.

Fifthly, as different operations yield qualitatively different modes of being conscious subjects, so too they yield qualitatively different modes of intending. The intending of our senses is an attending; it normally is selective but not creative. What is grasped in insight, is neither an actually given datum of sense nor a creation of the imagination but an intelligible organization that may or may not be relevant to data. The intending that is conception puts together both the content of the insight and as much of the image as is essential to the occurrence of the insight; the result is the intending of any concrete being selected by an incompletely determinate (and, in that sense, abstract) content.

However, the most fundamental difference in modes of intending lies between the categorial and the transcendental. Categories are determinations. They have a limited denotation. They vary with cultural variations. They may be illustrated by the type of classification associated with totemism and recently argued to be essentially a classification by homology. They may be reflectively known as categories, as were the Aristotelian substance, quantity, quality, relation, action, passion, place, time, posture, habit. They need not be called categories, as were the four causes, end agent, matter, form or the logical distinctions of genus, difference, species, property, accident. They may be the fine products of scientific achievement as the concepts of modern physics, the chemist's periodic table, the biologist's evolutionary tree.

In contrast, the transcendentals are comprehensive in connotation, unrestricted in denotation, invariant over cultural change. While categories are needed to put determinate questions and give determinate answers, the transcendentals are contained in questions prior to the answers. They are the radical intending that moves us from ignorance to knowledge. They are a priori because they go beyond what we know to seek what we do not know yet. They are unrestricted because answers are never complete and so only give rise to still further questions. They are comprehensive because they intend the unknown whole or totality of which our answers reveal only part. So intelligence takes us beyond experiencing to ask what and why and how and what for. Reasonableness takes us beyond the answers of intelligence to ask whether the answers are true and whether what they mean really is so. Responsibility goes beyond fact and desire and possibility to discern between what truly is good and what only apparently is good. So if we objectify the content of intelligent intending, we form the transcendental concept of the intelligible. If we objectify the content of reasonable intending, we form the transcendental concepts of the true and the real. If we objectify the content of responsible intending, we get the transcendental concept of value, of the truly good. But quite distinct from such transcendental concepts, which can be misconceived and often are, there are the prior transcendental notions that constitute the very dynamism of our conscious intending, promoting us from mere experiencing towards understanding, from mere understanding towards truth and reality, from factual knowledge to responsible action. That dynamism, so far from being a product of cultural advance, is the condition of its possibility; and any ignorance or error, any negligence or malice, that misrepresents or blocks that dynamism is obscurantism in its most radical form.

Sixthly, we began by speaking of operations intending objects. Now we must distinguish between elementary and compound objects, elementary and compound knowing. By elementary knowing is meant any cognitional operation, such as seeing, hearing, understanding, and so on. By the elementary object is meant what is intended in elementary knowing. By compound knowing is meant the conjunction of several instances of elementary knowing into a single knowing. By the compound object is meant the object constructed by uniting several elementary objects.

Now the process of compounding is the work of the transcendental notions which, from the beginning, intend the unknown that, gradually, becomes better known. In virtue of this intending, what is experienced can be the same as what is understood; what is experienced and understood can be the same as what is conceived, can be the same as what is affirmed to be real; what is experienced, understood, conceived, affirmed, can be the same as what is approved as truly good. So the many elementary objects are constructed into a single compound object, and in turn the many compound objects will be ordered in a single universe.

Seventhly, we have distinguished many conscious and intentional operations and arranged them in a succession of different levels of consciousness. But as the many elementary objects are constructed into larger wholes, as the many operations are conjoined in a single compound knowing. so too the many levels of consciousness are just successive stages in the unfolding of a single thrust, the eros of the human spirit.

Transcendental Method

What we have been describing as the basic pattern of operations is transcendental method. It is a method, for it is a normative pattern of recurrent and related operations yielding cumulative and progressive results. It is a transcendental method, for the results envisaged are not confined categorically to some particular field or subject, but regard any result that could be intended by the completely open transcendental notions. Where other methods aim at meeting the exigences and exploiting the opportunities proper to particular fields, transcendental method is concerned with meeting the exigencies and exploiting the opportunities presented by the human mind itself. It is a concern that is both foundational and universally significant and relevant.

Now in a sense everyone knows and observes transcendental method. Everyone does so, precisely in the measure that he is attentive, intelligent, reasonable, responsible. But in another sense it is quite difficult to be at home in transcendental method, for that is not to be achieved by reading books or listening to lectures or analyzing language. It is a matter of heightening one's consciousness by objectifying it, and that is something that each one, ultimately, has to do in himself and for himself. . . .

The operations are to be experienced not only singly but in their relations, for there are not merely conscious operations but also conscious processes. Where sensitive perception does not reveal intelligible relations so that, as Hume contended, we perceive not causality but succession, our own consciousness is a different matter. On the empirical level, it is true, process is spontaneous sensitivity; it is intelligible only in the sense that it is understood. But with inquiry the intelligent subject emerges, and process becomes intelligent; it is not merely an intelligible that can be understood, but the active correlative of intelligibility, the intelligence that intelligently seeks understanding, comes to understand, and operates in the light of having understood. When inquiry comes to a term, or an impasse, intelligence intelligently yields place to critical reflection; as critically reflective, the subject stands in conscious relation to an absolute—the absolute that makes us regard the positive content of the sciences not as true and certain but only as probable. Finally, the rational subject, having achieved knowledge of what is and could be, rationally gives way to conscious freedom and conscientious responsibility.

The operations, then, stand within a process that is formally dynamic, that calls forth and assembles its own components, that does so intelligently, rationally, responsibly. Such, then, is the unity and relatedness of the several operations. It is a unity and relatedness that exists and functions before we manage to advert to it explicitly, understand it, objectify it. It is a unity and relatedness quite different from the intelligible unities and relations by which we organize the data of sense, for they are merely intelligible, while the unity and relatedness of conscious process is intelligent, reasonable, responsible.

We have considered, first, experiencing the operations and, secondly, understanding their unity and relatedness. There arises the question for reflection. Do these operations occur? Do they occur in the described pattern? Is not that pattern just hypothetical, sooner or later due for revision and, when revised, sooner or later due for still further revision?

First, the operations exist and occur. Despite the doubts and denials of positivists and behaviorists, no one, unless some of his organs are deficient, is going to say that never in his life did he have the experience of seeing or of hearing, of touching or smelling or tasting, of imaging or perceiving, of feeling or moving; or that if he appeared to have such experience, still it was mere appearance, since all his life long he has gone about like a somnambulist without any awareness of his own activities.

The Functions of Transcendental Method

We have been inviting the reader to discover in himself the original normative pattern of recurrent and related operations that yield cumulative and progressive results. We have now to consider what uses or functions are served by that basic method.

First, then, there is the normative function. All special methods consist in making specific the transcendental precepts. Be attentive, Be intelligent, Be reasonable, Be responsible. But before they are ever formulated in concepts and expressed in words, those precepts have a prior existence and reality in the spontaneous, structured dynamism of human consciousness. Moreover, just as the transcendental precepts rest simply on a study of the operations themselves, so specific categorial precepts rest on a study of the mind operating in a given field. The ultimate basis of both transcendental and categorial precepts will be advertence to the difference between attention and inattention, intelligence and stupidity, reasonableness and unreasonableness, responsibility and irresponsibility.

Secondly, there is the critical function. The scandal still continues that men, while they tend to agree on scientific questions, tend to disagree in the most outrageous fashion on basic philosophic issues. So they disagree about the activities named knowing about the relation of those activities to reality, and about reality itself. However, differences on the third, reality, can be reduced to differences about the first and second, knowledge and objectivity. Differences on the second, objectivity, can be reduced to differences on the first, cognitional theory. Finally, differences in cognitional theory can be resolved by bringing to light the contradiction between a mistaken cognitional theory and the actual performance of the mistaken theorist. To take the simplest instance, Hume thought the human mind to be a matter of impressions linked together by custom. But Hume's own mind was not what Hume considered the human mind to be.

Thirdly, there is the dialectical function. For the critical use of transcendental method can be applied to every mistaken cognitional theory, whether expressed with philosophic generality or presupposed by a method of hermeneutics, of historical investigation, of theology, or demythologization. Moreover, these applications can be extended to concomitant views on epistemology and metaphysics. In this fashion one can determine the dialectical series of basic positions, which criticism confirms, and of basic counterpositions, which criticism confounds.

Fourthly, there is the systematic function. For in the measure that transcendental method is objectified, there are determined a set of basic terms and relations, namely, the terms that refer to the operations of cognitional process, and the relations that link these operations to one another. Such terms and relations are the substance of cognitional theory. They reveal the ground for epistemology. They are found to be isomorphic with the terms and relations denoting the ontological structure of any reality proportionate to human cognitional process. . . .

Sixthly, there is the heuristic function. Every inquiry aims at transforming some unknown into a known. Inquiry itself, then, is something between ignorance and knowledge. It is less than knowledge, else there would be no need to inquire. It is more than sheer ignorance, for it makes ignorance manifest and strives to replace it with knowledge. This intermediary between ignorance and knowing is an intending, and what is intended is an unknown that is to be known.

Now fundamentally all method is the exploitation of such intending, for it outlines the steps to be taken if one is to proceed from the initial intending of the question to the eventual knowing of what has been intended all along. Moreover, within method the use of heuristic devices is fundamental. They consist in designating and naming the intended unknown, in setting down at once all that can be affirmed about it, and in using this explicit knowledge as a guide, a criterion, and/or a premise in the effort to arrive at a fuller knowledge. Such is the function in algebra of the unknown x, in the solution of problems. Such is the function in physics of indeterminate or generic functions and of the classes of functions specified by differential equations.

Now transcendental method fulfills a heuristic function. It reveals the very nature of that function by bringing to light the activity of intending and its correlative, the intended that, though unknown, at least is intended. Moreover, inasmuch as the systematic function has provided sets of basic terms and relations, there are to hand basic determinations that may be set down at once whenever the unknown is a human subject or an object proportionate to human cognitional process, i.e. an object to be known by experiencing, understanding, and judging.

Seventhly, there is the foundational function. Special methods derive their proper norms from the accumulated experience of investigators in their several fields. But besides the proper norms there are also common norms. Besides the tasks in each field there are interdisciplinary problems. Underneath the consent of men as scientists, there is their dissent on matters of ultimate significance and concern. It is in the measure that special methods acknowledge their common core in transcendental method, that norms common to all the sciences will be acknowledged, that a secure basis will be attained for attacking interdisciplinary problems, and that the sciences will be mobilized within a higher unity of vocabulary, thought, and orientation, in which they will be able to make their quite significant contribution to the solution of fundamental problems.

Eighthly, transcendental method is relevant to theology. This relevance, of course, is mediated by the special method proper to theology and developed through the reflection of theologians on the successes and failures of their efforts past and present. But this special method, while it has its own special classes and combinations of operations, none the less is the work of human minds performing the same basic operations in the same basic relations as are found in other special methods. In other words, transcendental method is a constituent part in the special methods proper to the natural and to the human sciences. However true it is that one attends, understands, judges, decides differently in the natural sciences, in the human sciences, and in theology, still these differences in no way imply or suggest a transition from attention to inattention, from intelligence to stupidity, from reasonableness to silliness, from responsibility to irresponsibility. . . .

Tenthly, to assign to transcendental method a role in theology adds no new resource to theology but simply draws attention to a resource that has always been used. For transcendental method is the concrete and dynamic unfolding of human attentiveness, intelligence, reasonableness, and responsibility. That unfolding occurs whenever anyone uses his mind in an appropriate fashion. Hence, to introduce transcendental method introduces no new resource into theology, for theologians always have had minds and always have used them. . . .

In the twelfth place, the introduction of transcendental method abrogates the old metaphor that describes philosophy as the handmaid of theology and replaces it by a very precise fact. Transcendental method is not the intrusion into theology of alien matter from an alien source. Its function is to advert to the fact that theologies are produced by theologians, that theologians have minds and use them, that their doing so should not be ignored or passed over but explicitly acknowledged in itself and in its implications. Again, transcendental method is coincident with a notable part of what has been considered philosophy, but it is not any philosophy or all philosophy. Very precisely, it is a heightening of consciousness that brings to light our conscious and intentional operations and thereby leads to the answers to three basic questions. What am I doing when I am knowing? Why is doing that knowing? What do I know when I do it? The first answer is a cognitional theory. The second is an epistemology. The third is a metaphysics where, however, the metaphysics is transcendental, an integration of heuristic structures, and not some categorial speculation that reveals that all is water, or matter, or spirit, or process, or what have you. . . .

27. Karl Rahner, *Knowledge of God*

Transcendental and *a Posteriori* Knowledge of God

What we are calling transcendental knowledge or experience of God is an *a posteriori* knowledge insofar as man's transcendental experience of his free subjectivity takes place only in his encounter with the world and especially with other people. . . . Hence our transcendental knowledge or experience has to be called *a posteriori* insofar as every transcendental experience is mediated by a categorical encounter with concrete reality in our world, both the world of things and the world of persons. This is also true of the knowledge of God. To that extent we can and we must say that all knowledge of God is an *a posteriori* knowledge which comes from and through encountering the world, to which, of course, we ourselves also belong.

The knowledge of God is, nevertheless, a *transcendental* knowledge because man's basic and original orientation towards absolute mystery, which constitutes his fundamental experience of God, is a permanent existential of man as a spirit subject. This means that the explicit, conceptual and thematic knowledge, which we usually think of when we speak of the knowledge of God or of proofs for God's existence, is a reflection upon man's transcendental orientation towards mystery, and some degree of reflection is always necessary. It is not, however, the original and foundational mode of the transcendental experience of this mystery. It belongs necessarily to the very nature of human knowledge that thought is self-reflexive, that we think of a concrete object within the infinite and apparently empty horizon of thinking itself, that thinking is conscious of itself. We must get used to taking account of the fact that when we think and when we exercise freedom we are always dealing with more and always have to do with more than that which we are talking about in our words and concepts, and that with which we are occupied here and now as the concrete object of our activity. If one cannot see both the distinction and the unity in this bipolarity in knowledge and in freedom, that is, objective consciousness and subjective consciousness, or, as Blondel puts it, willed will and willing will, then basically he cannot see the point of what we are saying: that speaking of God is the reflection which points to a more original, unthematic and unreflexive knowledge of God.

We become conscious of ourselves and of the transcendental structures that are given with our subjectivity only in the fact that the world presents itself to us concretely and in quite definite ways, and hence in the fact that we are involved in the world both passively and actively. This is also true of the knowledge of God. In this sense it is not a knowledge which is grounded entirely in itself. But neither is it simply a mystical process within our own personal inferiority, nor, in the light of this, does it have the character of a personal, divine self-revelation. But the *a posteriori* character of the knowledge of God would be misunderstood if we were to overlook the transcendental element in it and understand the knowledge of God after the model of an a posteriori knowledge whose object comes entirely from without and appears in a neutral faculty of knowledge. In the knowledge of God a posteriority does not mean that we look out into the world with a neutral faculty of knowledge and then think that we can discover God there directly or indirectly among the realities that present themselves to us objectively, or that we can prove his existence indirectly.

We are oriented towards God. This original experience is always present, and it should not be confused with the objectifying, although necessary, reflection upon man's transcendental orientation towards mystery. This does not destroy the *a posteriori* character of the knowledge of God, but neither should this a posteriority be misunderstood in the sense that God could simply be indoctrinated from without as an object of our knowledge.

This unthematic and ever-present experience, this knowledge of God which we always have even when we are thinking of and concerned with anything but God, is the permanent ground from out of which that thematic knowledge of God emerges which we have in explicitly religious activity and in philosophical reflection. It is not in these latter that we discover God just as we discover a particular object of our experience within the world. Rather, both in this explicitly religious activity directed to God in prayer and in metaphysical reflection we are only making explicit for ourselves what we already know implicitly about ourselves in the depths of our personal self-realization. Hence we know our subjective freedom, our transcendence and the infinite openness of the spirit even where and when we do not make them thematic at all. We also know them when such a conceptual, objectifying thematization and verbal expression of this original knowledge perhaps does not succeed at all, or succeeds very imperfectly and distortedly. Indeed we even know them when we refuse to engage at all in such a process of thematization.

For this reason the meaning of all explicit knowledge of God in religion and in metaphysics is intelligible and can really be understood only when all the words we use there point to the unthematic experience of our orientation towards the ineffable mystery. And just as it is of the nature of transcendent spirit, because it is constituted in an objective world, always to offer along with this objectivity the possibility, both in theory and in practice, of running away from its own subjectivity, from taking responsibility for itself in freedom, so too a person can also hide from himself his transcendental orientation towards the absolute mystery which we call God. As scripture says (Rom. 1:18), he can in this way suppress the most real truth about himself.

The individual realities with which we are usually dealing in our lives always become clearly intelligible and comprehensible and manipulable because we can differentiate them from other things. There is no such way of knowing God. Because God is something quite different from any of the individual realities which appear within the realm of our experience or which are inferred from it, and because the knowledge of God has a quite definite and unique character and is not just an instance of knowledge in general, it is for these reasons very easy to overlook God. The concept "God" is not a grasp of God by which a person masters the mystery, but it is letting oneself be grasped by the mystery which is present and yet ever distant. This mystery remains a mystery even though it reveals itself to man and thus continually grounds the possibility of man being a subject. There can then follow from this ground, of course, the so-called concept of God, explicit language about him, words and what we mean by them and try to say to ourselves reflexively, and certainly a person ought not to avoid the effort involved in this process of reflexive conceptualization. But in order to remain true, all metaphysical ontology about God must return again and again to its source, must return to the transcendental experience of our orientation towards the absolute mystery, and to the *existentiell* practice of accepting this orientation freely. This acceptance takes place in unconditional obedience to conscience, and in the open and trusting acceptance of the uncontrollable in one's own existence in moments of prayer and quiet silence.

Since the original experience of God is not an encounter with an individual object alongside of other objects, and since in the human subject's transcendental experience God is absolutely beyond us in his transcendence, we can speak of God and the experience of God, and of creatureliness and the experience of creatureliness only together, in spite of the difference of what is meant in each instance.

It could be asked at this point: But if these two things are connected in this way, then are we only able to say something about what God is for us, and not able to say anything about what God is in himself? But if we have understood what is meant by the absolutely unlimited transcendentality of the human spirit, then we can say that the alternative of such a radical distinction between a statement about "God in himself" and "God for us" is not even legitimate. What is meant by the deepest characteristic of the human subject in his freedom and his dependence, and hence in his creatureliness, and what is meant by God himself can be understood only by taking into account that basic situation in which human existence finds itself, a situation in which man is in possession of himself and is radically alienated from himself because of the fact that the mystery addresses him in its absoluteness and remains at a distance as distinct from man. For this reason neither can we form a concept of God in the proper sense and then ask afterwards if it exists in the real order. The concept in its original ground and the reality itself to which this concept refers move beyond us and enter the unknown together. . . .

Transcendental Knowledge of God as Experience of Mystery

The knowledge of God we are referring to here is rooted in that subjectivity and free transcendence and in that situation of not being at one's own disposal which we tried at least to sketch. Now this transcendental experience, which is always mediated by a categorical experience of the concrete and individual data of our experience in the world and in time and space (all of our experience, including so-called "secular" experience), may not be understood as a neutral power by which, among other things, God can be known. It is rather the basic and original way of knowing God, so much so that the knowledge of God we are referring to here simply constitutes the very essence of this transcendence.

The transcendence in which God is already known, although unthematically and nonconceptually, may not be understood as an active mastering of the knowledge of God by one's own power, and hence also as a mastery of God himself. For this transcendence appears as what it is only in the self-disclosure of that towards which the movement of transcendence tends. It exists by means of that which gives itself in this transcendence as the other, the other which distinguishes this transcendence from itself and enables it to be experienced as mystery by the subject who is constituted as such by this transcendence. By its very nature subjectivity is always a transcendence which listens, which does not control, which is overwhelmed by mystery and opened up by mystery. In the midst of its absolute infinity transcendence experiences itself as empty, as merely formal, as necessarily mediated to itself by finiteness, and hence as a finite infinity. If it does not want to mistake itself for an absolute subject and divinize itself, it recognizes itself as a transcendence which has been bestowed upon it, which is grounded in mystery, and is not at its own disposal. For all its infinity it experiences itself as radically finite. It is precisely in and through the infinity of its transcendence that it is a transcendence which can grasp its own finiteness and must grasp it.

Transcendence strictly as such knows only God and nothing else, although it knows him as the condition which makes possible categorical knowledge, history and concrete freedom. Transcendence exists only by opening itself beyond itself, and, to put it in biblical language, it is in its origin and from the very beginning the experience of being known by God himself. The word which says everything by saying "God" is always experienced in its origin and by its very nature as a response in which the mystery, while remaining mystery, offers himself to man.

The unity between transcendence and its term cannot be understood as a unity between two elements related equally to each other, but only as the unity between that which grounds and disposes freely and that which is grounded. It is a unity in the sense of a unity between an original word and the response to it which is made possible by the word. This unity can be described in different ways because the unity as well as the primary and the ultimate element in it can only be expressed helplessly by means of the second and conditioned element, which never really comprehends the first element. We can speak of transcendence only by speaking of its term, and we can make the specific nature of the term intelligible only by speaking about the specific nature of transcendence as such.

If we wanted to understand this basic and original knowledge of God in transcendence only from its subjective pole, that is, if we wanted to clarify the nature of transcendence in order to clarify from this vantage point what the term towards which the transcendence moves really is, then we would have the difficulty of having to describe intentionality as such without discussing its term. Besides that, we would also have the burden of having to look for an *existentiell* mystagogy which would describe and focus the attention of each individual in his concrete existence on those experiences in which he in his individuality had the experience of transcendence and of being taken up out of himself into the ineffable mystery. Since the clarity and persuasiveness of the various individual experiences of this kind—for example, in anxiety, in the subject's absolute concern, in love's unshrinking acceptance of responsibility in freedom, in joy, and so on—vary a great deal in individual persons corresponding to the differences in their historical existence, such a mystagogy into one's own personal and individual experience of transcendence would have to vary a great deal from person to person. Such a mystagogy, in which the individual person is made aware of the fact that this experience of transcendence really takes place repeatedly and without being called such in his immediate involvement with the concrete world, could be possible for the individual person only in individual conversation and in individual logotherapy.

Therefore, we want to attempt a description of this basic and original knowledge of God here by pointing out where this transcendence is directed and what it encounters, or better, what is the source by which it is opened up. But the situation is such that our description of the term or the source of transcendence can only be understood if it calls attention repeatedly to transcendental experience as such, which is so obvious and unobtrusive that it can easily be overlooked.

Even when we look to the term and the source of transcendence in order to call attention to the original and unthematic knowledge of God, the difficulty of bringing this knowledge to awareness is still not overcome. For the names which have been given to the term and source of transcendence in the history of man's reflexive self-interpretation as transcending spirit are very numerous. Nor does each of these names mediate for each individual in the concrete experience of his existence in an equal and equally accessible way a reflexive approach to this original experience of God.

To begin with, this term and source by which transcendence is borne can be called "God." We can also speak of being, of ground, of ultimate cause, of illuminating, revealing logos, and we can appeal to what is meant by a thousand other names. When we say "God" or "primordial ground" or "abyss," then of course such a word is always fraught with images which go beyond what the word really wants to say, and which have nothing to do with what it really means. Each of these notions always has the patina of history on it, including the individual's history, so much so that what is really meant by such a word is hardly discernible any more. When we call God "Father" with the Bible and with Jesus himself, and notice the criticism which this name provokes today, we can understand how a word like this, a word in which Jesus dared to express his ultimate understanding of God and his relationship to God, can be misunderstood or not understood at all.

The philosopher might give further reflection especially to the question of how a transcendental relationship to what he calls being, and a transcendental relationship to God are related and how they are to be distinguished.

Since we want to consider directly only the original, transcendental knowledge of God, which is antecedent to and is not able to be recaptured completely by reflexive ontology, we can take a shorter, although to be sure less cautious, route here, because the hesitant caution of philosophy cannot become a substitute for risking an understanding of existence which is always prior to philosophy.

But this still does not solve the difficulty of what name we should give to the term and the source of our original experience of transcendence. We could, of course, following the venerable tradition of the whole of Western philosophy, a tradition to which we are certainly responsible, simply call it "absolute being" or "being in an absolute sense" or the "ground of being" which establishes everything in original unity. But when we speak this way of "being" and "ground of being" we run the deadly risk that many contemporaries can hear the word "being" only as an empty and subsequent abstraction from the multiple experience of the individual realities which encounter us directly. For this reason we want to try to call the term and the source of our transcendence by another name, a name, of course, which cannot claim to be the key which opens every door. But maybe, nevertheless, it clarifies what we mean by circumventing the problematic about "being" which we just mentioned. We want to call the term and source of our transcendence "the holy mystery," although this term must be understood, deepened, and then gradually shown to be identical with the word "God," and although we shall have to revert frequently to other terms which are available elsewhere in the humane and philosophical traditions. We shall have to consider later in a separate reflection why we call this mystery "holy."

We are considering the term of the experience of transcendence and we are defining it as the holy mystery not in order to express it in the most unintelligible and complicated way, but for another reason. For if we were simply to say that "God" is the term of our transcendence, then we would have to be continually afraid of the misunderstanding that we were speaking of God in the way that he is already expressed, known and understood beforehand in an objectifying set of concepts.

If we use a less familiar and less well-defined phrase like "holy mystery," in order to express the term of transcendence and the source from which it comes, then the danger of misunderstanding is somewhat less than when we say: "The term of transcendence is God." We must first describe the experience and the term of the experience together before what is experienced can be called "God."

The Term of Transcendence as the Infinite, the Indefinable and the Ineffable

The term of our experience of transcendence, for which we first of all have to look for a name, is always present as nameless and indefinable, as something not at our disposal. For every name defines, every name distinguishes and characterizes something by giving what it means a particular name selected from among many names. The infinite horizon, which is the term of transcendence and which opens us to unlimited possibilities of encountering this or that particular thing, cannot itself be given a name. For this name would situate the term among the realities which are understood within the horizon of this term and this source. Indeed we can and must reflect upon the mysterious and the incomprehensible which can never be situated within our system of coordinates, and can never be defined by being distinguished from something else. For that would be to objectify it, to understand it as one object among other objects, and to define it conceptually. Indeed we must express it as something distinct from everything else because, as the absolute ground of every particular existent, it cannot be the subsequent sum of these many individual existents. But all the conceptualizing which we have to do remains true only to the extent that, in this act of defining and expressing objectively the term of transcendence as the act's condition of possibility, once again an act of transcendence towards the infinite term of this transcendence takes place. In the act of reflection, which only intends to reflect upon and objectify transcendence, another original act of transcendence takes place.

Hence this original transcendence's pre-apprehension reaches out towards what is nameless and what originally and by its very nature is infinite. By its very nature the condition which makes possible distinguishing and naming cannot itself have a name. We can call this condition the nameless one or the nameless thing, that which or that who is distinct from everything finite, or the "infinite," but in doing this we have not given the term and source of transcendence a name, but have called it nameless. We have really understood this process of naming only if we understand it as simply pointing to the silence of transcendental experience.

What transcendence moves towards, then, is also indefinable. By the fact that the horizon or the term of transcendence extends beyond our reach and thus offers to knowledge the space for its individual objects of knowledge and love, this horizon or term always and essentially and by its very nature is distinct from anything which appears within it as an object of knowledge. To this extent the differentiation between this ineffable term and the finite is obviously not only a distinction which has to be made, but this differentiation is the one and original distinction which is experienced. This is so because it is the condition which makes possible all distinguishing of objects, both from the horizon of transcendence itself and among themselves. But this means that this ineffable term of transcendence is itself indefinable, for as the condition of possibility for all categorical distinguishing and differentiating it cannot itself be differentiated from others by means of the same norms for distinguishing.

It is in the light of the distinction between the transcendental term and individual categorical objects on the one hand, and the differentiation of categorical objects among themselves on the other hand, that we can understand the error involved both in a real *pantheism* as well as in a more popular form of *dualism* which places God and the nondivine simply as two things alongside of each other, a dualism which is also found in religion.

When we say against pantheism that God and the world are different, this statement is radically misunderstood if it is interpreted in a dualistic way. The difference between God and the world is of such a nature that God establishes and is the difference of the world from himself, and for this reason he establishes the closest unity precisely in the differentiation. For if the difference itself comes from God, and, if we can put it this way, is itself identical with God, then the difference between God and the world is to be understood quite differently than the difference between categorical realities. Their difference is antecedent to them because they presuppose as it were a space which contains and differentiates them, and no one of these categorically distinct realities itself establishes its difference from the other or is this difference. Pantheism could therefore be called a sensitivity to (or better, the transcendental experience of) the fact that God is the absolute reality, the original ground and the ultimate term of transcendence. This is the element of truth in pantheism.

Conversely, a religious dualism which in a primitive and naive way understands the difference between God and the reality of the world created by him simply as a categorical difference is basically very unreligious because it does not grasp what God really is, that is, because it understands God as an element within a larger whole, as a part of the whole of reality.

God to be sure is different from the world. But he is different in the way in which this difference is experienced in our original, transcendental experience. In this experience this peculiar and unique difference is experienced in such a way that the whole of reality is borne by this term and this source and is intelligible only within it. Consequently, it is precisely the difference which establishes the ultimate unity between God and the world, and the difference becomes intelligible only in this unity.

These very abstract sounding things are fundamental for an understanding of God which can have religious meaning for people today. For that God really does not exist who operates and functions as an individual existent alongside of other existents, and who would thus as it were be a member of the larger household of all reality. Anyone in search of such a God is searching for a false God. Both atheism and a more naive form of theism labor under the same false notion of God, only the former denies it while the latter believes that it can make sense out of it. Both are basically false: the latter, the notion that naive theism has, because this God does not exist; and the former, atheism, because God is the most radical, the most original, and in a certain sense the most self-evident reality.

The term of transcendence is indefinable because the horizon itself cannot be present within the horizon, because the term of transcendence cannot itself really be brought within the scope of transcendence and thus distinguished from other things. The ultimate measure cannot itself be measured. The limit by which everything is "defined" cannot itself be defined by a still more ultimate limit. The infinite expanse which can and does encompass everything cannot itself be encompassed. But then this nameless and indefinable term of transcendence, which is distinguished from everything else only from its own side, and hence differentiates everything else from itself, and which is the norm for everything and is beyond all other norms, this term becomes that which is absolutely beyond our disposal. It is always present only as that which disposes.

It is beyond the control of the finite subject not only physically, but also logically. The moment the subject would define this nameless term with the hope of his formal logic and his ontology, the defining itself takes place by means of a pre-apprehension of that which is supposed to be defined. Ontology is that mysterious process in which the first principles show themselves to be unable to be measured, and man recognizes that he is what is measured. The term of transcendence admits of no control over itself because then we would be reaching beyond it and incorporating it within another, higher and broader horizon. This contradicts the very nature of this transcendence and of the real term of this transcendence. This infinite and silent term is what disposes of us. It presents itself to us in the mode of withdrawal, of silence, of distance, of being always inexpressible, so that speaking of it, if it is to make sense, always requires listening to its silence. . . .

The Term of Transcendence as the "Holy Mystery"

We have already and by way of anticipation called the term of transcendence the holy mystery. The reason why we had to call it "mystery" consisted ultimately in the fact that we experience it as that which cannot be encompassed by a pre-apprehension which reaches beyond it, and hence it cannot be defined. But why do we characterize it as the "holy" mystery? . . .

When we speak of transcendence we do not mean only and exclusively the transcendence which is the condition of possibility for categorical knowledge as such. We mean also and just as much the transcendence of freedom, of willing, and of love. This transcendence, which is constitutive of the subject as a free and personal subject of action within an unlimited realm of action, is just as important, and is basically just another aspect of the transcendence of a spiritual, and therefore knowing, and precisely for this reason free subject. Freedom is always the freedom of a subject who exists in interpersonal communication with other subjects. Therefore it is necessarily freedom vis-à-vis another subject of transcendence, and this transcendence is not primarily the condition of possibility for knowing things, but is the condition of possibility for a subject being present to himself and just as basically and originally being present to another subject. But for a subject who is present to himself to affirm freely vis-à-vis another subject means ultimately to love.

Hence when we reflect here upon transcendence as will and as freedom, we must also take into account the character of the term and source of transcendence as love. It is a term which possesses absolute freedom, and this term is at work in freedom and in love as that which is nameless and which is not at our disposal, for we are completely at its disposal. It is what opens up my own transcendence as freedom and as love. But the term of transcendence is always and originally the source of the mystery which offers itself. This term itself opens our transcendence; it is not established by us and by our own power as though we were absolute subjects. Hence if transcendence moves in freedom and in love towards a term which itself opens this transcendence, then we can say that that which is nameless and which is not at our disposal, and at whose complete disposal we exist, that this very thing is present in loving freedom, and this is what we mean when we say "holy mystery."

For what else would we call that which is nameless, that at whose disposal we exist and from which we are distanced in our finiteness, but which nevertheless we affirm in our transcendence though freedom and love, what else would we call this if not "holy"? And what could we call "holy" if not this, or to whom would the name "holy" belong more basically and more originally than to this infinite term of love, which love in the presence of the incomprehensible and the ineffable necessarily becomes worship.

In transcendence, therefore, dwells the holy, nameless and infinite, disposing but not being disposed, forbidding and distant. And this we call mystery, or somewhat more explicitly, the holy mystery, lest in focusing upon the knowledge element we overlook the transcendentality of freedom and love, and so that both elements remain present in their original and personal unity. The two words "holy mystery," which are understood as a unity, but between which nevertheless there is an intrinsic difference, express equally the transendentality both of knowledge and of freedom and love.

Every experience of transcendence is a basic and original experience which is not derived from something prior, and it receives this character of being underived and irreducible from what is encountered and becomes manifest in it. The designation of this term of transcendence as the "holy mystery," therefore, does not employ concepts derived from elsewhere and applied extrinsically to this term. It derives them rather from this original "object," which is its own ground and the ground and horizon of the knowledge of it, and which discloses itself in and through transcendental experience itself.

If we have arrived in this way at the basic and original idea of mystery and of the holy, and if it is correct to designate the term of transcendence by this name, there can be no question, of course, of giving a definition of the essence of this holy mystery. Mystery is as indefinable as every other transcendental "concept." They do not admit of definition because what is expressed in them is known only in transcendental experience, and transcendental experience, as always and everywhere given antecedently, has nothing outside of itself by which it and its term could be defined. . . .

11

Theology and Language

In English-speaking countries, where the Enlightenment was first nurtured, a particular sort of the Enlightenment's critique of theology continued through the nineteenth and twentieth centuries independently of developments in Germany. David Hume stated it classically, in his *Enquiry Concerning Human Understanding:* "If we take in our hand any volume; of divinity, or school metaphysics, for instance; let us ask, Does it contain any abstract reasoning concerning quantity or number? No. Does it contain any experimental reasoning concerning matter of fact and existence? No. Commit it then to the flames. For it can contain nothing but sophistry and illusion."

The charge is not that sentences of "metaphysics" or "divinity" are false, but that they are empty. They are "illusion" in the sense of appearance that has no reality behind it; thus a sentence like "There is a loving God" only *seems,* according to Hume, to say something. "Experimental reasoning concerning matter of fact and existence," that is, the setting forth of hypotheses capable of empirical testing and the discourse involved in so testing them, is a mode of discourse justified by its manifest practical success. And the propositions of logic and mathematics are justified by their self-evidence. But consider such a metaphysical proposition as Leibnitz' principle that there is a "sufficient reason" for whatever happens, or the theological proposition that all things are "redeemed." What, finally, do they explain? How could we find out whether they are true? What practical difference would it make if they *were* true? Hume's answers to these questions are, respectively, Nothing, No way, and None.

The debunking of theology in this fashion, and attempts of theologians to respond, have, since Hume, never been absent from English and American thought. Around the middle of the twentieth century, a particularly vigorous flurry of both origins produced a body of literature that must appear on our map. One book especially, the collection *New Essays in Philosophical Theology,* edited by Antony Flew (1923–) and Alasdair MacIntyre (1929–), became a staple of discussion. From this collection we reprint a central group of short essays, together with a selection from the most notable participant in the same discussion, Ian Ramsey.

I

In the twentieth-century discussion, Hume's challenge to metaphysics and theology took a form determined by the "linguistic turn" of Anglo-American philosophy. The "linguistic" form of Hume's attack is the suspicion that the questions of metaphysics and theology are in confusion simply as pieces of language, and appear profound only because this confusion stymies all possible answers.

In the first period of this discussion, in the 1930s and 1940s, the assault was carried by the "logical positivists," wielding the razor of "verification." Their intellectual base was in the logic of the sciences. Their leading question was, How can we tell when a sentence is informative in the way that right scientific propositions must be? They proposed that a sentence is an informative proposition if we can say how it would be possible to decide by stated procedures whether it is true or false. If it is proposed that "water is H_2O," we can work out what, at least in principle, must be done to verify or falsify the proposition.

Sentences about God seem not to be verifiable in this or any closely analogous way. The positivists granted that this by itself does not disqualify the sentences as discourse; neither are the sentences of poetry or moral exhortation verifiable. But these do not pretend to be factually informative, whereas a sentence like "God is loving" does. It is a "pseudo-statement," a form of words disguised as a kind of discourse it cannot in fact be.

It will be seen that the positivists were operating with the same three categories of discourse as had Hume: empirical, logical-mathematical, and everything else. Further reflection on these matters was enabled when less ideological analysts, often inspired by Ludwig Wittgenstein (1889–1951), observed that the Humean everything-else grab bag must contain many and very *different* modes of discourse. There are various "games" that we play using words; moreover, by what rules any of these discourses are related to extra linguistic reality can only be discovered from case to case. The questions directed to "God-talk" must therefore be more nuanced: What specific language-game is afoot here? Is it a *cognitive* use of language? If it is, how specifically? *New Essays* belongs to this stage of the discussion.

The exchanges were given their standard shape by a paper simply entitled "Gods," by John Wisdom (1909–). The paper's centerpiece was a parable. Flew retells the parable for his own use in the essay reprinted in this chapter, but readers should have also Wisdom's original before them:

> Two people return to their long neglected garden and find among the weeds a few of the old plants surprisingly vigorous. One says to the other, "It must be that a gardener has been coming and doing something about these plants." Upon inquiry they find that no neighbor has ever seen anyone at work in their garden. The first man says to the other, "He must have worked

while people slept." The other says, "No, someone would have heard him and besides, anybody who cared about the plants would have kept down these weeds." The first man says, "Look at the way these plants are arranged. There is purpose and a feeling for beauty here. I believe that someone comes, someone invisible to mortal eyes. I believe that the more carefully we look the more we shall find confirmation of this." They examine the garden ever so carefully and sometimes they come on new things suggesting that a gardener comes and sometimes they come on new things suggesting the contrary and even that a malicious person has been at work. Besides examining the garden carefully they also study what happens to gardens left without attention. Each learns all the other learns about this and about the garden. Consequently, when after all this, one says, "I still believe a gardener comes," while the other says, "I don't" their different words now reflect no difference as to what they have found in the garden, no difference as to what they would find in the garden if they looked further, and no difference about how fast untended gardens fall into disorder. At this stage, in this context, the gardener hypothesis has ceased to be experimental. . . .

Wisdom's parable was widely accepted as illuminating. Three moves are possible if the parable is taken as is, all of which continue to be supported.

Wisdom's own intention was to suggest there can be disagreement that is genuinely about fact even though it is not experimentally decidable, and that the difference between "There is a good God" and "There is not a good God" is of this sort. Wisdom adduces a court case about whether someone, of whose conduct there is a detailed agreed record, was or was not "negligent" in so behaving. The court will examine behavior just as the gardeners examined their garden, tracing patterns, emphasizing or debunking connections between the agreed facts, and so on. At the end, the court will have to rule that the accused was or was not in fact "negligent"; the ruling will not be arbitrary since it will have been arrived at by rational procedures; and it will state a fact of some sort. Several writers, including Ian Ramsey (1915–1972) and Basil Mitchell (1917–) followed Wisdom on this general line.

Flew, on the other hand, used the parable to enforce Humean suspicion that theological utterance is, as such, cognitively vacuous. If the one who says "There is a Gardener" and the one who says "There is not" acknowledge exactly the same set of present circumstances *and* do not differ in what they expect from future experience, how can they be said to have any real disagreement? And if they do not really disagree, that is, if "There is God" and "There is not God" are not contradictory, what can "There is God" be supposed to *mean?*

A third group accepted Flew's conclusion, but argued that theological statements are none the worse for it. Theological statements indeed do not, this group held, state fact of any sort. What they do is express and/or trigger a certain attitude toward the facts, an attitude that has real consequences. R. M. Hare's (1919–) essay coined the term "blik" for an attitude toward the world that is indeed itself immune to evidence, but only because it determines what counts as evidence in the first place. It is thus by no means empty, has meaningful alternatives, and makes a great difference between those who hold it and those who hold an alternative. In some versions, the difference between this position and that of Wisdom is clear, in some it is not.

A fourth move, also proposed in the subsequent discussion, would be to rewrite the parable, to include discovery of what purports to be a promise by the Gardener finally to reveal himself. On this supposition, the contending hypotheses will after all be "verified" or falsified, by the fulfillment or failure of this promise, "eschatologically."

II

A second line of concern with language leads from the *German* Enlightenment and from German efforts to overcome or rejuvenate the Enlightenment, to a similar if more dramatic "deconstruction" of language's theological utility. The thinkers on this path have been German, then French, and, recently, American. Friedrich Nietzsche (1844–1900) and Sigmund Freud (1856–1939) are chief patrons, with Martin Heidegger (1889–1976) and his French epigones supporting. We may list the more immediately relevant movements by their slogans: phenomenology, structuralism, poststructuralism, deconstruction.

For present purpose, we may begin with the "structuralist" understanding of language, founded by Ferdinand de Saussure (1857–1913) at the turn of the century. A "language," in structuralist theory, is a system of signs, whether of words, gestures, or other cultural artifacts. Each such system functions as possible discourse merely by the internal relations of its constituent signs, independently of any relation to a world outside the system. A language system as such can therefore have no history, any more than the plan of a house can *as such* have a history. It simply perseveres for its time and then is replaced by another, built perhaps from its fragment-signs; a favorite term in this connection is "bricolage," the assembling of a new structure from fragments of former structures.

Structuralist hermeneutics must have disastrous consequences for a faith in which ancient texts are supposed to have authority. For, according to structuralism, an ancient text is the artifact of an earlier language system with which that of later interpreters can have no intrinsic continuity. What the text meant when it was written is therefore irrecoverable; its only meaning now is whatever "reading" it may accommodate within a current language. Thus, there can be no ultimate difference between what a text means and what it is interpreted to mean; and so the text cannot be used to correct its interpreters.

"Poststructuralism" combined structuralist understanding of language with an ontological position widely held in existentialist and related Continental thought: the personal self is said to be constituted in and by language, to subsist only as the act of self-interpretation. The consequences of the combination are comprehensively nihilistic, in two ways.

First, the user of language does not on this understanding of personhood transcend language; he or she therefore cannot control what is said by independent access to a world beyond the saying. But structuralism had already taught that language itself works by an internal system that is independent of any world outside itself. Thus, neither the structure of language nor the user of language can adjudicate the play of linguistic signs by its truth to a world. Discourse is now seen as a game subject to no umpire or rules beyond itself; therefore, it finally can be *about* nothing but itself. Human consciousness, according to Jacques Derrida, is the semiotic play of a "world of signs without fault [and] without truth. . . ."

Second, the human self inescapably does have history. But if the self is linguistic, constituted in self-interpretation, and if language's history is discontinuous, then so is the self's history—the self is constituted as an endless bricolage of succeeding self-interpretations. A human life can have no meaning as a whole, neither in an origin from which it proceeds nor in an end to which it goes.

Perhaps the most notable and theologically motivated response to such positions has been made by Paul Ricoeur (1913–), a Frenchman steeped in German thought who has spent much of his time in America. Ricoeur has worked a scholarly and constructive way through this entire tradition. His influence in America has perhaps had some of the same quality—though so far not the extent—as the earlier influence of Paul Tillich.

Ricoeur has accepted what he takes to be the truth of these movements, yet has resisted their nihilist outcome, for the sake of the hope which the gospel proclaims. His regular critique of usual structuralism and poststructuralism has been that *interpretation* never in fact occurs within a single language system. Precisely because a text—even the text of one's own past self-understanding—does indeed come from a language system other than that of the interpreter, interpretation always occurs as the *meeting* and often productive *conflict* of "languages." In themselves, languages may be, à la Saussure, closed systems, but in any actual event of interpretation they break each other open. Interpretation and language—and we with them—have history that is not just bricolage; it is even permitted to believe that they and we are being brought to some goal. What is created in interpretation's conflict of language systems is meaning that can transcend the merely mutual meanings of the signs constituting any one such system.

304

Ricoeur's work with language has thus been devoted to those features of language in which interpretation's conflict of language systems appears and which may therefore embody transcendent meaning. He has written on "symbol," in which a prelinguistic grasp of transcendent meaning reemerges through the cracks of a language; on "metaphor," by which the movements of language's history occur; and on "narrative," in which interpretation yearns toward eschatological meaning. The very long work here excerpted, *The Symbolism of Evil,* is at once an analysis of how "symbols" work and an exploration of a central and explicitly theological body of symbolism.

28. Antony Flew, R. M. Hare, and Basil Mitchell, *The University Discussion*

Antony Flew

Let us begin with a parable. It is a parable developed from a tale told by John Wisdom in his haunting and revelatory article "Gods." Once upon a time two explorers came upon a clearing in the jungle. In the clearing were growing many flowers and many weeds. One explorer says, "Some gardener must tend this plot." The other disagrees, "There is no gardener." So they pitch their tents and set a watch. No gardener is ever seen. "But perhaps he is an invisible gardener." So they set up a barbed-wire fence. They electrify it. They patrol with bloodhounds. (For they remember how H. G. Wells's *The Invisible Man* could be both smelt and touched though he could not be seen.) But no shrieks ever suggested that some intruder has received a shock. No movements of the wire ever betray an invisible climber. The bloodhounds never give cry. Yet still the Believer is not convinced. "But there is a gardener, invisible, intangible, insensible to electric shocks, a gardener who has no scent and makes no sound, a gardener who comes secretly to look after the garden which he loves." At last the Sceptic despairs, "But what remains of your original assertion? Just how does what you call an invisible, intangible, eternally elusive gardener differ from an imaginary gardener or even from no gardener at all?"

In this parable we can see how what starts as an assertion, that something exists or that there is some analogy between certain complexes of phenomena, may be reduced step by step to an altogether different status, to an expression perhaps of a "picture preference." The Sceptic says there is no gardener. The Believer says there is a gardener (but invisible, etc.). One man talks about sexual behaviour. Another man prefers to talk of Aphrodite (but knows that there is not really a superhuman person additional to, and somehow responsible for, all sexual phenomena). The process of qualification may be checked at any point before the original assertion is completely withdrawn and something of that first assertion will remain (Tautology). Mr. Wells's invisible man could not, admittedly, be

305

seen, but in all other respects he was a man like the rest of us. But though the process of qualification may be, and of course usually is, checked in time, it is not always judiciously so halted. Someone may dissipate his assertion completely without noticing that he has done so. A fine brash hypothesis may thus be killed by inches, the death by a thousand qualifications.

And in this, it seems to me, lies the peculiar danger, the endemic evil, of theological utterance. Take such utterances as "God has a plan," "God created the world," "God loves us as a father loves his children." They look at first sight very much like assertions, vast cosmological assertions. Of course, this is no sure sign that they either are, or are intended to be, assertions. But let us confine ourselves to the cases where those who utter such sentences intend them to express assertions. (Merely remarking parenthetically that those who intend or interpret such utterances as crypto-commands, expressions of wishes, disguised ejaculations, concealed ethics, or as anything else but assertions, are unlikely to succeed in making them either properly orthodox or practically effective.)

Now to assert that such and such is the case is necessarily equivalent to denying that such and such is not the case. Suppose then that we are in doubt as to what someone who gives vent to an utterance is asserting, or suppose that, more radically, we are skeptical as to whether he is really asserting anything at all, one way of trying to understand (or perhaps it will be to expose) his utterance is to attempt to find what he would regard as counting against, or as being incompatible with, its truth. For if the utterance is indeed an assertion, it will necessarily be equivalent to a denial of the negation of that assertion. And anything which would count against the assertion, or which would induce the speaker to withdraw it and to admit that it had been mistaken, must be part of (or the whole of) the meaning of the negation of that assertion. And to know the meaning of the negation of an assertion, is as near as makes no matter, to know the meaning of that assertion. And if there is nothing which a putative assertion denies then there is nothing which it asserts either: and so it is not really an assertion. When the Sceptic in the parable asked the Believer, "Just how does what you call an invisible, intangible, eternally elusive gardener differ from an imaginary gardener or even from no gardener at all?" he was suggesting that the Believer's earlier statement had been so eroded by qualification that it was no longer an assertion at all.

Now it often seems to people who are not religious as if there was no conceivable event or series of events the occurrence of which would be admitted by sophisticated religious people to be a sufficient reason for conceding "There wasn't a God after all" or "God does not really love us then." Someone tells us that God loves us as a father loves his children. We are reassured. But then we see a child dying of inoperable cancer of the throat. His earthly father is driven frantic in his efforts to help, but his Heavenly Father reveals no obvious sign of concern. Some qualification is made—God's love is "not a merely human love" or it is "an inscrutable love," perhaps—and we realize that such sufferings are quite compatible with the truth of the assertion that "God loves us as a father (but, of course, . . .)." We are reassured again. But then perhaps we ask: what is this assurance of God's (appropriately qualified) love worth, what is this apparent guarantee really a guarantee against? Just what would have to happen not merely (morally or wrongly) to tempt but also (logically and rightly) to entitle us to say "God does not love us" or even "God does not exist?" I therefore put to the succeeding symposiasts the simple central question, "What would have to occur or to have occurred to constitute for you a disproof of the love of, or the existence of, God?"

R. M. Hare

I wish to make it clear that I shall not try to defend Christianity in particular, but religion in general—not because I do not believe in Christianity, but because you cannot understand what Christianity is, until you have understood what religion is.

I must begin by confessing that, on the ground marked out by Flew, he seems to me to be completely victorious. I therefore shift my ground by relating another parable. A certain lunatic is convinced that all dons want to murder him. His friends introduce him to all the mildest and most respectable dons that they can find, and after each of them has retired, they say, "You see, he doesn't really want to murder you; he spoke to you in a most cordial manner; surely you are convinced now?" But the lunatic replies, "Yes, but that was only his diabolical cunning; he's really plotting against me the whole time, like the rest of them; I know it, I tell you." However many kindly dons are produced, the reaction is still the same.

Now we say that such a person is deluded. But what is he deluded about? About the truth or falsity of an assertion? Let us apply Flew's test to him. There is no behaviour of dons that can be enacted which he will accept as counting against his theory; and therefore his theory, on this test, asserts nothing. But it does not follow that there is no difference between what he thinks about dons and what most of us think about them—otherwise we should not call him a lunatic and ourselves sane, and dons would have no reason to feel uneasy about his presence in Oxford.

Let us call that in which we differ from this lunatic, our respective *bliks*. He has an insane *blik* about dons; we have a sane one. It is important to realize that we have a sane one, not no *blik* at all; for there must be two sides to any argument—if he has a wrong *blik*, then those who are right about dons must have a right one. Flew has shown that a *blik* does not consist in an assertion or system of them; but nevertheless it is very important to have the right *blik*.

Let us try to imagine what it would be like to have different *bliks* about other things than dons. When I am driving my car, it sometimes occurs to me to wonder whether my movements of the steering wheel will always continue to be followed by corresponding alterations in the direction of the car. I have never had a steering failure, though I have had skids, which must be similar. Moreover, I know enough about how the steering of my car is made, to know the sort of thing that would have to go wrong for the steering to fail—steel joints would have to part, or steel rods break, or something—but how do I know that this won't happen? The truth is, I don't know; I just have a *blik* about steel and its properties, so that normally I trust the steering of my car; but I find it not at all difficult to imagine what it would be like to lose this *blik* and acquire the opposite one. People would say I was silly about steel; but there would be no mistaking the reality of the difference between our respective *bliks*—for example, I should never go in a motor-car. Yet I should hesitate to say that the difference between us was the difference between contradictory assertions. No amount of safe arrivals or bench-tests will remove my *blik* and restore the normal one; for my *blik* is compatible with any finite number of such tests.

It was Hume who taught us that our whole commerce with the world depends upon our *blik* about the world; and that differences between *bliks* about the world cannot be settled by observation of what happens in the world. That was why, having performed the interesting experiment of doubting the ordinary man's *blik* about the world, and showing that no proof could be given to make us adopt one *blik* rather than another, he turned to backgammon to take his mind off the problem. It seems, indeed, to be impossible even to formulate as an assertion the normal *blik* about the world which makes me put my confidence in the future reliability of steel joints, in the continued ability of the road to support my car, and not gape beneath it revealing nothing below; in the general nonhomicidal tendencies of dons; in my own continued well-being (in some sense of that word that I may not now fully understand) if I continue to do what is right according to my lights; in the general likelihood of people like Hitler coming to a bad end. But perhaps a formulation less inadequate than most is to be found in the Psalms: "The earth is weak and all the inhibitors thereof: I bear up the pillars of it."

The mistake of the position which Flew selects for attack is to regard this kind of talk as some sort of *explanation*, as scientists are accustomed to use the word. As such, it would obviously be ludicrous. We no longer believe in God as an Atlas—*nous n'avons pas besoin de cette hypothesè*. But it is nevertheless true to say that, as Hume saw, without a *blik* there can be no explanation; for it is by our *bliks* that we decide what is and what is not an explanation. Suppose we believed that everything happened by pure chance. This would not of course be an assertion; for it is compatible with anything happening or not happening, and so, incidentally, is its contradictory. But if we had this belief, we should not be able to explain or predict or plan anything. Thus, although we should not be *asserting* anything different from those of a more normal belief, there would be a great difference between us; and this is the sort of difference that there is between those who really believe in God and those who really disbelieve in him.

The word "really" is important, and may excite suspicion. I put it in, because when people have had a good Christian upbringing, as have most of those who now profess not to believe in any sort of religion, it is very hard to discover what they really believe. The reason why they find it so easy to think that they are not religious, is that they have never got into the frame of mind of one who suffers from the doubts to which religion is the answer. Not for them the terrors of the primitive jungle. Having abandoned some of the more picturesque fringes of religion, they think that they have abandoned the whole thing—whereas in fact they still have got, and could not live without, a religion of a comfortably substantial, albeit highly sophisticated, kind, which differs from that of many "religious people" in little more than this, that "religious people" like to sing Psalms about theirs—a very natural and proper thing to do. But nevertheless there may be a big difference lying behind—the difference between two people who, though side by side, are walking in different directions. I do not know in what direction Flew is walking; perhaps he does not know either. But we have had some examples recently of various ways in which one can walk away from Christianity, and there are any number of possibilities. After all, man has not changed biologically since primitive times; it is his religion that has changed, and it can easily change again. And if you do not think that such changes make a difference, get acquainted with some Sikhs and some Mussulmans of the same Punjabi stock; you will find them quite different sorts of people.

There is an important difference between Flew's parable and my own which we have not yet noticed. The explorers do not mind about their garden; they discuss it with interest, but not with concern. But my lunatic, poor fellow, minds about dons; and I mind about the steering of my car; it often has people in it that I care for. It is because I mind very much about what goes on in the garden in which I find myself, that I am unable to share the explorers' detachment.

Basil Mitchell

Flew's article is searching and perceptive, but there is, I think, something odd about his conduct of the theologian's case. The theologian surely would not deny that the fact of pain counts against the assertion that God loves men. This very incompatibility generates the most intractable of theological problems—the problem of evil. So the theologian does recognize the fact of pain as counting against Christian doctrine. But it is true that he will not allow it—or anything— to count decisively against it; for he is committed by his faith to trust God. His attitude is not that of the detached observer, but of the believer.

Perhaps this can be brought out by yet another parable. In time of war in an occupied country, a member of the resistance meets one night a stranger who deeply impresses him. They spend that night together in conversation. The Stranger tells the partisan that he himself is on the side of the resistance—indeed that he is in command of it, and urges the partisan to have faith in him no matter what happens. The partisan is utterly convinced at that meeting of the Stranger's sincerity and constancy and undertakes to trust him.

They never meet in conditions of intimacy again. But sometimes the Stranger is seen helping members of the resistance, and the partisan is grateful and says to his friends, "He is on our side."

Sometimes he is seen in the uniform of the police handing over patriots to the occupying power. On these occasions his friends murmur against him: but the partisan still says, "He is on our side." He still believes that, in spite of appearances, the Stranger did not deceive him. Sometimes he asks the Stranger for help and receives it. He is then thankful. Sometimes he asks and does not receive it. Then he says, "The Stranger knows best." Sometimes his friends, in exasperation, say "Well, what *would* he have to do for you to admit that you were wrong and that he is not on our side?" But the partisan refuses to answer. He will not consent to put the Stranger to the test. And sometimes his friends complain, "Well, if *that's* what you mean by his being on our side, the sooner he goes over to the other side the better."

The partisan of the parable does not allow anything to count decisively against the proposition "The Stranger is on our side." This is because he has committed himself to trust the Stranger. But he of course recognizes that the Stranger's ambiguous behaviour *does* count against what he believes about him. It is precisely this situation which constitutes the trial of his faith.

When the partisan asks for help and doesn't get it, what can he do? He can (a) conclude that the Stranger is not on our side or (b) maintain that he is on our side, but that he has reasons for withholding help.

The first he will refuse to do. How long can he uphold the second position without its becoming just silly?

I don't think one can say in advance. It will depend on the nature of the impression created by the Stranger in the first place. It will depend, too, on the manner in which he takes the Stranger's behaviour. If he blandly dismisses it as of no consequence, as having no bearing upon his belief, it will be assumed that he is thoughtless or insane. And it quite obviously won't do for him to say easily, "Oh, when used of the Stranger the phrase 'is on our side' *means* ambiguous behaviour of this sort." In that case he would be like the religious man who says blandly of a terrible disaster, "It is God's will." No, he will only be regarded as sane and reasonable in his belief, if he experiences in himself the full force of the conflict.

It is here that my parable differs from Hare's. The partisan admits that many things may and do count against his belief, whereas Hare's lunatic who has a *blik* about dons doesn't admit that anything counts against his *blik*. Nothing *can* count against *bliks*.

This means that I agree with Flew that theological utterances must be assertions. The partisan is making an assertion when he says, "The Stranger is on our side."

Do I want to say that the partisan's belief about the Stranger is, in any sense, an explanation? I think I do. It explains and makes sense of the Stranger's behaviour: it helps to explain also the resistance movement in the context of which he appears. In each case it differs from the interpretation which the others put upon the same facts.

"God loves men" resembles "The Stranger is on our side" (and many other significant statements, e.g. historical ones) in not being conclusively falsifiable. They can both be treated in at least three different ways: (1) As provisional hypotheses to be discarded if experience tells against them; (2) As significant articles of faith; (3) As vacuous formulae (expressing, perhaps, a desire for reassurance) to which experience makes no difference and which make no difference to life.

The Christian, once he has committed himself, is precluded by his faith from taking up the first attitude: "Thou shalt not tempt the lord thy God." He is in constant danger, as Flew has observed, of slipping into the third. But he need not; and, if he does, it is a failure in faith as well as in logic.

Antony Flew

It has been a good discussion: and I am glad to have helped to provoke it. But now—at least in *University*—it must come to an end: and the Editors of *University* have asked me to make some concluding remarks. Since it is impossible to deal with all the issues raised or to comment separately upon each contribution, I will concentrate on Mitchell and Hare, as representative of two very different kinds of response to the challenge made in "Theology and Falsification."

The challenge, it will be remembered, ran like this. Some theological utterances seem to, and are intended to, provide explanations or express assertions. Now an assertion, to be an assertion at all, must claim that things stand thus and thus; *and not otherwise*. Similarly an explanation, to be an explanation at all, must explain why this particular thing occurs; *and not something else*. Those last clauses are crucial. And yet sophisticated religious people—or so it seemed to me—are apt to overlook this, and tend to refuse to allow, not merely that anything actually does occur, but that anything conceivably could occur, which would count against their theological assertions and explanations. But in so far as they do this their supposed explanations are actually bogus, and their seeming assertions are really vacuous.

Mitchell's response to this challenge is admirably direct, straightforward, and understanding. He agrees "that theological utterances must be assertions." He agrees that if they are to be assertions, there must be something that would count against their truth. He agrees, too, that believers are in constant danger of transforming their would-be assertions into "vacuous formulae." But he takes me to task for an oddity in my "conduct of the theologian's case. The theologian surely would not deny that the fact of pain counts against the assertion that God loves men. This very incompatibility generates the most intractable of theological problems, the problem of evil." I think he is right. I should have made a distinction between two very different ways of dealing with what looks like evidence against the love of God: the way I stressed was the expedient of qualifying the original assertion; the way the theologian usually takes, at first, is to admit that it looks bad but to insist that there is—there must be—some explanation which will show that, in spite of appearances, there really is a God who loves us. His difficulty, it seems to me, is that he has given God attributes which rule out all possible saving explanations. In Mitchell's parable of the Stranger it is easy for the believer to find plausible excuses for ambiguous behaviour: for the Stranger is a man. But suppose the Stranger is God. We cannot say that he would like to help but cannot: God is omnipotent. We cannot say that he would help if he only knew: God is omniscient. We cannot say that he is not responsible for the wickedness of others: God creates those others. Indeed an omnipotent, omniscient God must be an accessory before (and during) the fact to every human misdeed; as well as being responsible for every nonmoral defect in the universe. So, though I entirely concede that Mitchell was absolutely right to insist against me that the theologian's first move is to look for an *explanation*, I still think that in the end, if relentlessly pursued, he will have to resort to the avoiding action of *qualification*. And there lies the danger of that death by a thousand qualifications, which would, I agree, constitute "a failure in faith as well as in logic."

Hare's approach is fresh and bold. He confesses that "on the ground marked out by Flew, he seems to me to be completely victorious." He therefore introduces the concept of *blik*. But while I think that there is room for some such concept in philosophy, and that philosophers should be grateful to Hare for his invention, I nevertheless want to insist that any attempt to analyze Christian religious utterances as expressions or affirmations of a *blik* rather than as (at least would-be) assertions about the cosmos is fundamentally misguided. *First*, because thus interpreted they would be entirely unorthodox. If Hare's religion really is a *blik*, involving no cosmological assertions about the nature and activities of a supposed personal creator, then surely he is not a Christian at all? *Second*, because thus interpreted, they could scarcely do the job they do. If they were not even intended as assertions then many religious activities would become fraudulent, or merely silly. If "You ought because it is God's will" asserts no more than "You ought," then the person who prefers the former phraseology is not really giving a reason, but a fraudulent substitute for one, a dialectical dud cheque. If "My soul must be immortal because God loves his children, etc." asserts no more than "My soul must be immortal," then the man who reassures himself with theological arguments for immortality is being as silly as the man who tries to clear his overdraft by writing his bank a cheque on the same account. (Of course neither of these utterances would be distinctively Christian: but this discussion never pretended to be so confined.) Religious utterances may indeed express false or even bogus assertions, but I simply do not believe that they are not both intended and interpreted to be or at any rate to presuppose assertions, at least in the context of religious practice; whatever shifts may be demanded, in another context, by the exigencies of theological apologetic.

One final suggestion. The philosophers of religion might well draw upon George Orwell's last appalling nightmare *1984* for the concept of *doublethink*. "*Doublethink* means the power of holding two contradictory beliefs simultaneously, and accepting both of them. The party intellectual knows that he is playing tricks with reality, but by the exercise of *doublethink* he also satisfies himself that reality is not violated" *(1984,* p. 220). Perhaps religious intellectuals too are sometimes driven to doublethink in order to retain their faith in a loving God in face of the reality of a heartless and indifferent world. But of this more another time, perhaps. . . .

29. Ian T. Ramsey, *Religious Language*

In this small book I hope to show how the contemporary philosophical interest in language, far from being soul-destroying, can be so developed as to provide a novel inroad into the problems and controversies of theology, illuminating its claims and reforming its apologetic. If that seems an astounding suggestion, my hope is that the book will make it less incredible than at first sight it appears.

Let us begin with a brief survey of the historical origins of the contemporary scene. We might perhaps back-date the present philosophical interest in language to the turn of the century when people like G. E. Moore and Bertrand Russell protested against the kind of language being used by the neo-Hegelians who at that time dominated philosophy. To Moore and Russell the language of these neo-Hegelians seemed pretentious, woolly, and confused. There was this talk, for instance, of "Being" which when "freely-floating . . . in the air" provided the subject matter of logic. Many of the characteristic claims such as "time is unreal" seemed to depend on mere juggling with language. Against this, the watchword for Russell, and especially for Moore, was "clarify." They would warn us not to think that a philosopher or a theologian is good and impressive because we cannot understand him. What can be said, can be said plainly. If it cannot be said plainly, we should be suspicious of its claim to be said at all. . . .

As the interest in clarification developed, emphasis came to be centered on the Verification Principle which came to these islands by way of Austria, and is associated with names like Carnap, Schlick and Wittgenstein. This Principle claims, we might say, to give a touchstone for clear and unambiguous language. According to the Verification Principle we must exclude from language all propositions which cannot, at any rate in principle, be verified by sense experience—by what is seen, heard, touched, tasted and smelt. Restrict ourselves to propositions of sense experience and all will be well. Unfortunately, as it seemed to some, not much of language is then left, and in particular ethics and theology would have to be excluded from meaningful language in so far as they claimed to be about anything more than sense-objects. . . .

Mellowing came with the realization that the Verification Principle may only be *one* clue to meaning, so that propositions, however odd by verificationist tests, may yet have a meaning of their own. In other words the view arises that apparently homogeneous language may exhibit all kinds of logical differences.

Here we have the third stage in the development of recent thought: logical empiricism. But let us not think that the mellowing of the verificationist outlook means that the challenge of contemporary philosophy is weakened. It is, in fact, all the stronger for being the more subtle. The third stage has in its turn led naturally to a denial of the possibility of metaphysics, and in this way. If it is the case that language can exhibit all kinds of logical differences, may not all so-called ultimate problems arise from confounding these logical differences and in this way misusing words? Confound logic differences and you will have *pseudo-problems*. "The Army," we are told, "marches on its stomach." If we suppose this is a straightforward assertion, we shall then ask: What kind of animal can the Army be? Is it some kind of cross between a snake and a dachshund? Is it some special kind of Being? So puzzles develop from a misallocation of the original assertion. Or again, confound logical differences and we will have *pseudo-theories* such as the typically scientific claim that "My table is really only electrons and space . . . ," a pseudo-theory which arises from confounding the languages of common sense and physics. When we come to "God" we find that believers wish on the one hand to claim that he is indescribable and ineffable, and yet on the other hand to talk a great deal about him. Nay more, when they speak of God they say that he is transcendent and immanent, impassible yet loving, and so on. But if we speak like this, are we talking significantly at all? . . .

Now it is true that philosophers do not claim as vigorously as they might have done even five years ago, that all the ultimate problems of metaphysics have been created by confounding logics; that these ultimate problems are just category blunders. Nevertheless it is plain that contemporary philosophy lays on us an urgent task and duty, *viz.* to elucidate the logic of theological assertions . . . . How then do we face the challenge? The answer is, by asking at the outset, and as a leading question: To what kind of situation does religion appeal? What kinds of empirical anchorage have theological words?

To answer that question, let our memories first go back to Joseph Butler who in the eighteenth century and in his own way likewise attempted Christian apologetic in the face of contemporary empiricism. If we take up again *The Analogy of Religion Natural and Revealed to the Constitution and Course of Nature*, we shall find Butler makes two points of special interest for our present purpose. . . .

Butler suggests that religion claims (a) a fuller discernment, to which we respond with (b) a total commitment. Such a commitment without any discernment whatever is bigotry and idolatry; to have the discernment without an appropriate commitment is the worst of all religious vices. It is insincerity and hypocrisy.

If then we are to meet squarely the challenge of contemporary philosophy; if we are to make clearer to the unbeliever the kind of empirical anchorage which theological words possess; if we are to enliven apologetic, our first task will be to make clearer what is meant by speaking of situations in terms of "discernment" and "commitment." To do this I suggest that we ask ourselves whether we can find other situations in ordinary life reminiscent of these to which religion appeals? Can we find any parallels from ordinary experience to the twofold characterization of religion as a discernment–commitment? I think we can. . . .

The first group of situations, illustrating in the main what we have called "religious discernment," are those about which, and not surprisingly, we use phrases that are in certain ways odd, peculiar and unusual. We should say, for instance, of these situations at the point where they provide parallels to religious discernment, that they "come alive"; that the "light dawns"; that the "ice breaks"; that the "penny drops," and so on.

For our first example let us recall the setting of a High Court—all very impersonal, all very formal, quite lacking in "depth" and "vision." The name of the judge is made as suitably abstract as possible—Mr. Justice Brown. The wigs and scarlet are meant to conceal the fact that Mr. Justice Brown is after all a human being. If he has rushed to the Court from riding, or mending the car, he would never think of appearing there in riding breeches or overalls. Whatever clothes he wore to play with the children will at least be covered with scarlet and ermine. Nor is the argument of the Court interested in persons. We have, instead, "the Crown," "the accused" and "the prosecution." Here is a situation as impersonal as may be; a mere facade of human existence. Then, one morning, Mr. Justice Brown enters the Court to see as the "accused" the closest friend of his undergraduate days; or, if we may be more melodramatic, his long-lost wife. "Eye meets eye"; astonishment; an odd word is uttered. It may be from the undergraduate friend "Sammy!"; from the wife "Penny!"; and the result is (as the papers will tell us next day) that the Court is "electrified." An impersonal situation has "come alive." Mr. Justice Brown has seen in the "accused" something he has never seen before, and the accused has seen in the judge of the Queen's Bench Division, something which scarlet and ermine did not express, something which goes far beyond the wigs and the legal language. "Eye meets eye," but if this phrase is used of the new situation it means far more than physiological positioning; and it is important to see that the significance of words like "Sammy" and "Penny" is proportionate to their comparative lack of empirical relevance. The situation has not "come alive" merely by containing an unusually large range of facts; rather, in stretching to include these facts, the situation has taken on "depth" as well—it has become in a certain way partly elusive. The very lack of observational ties which nicknames like "Penny" and "Sammy" possess, enables them all the better to claim a measure of spatio-temporal elusiveness about the situation of which they are appropriately used. "Sammy," for instance, may have been a word which, for some quite trivial reason, was associated once with Mr. Justice Brown—there may have been some pun on a Sam Browne belt—but it is not used with any observational unpacking in mind, its significance is that it has always belonged to *characteristically personal situations.* "Penny" may likewise have the thinnest empirical anchorage. Perhaps Mr. Justice Brown found a penny by the first stile which he and his wife crossed on the first day of their honeymoon, and with that beginning the word "Penny" has now come to be currency between them for all that which is most *characteristically personal.* At any rate my point now is that such words would be in violent contrast to the language used normally in the setting of the High Court, and that this violent contrast makes the point (or so I hope) that a characteristically personal situation cannot be contained or expressed in legal language and customs, as it cannot be contained in any "impersonal" object language. The situation is more than "what's seen," it has taken on "depth"; there is something akin to religious "insight," "discernment," "vision."

Our second example begins with a party all stiff and formal. Then, it happens that someone's dinner jacket splits unexpectedly up the back; or someone sits sedately on a chair which collapses beneath her. At once the party takes on "human warmth"; as we should say, "the ice breaks." Some theologians who were present might say the party had now entered a "new dimension." Once again let us notice that evoking the characteristically different situation is something odd—unusual—though this time it is not odd words but other odd, unusual symbols, like the torn jacket and the broken chair.

For a third example, let us recall the experience we have all had of an argument or a joke in relation to which there is no sort of mutual understanding. We say—and significantly—"I might just as well be talking to a brick wall." The situation is indeed, as the phrase suggests, impersonal.

But there is one way of assured success, and this will be found if (as we say) we know the weak points in his armour—and once again notice that his personality is concealed by this impersonal word "armour." It may be that he is never, as we should say, "more himself" than when he is fishing. Fishing moves him to tears, reaches the "roots" of his personality. Nothing so good as a river and fish for evoking "depth"; fishing is an "inspiration" to him. Let us suppose then that we are trying to argue the merits of "equal pay for equal work." We illustrate it from this angle and from that, but there is no penetration. The head always shakes, and the face looks blank. and then we remember the fishing and we say, "Look here, Jim, what I mean is 'equal fishing pay for equal fishing work,'" and he smiles; his face breaks significantly, the penny drops. He says: "Now I understand perfectly." Once again it is a word odd to the context which has evoked that characteristically different situation, which in this case occurs when an argument is grasped, and we "see" the conclusion in a way which is more than merely "entertaining" the appropriate proposition.

Incidentally we now have a glimpse of the logical grounds on which swearing has been condemned by religious people. For it is plain that in the story just told, the word "fishing" could have been replaced by an oath, e.g. "bloody." In fact there is a version of the story which does just this and which for reasons of delicacy I avoided. Now it is in situations of high frustration when nothing seems to yield; when a man realizes his powerlessness or finitude; when he is caught up in an entanglement of relationships, that he may be heard to swear. In such words are his cosmic protest, his label for this situation where in some way his existence is shown in its "authentic" character; when he sees the "existential" claim of his life; when he knows what "being-in-a-situation" is. Swearing expresses "heroic defiance"; it is an assertion of a man's "being *pour soi*" and so on. So swearing is rightly condemned by religious people because the logic of swearing is so very close to the logic of God. Both appeal to a characteristic situation of discernment and depth, but when a man swears, "God" is replaced by a word which, even if it is the same token word—made up of the same letters or sounding identical—has no logical connection with a theistic scheme. Swearing is rightly condemned when, in a situation of discernment, an oath takes the place of "God." . . .

The discernment which we have so far tried to parallel by recalling situations where, as it would be said, "the penny drops," "the ice breaks"—situations which "come alive"—this discernment can also be illustrated I believe by the use of such diagrams as are commonplace in Gestalt psychology.

Let us recall how there could be drawn twelve straight lines which at first sight might look no more than two squares with corners joined. But then there dawns on us "depth," and we see the twelve straight lines as a "unity." The lines indeed represent a cube and this cube may, as is well known, seem to enter into or stand out of the surface on which the lines are drawn. Here again is a characteristically different situation which dawns on us at some recognizable point. This is the point where twelve straight lines cease to be merely twelve straight lines, when a characteristically different situation is evoked which needs odd words like "depth" and "unity," or mathematically the idea of a "new dimension," "volume" besides "area."

Or again, there is the bread on sale in French shops.
We have bread like   ⌣
bread like   ⌒   and   ◦ ◦
and bread like   ○
but if we have been superimposing these shapes in telling the story, we shall then finish not with bread in a shop, but with a Frenchman: ☺
There is a disclosure: the "penny drops."

There are "disclosures" similar to those we have mentioned, when, for example, we are told someone's name. We may previously have known all kinds of facts about him. We may have had a very great deal of what Russell would have called "knowledge by description." We may first have known him as the man in the bowler hat who came to sit next to us in the train. He then appears opposite us at lunch, and we begin to see him regularly. We now know him as the man who invariably orders "Double Diamond"; the man who does the *Times* crossword in fifteen minutes; and as the weeks pass we come to know him as the man who has a wife and three children; too much herbaceous border to weed in the evenings, too few vegetables left after the frost, too little money left at the end of the month. But one day he says, offering his hand: "Look here—I'm Nigel Short." At that moment there is a "disclosure," an individual becomes a "person," the ice does not continue to melt, it *breaks*. We have not discovered just one more fact to be added to those we have been collecting day by day. There has now been some significant "encounter," which is not just a moving of palm on palm, no mere correlation of mouth noises, not just heads nodding in some kind of mutual harmony. The little labels at conferences do not merely give ostensive definitions of the people behind them; nor do they provoke conversation simply because they associate those people with a background we already know. Not for nothing do people say that the labels "break the ice"—evoke "depth," break down the impersonality.

The same kind of "disclosure" occurs when hills or buildings are named. Suppose we are on a railway or car journey. The countryside might look very much like anywhere else: hills, houses, churches and so on. But then someone has a map or a guide: "There's Winter Hill," "That's the Manor House," "Here is St. Lawrence's Church—going back to Saxon times." Is it no more than additional information? Do we delight to know these details simply because we want to know more facts? Or is it that, with such details, our surroundings become familiar, that this familiarity develops into a feeling of friendship which finally evokes a sense of cosmic kinship where before there were only unknown objects. We not only see the hills, houses, churches, around us, but the landscape "comes alive." May not the use of maps and guide books, then, witness to the occurrence of situations parallel to those in which religion is founded?

This first group of examples could plainly continue much further, but I think they will have given some kind of indication of what is meant when religious people talk of an odd "discernment" and a "characteristically different" situation. Let no one condemn the examples I have given on the grounds that they assimilate religion to psychology. Let me repeat that the examples are certainly psychological in so far as they appeal to situations which are experienced, but they are not psychological in so far as they would reduce religion to what would be called "subjective experiences"—whatever that phrase may mean. There is no question of a characteristically religious situation being merely "emotional," if that word is thought to claim that the characteristic features we have been mentioning are entirely (in some sense or other) "subjective." Let us emphasize, without any possibility of misunderstanding, that all these situations, all these characteristically different situations, when they occur, have an *objective* reference and are, as all situations, *subject-object* in structure. When situatons "come alive," or the "ice breaks," there is objective "depth" in these situations along with and alongside any subjective changes.

30. Paul Ricoeur, *Myth and Symbol*

Speculation, Myth, and Symbol

How shall we make the transition from the possibility of evil in man to its reality, from fallibility to fault? We will try to surprise the transition in the act by "re-enacting" in ourselves the confession that the religious consciousness makes of it. . . .

It seems tempting, at first, to begin with the most elaborate, the most rationalized expressions of that confession, in the hope that those expressions will be closest to the language of philosophy in virtue of their "explanatory" character. Thus, one will be inclined to think that it is against the late constructions of the Augustinian epoch concerning *original sin* that philosophy is challenged to measure itself. Many philosophies, classical and modern, take this supposed concept as a religious and theological datum and reduce the philosophical problem of fault to a critique of the idea of original sin.

Nothing is less amenable to a direct confrontation with philosophy than the concept of original sin, for nothing is more deceptive than its appearance of rationality. On the contrary, it is to the least elaborate, the most inarticulate expressions of the confession of evil that philosophic reason must listen. Therefore we must proceed regressively and revert from the "speculative" expressions to the "spontaneous" ones. In particular, it is essential to be convinced from the start that the concept of original sin is not at the beginning but at the end of a cycle of living experience, the Christian experience of sin. . . .

To what does speculation refer us? To living experience? Not yet. Behind speculation, and beneath gnosis and anti-gnostic constructions, we find *myths*. Myth will here be taken to mean what the history of religions now finds in it: not a false explanation by means of images and fables, but a traditional narration which relates to events that happened at the beginning of time and which has the purpose of providing grounds for the ritual actions of men of today and, in a general manner, establishing all the forms of action and thought by which man understands himself in his world. For us, moderns, a myth is *only* a myth because we can no longer connect that time with the time of history as we write it, employing the critical method, nor can we connect mythical places with our geographical space. This is why the myth can no longer be an explanation; to exclude its etiological intention is the theme of all necessary demythologization. But in losing its explanatory pretensions the myth reveals its exploratory significance and its contribution to understanding, which we shall later call its symbolic function—that is to say, its power of discovering and revealing the bond between man and what he considers sacred. Paradoxical as it may seem, the myth, when it is thus demythologized through contact with scientific history and elevated to the dignity of a symbol, is a dimension of modern thought. . . .

Shall we begin, then, with an interpretation of the myths about the origin and the end of evil? Not yet. The stratum of myths, to which we are referred by pseudo-rational speculation, refers us to its turn back to an experience lying at a lower level than any narration or any gnosis. Thus, the account of the fall in the Bible, even if it comes from traditions older than the preaching of the prophets of Israel, gets its meaning only from an experience of sin which is itself an attainment of Jewish piety. It is the "confession of sins" in the cult and the prophetic appeal for "justice and righteousness" that furnish the myth with a substructure of meaning.

Thus, speculation on original sin sends us back to the myth of the fall, and this, in its turn, sends us back to the confession of sins. The myth of the fall is so far from being the cornerstone of the Judeo-Christian conception of sin that the figure of Adam, placed by the myth at the origin of the history of human evil, remained a mute figure for practically all of the writers of the Old Testament. Abraham, the father of believers, the founder-ancestor of the elect people, and Noah, the father of postdiluvian humanity, produced more of an echo in the Biblical theology of history than the figure of Adam, which remained in a state of suspended animation, so to speak, until St. Paul revived it by making it parallel to the second Adam, Jesus Christ. At the same time, the "event" of the Christ transformed the fall of Adam retroactively into a similar "event"; the historicity of the second Adam, by reflection, conferred upon the first Adam a comparable historicity and an individuality corresponding to the Christ's. The demythologization of the story of the fall was made more urgent by this retroactive action of Paulinian Christology on the Adamic symbol.

Now this dimension of the symbol can only be recovered by the "re-enactment" of the experience made explicit by the myth. It is, then, to this experience that we must try to penetrate.

But is this re-enactment possible? Does not the mediative role that we have granted to speculation and myth condemn in advance the attempt to restore the pre-mythical and pre-speculative foundation? The venture would be hopeless if, lower than gnosis and myth, there were no longer any language. But this is not the case; there is the language of *confession*, which in the languages of myth and speculation is raised to the second and third degrees.

This language of confession is the counterpart of the triple character of the experience it brings to light: blindness, equivocalness, scandalousness.

The experience of which the penitent makes confession is a blind experience, still embedded in the matrix of emotion, fear, anguish. It is this emotional note that gives rise to objectification in discourse; the confession expresses, pushes to the outside, the emotion which without it would be shut up in itself, as an impression in the soul. Language is the light of the emotions. Through confession the consciousness of fault is brought into the light of speech; through confession man remains speech, even in the experience of his own absurdity, suffering, and anguish.

Moreover, this experience is complex. Instead of the simple experience that one might expect, the confession of sins reveals several layers of experience. "Guilt," in the precise sense of a feeling of the unworthiness at the core of one's personal being, is only the advanced point of a radically individualized and interiorized experience. This feeling of guilt points to a more fundamental experience, the experience of "sin," which includes *all* men and indicates the *real* situation of man before God, whether man knows it or not. It is this sin of which the myth of the fall recounts the entry into the world and which speculation on original sin attempts to erect into a doctrine. But sin, in its turn, is a correction and even a revolution with respect to a more archaic conception of fault—the notion of "defilement" conceived in the guise of a strain or blemish that infects from without. Guilt, sin, and defilement thus constitute a primitive diversity in experience. Hence, the feeling involved is not only blind in virtue of being emotional; it is also equivocal, laden with a multiplicity of meanings. This is why language is needed a second time to elucidate the subterranean crisis of the consciousness of fault.

Finally, the experience of which the believer makes avowal in the confession of sins creates a language for itself by its very strangeness; the experience of being oneself but alienated from oneself gets transcribed immediately on the plane of language in the mode of interrogation. Sin, as alienation from oneself, is an experience even more astonishing, disconcerting, and scandalous, perhaps, than the spectacle of nature, and for this reason it is the richest source of interrogative thought. In the oldest Babylonian psalters the believer asks: "How long, O Lord? What god have I sinned against? What sin have I committed?" Sin makes me incomprehensible to myself: God is hidden; the course of things no longer has meaning. It is in line with this questioning and for the purpose of warding off the threat of meaninglessness that the myth relates "how that began," and that gnosis elaborates the famous question: πόθεν τὰ κακά? (Whence come evils?) and mobilizes all its resources for explanation. Sin is perhaps the most important of the occasions for questioning, but also for reasoning incorrectly by giving premature answers. But just as the transcendental illusion, according to Kant, testifies by its very perplexities that reason is the faculty of the unconditioned, so the unseasonable answers of gnosis and of the etiological myths testify that man's most moving experience, that of being lost as a sinner, communicates with the need to understand and excites attention by its very character as a scandal.

By this threefold route man's living experience of fault gives itself a language: a language that expresses it in spite of its blind character; a language that makes explicit its contradictions and its internal revolutions; a language, finally, that reveals the experience of alienation as astonishing.

Now, the Hebraic and Hellenic literatures give evidence of a linguistic inventiveness that marks the existential eruptions of this consciousness of fault. It is by discovering the motivations of those linguistic inventions that we re-enact the passage from defilement to sin and guilt. Thus, the Hebrew and Greek words that express the consciousness of fault have a sort of wisdom of their own which we must make explicit and take as our guide in the labyrinth of living experience. We are not, therefore, reduced to the ineffable when we try to dig beneath the myths of evil; we still come up with a language.

Moreover, the merely semantic understanding that we can acquire from the vocabulary of fault is an exercise preparatory to the hermeneutics of myths. Indeed, it is itself already a hermeneutics, for *the most primitive and least mythical language is already a symbolic language*: defilement is spoken of under the symbol of a stain or blemish, sin under the symbol of missing the mark, of a torturous road, of trespass, etc. In short, the preferred language of fault appears to be indirect and based on imagery. There is something quite astonishing in this: the consciousness of self seems to constitute itself at its lowest level by means of symbolism and to work out an abstract language only subsequently, by means of a spontaneous hermeneutics of its primary symbols. We shall see later the extensive implications of this assertion. For the moment it is enough to have established that the "re-enactment" in sympathetic imagination always moves in the element of language as reflection reverts from gnosis to myth and from myth to the primary symbolic expressions brought into play in the confession of fault. This reversion to the primary symbols permits us henceforth to consider myths and gnosis as secondary and tertiary symbols, an interpretation of which rests on the interpretation of the primary symbols.

We must therefore take as a whole the elementary language of confession, the developed language of myths, and the elaborated language of gnosis and counter-gnosis. Speculation is not autonomous and myths themselves are secondary; but neither is there any immediate consciousness of fault that can do without the secondary and tertiary elaborations. It is the whole circle, made up of confession, myth, and speculation, that we must understand. . . .

Criteriology of Symbols

Confession, we have said, always manifests itself in the element of language. Now, that language is essentially symbolic. Hence a philosophy that is concerned to integrate confession with the consciousness of self cannot escape the task of elaborating, at least in outline, a criteriology of symbols.

Before proceeding to a direct intentional analysis of symbolism, we must determine the extent and the variety of its zones of emergence. One cannot, in fact, understand the reflective use of symbolism—as one sees, for example, in the examination of conscience of the penitent of Babylonia or Israel—without reverting to its naive forms, where the prerogatives of reflective consciousness are subordinated to the cosmic aspect of hierophanies, to the nocturnal aspect of dream productions, or finally to the creativity of the poetic word. These three dimensions of symbolism—cosmic, oneiric, and poetic—are present in every authentic symbol. The reflective aspect of symbols, which we shall examine further on (defilement, deviation, straying, exile, weight of fault, etc.), is intelligible only if it is connected with these three functions of symbols.

Man first reads the sacred *on* the world, *on* some elements or aspects of the world, on the heavens, on the sun and moon, on the waters and vegetation. Spoken symbolism thus refers back to manifestations of the sacred, to hierophanies, where the sacred is shown in a fragment of the cosmos, which, in return, loses its concrete limits, gets charged with innumerable meanings, integrates and unifies the greatest possible number of the sectors of anthropocosmic experience. First of all, then, it is the sun, the moon, the waters—that is to say, cosmic realities—that are symbols. Shall we say, therefore, that symbols, in their cosmic aspect, are anterior to language, or even foreign to it? Not at all. For these realities to be symbol is to gather together at one point a mass of significations which, before giving rise to thought, give rise to speech. The symbolic *manifestation* as a *thing* is a matrix of symbolic meanings as words. We have never ceased to find meaning in the sky (to take the first example on which Eliade practices his comparative phenomenology). It is the same thing to say that the sky *manifests* the sacred and to say that it *signifies* the most high, the elevated and the immense, the powerful and the orderly, the clairvoyant and the wise, the sovereign, the immutable. The manifestation through the thing is like the condensation of an infinite discourse; manifestation and meaning are strictly contemporaneous and reciprocal; the concretion in the thing is the counterpart of the surcharge of inexhaustible meaning which has ramifications in the cosmic, in the ethical, and in the political. Thus, the symbol-thing is the potentiality of innumerable spoken symbols which, on the other hand, are knotted together in a single cosmic manifestation. . . .

These cosmic resonances, reaching even into reflective consciousness, are less surprising if the second dimension of symbolism is taken into consideration—the oneiric dimension. It is in dreams that one can catch sight of the most fundamental and stable symbolisms of humanity passing from the "cosmic" function to the "psychic" function. We should not be able to comprehend how symbols can signify the bond between the being of man and total being if we opposed to one another the hierophanies described by the phenomenology of religion and the dream productions described by Freudian and Jungian psychoanalysis (at least those which, by Freud's own admission, go beyond the projections of individual history and plunge beneath the private archeology of a subject into the common representations of a culture, or into the folklore of humanity as a whole). To manifest the "sacred" *on* the "cosmos" and to manifest it *in* the "psyche" are the same thing. . . .

Cosmos and Psyche are the two poles of the same "expressivity"; I express myself in expressing the world; I explore my own sacrality in deciphering that of the world.

Now, this double "expressivity"—cosmic and psychic—has its complement in a third modality of symbols: poetic imagination. But, to understand it properly, it is necessary firmly to distinguish imagination from image, if by image is understood a function of absence, the annulment of the real in an imaginary unreal. This image representation, conceived on the model of a portrait of the absent, is still too dependent on the thing that it makes unreal; it remains a process for *making present* to oneself the things of the world. A poetic image is much closer to a word than to a portrait. As M. Bachelard excellently says, it "puts us at the origin of the speaking being"; "it becomes a new being of our language, it expresses us in making us that which it expresses." Unlike the two other modalities of symbols, hierophanic and oneiric, the poetic symbol shows us expressivity in its nascent state. In poetry the symbol is caught at the moment when it is a welling up of language, "when it puts language in a state of emergence," instead of being regarded in its hieratic stability under the protection of rites and myths, as in the history of religions, or instead of being deciphered through the resurgences of a suppressed infancy.

It should be understood that there are not three unconnected forms of symbols. The structure of the poetic image is also the structure of the dream when the latter extracts from the fragments of our past a prophecy of our future, and the structure of the hierophanies that make the sacred manifest in the sky and in the waters, in vegetation and in stones.

Can we arrive at this one structure by a direct eidetic analysis, which would account for this remarkable convergence of religious symbolism, oneiric symbolism, and poetic symbolism? It is possible, up to a certain point, to reveal the unifying principle of the preceding enumeration by an intentional analysis. But, like all eidetic reflection, this intentional analysis consists solely in *distinguishing* a symbol from what is not a symbol, and thus directing attention to the more or less intuitive grasp of an identical nucleus of meaning.

We will proceed, then, by a series of increasingly close approximations to the essence of a symbol.

1. That symbols are signs is certain: they are expressions that communicate a meaning; this meaning is declared in an intention of signifying which has speech as its vehicle. Even when the symbols are elements of the universe (sky, water, moon) or things (tree, stone set up), it is still in the universe of discourse that

these realities take on a symbolic dimension (words of consecration or invocation, mythical utterances). As Dumézil very well says: "It is under the sign of *logos* and not under that of *mana* that research [in the history of religions] takes its stand today."

Similarly, dreams, although they are nocturnal spectacles, are originally close to words, since they can be told, communicated. Finally, it has been seen that poetic images themselves are essentially words.

2. But to say that the symbol is a sign is to draw too large a circle, which must now be made smaller. Every sign aims at something beyond itself and stands for that something; but not every sign is a symbol. We shall say that the symbol conceals in its aim a double intentionality. Take the "defiled," the "impure." This significant expression presents a first or literal intentionality that, like every significant expression, supposes the triumph of the conventional sign over the natural sign. Thus, the literal meaning of "defilement" is "stain," but this literal meaning is already a conventional sign; the words "stain," "unclean," etc., do not resemble the thing signified. But upon this first intentionality there is erected a second intentionality which, through the physically "unclean," points to a certain situation of man in the sacred which is precisely that of being defiled, impure. The literal and manifest sense, then, points beyond itself to something that is like a stain or spot. Thus, contrary to perfectly transparent technical signs, which say only that they want to say in positing that which they signify, symbolic signs are opaque, because the first, literal, obvious meaning itself points analogically to a second meaning which is not given otherwise than in it (we shall return to this point in order to distinguish symbol from allegory). This opacity constitutes the depth of the symbol, which, it will be said, is inexhaustible.

3. But let us correctly understand the analogical bond between the literal meaning and the symbolic meaning. While analogy is inconclusive reasoning that proceeds by fourth proportional—A is to B as C is to D—in the symbol, I cannot objectify the analogical relation that connects the second meaning with the first. It is by living in the first meaning that I am led by it beyond itself; the symbolic meaning is constituted in and by the literal meaning which effects the analogy in giving the analogue. Maurice Blondel said: "Analogies are based less on notional resemblances (*similitudines*) than on an interior stimulation, on an assimilative solicitation (*intentio ad assimilationem*)." In fact, unlike a comparison that we *consider* from outside, the symbol is the movement of the primary meaning which makes us participate in the latent meaning and thus assimilates us to that which is symbolized without our being able to master the similitude intellectually. It is in this sense that the symbol is donative; it is donative because it is a primary intentionality that gives the second meaning analogically.

4. The distinction between symbol and allegory is an extension of our remarks on the analogy effected by the literal meaning itself. M. Pepin has elucidated this problem very well: in an allegory what is primarily signified—that is

to say, the literal meaning—is contingent, and what is signified secondarily, the symbolic meaning itself, is external enough to be directly accessible. Hence, there is a relation of translation between the two meanings; once the translation is made, the henceforth useless allegory can be dropped. Now the specific character of the symbol as opposed to the allegory has been brought to light slowly and with difficulty. Historically, allegory has been less a literary and rhetorical procedure of artificial construction of pseudo-symbols than a mode of treating myths as allegories. Such is the case with the Stoic interpretation of the myths of Homer and Hesiod, which consists in treating the myths as a disguised philosophy. To interpret is then to penetrate the disguise and thereby to render it useless. In other words, allegory has been a modality of hermeneutics much more than a spontaneous creation of signs. It would be better, therefore, to speak of allegorizing interpretation rather than of allegory. Symbol and allegory, then, are not on the same footing: symbols precede hermeneutics; allegories are already hermeneutic. This is so because the symbol presents its meaning transparently in an entirely different way than by translation. One would say rather that it evokes its meaning or suggests it, in the sense of the Greek αἰνίττεσθαι (from which the word "enigma" comes). It presents its meaning in the opaque transparency of an enigma and not by translation. Hence, I oppose the *donation of meaning in trans-parency* in symbols to the interpretation by *trans-lation* of allegories.

5. Is it necessary to say that the sort of symbol which will be in question here has nothing to do with that which symbolic logic calls by the same name? Indeed, it is the inverse of it. But it is not enough to say so; one must know why. For symbolic logic, symbolism is the acme of formalism. Formal logic, in the theory of the syllogism, had already replaced "terms" by signs standing for anything whatever; but the relation—for example, the expressions "all," "some," "is," "implies"—had not been cut loose from the ordinary linguistic expressions. In symbolic logic these expressions are themselves replaced by letters, or written signs, which need no longer be spoken and by means of which it is possible to calculate without asking oneself how they are incorporated in a deontology of reasoning. These, then, are no longer abbreviations of familiar verbal expressions, but "characters" in the Leibnitzian sense of the words—that is to say, elements of a calculus. It is clear that the kind of symbol with which we are concerned here is the contrary of a character. Not only does it belong to a kind of thinking that is bound to its contents, and therefore not formalized, but the intimate bond between its first and second intentions and the impossibility of presenting the symbolic meaning to oneself otherwise than by the actual operation of analogy make of the symbolic language a language essentially *bound*, bound to its content and, through its primary content, to its secondary content. In this sense, it is the absolute inverse of an absolute formalism. One might be astonished that the symbol has two such rigorously inverse uses. Perhaps the reason should be sought in the structure of signification, which is at once a function of absence and a

function of presence: a function of absence because to signify is to signify "vacuously," it is to say things without the things, in substituted signs; a function of presence because to signify is to signify "something" and finally the world. Signification, by its very structure, makes possible at the same time both total formalization—that is to say, the reductions of signs to "characters" and finally to elements of a calculus—and the restoration of a full language, heavy with implicit intentionalities and analogical references to something else, which it presents enigmatically.

6. Last criterion: how to distinguish myth and symbol? It is relatively easy to contrast myth and allegory, but much less easy to distinguish clearly between myth and symbol. Sometimes it seems that symbols are a manner of taking myths in a nonallegorical way. Thus, symbol and allegory would be intentional attitudes or dispositions of hermeneutics; and the symbolic and allegorical interpretations would then be two directions of interpretations bearing on the same mythical content. Contrarily to this interpretation, I shall always understand by symbol, in a much more primitive sense, analogical meanings which are spontaneously formed and immediately significant, such as defilement, analogue of stain; sin, analogue of deviation; guilt, analogue of accusation. These symbols are on the same level as, for example, the meaning of water as threat and as renewal in the flood and in baptism, and finally on the same level as the most primitive hierophanies. In this sense, symbols are more radical than myths. I shall regard myths as a species of symbols, as symbols developed in the form of narrations and articulated in a time and a space that cannot be co-ordinated with the time and space of history and geography according to the critical method. For example, exile is a primary symbol of human alienation, but the history of the expulsion of Adam and Eve from Paradise is a mythical narration of the second degree, bringing into play fabulous personages, places, times, and episodes. Exile is a primary symbol and not a myth, because it is a historical event made to signify human alienation analogically; but the same alienation creates for itself a fanciful history, the exile from Eden, which, as history that happened *in illo tempore*, is myth.

12

Process Theology

Process theology derives its name from the idea of process in the metaphysics of Alfred North Whitehead (1861–1947), reflected in the title of his classic work on the subject, *Process and Reality*. The term *process* is well chosen because it suggests that all reality, God and the world, nature, history, and culture, is a movement of dynamic change opening toward an unending future.

In early Greek philosophy, there were two rival philosophical visions, those of Heraclitus and Parmenides. Heraclitus, who stressed the primacy of "becoming" over "being," once observed that you can never step into the same river twice; when you try, the waters of the river have already moved downstream. Parmenides countered with the notion that beneath all appearances of change and flux lies the permanence of being. Western philosophy, due to the towering influence of Plato's thought, pursued Parmenides' line, a metaphysics of being, substance, and essences, rather than Heraclitus' vision of reality as fundamentally becoming, process, and novel change.

Process metaphysics reflects the profound change in the modern perception of the world brought about by Charles Darwin's theory of biological evolution and Albert Einstein's theory of relativity in physics. Darwin showed that the species were never fixed (each "after its kind") but are the result of ever-evolving new forms of life; and Einstein, that the world is not like a machine as in Newton's physics but more like a living organism made of cells of energy in a nexus of relations. The ideas of evolution and relativity were subsequently applied to all fields of study, beyond the natural sciences to history, culture, and philosophy. Process thought in philosophy and theology represents the application of the new scientific thinking in biology and physics to the interrelations of God and the world.

I

Process theology unapologetically makes use of the philosophical categories of Whitehead to express a new Christian understanding of God's dynamic and intimate relationship with the world. In the final chapter of *Process and Reality*, entitled "God and the World," Whitehead opposes ideas of God found in the Western traditions of religion, philosophy, and theology. Whether the "unmoved mover" of Aristotle, the "ruthless moralist" of the Old Testament, or the "imperial ruler" of ancient Christianity, none is suitable to the new meaning of God advanced by process theologians. The problem with all such images is that they picture God as one who exists independently over against the world, ontologically other than the stuff of which the world is made. But for process thought that is not the case: "God is not to be treated as an exception to all metaphysical principles, invoked to save their collapse. He is their chief exemplification." (In their place Whitehead takes a cue from what he calls "the Galilean origin of Christianity," referring to Jesus' teaching of God as love, the source of "the tender elements in the world.")

It is impossible to think like a process theologian without mastering a whole new vocabulary, or learning new meanings for old words. "Actual entities" or "occasions" are the basic irreducible elements of which the world is made, and there is no way of going behind them to an underlying substance that is more real. These actual entities are not tiny bits of matter but more like moments of experience. They are always in transition, always in process of becoming something new. In addition to actual entities, there are "eternal objects." They are something like Plato's ideal forms or Aristotle's universals. They do not actually exist on their own, but are manifest in the actual entities in which they become concrete, a process that Whitehead calls "concrescence." Another important word is "prehension"; this refers to the way actual entities enter into relations with each other. When actual entities cluster together in a set of relations, they form a "nexus."

All of this language is "theological" because a depth description of the world is at once a representation of the physical side of God, which Whitehead calls his "consequent nature." Whitehead holds a dipolar conception of God; as an actual entity God has two natures, "primordial" and "consequent." God's primordial nature contains in a purely abstract way the totality of possibilities inherent in the world's becoming, all the eternal objects that might be concretely actualized.

The question many critics have raised is whether in relating God so intimately to the totality of reality, has God ceased to have any existence of his own? Has God been reduced to the reality of the world in process, losing his transcendence as well as his power and freedom to live as an eternal communion of divine persons, not dependent on the world for his life? Whitehead's God needs the world as much as the world needs God. Whitehead boldly says, "It is as true to say that God creates the World, as that the World creates God." What are the implications of this assertion for the Christian doctrine of God's creation of the world "out of nothing" (*ex nihilo*)?

II

Whitehead's doctrine of God and the world has been enriched and elaborated by the philosophical theology of Charles Hartshorne (1897–). Hartshorne's technical term to denote God's relation to the world is "panentheism." In his usage, the world is not ontologically distinct from God but is a constituent part of God's being, similar to Whitehead's idea of God's "consequent nature." We may think of God's relation to the world as being analogous to the relation of the human mind to the body. "In this sense the world is God's body." The implication is clear; as the human mind cannot exist without the body in which it indwells, so also God cannot exist without the world and never has. Therefore the world enjoys the same ability as God to endure throughout all time. As the body and mind need each other, so do God and the world. There never was a time when the world was not.

In place of the doctrine of creation *ex nihilo,* Hartshorne substitutes his notion of "transformative creation." This universe results from the creative transformation of a previous one, and that in turn from an earlier one; the series of actual and possible universes stretches backward and forward infinitely. Process theologians find this notion of God as creative transformer religiously appealing for two reasons: (a) it integrates the human factor of response into the creative process, and (b) it involves God in the sufferings and tragedies of human experience. The same cannot be said of the distant Absolute of traditional theism, nor of such categories of the Absolute as pure actuality or being itself. They claim that their process view of God as finite, temporal, and conditioned by interpersonal experience is more consonant with the biblical picture of God as persuasive love and the intercommunicative nature of prayer. For the presupposition of prayer, Hartshorne maintains, is that it may have an effect on God and that the world may be changed on account of it.

III

Whitehead and Hartshorne developed their metaphysical concepts of God and the world without mediating them through christological reflection, as is almost invariably the case in continental theology, from Barth and Bultmann to Ebeling and Pannenberg. Whitehead and Hartshorne acknowledge Jesus of Nazareth as one of the great figures of history and uniquely influential in the founding of the Christian religion, but they showed no interest in thinking christologically about God and the world. Hartshorne said, "I have no Christology to offer, beyond the simple suggestion that Jesus appears to be the supreme symbol furnished to us by history of the notion of God genuinely and literally 'sympathetic'—receiving into his own experience the sufferings as well as the joys of the world."

There is, however, another contemporary stream of process theology that is decidedly christocentric from beginning to end. That is the evolutionary theology of Teilhard de Chardin (1881–1955), the Jesuit priest and paleontologist whose theological thought became known worldwide only after his death, because he was prohibited by papal authority from publishing his writings during his lifetime. During and after Vatican II, Teilhard's system became the rallying point for many progressive theologians committed to the modernization of Catholic theology. His driving interest was to reconcile and synthesize the two separated worlds of science and Christianity. Teilhard's question was: "What does it mean to believe in Christ in an evolutionary perspective?" The key to his answer was to show that the cosmic Christ of Paul was the power working backward from the future to draw all individuals and the universe into a creative unity.

Teilhard equated the eschatological Christ of biblical revelation with the Omega Point of cosmic evolution. He wrote a great deal about the cosmic Christ, very little about the historical Jesus. Teilhard had his eye on the grand destiny of all things attaining their goal in Christ (Christification) and not on the history of the afflicted man hanging on a cross.

There lies, however, an ambiguity in Teilhard's idea of the eschatological future. His basic idea of the future was teleological. Teilhard's main access to thinking about the cosmic future was, in his own terms, scientific extrapolation. By studying the past, he believed, a scientist could extend a curve beyond the facts, that is, extrapolate. The evolutionary swing upward from the inorganic to the organic, from prehuman to human forms, may be extended to ultrahuman forms that lie in the future. This way of thinking, however, is related more to scientific futurology than to biblical eschatology, and is therefore hardly the basis of Christian "hope against hope." The evolutionary process, even if God is posited out in front, provides a model of a teleological conception that inadequately translates into a modern idiom the eschatological hope of Christian faith grounded in the story of Jesus' life, death, and resurrection.

IV

Process theology has not been timid about restoring philosophy to its place of historic importance in the theological curriculum. The argument is that just as Augustine used Platonism and Aquinas used Aristotle, so now the future of Christian theology, its rationality and persuasiveness, depends on appropriating the categories of a modern philosophy in harmony with the natural sciences. Critics of process theology have not failed to point out a significant difference, however. Both Augustine and Aquinas used philosophy, but when they found it in conflict with the Christian tradition, they were willing to revise or even reject it. Theology

331

was the queen of the sciences and philosophy but her handmaid, to use the medieval image. Among the better known process theologians— Bernard Meland, Schubert Ogden, John Cobb, David Griffin—the relationship between philosophy and theology seems to be the other way around. In case of conflict between Christian doctrine and Whiteheadian metaphysics, the doctrine is surrendered or so reinterpreted as to land in one of the heresies (e.g., Pelagianism, Arianism, or Sabellianism) rejected by the ancient councils of the Church. John Cobb writes, "Process theology is not interested in formulating distinctions within God for the sake of conforming with traditional Trinitarian notions."

In conclusion, it should be pointed out that the process view of reality is not limited to the schools of thought influenced by Whitehead, Hartshorne, or Teilhard. The rejection of a static concept of being and criticism of substance metaphysics, coupled with a sense of becoming in God and a dynamic sense of reality as history, are features common to almost all contemporary theologies. Theologians influenced by G. F. W. Hegel—for example, Wolfhart Pannenberg and Eberhard Jüngel—provide alternative visions of God and the world equally committed to dynamic categories of interpretation rather than static essences, substances, and natures.

31. Pierre Teilhard de Chardin, *Evolution and the Christian Future*

The Attributes of the Omega Point

After allowing itself to be captivated in excess by the charms of analysis to the extent of falling into illusion, modern thought is at last getting used once more to the idea of the creative value of synthesis in evolution. It is beginning to see that there is definitely more in the molecule than in the atom, more in the cell than in the molecule, more in society than in the individual, and more in mathematical construction than in calculations and theorems. We are now inclined to admit that at each further degree of combination something which is irreducible to isolated elements emerges in a new order. And with this admission, consciousness, life and thought are on the threshold of acquiring a right to existence in terms of science. But science is nevertheless still far from recognizing that this something has a particular value of independence and solidity. For, born of an incredible concourse of chances on a precariously assembled edifice, and failing to create any measurable increase of energy by their advent, are not these "creatures of synthesis," from the experimental point of view, the most beautiful as well as the most fragile of things? How could they anticipate or survive the ephemeral union of particles on which their souls have alighted? So in the end, in spite of a halfhearted conversion to spiritual views, it is still on the elementary side — that is, towards matter infinitely diluted — that physics and biology look to find the eternal and the Great Stability.

In conformity with this state of mind the idea that some Soul of souls should be developing at the summit of the world is not as strange as might be thought from the present-day views of human reason. After all, is there any other way in which our thought can generalize the Principle of Emergence? At the same time, as this Soul coincides with a supremely improbable coincidence of the totality of elements and causes, it remains understood or implied that it could not form itself save at an extremely distant future and in a total dependence on the reversible laws of energy.

Yet it is precisely from these two restrictions (fragility and distance), both incompatible to my mind with the nature and function of Omega, that we want to rid ourselves — and this for two positive reasons, one of love, the other of survival.

First of all the reason of love. Expressed in terms of internal energy, the cosmic function of Omega consists in initiating and maintaining within its radius the unanimity of the world's "reflective" particles. But how could it exercise this action were it not in some sort loving and lovable at this very moment? Love, I said, dies in contact with the impersonal and the anonymous. With equal infallibility it becomes impoverished with remoteness in space — and still more, much more, with difference in time. For love to be possible there must be coexistence. Accordingly, however marvelous its foreseen figure, Omega could never even so much as equilibrate the play of human attractions and repulsions if it did not act with equal force, that is to say with the same stuff of proximity. With love, as with every other sort of energy, it is within the existing datum that the lines of force must at every instant come together. Neither an ideal centre, nor a potential centre could possibly suffice. A present and real noosphere goes with a real and present centre. To be supremely attractive, Omega must be supremely present.

In addition, the reason of survival. To ward off the threat of disappearance, incompatible with the mechanism of reflective activity, man tries to bring together in an ever vaster and more permanent subject the collective principle of his acquisitions — civilization, humanity, the spirit of the earth. Associated in these enormous entities, with their incredibly slow rhythm of evolution, he has the impression of having escaped from the destructive action of time.

But by doing this he has only pushed back the problem. For after all, however large the radius traced within time and space, does the circle ever embrace anything but the perishable? So long as our constructions rest with all their weight on the earth, they will vanish with the earth. The radical defect in all forms of belief in progress, as they are expressed in positivist credos, is that they do not definitely eliminate death. What is the use of detecting a focus of any sort in the van of evolution if that focus can and must one day disintegrate? To satisfy the ultimate requirements of our action, Omega must be independent of the collapse of the forces with which evolution is woven.

Actuality, irreversibility. There is one way in which our minds can integrate into a coherent picture of noogenesis these two essential properties of the autonomous centre of all centres, and that is to resume and complement our Principle of Emergence. In the light of our experience it is abundantly clear that emergence in the course of evolution can only happen successively and with mechanical dependence on what precedes it. First the grouping of the elements; then the manifestation of 'soul' whose operation only betrays, from the point of view of energy, a more and more complex and sublimated involution of the powers transmitted by the chains of elements. The radial function of the tangential: a pyramid whose apex is supported from below: that is what we see during the course of the process. And it is in the very same way that Omega itself is discovered to us at the end of the whole process, inasmuch as in it the movement of synthesis culminates. Yet we must be careful to note that under this evolutive facet Omega still only reveals half of itself. While being the last term of its series, it is also outside all series. Not only does it crown, but it closes. Otherwise the sum would fall short of itself, in organic contradiction with the whole operation. When, going beyond the elements, we come to speak of the conscious Pole of the world, it is not enough to say that it emerges from the rise of consciousness: we must add that from this genesis it has already emerged; without which it could neither subjugate into love nor fix in incorruptibility. If by its very nature it did not escape from the time and space which it gathers together, it would not be Omega.

Autonomy, actuality, irreversibility, and thus finally transcendence are the four attributes of Omega. In this way we round off without difficulty the scheme left incomplete . . . , where we sought to enclose the energy-complex of our universe.

In Omega we have in the first place the principle we needed to explain both the persistent march of things towards greater consciousness, and the paradoxical solidity of what is most fragile. Contrary to the appearances still admitted by physics, the Great Stability is not at the bottom in the infraelementary sphere, but at the top in the ultrasynthetic sphere. It is thus entirely by its tangential envelope that the world goes on dissipating itself in a chance way into matter. By its radical nucleus it finds its shape and its natural consistency in gravitating against the tide of probability towards a divine focus of mind which draws it onward.

Thus something in the cosmos escapes from entropy, and does so more and more.

During immense periods in the course of evolution, the radial, obscurely stirred up by the action of the Prime Mover ahead, was only able to express itself, in diffuse aggregates, in animal consciousness. And at that stage, above them, not being able to attach themselves, to a support whose order of simplicity was greater than their own, the nuclei were hardly formed before they began to disaggregate. But as soon as, through reflection, a type of unity appeared no longer closed or even centred, but punctiform, the sublime physics of centres came into play. When they became centres, and therefore persons, the elements could at last begin to react, directly as such, to the personalizing action of the centre of centres. When consciousness broke through the critical surface of hominization, it really passed from divergence to convergence and changed, so to speak, both hemisphere and pole. Below that critical "equator" lay the relapse into multiplicity; above it, the plunge into growing and irreversible unification. Once formed, a reflective centre can no longer change except by involution upon itself. To outward appearance, admittedly, man disintegrated just like any animal. But here and there we find an inverse function of the phenomenon. By death, in the animal, the radial is reabsorbed into the tangential, while in man it escapes and is liberated from it. It escapes from entropy by turning back to Omega: the hominization of death itself.

Thus from the grains of thought forming the veritable and indestructible atoms of its stuff, the universe—a well-defined universe in the outcome—goes on building itself above our heads in the inverse direction of matter which vanishes. The universe is a collector and conservator, not of mechanical energy, as we supposed, but of persons. All round us, one by one, like a continual exhalation, "souls" break away, carrying upwards their incommunicable load of consciousness. One by one, yet not in isolation. Since, for each of them, by the very nature of Omega, there can only be one possible point of definitive emersion—that point at which, under the synthesizing action of personalizing union, the noosphere (furling its elements upon themselves as it too furls upon itself) will reach collectively its point of convergence—at the "end of the world."

The Christian Phenomenon

Neither in the play of its elemental activities, which can only be set in motion by the hope of an "imperishable"; nor in the play of its collective affinities, which require for their coalescence the action of a conquering love, can reflective life continue to function and to progress unless, above it, there is a pole which is supreme in attraction and consistence. By its very structure the noosphere could not close itself either individually or socially in any way save under the influence of the centre we have called Omega.

That is the postulate to which we have been led logically by the integral application to man of the experimental laws of evolution. The possible, or even the probable, repercussion of this conclusion, however theoretical in the first approximation, upon experience will now be obvious.

If Omega were only a remote and ideal focus destined to emerge at the end of time from the convergence of terrestrial consciousness, nothing could make it known to us in anticipation of this convergence. At the present time no other energy of a personal nature could be detected on earth save that represented by the sum of human persons.

If, on the other hand, Omega is, as we have admitted, *already in existence* and operative at the very core of the thinking mass, then it would seem inevitable that its existence should be manifested to us here and now through some traces. To animate evolution in its lower stages, the conscious pole of the world could of course only act in an impersonal form and under the veil of biology. Upon the thinking entity that we have become by hominization, it is now possible for it to radiate from the one centre to all centres—*personally*. Would it seem likely that it should not do so?

Either the whole construction of the world presented here is vain ideology or, somewhere around us, in one form or another, some excess of personal, extra-human energy should be perceptible to us if we look carefully, and should reveal to us the great Presence. It is at this point that we see the importance for science of *the Christian phenomenon*.

At the conclusion of a study of *the human phenomenon* I have not chosen those words haphazardly, nor for the sake of mere verbal symmetry. They are meant to define without ambiguity the spirit in which I want to speak.

As I am living at the heart of the Christian world, I might be suspected of wanting to introduce an apologia by artifice. But, here again, so far as it is possible for a man to separate in himself the various planes of knowledge, it is not the convinced believer but the naturalist who is asking for a hearing.

The Christian fact stands before us. It has its place among the other realities of the world.

I would like to show how it seems to me to bring to the perspectives of a universe dominated by energies of a personal nature the crucial confirmation we are in need of, firstly by the substance of its creed, next by its existence-value, and finally by its extraordinary power of growth.

Axes of Belief

To those who only know it outwardly, Christianity seems desperately intricate. In reality, taken in its main lines, it contains an extremely simple and astonishingly bold solution of the world.

In the centre, so glaring as to be disconcerting, is the uncompromising affirmation of a personal God: God as providence, directing the universe with loving, watchful care; and God the revealer, communicating himself to man on the level of and through the ways of intelligence. It will be easy for me, after all I have said, to demonstrate the value and actuality of this tenacious personalism, not long since condemned as obsolete. The important thing to point out here is the way in which such an attitude in the hearts of the faithful leaves the door open to, and is easily allied to, everything that is great and healthy in the universal.

In its Judaic phase, Christianity might well have considered itself the particular religion of one people. Later on, coming under the general conditions of human knowledge, it came to think that the world around it was much too small. However that may be, it was hardly constituted before it was ceaselessly trying to englobe in its constructions and conquests the totality of the system that it managed to picture to itself.

Personalism and universalism: in what form have these two characters been able to unite in its theology?

For reasons of practical convenience and perhaps also of intellectual timidity, the City of God is too often described in pious works in conventional and purely moral terms. God and the world he governs are seen as a vast association, essentially legalistic in its nature, conceived in terms of a family or government. The fundamental root from which the sap of Christianity has risen from the beginning and is nourished, is quite otherwise. Led astray by a false evangelism, people often think they are honouring Christianity when they reduce it to a sort of gentle philanthropism. Those who fail to see in it the most realistic and at the same time the most cosmic of beliefs and hopes, completely fail to understand its "mysteries." Is the Kingdom of God a big family? Yes, in a sense it is. But in another sense it is a prodigious biological operation—that of the Redeeming Incarnation.

As early as in St. Paul and St. John we read that to create, to fulfil and to purify the world is, for God, to unify it by uniting it organically with himself. How does he unify it? By partially immersing himself in things, by becoming "element," and then, from this point of vantage in the heart of matter, assuming the control and leadership of what we now call evolution. Christ, principle of universal vitality because sprung up as man among men, put himself in the position (maintained ever since) to subdue under himself, to purify, to direct and superanimate the general ascent of consciousness into which he inserted himself. By a perennial act of communion and sublimation, he aggregates to himself the total psychism of the earth. And when he has gathered everything together and transformed everything, he will close in upon himself and his conquests, thereby rejoining, in a final gesture, the divine focus he has never left. Then, as St. Paul tells us, God shall be all in all. This is indeed a superior form of "pantheism" without trace of the poison of adulteration or annihilation: the expectation of perfect unity, steeped in which each element will reach its consummation at the same time as the universe.

Existence Value

It is relatively easy to build up a theory of the world. But it is beyond the powers of an individual to provoke artificially the birth of a religion. Plato, Spinoza and Hegel were able to elaborate views which compete in amplitude with the perspectives of the Incarnation. Yet none of these metaphysical systems advanced beyond the limits of an ideology. Each in turn has perhaps brought light to men's minds, but without ever succeeding in begetting life. What to the eyes of a "naturalist" comprises the importance and the enigma of the Christian phenomenon is its existence-value and reality-value.

Christianity is in the first place real by virtue of the spontaneous amplitude of the movement it has managed to create in mankind. It addresses itself to every man and to every class of man, and from the start it took its place as one of the most vigorous and fruitful currents the noosphere has ever known. Whether we adhere to it or break off from it, we are surely obliged to admit that its stamp and its enduring influence are apparent in every corner of the earth today.

It is doubtless a quantitative value of life if measured by its radius of action; but it is still more a qualitative value which expresses itself—like all biological progress—by the appearance of a specifically new state of consciousness.

I am thinking here of Christian love.

Christian love is incomprehensible to those who have not experienced it. That the infinite and the intangible can be lovable, or that the human heart can beat with genuine charity for a neighbor, seems impossible to many people I know—in fact almost monstrous. But whether it be founded on an illusion or not, how can we doubt that such a sentiment exists, and even in great intensity? We have only to note crudely the results it produces unceasingly all round us. Is it not a positive fact that thousands of mystics, for twenty centuries, have drawn from its flame a passionate fervour that outstrips by far in brightness and purity the urge and devotion of any human love? Is it not also a fact that, having once experienced it, further thousands of men and women are daily renouncing every other ambition and every other joy save that of abandoning themselves to it and labouring within it more and more completely? Lastly, is it not a fact, as I can warrant, that if the love of God were extinguished in the souls of the faithful, the enormous edifice of rites, of hierarchy and of doctrines that comprise the church would instantly revert to the dust from which it rose?

It is a phenomenon of capital importance for the science of man that, over an appreciable region of the earth, a zone of thought has appeared and grown in which a genuine universal love has not only been conceived and preached, but has also been shown to be psychologically possible and operative in practice. It is all the more capital inasmuch as, far from decreasing, the movement seems to wish to gain still greater speed and intensity.

Power of Growth

For almost all the ancient religions, the renewal of cosmic outlook characterizing "the modern mind" has occasioned a crisis of such severity that, if they have not yet been killed by it, it is plain they will never recover. Narrowly bound to untenable myths, or steeped in a pessimistic and passive mysticism, they can adjust themselves neither to the precise immensities, nor to the constructive requirements, of space-time. They are out of step both with our science and with our activity.

But under the shock which is rapidly causing its rivals to disappear, Christianity, which might at first have been thought to be shaken too, is showing, on the contrary, every sign of forging ahead. For, by the very fact of the new dimensions assumed by the universe as we see it today, it reveals itself both as inherently more vigorous in itself and as more necessary to the world than it has ever been before.

More vigorous. To live and develop the Christian outlook needs an atmosphere of greatness and of connecting links. The bigger the world becomes and the more organic become its internal connections, the more will the perspectives of the Incarnation triumph. That is what believers are beginning, much to their surprise, to find out. Though frightened for a moment by evolution, the Christian now perceives that what it offers him is nothing but a magnificent means of feeling more at one with God and of giving himself more to him. In a pluralistic and static Nature, the universal domination of Christ could, strictly speaking, still be regarded as an extrinsic and superimposed power. In a spiritually converging world this "Christic" energy acquires an urgency and intensity of another order altogether. If the world is convergent and if Christ occupies its centre, then the Christogenesis of St. Paul and St. John is nothing else and nothing less than the extension, both awaited and unhoped for, of that noogenesis in which cosmogenesis—as regards our experience—culminates. Christ invests himself organically with the very majesty of his creation. And it is in no way metaphorical to say that man finds himself capable of experiencing and discovering his God in the whole length, breadth and depth of the world in movement. To be able to say literally to God that one loves him, not only with all one's body, all one's heart and all one's soul, but with every fibre of the unifying universe—that is a prayer that can only be made in space-time.

More necessary. To say of Christianity that, despite appearances to the contrary, it is acclimatizing itself and expanding in a world enormously enlarged by science, is to point to no more than one half of the picture. Evolution has come to infuse new blood, so to speak, into the perspectives and aspirations of Christianity. In return, is not the Christian faith destined, is it not preparing, to save and even to take the place of evolution?

I have tried to show that we can hope for no progress on earth without the primacy and triumph of the *personal* at the summit of *mind*. And at the present moment Christianity is the *unique* current of thought, on the entire surface of the noosphere, which is sufficiently audacious and sufficiently progressive to lay hold of the world, at the level of effectual proactive, in an embrace, at once already complete, yet capable of indefinite perfection, where faith and hope reach their fulfillment in love. *Alone,* unconditionally alone, in the world today, Christianity shows itself able to reconcile, in a single living act, the All and the Person. Alone, it can bend our hearts not only to the service of that tremendous movement of the world which bears us along, but beyond, to embrace that movement in love.

In other words can we not say that Christianity fulfills all the conditions we are entitled to expect from a religion of the future; and that hence, through it, the principal axis of evolution truly passes, as it maintains?

Now let us sum up the situation:

i. Considered objectively as a phenomenon, the Christian movement, through its rootedness in the past and ceaseless developments, exhibits the characteristics of a *phylum*.
ii. Reset in an evolution interpreted as an ascent of consciousness, this phylum, in its trend towards a synthesis based on love, progresses precisely in the direction presumed for the leading-shoot of biogenesis.
iii. In the impetus which guides and sustains its advance, this rising shoot implies essentially *the consciousness of finding itself in actual relationship* with a spiritual and transcendent pole of universal convergence.

To confirm the presence at the summit of the world of what we have called the Omega Point, do we not find here the very cross-check we were waiting for? Here surely is the ray of sunshine striking through the clouds, the reflection onto what is ascending of that which is already on high, the rupture of our solitude. The palpable influence on our world of *an other* and supreme Someone. . . . Is not the Christian phenomenon, which rises upwards at the heart of the social phenomenon, precisely that?

In the presence of such perfection in coincidence, even if I were not a Christian but only a man of science, I think I would ask myself this question.

32. Alfred North Whitehead, *God and the World*

So long as the temporal world is conceived as a self-sufficient completion of the creative act, explicable by its derivation from an ultimate principle which is at once eminently real and the unmoved mover, from this conclusion there is no escape: the best that we can say of the turmoil is, "For so he giveth his beloved-sleep." This is the message of religions of the Buddhistic type, and in some sense it is true. In this final discussion we have to ask, whether metaphysical principles impose the belief that it is the whole truth. The complexity of the world must be reflected in the answer. It is childish to enter upon thought with the simple-minded question, What is the world made of? The task of reason is to fathom the deeper depths of the many-sidedness of things. We must not expect simple answers to far-reaching questions. However far our gaze penetrates, there are always heights beyond which block our vision.

The notion of God as the "unmoved mover" is derived from Aristotle, at least so far as Western thought is concerned. The notion of God as "eminently real" is a favorite doctrine of Christian theology. The combination of the two into the doctrine of an aboriginal, eminently real, transcendent creator, at whose fiat the world came into being, and whose imposed will it obeys, is the fallacy which has infused tragedy into the histories of Christianity and of Mahometanism.

When the Western world accepted Christianity, Caesar conquered; and the received text of Western theology was edited by his lawyers. The code of Justinian and the theology of Justinian are two volumes expressing one movement of the human spirit. The brief Galilean vision of humility flickered throughout the ages, uncertainly. In the official formulation of the religion it has assumed the trivial form of the mere attribution to the Jews that they cherished a misconception about their Messiah. But the deeper idolatry of the fashioning of God in the image of the Egyptian, Persian, and Roman imperial rulers, was retained. The church gave unto itself the attributes which belonged exclusively to Caesar.

In the great formative period of theistic philosophy, which ended with the rise of Mahometanism, after a continuance coeval with civilization, three strains of thought emerged which, amid many variations in detail, respectively fashion God in the image of an imperial ruler, God in the image of a personification of moral energy, God in the image of an ultimate philosophical principle. Hume's *Dialogues* criticize unanswerably these modes of explaining the system of the world.

The three schools of thought can be associated respectively with the divine Caesars, the Hebrew prophets, and Aristotle. But Aristotle was antedated by Indian, and Buddhistic, thought; the Hebrew prophets can be paralleled in traces of earlier thought: Mahometanism and the divine Caesars merely represent the most natural, obvious, theistic idolatrous symbolism, at all epochs and places.

The history of theistic philosophy exhibits various stages of combination of these three diverse ways of entertaining the problem. There is, however, in the Galilean origin of Christianity yet another suggestion which does not fit very well with any of the three main strands of thought. It does not emphasize the ruling Caesar, or the ruthless moralist, or the unmoved mover. It dwells upon the tender elements in the world, which slowly and in quietness operate by love; and it finds purpose in the present immediacy of a kingdom not of this world. Love neither rules, nor is it unmoved; also it is a little oblivious as to morals. It does not look to the future; for it finds its own reward in the immediate present.

II

Apart from any reference to existing religions as they are, or as they ought to be, we must investigate dispassionately what the metaphysical principles, here developed, require on these points, as to the nature of God. There is nothing here in the nature of proof. There is merely the confrontation of the theoretic system with a certain rendering of the facts. The unsystematized report upon the facts is itself highly controversial, and the system is confessedly inadequate. The deductions from it in this particular sphere of thought cannot be looked upon as more than suggestions as to how the problem is transformed in the light of that system. What follows is merely an attempt to add another speaker to that masterpiece, Hume's *Dialogues Concerning Natural Religion*. Any cogency of argument entirely depends upon elucidation of somewhat exceptional elements in our conscious experience—those elements which may roughly be classed together as religious and moral intuitions.

In the first place, God is not to be treated as an exception to all metaphysical principles, invoked to save their collapse. He is their chief exemplification.

Viewed as primordial, he is the unlimited conceptual realization of the absolute wealth of potentiality. In this aspect, he is not *before* all creation, but *with* all creation. But, as primordial, so far is he from "eminent reality," that in this abstraction he is "deficiently actual"—and this in two ways. His feelings are only conceptual and so lack the fullness of actuality. Secondly, conceptual feelings, apart from complex integration with physical feelings, are devoid of consciousness in their subjective forms.

Thus, when we make a distinction of reason, and consider God in the abstraction of a primordial actuality, we must ascribe to him neither fullness of feeling, nor consciousness. He is the unconditioned actuality of conceptual feeling at the base of things; so that, by reason of this primordial actuality, there is an order in the relevance of eternal objects to the process of creation. His unity of conceptual operations is a free creative act, untrammeled by reference to any particular course of things. It is deflected neither by love, nor by hatred, for what in fact comes to pass. The *particularities* of the actual world presuppose *it*; while *it* merely presupposes the *general* metaphysical character of creative advance, of which it is the primordial exemplification. The primordial nature of God is the acquirement by creativity of a primordial character.

His conceptual actuality at once exemplifies and establishes the categoreal conditions. The conceptual feelings, which compose his primordial nature, exemplify in their subjective forms their mutual sensitivity and their subjective unity of subjective aim. These subjective forms are valuations determining the relative relevance of eternal objects for each occasion of actuality.

He is the lure for feeling, the eternal urge of desire. His particular relevance to each creative act as it arises from its own conditioned standpoint in the world, constitutes him the initial "object of desire" establishing the phase of each subjective aim. A quotation from Aristotle's *Metaphysics* expresses some analogies to, and some differences from, this line of thought: "And since that which is moved and mover is intermediate, there is a mover which moves without being moved, being eternal, substance, and actuality. And the object of desire and the object of thought are the same. For the apparent good is the object of appetite, and the real good is the primary object of rational desire. But desire is consequent on opinion rather than opinion on desire; for the thinking is the starting point. And thought is moved by the object of thought, and one side of the list of opposites is in itself the object of thought; . . . ." Aristotle had not made the distinction between conceptual feelings and the intellectual feelings which alone involve consciousness. But if "conceptual feeling," with its subjective form of valuation, be substituted for "thought," "thinking," and "opinion," in the above quotation, the agreement is exact.

III

There is another side to the nature of God which cannot be omitted. Throughout this exposition of the philosophy of organism we have been considering the primary action of God on the world. From this point of view, he is the principle of concretion—the principle whereby there is initiated a definite outcome from a situation otherwise riddled with ambiguity. Thus, so far, the primordial side of the nature of God has alone been relevant.

But God, as well as being primordial, is also consequent. He is the beginning and the end. He is not the beginning in the sense of being in the past of all members. He is the presupposed actuality of conceptual operation, in unison of becoming with every other creative act. Thus by reason of the relativity of all things, there is a reaction of the world on God. The completion of God's nature into a fullness of physical feeling is derived from the objectification of the world in God. He shares with every new creation its actual world; and the concrescent creature is objectified in God as a novel element in God's objectification of that actual world. This prehension into God of each creature is directed with the subjective aim, and clothed with the subjective form, wholly derivative from his all-inclusive primordial valuation. God's conceptual nature is unchanged, by reason of its final completedness. But his derivative nature is consequent upon the creative advance in the world.

Thus, analogously to all actual entities, the nature of God is dipolar. He has a primordial nature and a consequent nature. The consequent nature of God is conscious; and it is the realization of the actual world in the unity of his nature, and through the transformation of his wisdom. The primordial nature is conceptual, the consequent nature is the weaving of God's physical feelings upon his primordial concepts.

One side of God's nature is constituted by his conceptual experience. This experience is the primordial fact in the world, limited by no actuality which is presupposed. It is therefore infinite, devoid of all negative prehensions. This side of his nature is free, complete, primordial, eternal, actually deficient, and unconscious. The other side originates with physical experience derived from the temporal world, and then acquires integration with the primordial side. It is determined, incomplete, consequent, "everlasting," fully actual, and conscious. His necessary goodness expresses the determination of his consequent nature.

Conceptual experience can be infinite, but it belongs to the nature of physical experience that it is finite. An actual entity in the temporal world is to be conceived as originated by physical experience with its process of completion motivated by consequent, conceptual experience initially derived from God. God is to be conceived as originated by conceptual experience with his process of completion motivated by consequent, physical experience, initially derived from the temporal world.

IV

The perfection of God's subjective aim, derived from the completeness of his primordial nature, issues into the character of his consequent nature. In it there is no loss, no obstruction. The world is felt in a unison of immediacy. The property of combining creative advance with the retention of mutual immediacy is what in the previous section is meant by the term "everlasting."

The wisdom of subjective aim prehends every actuality for what it can be in such a perfected system—its sufferings, its sorrows, its failures, its triumphs, its immediacies of joy—woven by rightness of feeling into the harmony of the universal feeling, which is always immediate, always many, always one, always with novel advance, moving onward and never perishing. The revolts of destructive evil, purely self-regarding, are dismissed into their triviality of merely individual facts; and yet the good they did achieve in individual joy, in individual sorrow, in the introduction of needed contrast, is yet saved by its relation to the completed whole. The image—and it is but an image—the image under which this operative growth of God's nature is best conceived, is that of a tender care that nothing be lost.

The consequent nature of God is his judgment on the world. He saves the world as it passes into the immediacy of his own life. It is the judgment of a tenderness which loses nothing that can be saved. It is also the judgment of a wisdom which uses what in the temporal world is mere wreckage.

Another image which is also required to understand his consequent nature, is that of his infinite patience. The universe includes a threefold creative act composed of (i) the one infinite conceptual realization, (ii) the multiple solidarity of free physical realizations in the temporal world, (iii) the ultimate unity of the multiplicity of actual fact with the primordial conceptual fact. If we conceive the first term and the last term in their unity over against the immediate multiple freedom of physical realizations in the temporal world, we conceive of the patience of God, tenderly saving the turmoil of the intermediate world by the completion of his own nature. The sheer force of things lies in the intermediate physical process: this is the energy of physical production. God's role is not the combat of productive force with productive force, of destructive force with destructive force; it lies in the patient operation of the overpowering rationality of his conceptual harmonization. He does not create the world, he saves it: or, more accurately, he is the poet of the world, with tender patience leading it by his vision of truth, beauty, and goodness.

V

The vicious separation of the flux from the permanence leads to the concept of an entirely static God, with eminent reality, in relation to an entirely fluent world, with deficient reality. But if the opposites, static and fluent, have once been so explained as separately to characterize diverse actualities, the interplay between the thing which is static and the things which are fluent involves contradiction at every step in its explanation. Such philosophies must include the notion of "illusion" as a fundamental principle—the notion of "mere appearance." This is the final platonic problem.

Undoubtedly, the intuitions of Greek, Hebrew, and Christian thought have alike embodied the notions of a static God condescending to the world, and of a world either thoroughly fluent, or accidentally static, but finally fluent— "heaven and earth shall pass away." In some schools of thought, the fluency of the world is mitigated by the assumption that selected components in the world are exempt from this final fluency, and achieve a static survival. Such components are not separated by any decisive line from analogous components for which the assumption is not made. Further, the survival is construed in terms of a final pair of opposites, happiness for some, torture for others.

Such systems have the common character of starting with a fundamental intuition which we do mean to express, and of entangling themselves in verbal expressions, which carry consequences at variance with the initial intuition of permanence in fluency and of fluency in permanence.

But civilized intuition has always, although obscurely, grasped the problem as double and not as single. There is not the mere problem of fluency and permanence. There is the double problem: actuality with permanence, requiring fluency as its completion; and actuality with fluency, requiring permanence as its completion. The first half of the problem concerns the completion of God's primordial nature by the derivation of his consequent nature from the temporal world. The second half of the problem concerns the completion of each fluent actual occasion by its function of objective immortality, devoid of "perpetual perishing," that is to say, "everlasting."

This double problem cannot be separated into two distinct problems. Either side can only be explained in terms of the other. The consequent nature of God is the fluent world become "everlasting" by its objective immortality in God. Also the objective immortality of actual occasions requires the primordial permanence of God, whereby the creative advance ever re-establishes itself endowed with initial subjective aim derived from the relevance of God to the evolving world.

But objective immortality within the temporal world does not solve the problem set by the penetration of the finer religious intuition. "Everlastingness" has been lost; and "everlastingness" is the content of that vision upon which the finer religions are built—the "many" absorbed everlastingly in the final unity. The problems of the fluency of God and of the everlastingness of passing experience are solved by the same factor in the universe. This factor is the temporal world perfected by its reception and its reformation, as a fulfillment of the primordial appetition which is the basis of all order. In this way God is completed by the individual, fluent satisfactions of finite fact, and the temporal occasions are completed by their everlasting union with their transformed selves, purged into conformation with the eternal order which is the final absolute "wisdom." The final summary can only be expressed in terms of a group of antitheses, whose apparent self-contradiction depends on neglect of the diverse categories of existence. In each antithesis there is a shift of meaning which converts the opposition into a contrast.

It is as true to say that God is permanent and the World fluent, as that the World is permanent and God is fluent.

It is as true to say that God is one and the World many, as that the World is one and God many.

It is as true to say that, in comparison with the World, God is actual eminently, as that, in comparison with God, the World is actual eminently.

It is as true to say that the World is immanent in God, as that God is immanent in the World.

It is as true to say that God transcends the World, as that the World transcends God.

It is as true to say that God creates the World, as that the World creates God.

God and the World are the contrasted opposites in terms of which Creativity achieves its supreme task of transforming disjoined multiplicity, with its diversities in opposition, into concrescent unity, with its diversities in contrast. In each actuality there are two concrescent poles of realization—"enjoyment" and "appetition," that is, the "physical" and the "conceptual." For God the conceptual is prior to the physical, for the World the physical poles are prior to the conceptual poles.

A physical pole is in its own nature exclusive, bounded by contradiction: a conceptual pole is in its own nature all-embracing, unbounded by contradiction. The former derives its share of infinity from the infinity of appetition; the latter derives its share of limitation from the exclusiveness of enjoyment. Thus, by reason of his priority of appetition, there can be but one primordial nature for God; and, by reason of their priority of enjoyment, there must be one history of many actualities in the physical world.

God and the World stand over against each other, expressing the final metaphysical truth that appetitive vision and physical enjoyment have equal claim to priority in creation. But no two actualities can be torn apart: each is all in all. Thus each temporal occasion embodies God, and is embodied in God. In God's nature, permanence is primordial and flux is derivative from God. Also the World's nature is a primordial datum for God; and God's nature is a primordial datum for the World. Creation achieves the reconciliation of permanence and flux when it has reached its final term which is everlastingness—the Apotheosis of the World.

Opposed elements stand to each other in mutual requirement. In their unity, they inhibit or contrast. God and the World stand to each other in this opposed requirement. God is the infinite ground of all mentality, the unity of vision seeking physical multiplicity. The World is the multiplicity of finites, actualities seeking a perfected unity. Neither God, nor the World, reaches static completion. Both are in the grip of the ultimate metaphysical ground, the creative advance into novelty. Either of them, God and the World, is the instrument of novelty for the other.

In every respect God and the World move conversely to each other in respect to their process. God is primordially one, namely, he is the primordial unity of relevance of the many potential forms: in the process he acquires a consequent multiplicity, which the primordial character absorbs into its own unity. The World is primordially many, namely, the many actual occasions with their physical finitude; in the process it acquires a consequent unity, which is a novel occasion and is absorbed into the multiplicity of the primordial character. Thus God is to be conceived as one and as many in the converse sense in which the World is to be conceived as many and as one. The theme of Cosmology, which is the basis of all religions, is the story of the dynamic effort of the World passing into everlasting unity, and of the static majesty of God's vision, accomplishing its purpose of completion by absorption of the World's multiplicity of effort.

VI

The consequent nature of God is the fulfillment of his experience by his reception of the multiple freedom of actuality into the harmony of his own actualization. It is God as really actual, completing the deficiency of his mere conceptual actuality.

Every categoreal type of existence in the world presupposes the other types in terms of which it is explained. Thus the many eternal objects conceived in their bare isolated multiplicity lack any existent character. They require the transition to the conception of them as efficaciously existent by reason of God's conceptual realization of them.

But God's conceptual realization is nonsense if thought of under the guise of a barren, eternal hypothesis. It is God's conceptual realization performing an efficacious role in multiple unifications of the universe, which are free creations of actualities arising out of decided situations. Again this discordant multiplicity of actual things, requiring each other and neglecting each other, utilizing and discarding, perishing and yet claiming life as obstinate matter of fact, requires an enlargement of the understanding to the comprehension of another phase in the nature of things. In this later phase, the many actualities are one actuality, and the one actuality is many actualities. Each actuality has its present life and its immediate passage into novelty; but its passage is not its death. This final phase of passage in God's nature is ever enlarging itself. In it the complete adjustment of the immediacy of joy and suffering reaches the final end of creation. This end is existence in the perfect unity of adjustment as means, and in the perfect multiplicity of the attainment of individual types of self-existence. The function of being a means is not disjoined from the function of being an end. The sense of worth beyond itself is immediately enjoyed as an overpowering element in the individual self-attainment. It is in this way that the immediacy of sorrow and pain is transformed into an element of triumph. This is the notion of redemption through suffering, which haunts the world. It is the generalization of its very minor exemplification as the aesthetic value of discords in art.

Thus the universe is to be conceived as attaining the active self-expression of its own variety of opposites—of its own freedom and its own necessity, of its own multiplicity and its own unity, of its own imperfection and its own perfection. All the "opposites" are elements in the nature of things, and are incorrigibly there. The concept of "God" is the way in which we understand this incredible fact— that what cannot be, yet is.

VII

Thus the consequent nature of God is composed of a multiplicity of elements with individual self-realization. It is just as much a multiplicity as it is a unity; it is just as much one immediate fact as it is an unresting advance beyond itself. Thus the actuality of God must also be understood as a multiplicity of actual components in process of creation. This is God in his function of the kingdom of heaven.

Each actuality in the temporal world has its reception into God's nature. The corresponding element in God's nature is not temporal actuality, but is the transmutation of that temporal actuality into a living, ever-present fact. An enduring personality in the temporal world is a route of occasions in which the successors with some peculiar completeness sum up their predecessors. The correlate fact in God's nature is an even more complete unity of life in a chain of elements for which succession does not mean loss of immediate unison. This element in God's nature inherits from the temporal counterpart according to the same principle as in the temporal world the future inherits from the past. Thus in the sense in which the present occasion is the person now, and yet with his own past, so the counterpart in God is that person in God.

But the principle of universal relativity is not to be stopped at the consequent nature of God. This nature itself passes into the temporal world according to its gradation of relevance to the various concrescent occasions. There are thus four

348

creative phases in which the universe accomplishes its actuality. There is first the phase of conceptual origination, deficient in actuality, but infinite in its adjustment of valuation. Secondly, there is the temporal phase of physical origination, with its multiplicity of actualities. In this phase full actuality is attained; but there is deficiency in the solidarity of individuals with each other. This phase derives its determinate conditions from the first phase. Thirdly, there is the phase of perfected actuality, in which the many are one everlastingly, without the qualification of any loss either of individual identity or of completeness of unity. In everlastingnesss, immediacy is reconciled with objective immortality. This phase derives the conditions of its being from the two antecedent phases. In the fourth phase, the creative action completes itself. For the perfected actuality passes back into the temporal world, and qualifies this world so that each temporal actuality includes it as an immediate fact of relevant experience. For the kingdom of heaven is with us today. The action of the fourth phase is the love of God for the world. It is the particular providence for particular occasions. What is done in the world is transformed into a reality in heaven, and the reality in heaven passes back into the world. By reason of this reciprocal relation, the love in the world passes into the love in heaven, and the reality in heaven passes back into the world. By reason of this reciprocal relation, the love in the world passes into the love in heaven, and floods back again into the world. In this sense, God is the great companion—the fellow-sufferer who understands.

We find here the final application of the doctrine of objective immortality. Throughout the perishing occasions in the life of each temporal Creature, the inward source of distaste or of refreshment, the judge arising out of the very nature of things, redeemer or goddess of mischief, is the transformation of Itself, everlasting in the Being of God. In this way, the insistent craving is justified—the insistent craving that zest for existence be refreshed by the ever-present, unfading importance of our immediate actions, which perish and yet live for evermore.

33. Charles Hartshorne, *The Divine Self-Creation*

A possible objection to the temporalistic view of God . . . is that it conflicts with the classical idea of creation as creation *ex nihilo.* One can no longer contrast God as purely eternal with his creation as temporal, and if God is to be viewed as essentially temporal, one can no more admit a beginning of the temporal as such than of God himself. Does not the world then become a second primordial and everlasting entity over against rather than created by God? The answer is that the question is full of ambiguities. "The world," if that means the system of atoms and stars we see, or anything in any particular respect like it, is not everlasting but a created product. It is created, to be sure, not out of nothing—whatever that would mean—but out of an earlier world and its potentialities for transformation. This earlier world was similarly created. The world as preserving its identity through all these transformations is something infinitely protean and infinitely endowed with power to assimilate variety into unity. Indeed, the world in this sense is identical with God, not a second entity. God is the self-identical individuality of the world somewhat as a man is the self-identical individuality of his ever-changing system of atoms. The only everlasting (and primordial) entity upon which God acts in creation is himself; all individuals, other than himself, which are influenced by his action are less than everlasting, or at least less than primordial. To contrast the world as creation to God as creator is one of three things: it is to contrast the multitude of nonprimordial individuals with the single primordial individual which alone makes of this multitude a single inclusive individual with self-identity throughout all time; or it is to contrast the concrete totality of God's being—his "consequent nature" (Whitehead)—as at a given world moment with the abstract essence of God as purely the same at all times, all accidents being left out of account; or finally it is to contrast God at one moment with himself as in a preceding moment about to create for himself an appropriate subsequent state.

The term creator can perfectly well be used by one who denies creation *ex nihilo*. For to "make the world" out of a preceding world is not only no abuse of language but the very meaning that language supports. All making we ever encounter is transformation, enrichment of something already there. The word creation is standard usage for all the more exalted examples of such transformation, for instance, for composing music, writing poetry, imagining striking characters in a novel. Of course divine creation is intended to be a unique case, but the uniqueness of God is his maximality. He makes on a supreme, that is cosmic, scale; he makes the whole, not just certain parts; and he makes not for a limited time but during infinite time. These functions are strictly unique and unrivaled, not a whit the less so because the making is still transformation, enrichment. And it is not as if the given world which is utilized in creation were simply imposed upon God from without as something alien, for the given world too is his creation, though made from an earlier world which he created out of an earlier one, and so on. The highest authority in traditional theology, Thomas Aquinas, admitted that this conception is open to no objections except those derived from revelation. And since Protestant views of revelation render these objections thoroughly questionable, the issue reduces to the Roman Catholic issue, which is irrelevant to the subject of this chapter. Thus there is no reason why the "creator" need be supposed to have created out of nothing.

From another point of view theologians ought not to have been so averse to the notion of transformative creation. For they were committed to this notion in another guise. Namely, creation was not really out of nothing, but out of the potentialities, essences, or natures of all things, as embraced eternally in the divine essence. These were transformed or transferred from their status of mere possibilities, in which some of them, the uncreated but possible creatures, remained, into the status of actualities, whatever the difference between the one status and the other may be. We are more inclined today to say that the natures of things which come into existence are really created *de novo*, utilizing only the natures of other things already in existence. Thus there is more genuine creation in this view than in the old. For there is hardly any meaning to the idea that God "made" what is (on the usual older account) part of his necessary essence, the eternal essences of things. Just in knowing himself he knew his possible effects. On the new view God chooses not only what is to be but even what is to be a definite possibility. Of course he could not have chosen to make definitely impossible what he has made definitely possible, but he could have left possibility indefinite in certain respects, so that there would have been no truth about either the possibility or impossibility of the thing in question. Descartes' famous view that God made possibilities as well as actualities by a free act of will may thus be given an acceptable interpretation. This is an example, out of many, of the power of second-type theism to reconcile age-old oppositions of doctrine.

The final defense of the idea of creation not *ex nihilo* but out of a pre-existing state of affairs is that the idea of a beginning of time is self-contradictory, as Aristotle pointed out. Even a beginning is a change, and all change requires something changing that does not come to exist through that same change. The beginning of the world would have to happen to something other than the world, something which as the subject of happening would be in a time that did not begin with the world. God as changing furnishes such a subject, since he is in one respect (in Whitehead's terms, his primordial nature) ever identical, in another (his consequent nature) ever partly novel, and yet also—by the indestructibility of the past—containing all that he ever was as part of what at any subsequent time becomes.

13

Neo-Protestantism in America

In his book *The Kingdom of God in America,* H. Richard Niebuhr (1894–1962) demonstrated that the biblical idea of the kingdom of God has been the driving force in American Christianity. There is both greatness and tragedy in the story that Niebuhr tells. The vision of America as God's righteous empire was originally inspired by the Puritans' belief in the sovereign rule of God in history and their sense of being elected for a divine mission in the new world. Mircea Eliade observed that "the most popular religious doctrine in the Colonies was that America had been chosen among all the nations of the earth as the place of the Second Coming of Christ." Niebuhr recounts how various Christian groups have striven to realize the kingdom in their personal lives and communities. Providing an overview that spans several centuries of American experience, Niebuhr writes, "If the seventeenth century was the century of the sovereignty and the eighteenth the time of the kingdom of Christ, the nineteenth may be called the period of the coming kingdom."

I

The "Social Gospel Movement," under the leadership of Walter Rauschenbusch (1861–1918) and Shailer Matthews (1863–1941), carried forward God's "grand experiment" (Horace Bushnell) to transform all of human society into the kingdom of God. Even after the optimism of the Social Gospel liberals was shattered by World War I and the Great Depression, and their belief in progress gave way to a more pessimistic estimate of human possibilities that came in the aftermath of such catastrophic world events, American Protestant theologians continued to be primarily concerned about the social application of the Christian faith. The Niebuhr brothers, Reinhold and H. Richard, although critical of the Social Gospel theology, retained its concern for society and the life of the world beyond the church. It is significant that Reinhold Niebuhr (1892–1971) held the chair in Applied Christianity at Union Theological Seminary in New York, and H. Richard's legacy in subsequent American theology has been evident primarily in the field of ethics. Even among conservative evangelicals to the right—Carl F. H. Henry, for example—there has been a concerted effort to go beyond Fundamentalism's separatistic orientation to culture and to become involved in the Christianization of society in all areas: politics, economics, education, entertainment, and the media.

The idea of the kingdom of God reached its high point in Rauschenbusch's classic, *A Theology for the Social Gospel*. Rauschenbusch complained that theology had allowed this biblical idea "to lead a decrepit, bed-ridden, and senile existence in that museum of antiquities which we call eschatology." The doctrine lost its social relevance when it became merely another world into which individuals entered one by one after death. When the kingdom is thought of statically as existing at the remote end of history, the church tends to become a stationary structure in history, irrelevant to the ordering of society. Rauschenbusch saw the kingdom as the power of God working with revolutionary force to bring about social righteousness and to call the church to do battle with the forces of evil.

Rauschenbusch studied theology in Germany and came under the influence of the Ritschlian school of theology. His idea of the kingdom repeated the same serious mistake of the Ritschlians in confusing the growth of the kingdom with belief in the progress of history. Rauschenbusch, for example, could speak of "the progress of the Kingdom of God in the flow of history." Sometimes he spoke of the kingdom as something that "grows" and "develops" in an organic way in history, something that can be equated with the ethical and spiritual progress of humanity. By identifying Jesus' promise of the kingdom with the progress of civilization, liberal theology was vulnerable in the face of oncoming crises and catastrophes.

II

Reinhold Niebuhr and H. Richard Niebuhr, who were of German evangelical background, have been credited with infusing insights from continental neo-orthodoxy into liberal Protestant theology in America. Both of them launched their theological careers with major criticisms of liberal theology. H. Richard Niebuhr wrote the epitaph for the tombstone of liberal Protestant Christianity: "A God without wrath brought men without sin into a kingdom without judgment through the ministrations of a Christ without a cross." Reinhold Niebuhr was more relentless in exposing the faults in the liberal synthesis. Upon hearing that Wolfhart Pannenberg was engaged in rehabilitating the idea of the kingdom of God in theology, Reinhold Niebuhr retorted, "Social thought that begins with the Kingdom of God, or even emphasizes it very much, inevitably ends up with utopianism. We've been through this business of the Kingdom before."

Reinhold Niebuhr spotted the fatal flaw of liberal theology in its anthropology. His Gifford Lectures, *The Nature and Destiny of Man,* offer a realistic assessment of the human predicament in accord with the biblical doctrines of God's creation of human beings, their fall from grace, and redemption from sin through God's atoning act in Christ. In terms of the doctrinal structure and substance of Niebuhr's thought, he was indebted to the theological traditions of the Protestant Reformation, in both its Calvinist and Lutheran streams. His decisive break with liberalism became most conspicuous in his treatment of sin. To Niebuhr, sin is basically pride, human pride that over-reaches creaturely finitude to attain the level of God. Standing in the Augustinian tradition, Niebuhr countered the Pelagianism of the Protestant liberals by reclaiming the notion of original sin. Sin is universal, unavoidable, and always disruptive of the creature's proper relation to God and the world of others.

Reinhold Niebuhr was more of a preacher and a prophet than an academic theologian. He often protested that he was not a theologian at all, by which he meant that he was not a systematic theologian in the German tradition, so eminently exemplified by his colleague Paul Tillich. Most of Niebuhr's writings aim to demonstrate the practical relevance of the Christian faith in addressing social and political problems. His intention was to speak to the problems of modern secular society more realistically and therefore to remain more true to the Christian faith than the liberals had been able to do.

III

H. Richard Niebuhr was more of a theologian's theologian. He undertook the seemingly impossible task of trying to cross-breed the theological perspectives of Ernst Troeltsch and Karl Barth. From Troeltsch he learned two things: (a) the truth of cultural relativism that history has no place for absolutes, and (b) the sociological analysis of Christianity in relation to culture. In *The Meaning of Revelation,* Niebuhr distinguishes between two kinds of history, outer and inner history. Outer history refers to the facts of history viewed from the perspective of an objective historian; inner history refers to the stories of origin and living tradition remembered by a particular community. A strictly scientific examination of external history provides no escape from pure relativism. For help, Niebuhr turned to Barth's concern for God's revelation which can only be narrated from an insider's point of view. "We can speak of revelation only in connection with our own history, without affirming or denying its reality in the history of other communities into whose inner life we cannot penetrate without abandoning ourselves and our community." Barth wrote his dogmatics as the church's account of its own internal history, which can never be subject to verification by objective historical research. Niebuhr bequeathed to the next generation the question, left to him by both Troeltsch and Barth, of how revelation, history, and faith relate to each other within a unified perspective. The problems of historical relativism and religious pluralism were lying in wait to draw the attention and consume the energies of the next generation of theologians now busily engaged in a search for answers.

In *Christ and Culture,* H. Richard Niebuhr expanded Troeltsch's threefold typology of Christianity in society—the church, the sect, and mystical groups—into a fivefold pattern: Christ against culture, Christ of culture, Christ above culture, Christ and culture in paradox, and Christ the transformer of culture. Niebuhr offered examples from church history for each type, but in a way typical of the Calvinist influence in American theology, whether liberal or conservative, Niebuhr opted for the fifth type, involving the church in society to transform it in line with the Christian vision of the kingdom of God.

H. Richard Niebuhr's influence on contemporary theology is still immense. In *Radical Monotheism and Western Culture,* he sets forth the idea of radical theocentrism as a form of faith and theology which he played off against a christocentric theology. He warned against letting Christ take the place of God and substituting the Lordship of Christ for the Lordship of God. Jesus Christ reveals the absolute One of radical theocentric monotheism. Niebuhr's influence lies behind the current trend to shift away from Christology in the interest of a theocentric pluralistic theology of the religions. Neither of the Niebuhr brothers contributed any useful insights to the renewal or development of classical trinitarian theology on American soil. They shared with liberal Protestantism a low Christology that maintained an ontological gulf between Jesus and God.

IV

Carl F. H. Henry (1913–) became the leader of the mass conservative evangelical exodus from American fundamentalism. As the founding editor of *Christianity Today,* his became the public voice of the new evangelicals who wanted to become involved in the mainstream of theological debates and to become engaged with the problems of society. Henry had the education, interest, and skills to provide the evangelicals with an apologetic rationale for the fundamentals of Christian truth and a comprehensive social program based on the moral principles of the Bible. In *The Uneasy Conscience of Modern Fundamentalism,* Henry charged fundamentalism with neglecting both the intellectual and the ethical challenges of American religion and culture. Its sin was letting itself drift into irrelevance, thus dooming it to be nothing but a sect on the sidelines. Henry had no quarrel with the standard fundamentalist doctrines; he denied not a one of them. His point was that in narrowing its agenda in the doctrines' defense, fundamentalism was losing the opportunity to represent the kingdom of God as a force for the transformation of not only individuals but the whole of society.

In his six-volume *magnum opus, God, Revelation and Authority,* Henry lays out and defends the classic doctrines of Christian orthodoxy and argues for their truth and superiority against all revisionist interpretations or modernist denials. Henry's outline is straightforward: God has revealed his mind through the Logos, his Word, which is both incarnate in Jesus Christ and expressly written down in Scripture. Christ is the eternal Son of God and Scripture infallibly communicates the truths of revelation in the form of cognitive propositions. Therefore, Scripture as the source and authority for all theological work is not only inspired but inerrant. Humans are capable of understanding revealed truth because they have been created in the image of God the Logos and when their minds are illuminated by the regenerating work of the Holy Spirit. Both human reason and a new birth play important roles in Henry's theological epistemology because they correlate with Christ the Logos and the work of the Holy Spirit in human beings.

Henry tried to be faithful to the classical Christian tradition, but as an evangelical theologian coming out of Protestant fundamentalism he could never escape its individualistic interpretation of Christianity and its failure to experience and understand the church as the universal body of Christ. Many evangelicals who learned from Henry have observed the ecclesiological deficit in his theology. In struggling to rediscover the church to support their evangelical experience, they have moved in a Catholic direction toward some form of either Anglicanism or Eastern Orthodoxy.

34. Walter Rauschenbusch, *Theology and the Social Gospel*

We have a social gospel. We need a systematic theology large enough to match it and vital enough to back it. . . .

We need not waste words to prove that the social gospel is being preached. It is no longer a prophetic and occasional note. It is a novelty only in backward social or religious communities. The social gospel has become orthodox. . . .

The social movement is the most important ethical and spiritual movement in the modern world, and the social gospel is the response of the Christian consciousness to it. Therefore it had to be. The social gospel registers the fact that for the first time in history the spirit of Christianity has had a chance to form a working partnership with real social and psychological science. It is the religious reaction on the historic advent of democracy. It seeks to put the democratic spirit, which the church inherited from Jesus and the prophets, once more in control of the institutions and teachings of the church.

The social gospel is the old message of salvation, but enlarged and intensified. The individualistic gospel has taught us to see the sinfulness of every human heart and has inspired us with faith in the willingness and power of God to save every soul that comes to him. But it has not given us an adequate understanding of the sinfulness of the social order and its share in the sins of all individuals within it. It has not evoked faith in the will and power of God to redeem the permanent institutions of human society from their inherited guilt of oppression and extortion. Both our sense of sin and our faith in salvation have fallen short of the realities under its teaching. The social gospel seeks to bring men under repentance for their collective sins and to create a more sensitive and more modern conscience. It calls on us for the faith of the old prophets who believed in the salvation of nations. . . .

The adjustment of the Christian message to the regeneration of the social order is plainly one of the most difficult tasks ever laid on the intellect of religious leaders. The pioneers of the social gospel have had a hard time trying to consolidate their old faith and their new aim. Some have lost their faith; others have come out of the struggle with crippled formulations of truth. Does not our traditional theology deserve some of the blame for this spiritual wastage because it left these men without spiritual support and allowed them to become the vicarious victims of our theological inefficiency? If our theology is silent on social salvation, we compel college men and women, workingmen, and theological students, to choose between an unsocial system of theology and an irreligious system of social salvation. It is not hard to predict the outcome. If we seek to keep Christian doctrine unchanged, we shall ensure its abandonment. . . .

The Kingdom of God

If theology is to offer an adequate doctrinal basis for the social gospel, it must not only make room for the doctrine of the kingdom of God, but give it a central place and revise all other doctrines so that they will articulate organically with it. . . .

To those whose minds live in the social gospel, the kingdom of God is a dear truth, the marrow of the gospel, just as the incarnation was to Athanasius, justification by faith alone to Luther, and the sovereignty of God to Jonathan Edwards. It was just as dear to Jesus. He too lived in it, and from it looked out on the world and the work he had to do.

Jesus always spoke of the kingdom of God. Only two of his reported sayings contain the word "church," and both passages are of questionable authenticity. It is safe to say that he never thought of founding the kind of institution which afterward claimed to be acting for him.

Yet immediately after his death, groups of disciples joined and consolidated by inward necessity. Each local group knew that it was part of a divinely founded fellowship mysteriously spreading through humanity, and awaiting the return of the Lord and establishing of his kingdom. This universal church was loved with the same religious faith and reverence with which Jesus had loved the kingdom of God. It was the partial and earthly realization of the divine Society, and at the parousia the church and the kingdom would merge.

357

But the kingdom was merely a hope, the church a present reality. The chief interest and affection flowed toward the church. Soon, through a combination of causes, the name and idea of "the kingdom" began to be displaced by the name and idea of the "church" in the preaching, literature, and theological thought of the church. Augustine completed this process in his *De Civitate Dei*. The kingdom of God which has, throughout human history, opposed the kingdom of sin, is today embodied in the church. The millennium began when the church was founded. This practically substituted the actual, not the ideal church for the kingdom of God. The beloved ideal of Jesus became a vague phrase which kept intruding from the New Testament. Like Cinderella in the kitchen, it saw the other great dogmas furbished up for the ball, but no prince of theology restored it to its rightful place. The Reformation, too, brought no renascence of the doctrine of the kingdom; it had only eschatological value, or was defined in blurred phrases borrowed from the church. The present revival of the kingdom idea is due to the combined influence of the historical study of the Bible and of the social gospel. . . .

The restoration of the doctrine of the kingdom has already made progress. Some of the ablest and most voluminous works of the old theology in their thousands of pages gave the kingdom of God but a scanty mention, usually in connection with eschatology, and saw no connection between it and the Calvinistic doctrines of personal redemption. The newer manuals not only make constant reference to it in connection with various doctrines, but they arrange their entire subject matter so that the kingdom of God becomes the governing idea.

In the following brief propositions I should like to offer a few suggestions, on behalf of the social gospel, for the theological formulation of the doctrine of the kingdom. Something like this is needed to give us "a theology for the social gospel."

1. The kingdom of God is divine in its origin, progress and consummation. It was initiated by Jesus Christ, in whom the prophetic spirit came to its consummation, it is sustained by the Holy Spirit, and it will be brought to its fulfillment by the power of God in his own time. The passive and active resistance of the kingdom of evil at every stage of its advance is so great, and the human resources of the kingdom of God so slender, that no explanation can satisfy a religious mind which does not see the power of God in its movements. The kingdom of God, therefore, is miraculous all the way, and is the continuous revelation of the power, the righteousness, and the love of God. The establishment of a community of righteousness in mankind is just as much a saving act of God as the salvation of an individual from his natural selfishness and moral inability. The kingdom of God, therefore, is not merely ethical, but has a rightful place in theology. This doctrine is absolutely necessary to establish that organic union between religion and morality, between theology and ethics, which is one of the characteristics of the Christian religion. When our moral

actions are consciously related to the kingdom of God they gain religious quality. Without this doctrine we shall have expositions of schemes of redemption and we shall have systems of ethics, but we shall not have a true exposition of Christianity. The first step to the reform of the churches is the restoration of the doctrine of the kingdom of God.

2. The kingdom of God contains the teleology of the Christian religion. It translates theology from the static to the dynamic. It sees, not doctrines or rites to be conserved and perpetuated, but resistance to be overcome and great ends to be achieved. Since the kingdom of God is the supreme purpose of God, we shall understand the kingdom so far as we understand God, and we shall understand God so far as we understand his kingdom. As long as organized sin is in the world, the kingdom of God is characterized by conflict with evil. But if there were no evil, or after evil has been overcome, the kingdom of God will still be the end to which God is lifting the race. It is realized not only by redemption, but also by the education of mankind and the revelation of his life within it.

3. Since God is in it, the kingdom of God is always both present and future. Like God it is in all tenses, eternal in the midst of time. It is the energy of God realizing itself in human life. Its future lies among the mysteries of God. It invites and justifies prophecy, but all prophecy is fallible; it is valuable in so far as it grows out of action for the kingdom and impels action. No theories about the future of the kingdom of God are likely to be valuable or true which paralyze or postpone redemptive action on our part. To those who postpone, it is a theory and not a reality. It is for us to see the kingdom of God as always coming, always pressing in on the present, always big with possibility, and always inviting immediate action. We walk by faith. Every human life is so placed that it can share with God in the creation of the kingdom, or can resist and retard its progress. The kingdom is for each of us the supreme task and the supreme gift of God. By accepting it as a task, we experience it as a gift. By laboring for it we enter into the joy and peace of the kingdom as our divine fatherland and habitation.

4. Even before Christ, men of God saw the kingdom of God as the great end to which all divine leadings were pointing. Every idealistic interpretation of the world, religious or philosophical, needs some such conception. Within the Christian religion the idea of the kingdom gets its distinctive interpretation from Christ. (a) Jesus emancipated the idea of the kingdom from previous nationalistic limitations and from the debasement of lower religious tendencies, and made it worldwide and spiritual. (b) He made the purpose of salvation essential in it. (c) He imposed his own mind, his personality, his love and holy will on the idea of the kingdom. (d) He not only foretold it but initiated it by his life and work. As humanity more and more develops a racial consciousness in modern life, idealistic interpretations of the destiny of humanity will become more influential and important. Unless theology has a solidaristic vision, higher and fuller than any other, it can not maintain the spiritual leadership of mankind, but will be outdistanced. Its business is to infuse the distinctive qualities of Jesus Christ into its teachings

about the kingdom, and this will be a fresh competitive test of his continued head-ship of humanity.

5. The kingdom of God is humanity organized according to the will of God. Interpreting it through the consciousness of Jesus we may affirm these convictions about the ethical relations within the kingdom: (a) Since Christ revealed the divine worth of life and personality, and since his salvation seeks the restoration and fulfillment of even the least, it follows that the kingdom of God, at every stage of human development, tends toward a social order which will best guarantee to all personalities their freest and highest development. This involves the redemption of social life from the cramping influence of religious bigotry, from the repression of self-assertion in the relation of upper and lower classes, and from all forms of slavery in which human beings are treated as mere means to serve the ends of others. (b) Since love is the supreme law of Christ, the kingdom of God implies a progressive reign of love in human affairs. We can see its advance wherever the free will of love supersedes the use of force and legal coercion as a regulative of the social order. This involves the redemption of society from political autocracies and economic oligarchies; the substitution of redemptive for vindictive penology; the abolition of constraint through hunger as part of the industrial system; and the abolition of war as the supreme expression of hate and completest cessation of freedom. (c) The highest expression of love is the free surrender of what is truly our own, life, property, and rights. A much lower but perhaps more decisive expression of love is the surrender of any opportunity to exploit men. No social group or organization can claim to be clearly within the kingdom of God which drains others for its own ease, and resists the effort to abate this fundamental evil. This involves the redemption of society from private property in the natural resources of the earth, and from any condition in industry which makes monopoly profits possible. (d) The reign of love tends toward the progressive unity of mankind, but with the maintenance of individual liberty and the opportunity of nations to work out their own national peculiarities and ideals.

6. Since the kingdom is the supreme end of God, it must be the purpose for which the church exists. The measure in which it fulfills this purpose is also the measure of its spiritual authority and honour. The institutions of the church, its activities, its worship, and its theology must in the long run be tested by its effectiveness in creating the kingdom of God. For the church to see itself apart from the kingdom, and to find its aims in itself, is the same sin of selfish detachment as when an individual selfishly separates himself from the common good. The church has the power to save in so far as the kingdom of God is present in it. If the church is not living for the kingdom, its institutions are part of the "world." In that case it is not the power of redemption but its object. It may even become an anti-Christian power. If any form of church organization which formerly aided the kingdom now impedes it, the reason for its existence is gone.

7. Since the kingdom is the supreme end, all problems of personal salvation must be reconsidered from the point of view of the kingdom. It is not sufficient to

set the two aims of Christianity side by side. There must be a synthesis, and theology must explain how the two react on each other. The entire redemptive work of Christ must also be reconsidered under this orientation. Early Greek theology saw salvation chiefly as the redemption from ignorance by the revelation of God and from earthliness by the impartation of immortality. It interpreted the work of Christ accordingly, and laid stress on his incarnation and resurrection. Western theology saw salvation mainly as forgiveness of guilt and freedom from punishment. It interpreted the work of Christ accordingly, and laid stress on the death and atonement. If the kingdom of God was the guiding idea and chief end of Jesus—as we now know it was—we may be sure that every step in his life, including his death, was related to that aim and its realization, and when the idea of the kingdom of God takes its due place in theology, the work of Christ will have to be interpreted afresh.

8. The kingdom of God is not confined within the limits of the church and its activities. It embraces the whole of human life. It is the Christian transfiguration of the social order. The church is one social institution, alongside of the family, the industrial organization of society, and the State. The kingdom of God is in all these, and realizes itself through them all. During the Middle Ages all society was ruled and guided by the church. Few of us would want modern life to return to such a condition. Functions which the church used to perform, have now far outgrown its capacities. The church is indispensable to the religious education of humanity and to the conservation of religion, but the greatest future awaits religion in the public life of humanity.

35. H. Richard Niebuhr, *Revelation and Radical Monotheism*

Relations of Internal and External History

Though we may be persuaded that there is a valid distinction between history as lived and history as observed by the external spectator; though we may recognize a relative validity in either type while noting the close relation of faith and the life of selves to the practical knowledge of our destiny; yet questions about the relations of the two types of history are bound to arise in our minds. When we have understood that revelation must be looked for in the events that have happened to us, which live in our memory, we cannot refrain from asking ourselves how this history is related to the external accounts of our life. To such questions we must give some attention before we can proceed to a closer definition of the meaning of revelation.

The two-aspect theory of history, like the two-aspect theory of body and mind, may be made necessary by the recognition that all knowing is conditioned by the point of view, that the exaltation of differences of understanding into differences of being raises more problems than it solves, that the intimate relations of subjective and objective truth require the rejection of every extreme dualism. But it is evident that the theory does not solve the problem of unity in duality and duality in unity. It only states the paradox in a new form and every paradox is the statement of a dilemma rather than an escape from it. It is important, of course, that a paradox be correctly stated and that false simplicity be avoided. We have made some advance toward a correct statement of our dilemma, we believe, when we have recognized that the duality of the history in which there is revelation and of the history in which there is none, is not the duality of different groups or communities, or when we have understood that this dualism runs right through Christian history itself. We are enabled to see why we can speak of revelation only in connection with our own history without affirming or denying its reality in the history of other communities into whose inner life we cannot penetrate without abandoning ourselves and our community. The two-aspect theory allows us to understand how revelation can be in history and yet not be identifiable with miraculous events as visible to an external observer and how events that are revelatory in our history, sources of unconquerable certainty for us, can yet be analyzed in profane fashion by the observer. But the paradox remains. It is but another form of the two-world thinking in which Christianity is forever involved and we need not expect that in thinking about history we shall be able to escape the dilemma that confronts our faith in every other sphere. One-world thinking, whether as this-worldliness or as otherworldliness, has always betrayed Christianity into the denial of some of its fundamental convictions. It will do so in the case of history no less than in metaphysics and ethics. But how to think in two-worldly terms without lapsing into di-theism remains a problem of great import for faith.

There is no speculative escape from the dilemma, that is to say we cannot absorb internal history into external history nor yet transcend both practical and objective points of view in such a way as to gain a knowledge of history superior to both and able to unite them into a new whole. If we begin with the spectator's knowledge of events we cannot proceed to the participant's apprehension. There is no continuous movement from an objective inquiry into the life of Jesus to a knowledge of him as the Christ who is our Lord. Only a decision of the self, a leap of faith, a metanoia or revolution of the mind can lead from observation to participation and from observed to lived history. And this is true of all other events in sacred history.

It may be thought that the problem of the relation of inner and outer history can be solved by a determination of what the events, visible in two aspects, really are in themselves. But the idea of events-in-themselves like that of things-in-themselves is an exceedingly difficult one. The ultimate nature of an event is not what it is in its isolation only but what it is in its connection with all other events, not what it is for itself but also what it is from an inclusive point of view. The event, as it really is, is the event as it is for God who knows it at the same time and in one act from within as well as from without, in its isolation as well as in its community with all other events. Such knowledge of the nature of events is beyond the possibility of the finite point of view. Being finite souls with finite minds in finite bodies men are confined to a double and partial knowledge which is yet not knowledge of double reality.

Though there be no metaphysical or metahistorical solution of the problem of historical dualism there is a practical solution. Though we cannot speak of the way in which the two aspects of historical events are ultimately related in the event-for-God we can describe their functional relationship for us. Such a description must once more be given confessionally, not as a statement of what all men ought to do but as statement of what we have found it necessary to do in the Christian community on the basis of the faith which is our starting point. . . .

It is necessary for the Christian community, living in faith, to look upon all the events of time and to try to find in them the workings of one mind and will. This is necessary because the God who is found in inner history, or rather who reveals himself there, is not the spiritual life but universal God, the creator not only of the events through which he discloses himself but also of all other happenings. The standpoint of the Christian community is limited, being in history, faith and sin. But what is seen from this standpoint is unlimited. Faith cannot get to God save through historic experience as reason cannot get to nature save through sense-experience. But as reason, having learned through limited experience an intelligible pattern of reality, can seek the evidence of a like pattern in all other experience, so faith having apprehended the divine self in its own history, can and must look for the manifestation of the same self in all other events. Thus prophets, for whom the revelation of God was connected with his mighty acts in the deliverance of Israel from bondage, found the marks of that God's working in the histories of all the nations. The Christian community must turn in like manner from the revelation of the universal God in a limited history to the recognition of his rule and providence in all events of all times and communities. Such histories must be regarded from the outside to be sure; in events so regarded the meeting of human and divine selves cannot be recorded, but all the secondary causes, all the factors of political and social life can be approached with the firm conviction of an underlying unity due to the pervasive presence of the one divine self. It is not possible to describe external history by reference to miraculous deeds but the revelation of the one God makes it possible and necessary to approach the multiplicity of events in all times with the confidence that unity may be found, however hard the quest for it. Where faith is directed to many gods only pluralistic and unconnected histories can be written, if indeed there is any impulsion to understand or write history. Where, through a particular set of historical experiences, the conviction has been established that all events have one source and goal it becomes possible to seek out the uniformities, the dependable patterns of process. That such history, though a product of piety, is not pious history, designed to exalt the inner life of the religious factors in social life, must be evident. A faithful external history is not interested in faith but in the ways of God, and the more faithful it is the less it may need to mention his name or refer to the revelation in which he was first apprehended, or rather in which he first apprehended the believer. In this sense an external history finds its starting point or impulsion in an internal history.

Not only is the external history of other selves and communities a necessary and possible work of faith on the part of Christians but an external history of itself is its inescapable duty for two reasons. The revelation of God in history is, as we shall see, the revelation of a self. To know God is to be known of him, and therefore also to know the self as it is reflected in God. The church's external history of itself may be described as an effort to see itself with the eyes of God. The simultaneous, unified knowledge from within and from without that we may ascribe to God is indeed impossible to men, but what is simultaneous in his case can in a measure be successive for us. The church cannot attain an inclusive, universal point of view but it can attempt to see the reflection of itself in the eyes of God. What it sees in that reflection is finite, created, limited, corporeal being, alike in every respect to all the other beings of creation. To describe that vision in detail, to see the limited, human character of its founder, the connections between itself and a Judaism to which it often, in false pride, feels superior, between Catholicism and feudalism, Protestantism and capitalism, to know itself as the chief of sinners and the most mortal of societies—all this is required of it by a revelation that has come to it through its history.

Moreover, though there is no transition from external observation to internal participation save by decision and faith, yet it is also true that the internal life does not exist without external embodiment. The memory which we know within ourselves as pure activity must have some static aspect which an objective science, we may believe, will in time discover in the very structure of the neural system. What the neural system is to the memory of an individual self that books and monuments are to a common memory. Without the Bible and the rites of the institutional church the inner history of the Christian community could not continue, however impossible it is to identify the memory of that community with the documents. Though we cannot point to what we mean by revelation by directing attention to the historic facts as embodied and as regarded from without, we can have no continuing inner history through which to point without embodiment. "Words without thoughts never to heaven go" but thoughts without words never remain on earth. Moreover such is the alternation of our life that the thought which becomes a word can become thought again only through the mediation of the word; the word which becomes flesh can become word for us again only through the flesh. External history is the medium in which internal history exists and comes to life. Hence knowledge of its external history remains a duty of the church.

In all this we have only repeated the paradox of Chalcedonian Christology and of the two-world ethics of Christianity. But it is necessary to repeat it in our time, especially in view of the all too simple definitions of history and revelation that fail to take account of the duality in union which is the nature of Christian life and history.

We have not yet succeeded in saying what we mean by revelation but have indicated the sphere in which revelation is to be found. That sphere is internal history, the story of what happened to us, the living memory of the community. Our further efforts must be directed to a somewhat more precise determination of the area in which the revelatory event is to be found.

The Idea of Radical Monotheism

In ordinary discourse, the word "gods" has many meanings. Now we mean by it powers on which men call for help in time of trouble; now the forces which they summon up in their search for ecstasy; now the realities before which they experience awe and the sense of the holy; now the beings they posit in their speculative efforts to explain the origin and government of things; now the objects of adoration. The question whether religion in which all these attitudes and activities are present is a single movement of the mind, and with it the query whether the word "gods" refers to entities of one class, must be left to other contexts. We are concerned now with faith as dependence on a value center and as loyalty to a cause. Hence, when we speak of "gods" we mean the gods of faith, namely, such value centers and causes.

In this narrowed sense the plural term, "gods," alone seems appropriate. The religious and also the political institutions of the West have long been officially monotheistic, so that we do not easily regard ourselves as polytheists, believers in many gods, or as henotheists, loyal to one god among many. Using the word "god" without definition, we regard ourselves. . . .

For radical monotheism, the value-center is no closed society or the principle of such a society, but the principle of being itself; its reference is to no one reality among the many, but to One beyond all the many, whence all the many derive their being, and by participation in which they exist. As faith, it is reliance on the source of all being for the significance of the self and of all that exists. It is the assurance that because I am, I am valued; and because you are, you are beloved; and because whatever is, is there, therefore it is worthy of love. It is the confidence that whatever is, is good, because it exists as one thing among the many which all have their origin and their being in the One, the principle of being which is also the principle of value. In him, we live and move and have our being, not only as existent, but as worthy of existence and worthy in existence. It is not a relation to any finite, natural or supernatural, value-center that confers value on self and some of its companions in being, but it is value-relation to the One to whom all being is related. Monotheism is less than radical if it makes a distinction between the principle of being and the principle of value, so that while all being is acknowledged as absolutely dependent for existence on the One, only some beings are valued as having worth for it, or if, speaking in religious language, the Creator and the God of grace are not identified.

Radical monotheism is not in the first instance a theory about being and then a faith, as though the faith-orientation toward the principle of being as value-center needed to be preceded by an ontology that established the unity of the realm of being and its source in a single power beyond it. It is not at all evident that the One beyond the many, whether made known in revelation or always present to man in hiddenness, is principle of being before it is principle of value. Believing man does not say first, "I believe in a creative principle," and then, "I believe that the principle is gracious, that is, good toward what issues from it." He rather says, "I believe in God, the Father Almighty, Maker of heaven and earth." This is a primary statement, a point of departure and not a deduction. In it the principle of being is identified with the principle of value, and the principle of value with the principle of being. Neither is it evident, despite our intellectualist bias toward identifying ourselves with our reason, that the self is more itself as reasoning self than as faithful self, concerned about value. It is the "I" that reasons and the "I" that believes; it is present in its believing as in its reasoning. Yet the believing self must reason; there is always a reasoning in faith, so that rational efforts to understand the One beyond the many are characteristic of radical monotheism. But the orientation of faith toward the One does not wait on the development of theory.

As faith-reliance, radical monotheism depends absolutely and assuredly for the worth of the self on the same principle by which it has being; and since that principle is the same by which all things exist, it accepts the value of whatever is. As faith-loyalty, it is directed toward the principle and the realm of being as the cause for the sake of which it lives. Such loyalty, on the one hand, is claimed by the greatness and inclusiveness of the objective cause; on the other hand, it is given in commitment, since loyalty is the response of a self and not the compulsive reaction of a thing. The cause also has a certain duality. On the one hand, it is the principle of being itself; on the other, it is the realm of being. Whether to emphasize the one or the other may be unimportant, since the principle of being has a cause, namely, the realm of being, so that loyalty to the principle of being must include loyalty to its cause; loyalty to the realm of being, on the other hand, implies keeping faith with the principle by virtue of which it is, and is one realm. The counterpart, then, of universal faith-assurance is universal loyalty. Such universal loyalty cannot be loyalty to loyalty, as Royce would have it, but is loyalty to all existents as bound together by a loyalty that is not only resident in them but transcends them. It is not only their loyalty to each other that makes them one realm of being, but the loyalty that comes from beyond them, that originates and maintains them in their particularity and their unity. Hence, universal loyalty expresses itself as loyalty to each particular existent in the community of being and to the universal community. Universal loyalty does not express itself as loyalty to the loyal but to whatever is; not as reverence for the reverent but as reverence for being; not as the affirmation of world-affirmers but as world-affirmation. Such loyalty gives form to morality, since all moral laws and ends receive their form, though not their immediate content, from the form of faith-reliance and faith-loyalty. Love of the neighbor is required in every morality formed by a faith; but in polytheistic faith the neighbor is defined as the one who is near me in my interest group, *when* he is near me in that passing association. In henotheistic social faith my neighbor is my fellow in the closed society. Hence, in both instances the counterpart of the law of neighbor-love is the requirement to hate the enemy. But in radical monotheism my neighbor is my companion in being; if he is my enemy in some less than universal context, the requirement is to love the enemy. To give to everyone his due is required in every context; but what is due to him depends on the relation in which he is known to stand. All moral laws receive a universal form in the context of radically monotheistic faith, and it is an evidence of the influence of radical faith that all our mores are haunted by the presence to the conscience of a universal form of those laws that for the most part we interpret in pluralistic and closed-society fashion. To such a universal form, testimony is offered by Kant's categorical imperative, by the intuitions of universal equity and universal benevolence that Clarke and Sidgwick cannot escape, by the *prima facie* rightness of promise-keeping that Ross contends for. It is one thing to maintain that the universal form is given with reason or conscience itself; it is another thing to point out that where the universal form of moral law is acknowledged, the actuality of a universal community and the claim of a universal cause have also been recognized. . . .

Radical monotheism dethrones all absolutes short of the principle of being itself. At the same time it reverences every relative existent. Its two great mottoes are: "I am the Lord thy God; thou shalt have no other gods before me" and "Whatever is, is good."

36. Reinhold Niebuhr, *Human Nature and Politics*

The following pages are devoted to the task of analyzing the moral resource and limitations of human nature, of tracing their consequences and cumulative effect in the life of human groups, and of weighing political strategies in the light of the ascertained facts. The ultimate purpose of this task is to find political methods which will offer the most promise of achieving ethical social goals for society. Such methods must always be judged by two criteria: first, do they do justice to the moral resources and possibilities in human nature and provide for the exploitation of every latent moral capacity in man? Second, do they take account of the limitations of human nature, particularly those which manifest themselves in man's collective behavior?

Modern optimists would argue that the second question, with its implied pessimistic reservations upon their utopian dreams, is predicated upon the assumption that human nature does not change, while it is their own belief that human nature is surprisingly malleable and is to a large degree the product of its environment. The question is whether they have not confused human nature with human behavior. Human behavior is constantly changing under the influence of various stimuli. The differences in the behavior of a Chinese Buddhist monk, a British aristocrat, a Prussian general, an American go-getter, an expatriated artist, and a Russian worker are very considerable. But a certain common human nature underlies all this varied behavior. Its common characteristics have been obscured by the rationalistic illusions which began in the eighteenth century, and which lost sight of common human traits in their emphasis upon the variable factors of education and environment.

Recently a considerable number of political scientists have become aware of the relevance of Christian conceptions of human nature for the assessment of man's collective capacities and incapacities for justice and civic virtue. In secular political theory the tendency is to elaborate cynical and undemocratic social theories upon the basis of pessimistic interpretations of human nature; or to expound sentimental political theories upon the basis of a too optimistic interpretation of human nature. This contradiction between cynicism and sentimentality in political theory is partly derived from the separation of two elements in the Christian doctrine of man, the cynics emphasizing the sinful egoism of man and the sentimentalists emphasizing his dignity and greatness.

Humanist and Christian Views of Man

Western civilization rests upon two sources—Greek classical thought and biblical, Hebraic-Christian faith. These two sources are in agreement in their common appreciation of and emphasis upon the dignity and uniqueness of man. The alliance between them is, however, always uneasy, because they disagree on the character of man's unique gifts. For classical, as for modern secular, humanism, the emphasis lies heavily upon man's rational endowments, his logical and analytical faculties—in short, his "reason"—as the mark of his uniqueness. The biblical view regards man's reason as only a part of his unique endowment, which it defines as the "image of God" and which it describes as a radical form of freedom in the human person. It is the total person, in the unity of will, memory, and understanding, which bears the "image of God."

According to the classical and modern secular view every extension and development of the human mind represents a clear gain. This is why, in the modern period, man's rational conquest of nature increased the prestige of rational humanism so significantly, and why this humanism had such an optimistic view of the moral consequences of man's conquest of nature, and of the development of technical civilization.

According to the Christian view the dignity of man and the "misery" of man are inextricably interwoven in his freedom. Every extension of freedom therefore involves the possibility of both good and evil; for evil is never merely the inertia of "nature" against the operation of "mind." Evil is in the person and not in nature. It is man's inclination to "self-love," his undue concern for himself. This defect is not overcome by any extension of mind; for if the center of personality is not changed, the mind still remains the servant of the self.

One reason why the Christian view has achieved a new relevance today is because modern developments have proved that there is a more intimate relation between what Madison called man's reason and self-love than the rationalists have assumed. The force of sin is stronger than humanism understands; and therefore the necessity of "grace" is greater. By "grace" we must understand every force in life and history which persuades and beguiles self-centered man to forget himself and to realize himself by letting go of himself and seeking the good of his fellows.

Modern, like classical, humanism removes every mystery from human selfhood. Christianity, on the other hand, declares that man stands so far above and beyond all relations of nature and reason that he can understand himself only in his relation to God. Modern humanism tends to equate the "dignity" of man with his virtue. Christianity, on the other hand, recognizes that the "dignity" of man consists precisely of that freedom which makes it possible for man to sin.

Man as Creature and Free Spirit

As the classical view of man is determined by Greek metaphysical presuppositions, so the Christian view is determined by the ultimate presuppositions of the Christian faith. The Christian faith in God as Creator of the world transcends the canons and antinomies of rationality, particularly the antinomy between mind and matter, between consciousness and extension. God is not merely mind who forms a previously given formless stuff. God is both vitality and form and the source of all existence. He creates the world. This world is not God; but it is not necessarily evil simply because it is not God. Indeed, being God's creation, it is good.

The consequence of this conception of the world upon the view of human nature in Christian thought is to allow an appreciation of the unity of body and soul in human personality which idealists and naturalists have sought in vain. Furthermore it prevents the idealistic error of regarding the mind as essentially good or essentially eternal and the body as essentially evil. But it also obviates the romantic error of seeking for the good in man-as-nature and for evil in man-as-spirit or as reason. Man is, according to the biblical view, a created and finite existence in both body and spirit.

Thus, the Christian faith teaches that the world is not evil because it is temporal, that the body is not the source of sin in man, that individuality as separate and particular existence is not evil by reason of being distinguished from undifferentiated totality, and that death is not evil though it is an occasion for evil, namely the fear of death. The biblical view is that the finiteness, the dependence and the insufficiency of man's mortal life are facts which belong to God's plan of creation and must be accepted with reverence and humility.

Another characteristic of the Christian view of man is that he is understood primarily from the standpoint of God, rather than from the uniqueness of his rational faculties or his relation to nature. He is made in the "image of God." It has been the mistake of many Christian rationalists to assume that this term is no more than a religious-pictorial expression of what philosophy intends when it defines man as a rational animal. Whereas in fact the human spirit has the special capacity of standing continually outside itself in terms of indefinite regression. Consciousness is a capacity for surveying the world and determining action from a governing center. Self-consciousness represents a further degree of transcendence in which the self makes itself its own object in such a way that the ego is finally always subject and not object. The rational capacity of surveying the world, of forming general concepts and analyzing the order of the world, is thus but one aspect of what Christianity knows as "spirit." The self knows the world, insofar as it knows the world, because it stands outside both itself and the world, which means that it cannot understand itself except as it is understood from beyond itself and the world.

The essential homelessness of the human spirit is the ground of all religion; for the self which stands outside itself and the world cannot find the meaning of life in itself or the world. It cannot identify meaning with causality in nature; for its freedom is obviously something different from the necessary causal links of nature. Nor can it identify the principle of meaning with rationality, since it transcends its own rational processes, so that it may, for instance, ask the question whether there is a relevance between its rational forms and recurrences and forms of nature. It is this capacity of freedom which finally prompts great cultures and philosophies to transcend rationalism and to seek for the meaning of life in an unconditioned ground of existence.

While these paradoxes of human self-knowledge are not easily reduced to simpler formulae, they all point to two facts about man. The obvious fact is that man is a child of nature, subject to its vicissitudes, compelled by its necessities, driven by its impulses, and confined within the brevity of the years which nature permits its varied organic forms, allowing them some, but not too much, latitude. The other less obvious fact is that man is a spirit who stands outside of nature, life, himself, his reason and the world.

The behavior of collective man naturally has its source in this anatomy of human nature. If we examine the constants and variables in that behavior, the most apparent constant factors are obviously derived from those aspects of human nature which constitute man a creature of nature, namely his natural hungers and needs, and the natural forces of cohesion in his communities, such as the sense of kinship. But natural necessity is not the only source of the constant factors. Some are derived from the unvarying way in which man's unique freedom manifests itself, such as his yearning for an ultimate good and his inevitable abuse of his freedom. However, freedom is, of course, also the source of the unique and variable factors in social behavior and therefore of the unpredictable character of historical events.

In the Christian view, then, for man to understand himself truly means to begin with a faith that he is understood from beyond himself, that he is known and loved of God and must find himself in terms of obedience to the divine will. This relation of the divine to the human will makes it possible for man to relate himself to God without pretending to be God; and to accept his distance from God as a created thing, without believing that the evil of his nature is caused by this finiteness. Man's finite existence in the body and in history can be essentially affirmed, as naturalism wants to affirm it. Yet the uniqueness of man's spirit can be appreciated even more than idealism appreciates it, though always preserving a proper distinction between the human and the divine. Also the unity of spirit and body can be emphasized in terms of its relation to a Creator and Redeemer who created both mind and body. These are the ultra-rational foundations and presuppositions of Christian wisdom about man.

Man as Sinner

This conception of man's stature is not, however, the complete Christian picture of man. The high estimate of the human stature implied in the concept of "image of God" stands in paradoxical juxtaposition to the low estimate of human virtue in Christian thought. Man is a sinner.

Indeed, it is man's radical and boundless freedom which is the basis of the self's destructive as well as creative powers; and there is no simple possibility of making nice distinctions between human destructiveness and creativity. In the words of Pascal, the "dignity of man and his misery" have the same source. Man stands perpetually outside and beyond every social, natural, communal, and rational cohesion. He is not bound by any of them, which makes for his creativity. He is tempted to make use of all of them for his own ends; that is the basis of his destructiveness. One may go further and declare that the limitless character of man's ideals of perfection and the inordinacy of human lusts and ambitions have their common root in the capacity of man to stand out of, and survey, any historical or natural situation which surrounds him.

While the Bible consistently maintains that sin cannot be excused by, or inevitably derived from, any other element in the human situation than man himself, it does admit that man was tempted. In the myth of the Fall the temptation arises from the serpent's analysis of the human situation. The serpent depicts God as jealously guarding his prerogatives against the possibility that man might have his eyes opened and become "as God, knowing good and

371

evil." Man is tempted, in other words, to break and transcend the limits which God has set for him. The temptation thus lies in his situation of finiteness and freedom.

That is, the occasion for man's temptation lies in the two facts taken together: his greatness and his weakness, his unlimited and his limited knowledge. Man is both strong and weak, both free and bound, both blind and far-seeing. He stands at the juncture of nature and spirit; and is involved in both freedom and necessity. His sin is never the mere ignorance of his ignorance. It is always partly an effort to obscure his blindness by overestimating the degree of his sight and to obscure his insecurity by stretching his power beyond its limits.

In short, man is anxious. Anxiety is the inevitable concomitant of the paradox of freedom and finiteness in which man is involved. Anxiety is the internal precondition of sin, the internal description of the state of temptation.

It is not possible to make a simple separation between the creative and destructive elements in anxiety; and for that reason it is not possible to purge moral achievement of sin as easily as moralists imagine. The same action may reveal a creative effort to transcend natural limitations, and a sinful effort to give an unconditioned value to contingent and limited factors in human existence. Man may, in the same moment, be anxious because he has not become what he ought to be, and also anxious lest he cease to be at all.

The parent is anxious about his child and this anxiety reaches beyond the grave. Is the effort of the parent to provide for the future of the child creative or destructive? Obviously it is both.

The statesman is anxious about the order and security of the nation. But he cannot express this anxiety without an admixture of anxiety about his prestige as a ruler and without assuming unduly that only the kind of order and security which he establishes is adequate for the nation's health.

The philosopher is anxious to arrive at the truth; but he is also anxious to prove that his particular truth is the truth. He is never as completely in possession of the truth as he imagines. That may be the error of being ignorant of one's ignorance. But it is never simply that. The pretensions of final truth are always partly an effort to obscure a darkly felt consciousness of the limits of human knowledge. Man is afraid to face the problem of his limited knowledge, lest he fall into the abyss of meaninglessness. Thus fanaticism is always a partly conscious, partly unconscious attempt to hide the fact of ignorance and to obscure the problem of skepticism.

Anxiety, of course, must not be identified with sin because there is always the ideal possibility that faith will purge anxiety of the tendency toward sinful self-assertion. The ideal possibility is that faith in the ultimate security of God's love will overcome all immediate insecurities of nature and history. That is why Christian orthodoxy has consistently defined unbelief as the root of sin, or as the sin which precedes pride. It is significant that Jesus justifies his injunction, "Be not anxious" with the observation, "For your heavenly Father knoweth that ye have need of these things." The freedom from anxiety which he enjoins is a possibility only if perfect trust in divine security has been achieved.

Thus man's sin is defined as rebellion against God. The Christian estimate of human evil is so serious precisely because it places evil at the very center of human personality: in the will. This evil cannot be regarded complacently as the inevitable consequence of his finiteness or the fruit of his involvement in the contingencies and necessities of nature. Sin is occasioned precisely by the fact that man refuses to admit his "creatureliness" and to acknowledge himself as merely a member of a total unity of life. He pretends to be more than he is. Nor can he, as in both rationalistic and mystic dualism, dismiss his sins as residing in that part of himself which is not his true self, that is, that part of himself which is involved in physical necessity. In Christianity it is not the eternal man who judges the finite man; but the eternal and holy God who judges sinful man. Nor is redemption in the power of the eternal man who gradually sloughs off finite man. Man is not divided against himself so that the essential man can be extricated from the non-essential. Man contradicts himself within the terms of his true essence. His essence is free self-determination. His sin is the wrong use of his freedom and its consequent destruction.

Man is an individual but he is not self-sufficing. The law of his nature is love, a harmonious relation of life to life in obedience to the divine center and source of his life. This law is violated when man seeks to make himself the center and source of his own life. His sin is therefore spiritual and not carnal, though the infection of rebellion spreads from the spirit to the body and disturbs its harmonies also. Man, in other words, is a sinner not because he is one limited individual within a whole but rather because he is betrayed by his very ability to survey the whole to imagine himself the whole.

Pride and the Will-to-Power

The Bible defines sin in moral as well as religious terms. The religious dimension of sin is man's rebellion against God, his effort to usurp the place of God. The moral and social dimension of sin is injustice. The ego which falsely makes itself the center of existence in its pride and will-to-power inevitably subordinates other life to its will and thus does injustice to other life. Man is insecure and involved in natural contingency; he seeks to overcome his insecurity by a will-to-power which overreaches the limits of human creatureliness. Man is ignorant and involved in the limitations of a finite mind; but he pretends that he is not limited. He assumes that he can gradually transcend finite limitations until his mind becomes identical with universal mind. All of his intellectual and cultural pursuits, therefore, become infected with the sin of pride. Man's pride and will-to-power disturb the harmony of creation. We must now examine more carefully the ways in which sin expresses itself as both pride and the lust for power, and the consequences of these evils for social relations.

The most significant distinction between the human and the animal world is that the impulses of the latter are "spiritualized" in the human world. Human capacities for evil as well as for good are derived from this spiritualism. There is of course always a natural survival impulse at the core of all human ambition. But this survival impulse cannot be neatly disentangled from two forms of its spiritualization.

The one form is the desire to fulfill the potentialities of life and not merely to maintain its existence. Man is the kind of animal who cannot merely live. If he lives at all he is bound to seek the realization of his true nature; and to his true nature belongs his fulfillment in the lives of others.

The will-to-live is thus transmuted into the will to self-realization; and self-realization involves self-giving in relation to others. When this desire for self-realization is fully explored it becomes apparent that it is subject to the paradox that the highest form of self-realization is the consequence of self-giving, but that it cannot be the intended consequence without being prematurely limited. Thus the will-to-live is finally transmuted into its opposite in the sense that only in self-giving can the self be fulfilled, for: "He that findeth his life shall lose it; and he that loseth his life for my sake shall find it."

On the other hand the will-to-live is also spiritually transmuted into the will-to-power or into the desire for "power and glory." Man, being more than a natural creature, is not interested merely in physical survival but in prestige and social approval. Having the intelligence to anticipate the perils in which he stands in nature and history, he invariably seeks to gain security against these perils by enhancing his power, individually and collectively. Possessing a darkly unconscious sense of his insignificance in the total scheme of things, he seeks to compensate for his insignificance by pretensions of pride.

The conflicts between men are thus never simple conflicts between competing survival impulses. They are conflicts in which each man or group seeks to guard its power and prestige against the evil of competing expressions of power and pride. Since the very possession of power and prestige always involves some encroachment upon the prestige and power of others, this conflict is by its very nature a more stubborn and difficult one than the mere competition between various survival impulses in nature.

Since the survival impulse in nature is transmuted into two different and contradictory spiritualized forms, which we may briefly designate as the will-to-live-truly and the will-to-power, man is at variance with himself. The power of the second impulse places him more fundamentally in conflict with his fellow man than liberalism realizes. The fact that he cannot realize himself, except in organic relation with his fellows, makes the community more important than bourgeois individualism understands. The fact that the two impulses, though standing in contradiction to each other, are also mixed and compounded with each other on every level of human life, makes the simple distinctions between good and evil, between selfishness and altruism, with which liberal idealism has tried to estimate moral and political facts, invalid. The fact that the will-to-power inevitably justifies itself in terms of the morally more acceptable will to realize man's true nature means that the egoistic corruption of universal ideals is a much more persistent fact in human conduct than any moralistic creed is inclined to admit.

Intellectual, Moral and Spiritual Pride

The biblical and distinctively Christian conception of sin as pride and self-love finds various expressions in the observable behavior of men. Besides pride of power, two other types may be distinguished: pride of knowledge and pride of virtue. The third type, the pride of self-righteousness, rises to a form of spiritual pride, which is at once a fourth type and yet not a specific form of pride at all but pride and self-glorification in its inclusive and quintessential form.

The intellectual pride of man is of course a more spiritual sublimation of his pride of power. Sometimes it is so deeply involved in the more brutal and obvious pride of power that the two cannot be distinguished. Every ruling oligarchy of history has found ideological pretensions as important a bulwark of authority as its police power. But intellectual pride is confined neither to the political oligarchies nor to the savants of society. All human knowledge is tainted with an "ideological" taint. It pretends to be more true than it is. It is finite knowledge, gained from a particular perspective; but it pretends to be final and ultimate knowledge. Exactly analogous to the cruder pride of power, the pride of intellect is derived on the one hand from ignorance of the finiteness of the human mind and on the other hand from an attempt to obscure the known conditioned character of human knowledge and the taint of self-interest in human truth.

Moral pride is revealed in all "self-righteous" judgments in which the other is condemned because he fails to conform to the highly arbitrary standards of the self. Since the self judges itself by its own standards it finds itself good. It judges others by its own standards and finds them evil, when their standards fail to conform to its own. This is the secret of the relationship between cruelty and self-righteousness. When the self mistakes its standards for God's standards it is naturally inclined to attribute the very essence of evil to non-conformists.

One might add that the sin of self-righteousness is not only the final sin in the subjective sense but also in the objective sense. It involves us in the greatest guilt. It is responsible for our most serious cruelties, injustices and defamations against our fellow men. The whole history of racial, national, religious and other social struggles is a commentary on the objective wickedness and social miseries which result from self-righteousness.

The sin of moral pride, when it has conceived, brings forth spiritual pride. The ultimate sin is the religious sin of making the self-deification implied in moral pride explicit. This is done when our partial standards and relative attainments are explicitly related to the unconditioned good, and claim divine sanction. For this reason religion is not simply, as is generally supposed, an inherently virtuous human quest for God. It is merely a final battleground between God and man's self-esteem. In that battle even the most pious practices may be instruments of human pride. The same man may in one moment regard Christ as his judge and in the next moment seek to prove that the figure, the standards and righteousness of Christ bear a greater similarity to his own righteousness than to that of his enemy. The worst form of class domination is religious class domination in which, as for instance in the Indian caste system, a dominant priestly class not only subjects subordinate classes to social disabilities but finally excludes them from participation in any universe of meaning. The worst form of intolerance is religious intolerance in which the particular interests of the contestants hide behind religious absolutes. The worst form of self-assertion is religious self-assertion in which under the guise of contrition before God, he is claimed as the exclusive ally of our contingent self.

Christianity rightly regards itself as a religion, not so much of man's search for God, in the process of which he may make himself God; but as a religion of revelation in which a holy and loving God is revealed to man as the source and end of all finite existence, against whom the self-will of man is shattered and his pride abased. But as soon as the Christian assumes that he is, by virtue of possessing this revelation, more righteous, because more contrite, than other men, he increases the sin of self-righteousness and makes the forms of a religion of contrition the tool of his pride.

Indeed the final mystery of human sin cannot be understood if it is not recognized that the greatest teachers of this Reformation doctrine of the sinfulness of all men used it on occasion as the instrument of an arrogant will-to-power against theological opponents. There is no final guarantee against the spiritual pride of man. Even the recognition in the sight of God that he is a sinner can be used as a vehicle of that very sin. If that final mystery of the sin of pride is not recognized the meaning of the Christian gospel cannot be understood.

It must be added that it is not necessary to be explicitly religious in order to raise moral pride to explicit religious proportions. Stalin can be as explicit in making unconditioned claims as the pope; and a French revolutionist of the eighteenth century can be as cruel in his religious fervor as the "God-ordained" feudal system which he seeks to destroy. The hope of modern culture that the elimination of religion might result in the elimination of religious intolerance is fallacious. Religion, by whatever name, is the inevitable fruit of the spiritual stature of man; and religious intolerance and pride is the final expression of his sinfulness. A religion of revelation is grounded in the faith that God speaks to man from beyond the highest pinnacle of the human spirit; and that this voice of God will discover man's highest not only to be short of the highest but involved in the dishonesty of claiming that it is the highest.

37. Carl F. H. Henry, *God, Revelation and Authority*

Introduction to Theology

A century ago the French author Jules Verne wrote extravagantly imaginative stories in which he foresaw many remarkable scientific achievements of our own day, such as submarines, aircraft and television. What he did not foresee was the loss, equally remarkable, of what was once almost everywhere taken for granted, the reality of God. For our generation, is not theology a questionable concern at best? Contemporary man is far more sure of the landing of astronauts on the moon than he is of God's incarnation in Jesus Christ, more sure of scientists propelled into outer space than of the Logos "that came down from heaven" (John 3:13, KJV) as the eternal Word become flesh (John 1:14). To secular Western man in the late 1970s, no world seems more remote than that of theology.

Religion now has become "everyone's own kettle of fish"—a matter of personal preference rather than a truth-commitment universally valid for one and all. The notion seems to be widespread that theology—whether Christian or not—is not truly a rational enterprise at all, but rather an outmoded superstition, like alchemy or astrology, that has unfortunately survived from the ancient past or from the Dark Ages. Religious propagandists themselves for so long have recommended decision not for truth's sake but for the personal consolation and social stability it brings that untruths are increasingly thought to be the lifeblood of religion. Even neo-Protestant theologians today assert that divine revelation is to be believed without questioning, and that it cannot be integrated with any unified system of truth. One can more readily forgive Tertullian, who wrote to Marcion that because Christian assertions are absurd they are to be believed, than he can modern dialectical and existential theologians who uncritically espouse the same nonsense seventeen centuries later. So much has the leap of faith been exaggerated into a virtue that contemporary religionists have become more noted for their ingenious hurtling over rational objections than for their intelligible confrontation of the issues. That theology simply prepackages a platter of ideas to be hurriedly ingested rather than carefully savored by intellectual gourmets is a standard complaint of modern atheists and agnostics. The world religions offer, they say, a variety of man-made convenience frozen foods awaiting the moment when harried individuals run into unforeseen emergencies and are therefore willing to eat anything rather than starve.

If theology, then, is not dead, is it sheer bunk? Are we merely chasing a will-o'-the-wisp? Has theology not been taught for centuries by men ordained by the various world religions to raise their own flag? Is it, as someone has suggested, a specialized and rather bogus form of philosophy in which the conclusions are laid down before the argument begins? Is it a spurious form of philosophy that sets out with unquestioned and unquestionable assumptions, refuses to face problems, and corrals its converts into an irrational commitment that is academically closed and intellectually dishonest? Is the skeptic's doubt about Christianity to be overcome by a hurried appeal to Pascal's "wager"—a gambling of life on the view that even if a person is intellectually mistaken he stands to gain more by betting on God than on not-God?

Theology, we shall insist, sets out not simply with God as a speculative presupposition but with God known in his revelation. But the appeal to God and to revelation cannot stand alone, if it is to be significant; it must embrace also some agreement on rational methods of inquiry, ways of argument, and criteria for verification. For the critical question today is not simply, "What are the data of theology?" but "How does one proceed from these data to conclusions that commend themselves to rational reflection?" The fundamental issue remains the issue of truth, the truth of theological assertions. No work on theology will be worth its weight if that fundamental issue is obscured. Durable theology must revive and preserve the distinction between true and false religion, a distinction long obscured by neo-Protestant theologians. Either the religion of Jesus Christ is true religion or it is not worth bothering about.

The Crisis of Truth and Word

No fact of contemporary Western life is more evident than its growing distrust of final truth and its implacable questioning of any sure word. The prevalent mood, as Langdon Gilkey tells us, is "skeptical about all formulations of ultimate coherence or ultimate meaning, speculative as well as theological" and "doubts the possibility both of philosophical knowing and religious faith" (*Naming the Whirlwind*, p. 24). The "man from Missouri" long lampooned as a provincial doubting Thomas has now found a well-nigh universal and sophisticated counterpart. So widespread is the current truth-and-word crisis that, according to some observers, the night of nihilism—a new Dark Ages—may be swiftly engulfing the civilized world, and particularly the West which long has vaunted itself as the spearpoint of cosmic progress.

Underlying this clash over what and whose word is worthy flares a deep disagreement over which of the diverse media everywhere facing mankind reliably discloses the true nature and course of human events. . . .

The crisis of word and truth is not, however, in all respects peculiar to contemporary technocratic civilization. Its backdrop is not to be found in the mass media per se, as if these sophisticated mechanical instruments of modern communication were uniquely and inherently evil. Not even the French Revolution, which some historians now isolate as the development that placed human history under the shadow of continual revolution, can adequately explain the ongoing plunge of man's existence into endless crisis. Why is it that the magnificent civilizations fashioned by human endeavor throughout history have tumbled and collapsed one after another with apocalyptic suddenness? Is it not because, ever since man's original fall and onward to the present, sin has plummeted human existence into an unbroken crisis of word and truth? A cosmic struggle between truth and falsehood, between good and evil, shadows the whole history of mankind. The Bible depicts it as a conflict between the authority of God and the claims of the Evil One. Measured by the yardstick of God's holy purposes, all that man proudly designates as human culture is little but idolatry. God's Word proffers no compliments whatever to man's so-called historical progress; rather, it indicts man's pseudoparadises as veritable towers of Babel that obscure and falsify God's truth and Word. . . .

The world today vibrates under a communications cacophony. Twentieth-century technology has shaped a global village in which human beings are bombarded with more sights and sounds than in any previous generation in history. Words and events recovered from the ancient past, words and events of the pulsating present, words and events projected at tomorrow's frontiers clamor for attention and hearing. No generation since Babel has faced so massive a communications problem, and to none has belief in transcendent divine disclosure seemed more suspect, and the sense of divine authority less clear.

Yet neither scientific searching nor secular philosophizing has compensated for the tragic loss of revelational realities, nor have these realities been done to death. For our generation no less than for any other there remains the promise of a better prospect: "Eye hath not seen, nor ear heard, neither have entered into the heart of man, the things which God hath prepared . . ." (1 Cor. 2:9, KJV). Nothing can now relieve the modern crisis of truth and word other than a reconciliation and restoration of the media of human communication to the Mediator of divine disclosure in order to transcend the present costly conflict between the two. The Logos of God is the one ultimate medium of truth and the good; the mass media are multiple human means for reflecting and echoing the world of sound and sight in the context of either the truth and Word of God or of merely secular perspectives. The evangelical aim is to restore the wayward vocabulary of modern man to the clarity and vitality of the Word of God. The living God is the God who speaks for himself and shows himself. That God the Creator and Redeemer addresses good news to man in a verbally intelligible way and that the invisible Lord has become enfleshed and visible are emphases found conjoined in Christianity alone; to reborn modern men they are still more fascinating and rewarding than the technocratic marvels of our time.

If the church is to evangelize a world of four billion people, she must recover a theology abreast of divine invasion. This earth has indeed been invaded—from outside its own being, outside its own resources, outside its own possibilities; it has been and, moreover, continues to be invaded by the transcendent Logos made known in divine revelation. In this mass media age, the church's main mission is to overcome the eclipse of God. It must engage earnestly at the frontiers of human news and persuasion to uncover the currently obscured Word and truth of God.

The Dawn of a New Reformation

The need for a vital evangelicalism is proportionate to the world's need. The days are as hectic as Nero's Rome, and they demand attention as immediate as Luke's Macedonia.

The cries of suffering humanity today are many. No evangelicalism which ignores the totality of man's condition dares respond in the name of Christianity. Though the modern crisis is not basically political, economic or social—fundamentally it is religious—yet evangelicalism must be armed to declare the implications of its proposed religious solution for the politico-economic and sociological context for modern life.

However marred, the world vessel of clay is not without some of the influence of the Master Molder. God has not left himself entirely without witness in the global calamity; he discloses himself in the tragedies as well as the triumphs of history. He works in history as well as above history. There is a universal confrontation of men and women by the divine Spirit, invading all cultures and all individual lives. There is a constructive work of God in history, even where the redemptive gospel does not do a recreating work. The evangelical missionary message cannot be measured for success by the number of converts only. The Christian message has a salting effect upon the earth. It aims at a recreated society; where it is resisted, it often encourages the displacement of a low ideology by one relatively higher. Democratic humanitarianism furnishes a better context for human existence than political naturalism, except as it degenerates to the latter.

Modern evangelicalism need not substitute as its primary aim the building of "relatively higher civilizations." To do that is to fall into the error of yesterday's liberalism. Its supreme aim is the proclamation of redeeming grace to sinful humanity; there is no need for Fundamentalism to embrace liberalism's defunct social gospel. The divine order involves a supernatural principle, a creative force that enters society from outside its natural sources of uplift, and regenerates humanity. In that divine reversal of the self-defeating sinfulness of man is the only real answer to our problems—of whatever political, economic, or sociological nature. Is there political unrest? Seek first, not a Republican victory, or a labor victory, but the kingdom of God and his righteousness. Then there will be added—not necessarily a Republican or labor victory, but—political rest. Is there economic unrest? Seek first, not an increase of labor wages coupled with shorter hours, with its probable dog-eat-dog resultant of increased commodity cost, but the divine righteousness; this latter norm will involve fairness for both labor and management. But there will be added not only the solution of the problems of the economic man but also those of the spiritual man. There is no satisfying rest for modern civilization if it is found in a context of spiritual unrest.

This is but another way of declaring that the Gospel of redemption is the most pertinent message for our modern weariness, and that many of our other so-called solutions are quite impertinent, to say the least.

But that does not mean that we cannot cooperate in securing relatively higher goods, when this is the loftiest commitment we can evoke from humanity, providing we do so with appropriate warning of the inadequacy and instability of such solutions. The supernatural regenerative grace of God, proffered to the regenerate, does not prevent his natural grace to all men, regenerate and unregenerate alike. Because he brings rivers of living water to the redeemed, he does not on that account withhold the rain from the unjust and just alike. The realm of special grace does not preclude the realm of common grace. Just so, without minimizing the redemptive message, the church ministers by its message to those who stop short of commitment, as well as to regenerate believers.

The implications of this for evangelicalism seem clear. The battle against evil in all its forms must be pressed unsparingly; we must pursue the enemy, in politics, in economics, in science, in ethics—everywhere, in every field, we must pursue relentlessly. But when we have singled out the enemy—when we have disentangled him from those whose company he has kept and whom he has misled—we must meet the foe head-on, girt in the gospel armor. Others may resist him with inadequate weapons; they do not understand aright the nature of the foe, nor the requirements for victory. We join with them in battle, seeking all the while more clearly to delineate the enemy, and more precisely to state the redemptive formula.

These sub-Christian environments which result from an intermingling of Christian and non-Christian elements, however much they fail to satisfy the absolute demand of God, are for the arena of life more satisfactory than an atmosphere almost entirely devoid of its redemptive aspects. It is far easier, in an idealistic context, to proclaim the essential Christian message, than it is in a thoroughly naturalistic context. Life means more in a context of idealism, because true meaning evaporates in a context of naturalism; for that reason, the preaching of a more abundant life finds a more favorable climate in the former. Though neither is to be identified with the kingdom of God, Anglo-Saxon democracy is a relatively better atmosphere by far than German totalitarianism was, and what made it better is the trace of Hebrew-Christian ideology that lingers in it.

While it is not the Christian's task to correct social, moral and political conditions as his primary effort apart from a redemptive setting, simply because of his opposition to evils he ought to lend his endorsement to remedial efforts in any context not specifically anti-redemptive, while at the same time decrying the lack of a redemptive solution. In our American environment, the influences of Christian theism are still abroad with enough vigor that the usual solutions are non-redemptive, rather than anti-redemptive, in character. Such cooperation, coupled with the Gospel emphasis, might provide the needed pattern of action for condemning aggressive warfare in concert with the United Nations Organization, while at the same time disputing the frame of reference by which the attempt is made to outlaw such warfare; for condemning racial hatred and intolerance, while at the same time protesting the superficial view of man which overlooks the need of individual regeneration; for condemning the liquor traffic, while insisting that it is impossible by legislation actually to correct the heart of man; for seeking justice for both labor and management in business and industrial problems, while protesting the fallacy that man's deepest need is economic. This is to link the positive Christian message with a redemptive challenge to the world on its bitterest fronts. Christian ethics will always resist any reduction of the good of the community to something divorced from theism and revelation; its conviction that non-evangelical humanism cannot achieve any lasting moral improvements in the world as a whole, because of the lack of an adequate dynamic, will engender the vigorous affirmation of a Christian solution.

Not that evangelical action stops here; this is hardly the beginning of it. One of the fallacies of modern thought, with which non-evangelical groups have been so much taken up in recent years, is that the mere "passing of a resolution" or the "writing of a book" in which the proposed method was set forth, automatically constitutes a long step on the road to deliverance. But too often the action stopped with the resolution or the book. Western culture was flooded with solutions for deliverance, from every sort of idealism and humanism, during the very years that it walked most rapidly to its doom. The same danger attends any evangelical revival.

The evangelical task primarily is the preaching of the gospel, in the interest of individual regeneration by the supernatural grace of God, in such a way that divine redemption can be recognized as the best solution of our problems, individual and social. This produces within history, through the regenerative work of the Holy Spirit, a divine society that transcends national and international lines. The corporate testimony of believers, in their purity of life, should provide for the world an example of the divine dynamics to overcome evils in every realm. The social problems of our day are much more complex than in apostolic times, but they do not on that account differ in principle. When the twentieth-century church begins to "out-live" its environment as the first-century church outreached its pagan neighbors, the modern mind, too, will stop casting about for other solutions. The great contemporary problems are moral and spiritual. They demand more than a formula. The evangelicals have a conviction of absoluteness concerning their message, and not to proclaim it, in the assault on social evils, is sheer inconsistency.

Acknowledgments

The editors gratefully acknowledge the kind permission of the following publishers to excerpt material for this volume:

1. Albert Schweitzer, *The Quest of the Historical Jesus*, tr. W. Montgomery (New York: Macmillan, 1910), 398–402. Reprinted by permission.

2. Karl Barth, *The Word of God and the Word of Man*, tr. Douglas Horton (New York: Harper & Row, 1957), 28–50. Reprinted by permission.

3. Ernst Troeltsch, *The Absoluteness of Christianity*, tr. David Reid (Richmond: John Knox, 1971), 45–50, 66–76, 117–123. Reprinted by permission.

4. Karl Barth, *The Epistle to the Romans*, tr. W. Montgomery (New York: Macmillan, 1956), *passim*. Reprinted by permission. Karl Barth, *Der Römerbrief* (Munchen: Chr. Kaiser Verlag, 1922), *passim*, newly translated. Reprinted by permission.

5. Rudolf Bultmann, "The Question of 'Dialectical' Theology," *The Beginnings of Dialectical Theology*, ed. James Robinson, tr. K. R. Crim and L. De Grazia (Richmond: John Knox, 1968), 257–73. Reprinted by permission.

6. Emil Brunner, "Nature and Grace," *Natural Theology*, tr. Peter Fraenkel (London: Centenary Press, 1946), 17–32.

7. Karl Barth, "The Task of Church Dogmatics," *Church Dogmatics*, tr. G. T. Thomson (New York: Scribners, 1936), I/1:1–23; II/2:94–170. Reprinted by permission.

8. Paul Tillich, *Systematic Theology* (Chicago: University of Chicago Press, 1951–1963), I:2–64, II:118–34. Reprinted by permission.

9. Dietrich Bonhoeffer, *Letters and Papers from Prison*, tr. R. H. Fuller (New York: Macmillan, 1953), letters from April 30, May 5, June 27, June 30, July 8, July 18, July 21, 1944. Reprinted by permission.

10. Friedrich Gogarten, "Secularization and Christian Faith," *Despair and Hope for Our Time*, tr. T. Wieser (Philadelphia: Pilgrim Press, 1970), 9–22. Reprinted by permission.

ACKNOWLEDGMENTS

11. Rudolf Bultmann, "The Problem of Hermeneutics," *New Testament and Mythology*, tr. Schubert Ogden (Philadelphia: Fortress Press, 1984), 69–93. Reprinted by permission.

12. Gerhard Ebeling, "The Word of God and Hermeneutics," *Word and Faith*, tr. J. W. Leitch (Philadelphia: Fortress Press, 1963), 303–32. Reprinted by permission.

13. Ernst Fuchs, "The Essence of the 'Language Event' and Christology," *Studies of the Historical Jesus*, tr. A. Cobie (Naperville: Allenson, 1964), 213–28.

14. Wolfhart Pannenberg, *Revelation as History*, tr. D. Granskou (New York: Macmillan, 1968), 125–55. Reprinted by permission.

15. Jürgen Moltmann, *Theology of Hope*, tr. J. W. Leitch (New York: Harper & Row, 1967), 15–26. Reprinted by permission.

16. Johannes Metz, "The Church and the World in Light of 'Political Theology,'" *Theology of the World*, tr. W. Glen-Doepel (New York: Herder and Herder, 1968), 107–24. Reprinted by permission.

17. Karl Barth, "The Doctrine of the Trinity," *Church Dogmatics*, tr. G. T. Thomson (New York: Scribners, 1936), I/1:339–82. Reprinted by permission.

18. Karl Rahner, *The Trinity*, tr. J. Donceel (New York: Herder and Herder, 1970), 10–24. Reprinted by permission.

19. Eberhard Jungel, *The Doctrine of the Trinity*, tr. anon. (Grand Rapids: Eerdmans, 1976), 89–108. Reprinted by permission.

20. Paul Tillich, "The Significance of the History of Religions for the Systematic Theologian," *The Future of Religion* (New York: Harper & Row, 1966), 86–94. Reprinted by permission.

21. Hendrik Kraemer, *The Christian Message in a Non-Christian World* (New York: Harper Bros., 1938), 101–14. Reprinted by permission.

22. Karl Rahner, "Christianity and the Non-Christian Religions," *Theological Investigations*, vol. 5 (Baltimore: Helicon, 1966), 115–34. Reprinted by permission.

23. Werner Elert, "The Revelation of God," *The Christian Faith*, tr. M. W. Bertram and W. Bouman (unpub. ms.), 87–96. Reprinted by permission.

24. Anders Nygren, *Agape and Eros*, tr. P. S. Watson (Philadelphia: Westminster, 1946), 34–48. Reprinted by permission.

25. William Temple, "The Person of Christ," *Christus Veritas* (London: Macmillan, 1924), 124–53. Reprinted by permission.

26. Bernard J. F. Lonergan, *Method in Theology* (New York: Herder and Herder, 1972), 4–25. Reprinted by permission.

27. Karl Rahner, *Foundations of Christian Faith*, tr. W. V. Dych (New York: Seabury, 1978), 51–66. Reprinted by permission.

28. Antony Flew, R. M. Hare, and Basil Mitchell, "The University Discussion," *New Essays in Philosophical Theology*, ed. Antony Flew and Alasdair MacIntyre (London: SCM, 1955), 96–108. Reprinted by permission.

29. Ian T. Ramsey, *Religious Language* (London: SCM, 1957), 11–28. Reprinted by permission.

30. Paul Ricoeur, *The Symbolism of Evil*, tr. E. Buchanan (New York: Harper & Row, 1967), 3–18. Reprinted by permission.

31. Pierre Teilhard de Chardin, *The Phenomenon of Man* (London: Collins, 1959), 268–72, 291–98. Reprinted by permission.

32. Alfred North Whitehead, "God and the World," *Process and Reality* (New York: Macmillan, 1929), 519–33. Reprinted by permission.

33. Charles Hartshorne, "The Divine Self-Creation," *Man's Vision of God* (Chicago: Willet, Clark, 1941), 230–33.

34. Walter Rauschenbusch, *A Theology for the Social Gospel* (New York: Macmillan, 1917), 1–9, 131–45. Reprinted by permission.

35. H. Richard Niebuhr, *The Meaning of Revelation* (New York: Macmillan, 1955), 81–90; *Radical Monotheism and Western Civilization* (Lincoln: University of Nebraska Press, 1960), 17–34. Reprinted by permission.

36. Reinhold Niebuhr, "Human Nature and Politics," *Reinhold Niebuhr on Politics*, compiled by H. R. Davis and R. C. Good (New York: Scribners, 1960), 70–83. Reprinted by permission.

37. Carl F. H. Henry, *The Uneasy Conscience of Modern Fundamentalism*, vol. 1 of *God, Revelation and Authority* (Grand Rapids: Eerdmans, 1947), 84–88. Reprinted by permission.

Index

Agápe, 262
Apocalypticism, 148, 155
Apologetics, 195
Aristotelianism, 35
Authority, 1, 159

Catholicism, Roman, 11, 27, 50,
    231, 251, 276, 364
Christology, 7–10, 63, 76, 118, 138,
    185, 192, 268, 355, 364
Church, 31, 65, 173
Confessional theology, 247
Creation, 3, 43, 59, 64, 71, 74, 112,
    180, 329, 349, 354
Creator, 40, 49, 59, 73, 112, 114,
    187, 259, 350, 369, 371, 379
Cross, 46–47, 55, 90, 93, 234

Death, 47, 63, 163, 230
Dialectical theology, 39, 51, 62, 63,
    65, 94, 247
Docetism, 8
Dogma, 2, 67, 71, 185, 219
Dogmatics, 65

Ebionitism, 8
Election, 69
Enlightenment, 1–4, 6–7, 32, 41, 95,
    132, 168, 169, 276, 300, 303
Erlangen School, 11
Eros, 84, 265
Eschatology, 147, 160
Eschatological theology, 147, 173
Eternity, 40, 48, 63, 74, 75, 150, 201,
    220

Evangelicalism, 380
Existentialism, 6, 86, 102, 116,
    128–129

Faith, 10–11, 23, 25, 46, 63, 69, 96,
    138, 141, 145, 171, 258
Father, Son, Spirit, 80, 181, 195,
    202
Fundamentalism, 81, 353, 380

Gnosticism, 46, 111–13
God the Father, 9, 145, 187, 193
Gospel, 42–43, 47, 62, 64, 137, 228,
    236, 238, 244, 382
Gospels, 18, 20, 102, 170
Grace, 48, 60, 69, 70, 198, 204, 211,
    241, 243

Hermeneutics, 115, 130, 303
Historical Jesus, 7, 9–10, 17–20,
    118, 146
History, 31–35
Holy Spirit, 29–31, 52, 54, 60, 71,
    72, 79, 131, 356, 358, 382
Hope, 148–49, 162, 171

Image of God, 56–61, 74, 370
Incarnation, 8–9, 77, 101, 190, 191,
    226, 232, 272, 274, 377
Inspiration, verbal, 11

Jesus of Nazareth, 20, 77. *See also*
    Historical Jesus
Judgment, final, 147

Kingdom of God, 16–17, 46, 49, 86, 87, 88, 100, 173, 352, 353, 357
Knowledge of God, 37, 256, 289

Law, 47–48, 248, 252
Law/gospel dialectic, 117, 248, 254
Liberal theology, 39, 96, 210
Liberalism, 15–16
Logos, 36, 54, 82, 83, 85, 135, 149, 161, 191, 192, 196, 379
Love, 174, 175, 250, 272, 338, 360

Marxism, 7
Metaphysics. 3, 6, 7, 15, 96, 99, 249, 328
Monotheism, 361
Mystery, 297
Myth, 319

Neo-Protestantism, 12, 15, 39, 42, 62, 352
Neo-Protestant theology, 5, 377
Nestorianism, 8

Omega point, 332
Ontology, 84, 197, 297

Pantheism, 104, 296
Platonism, 35
Pluralism, 211, 232, 355
Political theology, 168
Predestination, 64, 71, 75
Process theology, 328
Protestant orthodoxy, 9, 248
Protestant theology, 47, 54, 202, 233
Protestantism, 11, 16, 364

Redemption, 43, 354
Reformation, 56, 248, 354, 358, 376

Religion, 4, 5, 15, 17, 26, 28, 32–33, 39–42, 46, 63, 94, 250, 270
Religions, 209, 234
    history of, 213
    non-Christian, 223, 231
    theology of, 210, 355
Resurrection, 24, 30, 43–47, 101, 140, 147–48, 150, 153, 154, 156, 163–64, 233
Revelation, 28, 38, 53–54, 56, 58, 59, 77, 86, 92, 99, 101, 128, 148, 150, 153, 154, 156, 158, 163, 180, 182, 198, 209, 244, 252, 354, 361
Righteousness, 47, 75

Salvation, 42, 56, 78, 97, 99, 128, 155, 170, 171, 226, 237, 356
Satan, 74, 75, 91
Secularization, 94, 107
Sin, 59–61, 102, 112–14, 140, 165, 238, 252, 255, 260, 321, 354, 355, 369, 373
Social Gospel, 356
Sola gratia, 55, 56, 61
Spirit. See Holy Spirit
Symbol, 319

Thomism, 276
Transcendental method, 285
Trinitarian theology, 179
Trinity, 9, 64, 70, 156, 179, 182, 190, 247
    economic and immanent Trinity, 181, 195
Truth, 29, 50–53, 68, 92

Word of God, 5, 50, 60, 61, 104, 117, 130, 139, 182, 234, 254, 271
Wrath of God, 253